DIRECTORY
OF BRITAIN'S
MILITARY
AIRCRAFT
VOLUME 2

Bombers and general-purpose types;
over-water reconnaissance and anti-submarine types;
transport and communications types; tankers;
airborne radar and long-range surveillance types; crew trainers

DIRECTORY
OF BRITAIN'S
MILITARY
AIRCRAFT
VOLUME 2

Bombers and general-purpose types;
over-water reconnaissance and anti-submarine types;
transport and communications types; tankers;
airborne radar and long-range surveillance types; crew trainers

TERRY HANCOCK

The
History
Press

Note

Volume 1 (published 2008) contains fighters, fighter-bombers, ground-attack and strike types; over-land reconnaissance, army-cooperation and army support types; pilot training and target-towing types.

The following manufacturers are covered in Volume 1 only: Auster; Bleriot; Bombardier; Brewster; British Aircraft Co.; British Taylorcraft; Britten-Norman; Chance-Vought; Cody; Dart; De Havilland Canada; DFS; Elliots; Etrich; Eurofighter; Flanders; Gloster; Grahame-White; Grob; Hiller; Lockheed-Martin; Martinsyde; McDonnell-Douglas; Morane-Saulnier; Nieuport; Panavia; Pemberton-Billing; Pilatus-Britten-Norman; Raytheon; Republic; RFD; Schemp-Hurth; Schleicher; Scneider; Sepecat; Spad; Sud Av.; Thomas; Vultee; Wright.

First published 2010

The History Press Ltd
The Mill, Brimscombe Port
Stroud, Gloucestershire, GL5 2QG
www.thehistorypress.co.uk

British Library Cataloguing in Publication Data.
A catalogue record for this book is available from the British Library.

ISBN 978 0 7524 4532 8

Typesetting and origination by The History Press Ltd.
Printed in Great Britain.
Manufacturing managed by Jellyfish Print Solutions Ltd.

Contents

Introduction to Volume 2

This volume, together with Volume 1 (which covers fighters, ground attack, strike, overland recon-naissance, pilot trainers and target tugs), provides brief but salient details of the approximately 650 types of aircraft (airships, aeroplanes, gliders and helicopters) which have seen operational and/or second-line service with the British armed forces since the *Nulli Secundus* airship of 1907, which was the first manned and powered type; it is thus a unique reference book and, in addition, its appendices cover engines, weapons, aircrew categories and provide the means of identifying which types were in service in which roles in any particular year. The criteria for inclusion are that the type must have carried a military serial and served with units of the Royal Engineers, Royal Flying Corps, Royal Naval Air Service, Royal Air Force, Fleet Air Arm or Army Air Corps; this definition excludes the following:

a) Prototypes and those types, or Marks of types, which served solely with the RAE, AAEE, ETPS, DERA or QiniteQ, or with 15 and 22 Sqns in the 1920s.
b) Types designed solely for record breaking, such as the Supermarine S6, Bristol 138 etc.
c) Types carrying civil registrations such as the pre-Second World War flying club aircraft used by the RAFVR, and the current Slingsby Fireflies and Grob Tutors/Herons.
d) Captured enemy aircraft.
e) Types or Marks which were used solely overseas by the British Commonwealth Air Training Plan, even when these were initially with RAF units and carried RAF serials – i.e. Anson Mk II and V. The Rhodesian Air Training Plan, however, has been treated as the RAF unit it was and remained as into the 1950s.
f) Types or Marks used solely by the Commonwealth Air Forces (except by those squadrons num-bered in the 400 range).
g) Types which continue in use with the BBMF, RN Historic Flt and AAC Historic Flt; in these cases the types are not counted as being still in service.
h) Types retained for ground training are not counted as being still in service.
i) Airliners from chartered airlines which carried temporary serials issued for trooping flights.
j) Tethered balloons and man-carrying kites.
k) Unmanned aircraft (UAVs).
l) Hovercraft.

Sources

The basis of this book are those 'bibles' by Owen Thetford, *Aircraft of the Royal Air Force* and *British Naval Aircraft*, plus J.M. Bruce's equally superb *Aircraft of the Royal Flying Corps – Military Wing*, all published by Putnam. However, much has been added to, or corrected by, reference over many years to books and magazines, notably the indispensable Air-Britain Files and RAF Registers and their books on the FAA and the annual *UK Air Arms* by Ian Carroll published by Mach III. Some fifty years of plastic modelling have also helped!

For the units I have used *RAF Squadrons* by W/C J. Jefford (Airlife), *Squadrons of the FAA* by R. Sturtivant (Air-Britain) and *Royal Air Force Training and Support Units* by R. Sturtivant (Air-Britain) as the base, supplemented by other books and magazine articles.

For piston-engines and engine powers I have taken *British Piston-Engines* by A. Lumsden as my base in this notoriously difficult area.

For serial numbers, total numbers and losses I have used the various Air-Britain RAF Registers, books on the FAA and type files.

Layout

The book is arranged alphabetically by the companies and then, under each company, is listed the types it produced, arranged chronologically by the year in which each type entered service – this date is important as the company may not always be the original design company – for example, the Argosy, designed by Armstrong-Whitworth, is the first entry under Hawker-Siddeley Aviation as that company had taken over Armstrong-Whitworth by the time the Argosy entered service. Conversely the Vulcan will be found under Avro because, at the time of its entry into service, Hawker-Siddeley Aviation had not taken over Avro. However, a type index is given in the appendices to help find the appropriate entry.

The Entries

Each entry contains the following information:

a) The type's name and Mark number including, from 1945 onwards, its role prefix. Under the first Mark covered there may be some general comments on the type as a whole. Mark numbers are given as Roman numerals until 1945 and then in Arabic numerals, as was done by the military.

b) A brief notation of its roles, crew numbers, armament, freight and passenger capacity and other information, followed by the year it entered service and with which unit, the number of units it served with, and the year it left service with the unit where possible. Also given are the wartime areas where the type saw active service or second-line duties and the countries in which it was based, or saw active service in, during so-called peacetime.

c) Armament is given as follows – the abbreviation 'mg' means the standard .303in calibre machine gun as used from the First World War to the 1940s; if given as in the wings or nose this signifies a fixed forward-firing gun; if given as in a gun position, i.e. rear cockpit, this signifies a manually operated omni-directional gun. Point 5in guns are shown as 0.5in and cannon by their calibre in millimetres, i.e. 20mm. Maximum bomb and store loads, with named missiles, are given together with the number of external hard points on wings or fuselage on which they can be carried. Appendix 3 outlines the weapons used by the British flying services.

d) The number, power and type of engines fitted (if not given, they are the same as the previous variant).

e) The serial numbers and totals of each variant; where possible these include only those aircraft which were actually delivered to the service and do not include examples of the type used only by the manufacturers, RAE, AAEE etc, thus sometimes considerably altering the numbers given in other publications.

f) A unique feature: where possible the number destroyed by hostile action and the number written off in accidents is given, with a percentage loss total for the type. Hostile action includes those shot down or destroyed on the ground and those missing in operational areas, as one would expect, but also includes those lost in shipping transit, destroyed by terrorist action or abandoned during retreats. Accidental losses include those aircraft missing in non-operational areas. These numbers can only be as accurate as surviving records permit but do give a reasonable idea of the losses suffered.

g) At the end of the entry for each type is a basic performance and dimensions table for comparison purposes.

Note: In listing the aircraft types and their variants the letters 'i' and 'o' have been omitted to avoid confusion with numerals.

1. Types of units

Sqn = operational squadron of the service operating the type (other services' squadrons are prefixed
by that services' initials), prefixed by its role if different from the type's stated role.

Flt = an operational Flight, specified as above.

Comms. unit = communications flights, units and unnumbered communications squadrons.

Training units' roles are defined in the text and by the abbreviations in Appendix 5.

Miscellaneous units = anything not covered by the above.

FAA and AAC second-line units, although numbered squadrons, are described in the same way as
are RAF training units (see above).

It should be noted that second-line units, especially communications squadrons and flights, used a
great variety of types, sometimes only one to a particular unit, but I have included these to show
how the RAF did, for example, use the 5,000 plus Ansons it took on charge. It should also be
noted that wings, squadrons and flying stations, until the 1960s, usually had one or two aircraft of
a variety of types (many of them impressed civil types during the Second World War) for communications – these are not, for reasons of space, included as units.

2. Geographical Areas

The countries are named as they were at the appropriate dates.

a) During wartime overland operations:

Northern Europe = the UK, northern France, Germany, Scandinavia and the Low Countries.

Russia = USSR.

Southern Europe = southern France, Italy, Sicily, Malta, Austria, Greece, the Greek Islands, the
Balkan states and Turkey.

The Middle East = Mesopotamia (First World War), Iraq, Palestine (now partly Israel), Jordan, Syria,
Iran, Aden (now Yemen) and the Persian Gulf.

North Africa = Egypt, Libya, Tunisia, Algeria and Morocco.

East Africa = British Somaliland, Italian Somaliland (both now Somalia), Kenya, Sudan, Uganda,
Tanganyika (now Tanzania) and Madagascar (now the Malagasy Republic).

West Africa = Sierra Leone, the Gambia, Nigeria and the Gold Coast (now Ghana).

South Africa = South Africa and Rhodesia (now Malawi, Zambia and Zimbabwe).

Far East = India (now India, Pakistan and Bangladesh), Ceylon (now Sri Lanka), Burma
(now Myanmah), Malaya (now Malaysia), Singapore, Hong Kong and the Dutch East Indies
(now Indonesia).

Australia = Australia.

North America = Canada and the USA.

BWI = British West Indies (now several different countries).

b) During wartime maritime operations, land or carrier based:

Home waters (First World War) = the seas surrounding the UK.

North Atlantic = over the Atlantic north of Gibraltar, including the Arctic, the North Sea and
English Channel.

South Atlantic = over the Atlantic south of and including Gibraltar.

The Mediterranean.

Indian Ocean = the whole Indian Ocean.

Western Indian Ocean = operations from African or Arabian bases.

The Pacific.

c) In peacetime the actual names of countries are given.

Photographs and Acknowledgements

Limitations as to space and availability make it impossible to include a photo of every type listed in this work, so a representative selection is given covering the vast majority; the captions to them are intentionally brief because the text itself is, in effect, the caption, and photos are included solely to give an idea of the appearance of the various types. Occasionally, photos of preserved examples have been used and for many of the types that were impressed I have used photos of preserved examples in civil markings. I am most grateful to all friends and fellow authors and enthusiasts who have allowed me to use their photos, particularly Alastair Goodrum, Peter Green, Jim Halley, Stuart Leslie and Mike Smith (Newark Air Museum). Also Charles Parker, John Fletcher, Mike French, Andrew Noland and Tony Hancock; the photos are all attributed but if any from my own collection are not properly acknowledged then I apologise unreservedly as they have been collected over the years, when this book was not intended for publication and notes were not made of their origin. Where photos of a type are not included I have provided a brief verbal description.

I am also grateful for information given by Lt Cdr N. Armstrong (750 Sqn, FAA), S/L Phil Bonner (RAF Waddington), S/L Roy Brocklebank (RAF Wainfleet), Ms Kathryn Cartlidge (771 Sqn, FAA), Cdr Niall Griffin (846 Sqn, FAA), F/L Si Kovac (60 R Sqn RAF), RAF Odiham and Mr Tim Lewis, MoD Press Office, whilst Steve and Martin, of Bob's Computers, Lincoln, gave great help on photo scanning. Amy Rigg, Jennifer Younger and The History Press team were as helpful as always.

The Evolution of the British Flying Services

During the century since the flight of the *Nulli Secundus* the British Military Services have seen many and continuing changes; the Royal Engineer's Balloon Section became, on 1 April 1911, the Air Battalion of the Royal Engineers, but a separate organisation was required to exploit the fast-growing science of aeronautics and the Royal Flying Corps was formed on 13 April 1912. The RFC consisted of a Central Flying School and Military and Naval Wings but the Admiralty was never happy to have its air arm under Army control and on 1 July 1914 the Naval Wing became the separate Royal Naval Air Service. The two Services had clearly defined roles at the beginning of the First World War – the RFC supported the Army for reconnaissance and spotting for the artillery; the RNAS carried out over-sea and coastal reconnaissance (so the airships were transferred to it), spotted for ship's guns and was also responsible for home defence. As the war progressed these roles became less clearly defined – the RFC took over air defence in 1916 and started bombing the battle areas, both services used fighters on the Western Front and the RNAS developed torpedo-bombers to operate from its ships and large land-based bombers to hit targets well behind enemy lines, as well as producing aircraft carriers. Their futures were decided politically and on 1 April 1918 the RFC and RNAS merged to form the Royal Air Force, not without dissent and ill-feeling on both sides. When the First World War ended the RAF was a very large organisation and had used most forms of air power.

The Service was run down quickly after the war and the Generals and Admirals tried hard to regain control of their respective air arms but Lord Trenchard, Chief of the Air Staff, managed to successfully resist the demise of the RAF and it began to grow again, seeing operational service in the Middle East and India. The Fleet Air Arm of the RAF pioneered the use of aircraft carriers but again the Admiralty argued for the return of its air force and achieved this on 17 February 1937 when the carrier-borne aircraft and some airfields transferred to the Royal Navy – but land-based anti-submarine and anti-shipping types remained under Coastal Command of the RAF, unlike most other countries where these too were operated by the navy.

So it was in this form that the two Services fought throughout the Second World War in virtually every part of the globe; initially much of their equipment and tactics were found wanting but lessons were quickly learnt and both the RAF and the FAA became very efficient and well-equipped forces, flying the best aircraft in the world of British, and later some American, design. The RAF entered the war still responsible for close support of the Army on the ground which was done by Army Co-Operation Command, some of whose pilots came from the Army; however its aircraft proved unsuitable for war and artillery spotting began to be carried out by small monoplanes flown by Royal Artillery pilots although still with RAF groundcrew. Later, men of the Glider Pilot Regiment flew their troop-carrying gliders into battle, towed by RAF transports so that, by the end of the Second World War, all three Services were once more heavily involved in air operations.

The end of the war meant, as after the First World War, a quick rundown of the RAF and FAA but the threat of attack by the USSR meant that this rundown was much less than that of 1919. Both Services pioneered the use of jet-powered aircraft and although they now lagged behind the United States in terms of aircraft performance and numbers they made a large contribution to NATO, whilst still performing the traditional role of air control in various British colonies until the 1960s. The success of the Army's air observation posts and gliders during the Second World War had not gone unnoticed and the War Office lobbied hard to gain control of these and, with helicopters coming into service, the Army Air Corps was formed on 1 September 1957, albeit with strict, RAF-imposed, rules on the roles it could undertake and the aircraft it could use for these roles; these have not always been followed! In 1968 the Admiralty, War Office and Air Ministry were merged into a combined Ministry of Defence and this meant that all three Services began to work more closely together, as evidenced during the Falklands War in 1982.

Following the end of the Cold War in the late 1980s, the RAF, FAA and AAC have become involved in peace-keeping operations around the world – the first Gulf War, the Balkans, Iraq, Sierra Leone and Afghanistan. These wars have seen the blurring of the traditional lines drawn between them with the RAF now flying Harriers and helicopters from RN carriers, the FAA's Harriers and helicopters operating from RAF bases in Afghanistan and AAC Apaches flying escort to RAF Chinooks, also in Afghanistan. Basic flying training was contracted out to private companies using civilian-registered aircraft. Despite these, sometimes unpopular, changes the British flying Services are still amongst the world's best, as is their equipment, but there is no doubt that they are overstretched and as there is little support from the British public as regards more money for defence it seems that this situation will continue for the foreseeable future; this is compounded by the financial crisis of 2008/9, the consequences of which on defence spending are still to be determined.

Since 1912, 136 companies have supplied a total of 241,308 aeroplanes to the Forces: 41,740 were for the RFC, 6,834 for the RNAS, 191,725 for the RAF, 28,554 for the FAA and 1,256 for the AAC. The disparity in totals is because the RFC/RAF passed aircraft on to the the RNAS/FAA, so these aircraft have been counted twice.

Aircraft Nomenclature

Aircraft need to identified individually so that their maintenance records are available and that proper accounting can be done! The RFC (and subsequently the RNAS) started to number each aeroplane in a surprisingly logical way, with serial numbers starting at No.1; it was decided that no more than five digits would be used so, at 9999, a new sequence started as A1–A9999, followed by B1–B9999 and so on. At the end of the First World War J serials were being used but a change took place as K came into use, five digits then becoming standard, starting with K1000 rather than K1. When Z9999 was reached in the first years of the Second World War AA100–999 was used, followed by AB100–999 etc and this sequence carries on to the present day with ZR being the current usage; after ZZ999 who knows but it is interesting to note that, very recently, 001–099 is starting to be used (as in ZK001) thus giving ninety-nine extra serial numbers in each letter sequence.

During the First World War there were no laid-down rules for the naming of aircraft types, most being known officially by their makers' designations which were often quite clumsy, so that Service personnel used their own nicknames which then became adopted for general usage; thus the Sopwith Scout F1 became the Camel, the Martinsyde G100 the Elephant, the Sopwith Type 9400/9700 the One-and-a-Half Strutter etc. In 1918 the RAF developed a naming system but this was short-lived and was successively replaced by different systems in 1921, 1927, 1932 and 1939, all being too detailed to reproduce in this book. Post-Second World War names seem to have been selected randomly and some earlier names have been repeated, such as Bulldog, Andover and Typhoon whilst still to come is the Wildcat; some types have not received a name, like the VC-10. (Particularly irritating to this author is the current predilection amongst serving personnel, aviation journalists and enthusiasts to ignore perfectly good RAF names and traditions and refer instead to F-4s, C-130s and E-3s, using USAF terminology, instead of Phantom, Hercules and Sentry.)

Once a type is named there has to be a method of distinguishing between different variants of that type and for this the British Services use Mark numbers, the first variant of a type being the Mark I (in Roman numerals until the mid-1940s, Arabic since) which after, say, re-engining becomes the Mark II or 2 and so on, some types, like the Mosquito and Spitfire, running to many different Marks. Role prefixes began to appear from 1940 on with photo-reconnaissance Spitfire conversions from the Mark I fighter being identified as the PR I, for example, and transport conversions of the Halifax bomber becoming A Vs rather than just the Mark V bomber. However, role prefixes became official towards the end of the war and were used thereafter together with the Mark number as, for example, in Canberra B (for Bomber) Mark 6, usually written as B 6; these role prefixes are detailed in Appendix 5 of this book. It should be noted that during the Second World War many civilian-owned trainers, tourers and airliners were 'impressed' by the RAF and FAA and were used for communications (i.e. as air taxis) and as transports; these were not allocated Mark numbers and were known by their original names and after the war, if they had survived, were returned to their owners. Those readers not sure of their Roman numerals might find the following helpful: I=1, II=2, III=3, IV=4, V=5, VI=6, VII=7, VIII=8, IX=9, X=10, XI=11, XII=12, XIII=13, XIV=14, XV=15, XVI=16, XVII=17, XVIII=18, XIX=19, XX=20, XXX=30 and so on.

Mark numbers altered because of fairly major changes in design but more minor changes were signified by putting a letter after the Mark number, i.e. Heyford IIA; until the 1950s this letter tended to be in lower case but since then capital letters have been used and are used throughout this work. Finally, very minor changes were denoted by a Series number as in the Stirling I Series III but this practice seems to have been rarely used after the Second World War.

This easily understood system has become confused during recent years – for example, the Agusta A109E Power has not been given a Mark number because it is leased.

The Aircraft

A.C. MOTOR (Thames Ditton, Surrey) Assembled GAL Hamilcar

ADMIRALTY AIR DEPARTMENT (London, England)
Designed one production type and supplied 28 examples.

1. A.D. Flying Boat
A reconnaissance and training type for the RNAS, with two crew in tandem cockpits, the front one right in the nose and armed with a Lewis mg. It was a two-bay un-staggered biplane, the upper wing having a longer span braced by 'goalpost' kingposts, with a rounded fuselage. The biplane tailplanes connected the two fins and elongated rudders and the two floats were faired to the lower wing. Built by Supermarine. In service 1917 at Grain Air Station, issued to 2xPTU until 1918, but saw little use.
Powered by one 150hp Hispano-Suiza 8Aa or 200hp 8Bb in-line pusher between the wings driving a four-blade propeller .
Serials: 1412–13 (2), N1290, N1520–1529 (10), N1710–1719 (10), N2450–54 (5).
Span: 50ft 4in/15.34m   Length: 30ft 7in/9.32m   Ceiling: 14,000ft/4,200m
Range: 150 miles/241km   Speed: 98mph/158kmph.
Total 28 but many not issued. No losses.

AERONCA (USA)
Founded in 1928 and famed for its light aircraft before and after the Second World War; supplied one example of one type.

2. Chief KCA
A high-wing tandem two-seat cabin monoplane impressed for communications work with the RAF.
In service 1941 with Dum-Dum SFlt, used by 2xcomms. units until 1943, Bengal SFlt.
Based overseas in the Far East, not operational in the UK.
Powered by one 50hp Continental A50 in-line.
Serial: Z2003.
Span: 36ft/10.98m   Length: 21ft/6.4m   Ceiling: 15,000ft/4,500m   Range: 450 miles/724km
Speed: 109mph/175 kmph.
Total 1 impressed. No losses.

AGUSTA-WESTLAND (International)
Formed in 2000 by the merger of the Italian company Agusta and the UK company Westland; supplied thirty-five examples of two types (A109A see Vol. 1).

3. A109E Power
A leased helicopter for VIP transport duties with the RAF, carrying two crew and eight passengers.
In service 2006 with 32 (Royal) Sqn, used by one sqn to the present 2010. ZR324-5 are not in service with 60RSqn but are used for foreign crew training.
Powered by two 900shp Turbomeca Arrius 2K1 turboprops
Serials: ZR321–325 (5).
Rotor diameter: 35ft 10in/11m   Length: 37ft 5in/11.41m   Ceiling: 19,600ft/5880m
Range: 599 miles/964km   Speed: 177mph/285kmph.
Total 5. No losses to date.

4. AW 139
A civil helicopter ordered for training foreign aircrew at the DHFS Shawbury and, although it carries RAF serials, is not in service with 60 (R) Sqn; carries two crew and 15 passengers if required. It is a medium-sized aircraft with a conventional tail-rotor pylon, a four-blade main rotor, retractable under-

carriage and three cabin windows each side.

In service 2009. Used by one TU to the present 2010.

Powered by two 1,679shp Pratt & Whitney PTC-6c turboprops.

Serials: ZR326–27. (2).

Rotor diameter: 45ft 3in/13.8m   Length: 54ft 7in/16.65m   Ceiling: 11,800ft/3,600m

Range: 400 miles/740km   Speed: 190mph/ 306kmph.

Total 2.

5. Lynx Wildcat HMA 1

A development of the FAA Westland Lynx (qv). Will be armed with the Future Anti-Surface Guided Weapon. No further details available.

Serials: ZZ400–427 (28).

Powered by two 1,361shp LHTEC CTS800-4n turboprops.

Total 28.

AIRBUS INDUSTRIE (International, UK partner BAE Systems)

Formed 1970 and has produced many successful airliners and just one military design. Will supply 39 examples of two types.

Agusta 109E Power, ZR321, 32 Sqn. (Andrew Nowland)

Agusta-Westland Lynx Wildcat HMA 1, artist's impression. (A-W)

Airbus A300-200, artist's impression.
(EADS)

Airbus A400M, artist's impression.
(EADS)

6. A330–200

A tanker-transport version of the airliner leased by the RAF under an agreement which means they can be operated as civil aircraft when not required by the RAF, although for military operations they will be controlled and flown by the RAF. They will carry three crew, 290 passengers and 44 tonnes of freight plus a fuel load of 132,300lb/60,064kg and will have underwing HDU pods, with some having a third refuelling point under the fuselage.

Due in service 2011.

Powered by two 71,000lb st RR Trent 772b turbofans.

Serials: ZZ330–343 (14).

Span: 198ft/60.3m   Length: 193ft/58.8m   Ceiling: 39,000ft/11,887m   Range: 7,500 miles/12,500km
Speed: 530mph/880kmph.

Total 14.

7. A400M

A tactical transport for the RAF with three or four crew and able to carry 116 passengers or 82,000lb/37,228kg of freight loaded through a rear ramp. Its hold is larger than that of the Lockheed Hercules (qv) and it can thus carry bulkier cargos.

Due in service 2013 at time of writing.

Powered by four 11,000shp EuroProp Int. TP400 D6 turboprops.

Serials: ZM400–424 (25).

Span: 139ft 1in/42.4m   Length: 143ft 8in/43.79m   Ceiling: 37,000ft/11,100m
Range: 3,000 miles/4,830km   Speed: 350mph/563kmph.

Total 25.

Airco DH 4, N6397, 202 Sqn.
(Newark Air Museum)

AIRCO (Hendon, Middlesex, UK)

The common abbreviation for the Aircraft Manufacturing Co., which was established in 1912 and started to build aircraft in 1914. Its Chief Designer was Geoffrey de Havilland and the designs which entered service carry his initials. However the lack of orders following the First World War saw the company fail in 1920. Supplied 11,467 examples of seven types (DH 1, DH 2, DH 5 and DH 6 see Vol. 1); also manufactured Curtiss H4, Maurice Farman S7 and S11, Henri Farman HF20, and Felixstowe F2A.

8. DH 4

A very successful two-seat day bomber for the RFC/RAF and RNAS, armed with one or two Vickers mg on the cowling, one/two Lewis mg in the rear cockpit and 460lb/210kg of bombs underwing.
Built by Airco, Berwick, Glendower, Palladium, Vulcan, and Westland. Nicknamed Flaming Coffin.
In service 1917 with 55 Sqn, RFC, used by 18 RFC/RAF sqns (18, 25, 27, 30, 49, 55, 57, 63, 72, 202, 211, 217, 220, 222, 223, 224, 226, 227), four coastal patrol sqns (212, 221, 233, 273) and eight RNAS units (2, 5, 6, 11, 12, 17 NSqns, 2 and 6W) until 1919, 57, 223 and 233 Sqns; also used by 15xTSqns, 13xTDSs, 3xSoN&BDs, 3xSoAGs, 1xSoAF, 2xFSs, 1xScout S, 1xFleet SoAF&G, 1xObsS, 1xObsSoAG, 1xSoP, 1xSoACo-op, 5xRNAS PTU, 1xRNAS CU, 2x comms. units and 2xRFC and 1xRNAS misc. units, until 1920.
Action: northern and southern Europe, home waters and the Middle East, also based overseas in Iraq.
Powered by one 230hp Siddeley Puma, 250hp RR Eagle III, 284hp Eagle IV, 275hp Eagle VI or Eagle VII, 260hp Fiat A12, or 200hp RAF 3a in-line.
Serials: 3962–63 (2), A2125–2174 (50), A7401–7142 (688), B1482, B2051–2150 (100), B3955–3968 (14 renumbered), B3987, B5451–5550 (100), B9434–39 (6), B9456, B9460–61 (2), B9470–71 (2), B9476–9500 (25), C4501–4541 (40), D1751–1775 (25), D8351–8430 (80), D9231–9280 (50), E4624–28 (5), F1551–52 (2), F2633–2715 (89), F5699–5798 (100), F7597–98 (2), H5290, H5894–5939 (46), N5960–6009 (50), N6380–6429 (41).
Total 1,499 plus 48 rebuilds making a total of 1,547 (83 RNAS). 478 accidental and 277 hostile losses.

8a. DH 4A

A conversion of the DH4 for communications work, the gunner's cockpit being replaced by a covered cabin for two passengers, with windows, and it had non-standard wings.
In service 1919 with 2 (Comms) Sqn, used by 2xcomms. units until 1919, Southern Comms. Sqn.
Powered by one 350hp Eagle VIII.
16 conversions of the DH4. Losses in the above.

	Span	Length	Ceiling	Endurance	Speed
DH4	42ft 5in/12.93m	29ft 8in to 30ft 8in /9.04m to 9.34m	22,000ft//6,600m	3.5hrs	36mph/219kmph
DH4A	"	30ft 6in /9.29m	21,000ft/6,300m	"	"

Total DH 4s = 1,449; in service 1917–20; 755 (48%) losses, including 277 hostile.

9. DH 9

Intended to replace the DH4 as the standard RAF day bomber but had a worse performance due to its unreliable engines; however, it was in large-scale production and was thus widely used. It was a two-seater, armed with one Vickers mg in the port fuselage-side and one/two Lewis mg in the rear cockpit, plus 460lb/210kg of bombs underwing or fuselage. Built by Airco, Alliance, Berwick, Cubitt, Mann-Egerton, National AF, Waring & Gillow, Weir and Whitehead.

In service 1918 with 99 Sqn, used by 27 sqns (17, 27, 47, 49, 55, 98, 99, 103, 104, 107, 108, 117, 119, 120, 142, 144, 202, 206, 211, 218, 220, 221, 223, 224, 226, 227, 236), 10 coastal patrol sqns (212, 219, 222, 233, 250, 254, 260, 269, 270, 273) and seven RNAS units (2, 6, 11, 17, 18, 19 NSqns, 1 W) until 1920 with 47 and 55 Sqns; also used by 14xTSqns, 28xTDS, 2xSoAF, 2xSoAF&G, 4xSoN&BD, 1xSASIObs, 1xSoAG, 4xFS, 2xMObsS, 1xSMOP, 2xFIS, 1xObsSoR&AP, 1xScout S, 1x Special Instructors Flt, 1xcomms. unit and 6xmisc. units, until 1920.

Action: in northern and southern Europe, home waters, North Africa, the Middle East and Russia, also based overseas in Turkey, Egypt, Sudan and India.

Powered by one 230hp BHP Galloway Adriatic, 230hp Siddeley Puma, or 260hp Fiat A12 in-line.

Serials: B7581–7680 (100), B9331–9430 (100), C1151–1448 (300), C2151–2232 (80), C6051–6350 (300), D451–812 (276), D1001–1451 (384), D1651–1750 (100), D2776–3275 (500), D5551–5850 (300), D7201–7251 (77), D7301–7380 (80), D9800–9885 (85), E601–701 (100), E5435–36 (2), E8857–9056 (200), F1101–1300 (200), F1767–1857 (25), H4216–4315 (100), H5541–5890 (350), H9113–9412 (300).

Total 3,959 plus 21 rebuilds making a total of 3,980 but many in later batches not issued. 467 accidental and 353 hostile losses.

9a. DH 9A

In order to cure the DH 9's problems it was re-engined and then became a stalwart of the post-war RAF, used as a bomber and general-purpose type with crew and armament as the DH 9; some FAA aircraft had three seats. It had a redesigned, fully cowled, nose, and more taper on the wingtips and tailplanes than did the DH 9. Built by Airco, Berwick, de Havilland, Mann-Egerton, Vulcan, Westland and Whitehead. Nicknamed Ninak.

Airco DH 9, C6051. (*MAP*)

Airco DH 9A, J7345. (Alastair Goodrum Collection)

In service 1918 with 110 Sqn, and used by 36 sqns: 8, 11, 12, 14, 15, 18 (First World War), 22, 24, 25, 27, 30, 35, 39, 45, 47, 55, 57, 60, 84, 99 (First World War), 100, 110 (First World War), 123, 155 (First World War), 156, 205, 207, 212 (First World War), 221, 501, 600, 601, 602, 603, 604, 605, one FAA sqn (3) and one FAA flt (420) until 1930, 501 Sqn; also used by 2xSoN&BD, 1xAir Pilot's S, 1xA&GS, 1xSoAG, 1xCDCo-opFlt, 1xCCFlt, 2xFS, 1xFleet SoAF&G, 6x FTS, RAFC, TB Leuchars, 1xTDS, 1xUASqn, 2x SoTT, 4xcomms. units and 13xmisc. units, until 1930. Action: in northern Europe (see the First World War sqns in list above), Russia and Iraq, also based overseas in Turkey, Aden, Egypt, Jordan, Sudan, Somaliland and India.

Powered by one 400hp Liberty 12a in-line.

Serials: E701–1041 (341), E8407–8806 (352), E9657–9756 (100), E9857–9956 (91), F951–1100 (150), F1603–1652 (50), F2733–2878 (170), H1–176 (200), H3396–3671 (376), J551–600 (50), J7249–7258 (10), J7700, J7787–819 (33), J7823–7890 (68), J8096–8225 (130).

Total 2,122 plus 179 rebuilds in J serials, making a total of 2,301 (52 FAA). 439 accidental and 50 hostile losses (38 First World War, 12 post-war).

9b. DH 9A (DC)

An advanced-trainer version, as the DH 9A but with armament removed and with dual-controls in a modified rear cockpit.

In service 1920, used by 6xFTS and other units as above until 1931, CFS.

Serials: J8460–8494 (35).

Total 35 plus an unknown number of conversions of the DH 9A. 6 accidental losses from these 35.

	Span	Length	Ceiling	Range	Speed
DH 9	42ft 5in/12.93m	30ft 5in/9.27m	17,500ft/5,250m	4.5hrs	117mph/188kmph
DH 9A	45ft 11in/14m	30ft 3in/9.22m	19,000ft/5,700m	620 miles /998kmph	120mph/ 193kmph

Total DH 9s = 6,116; in service 1918–31; 1,315 (22%) losses including 403 hostile.

10. DH 10 Amiens III

A twin-engined day bomber for the RAF which just missed service in the First World War and saw only limited use, often as a transport and route finder; three or four crew and armed with one/two Lewis mg in the nose and dorsal positions and one in the ventral position, plus 1,380lb/625kg of bombs internally. In service 1918 with 104 Sqn, used by four sqns (60, 97, 104, 216) until 1922, 216 Sqn; also used by 1xTDS, 1xFTS, and 1xSoN&BD.

Based overseas in Egypt and India.

Powered by two 400hp Liberty 12a in-lines, mounted between the wings.

Serials: E5437–5636 (200), E6037–6136 (60), E7837–7986 (18), E9057–9206 (48), F351–550 (5).

Total 331 but some not issued; 19 accidental losses.

10a. DH 10 Amiens IIIA

As the DH 10 but with the engines mounted on the lower wing, extended ailerons and heavy-duty wheels. In service 1920 to 1923 with 60 Sqn.

Based in India; no UK service.

Serials: F1867–82 (16), F8421–8495 (21).

Total 37; 1 accidental loss.

Amiens were built by Airco, Birmingham Carriage, Daimler, Mann-Egerton, National AF and Siddeley-Deasy.

	Span	Length	Ceiling	Endurance	Speed
Mk III	65ft 6in/19.96m	39ft 7in/12.07m	16,500ft/4,950m	5.75hrs	116mph/187kmph
Mk IIIA	"	"	17,500ft/5,250m	"	129mph/208kmph

Total Amiens = 368; in service 1918–23; 20 (5%) losses; nicknamed Kitehawk.

Airco DH 10A Amiens
III, F1869. (Newark Air
Museum)

AIRSHIPS

As airships are not normally attributed to a design firm all types are covered under this heading. 220 were
supplied, of 21 types (Nulli Secundus, Beta, Willows No.4 and Gamma see Vol. 1). Non-rigid ships had
an envelope inflated by the gas pressure inside; semi-rigid ships had an envelope inflated by gas but with
a metal keel from which hung the gondola; rigid ships had the envelope stretched over an aluminium
frame inside which were a series of gas-bags. Control and/or engine cars were carried below the envelope. The types listed below were non-rigids unless otherwise stated.

11. Delta

A two-seat unarmed training ship for the RFC, later RNAS, which also used it for patrol work. The
envelope tapered towards the rear and it had two small tailplanes and one ventral fin/rudder mounted on
the envelope. Built by Royal Aircraft Factory.
In service 1912 at Farnborough until 1915, RNAS.
Action: home waters.
Powered by two 105hp White & Popple pushers driving vertically swivelling propellers.
Serial: HMA 19.
Diameter: 39ft/11.89m   Length: 198ft/60.35m   Ceiling: n/k   Range: 400 miles/644km
Speed: 44mph/71kmph.
Total 1; no losses.

12. Eta

A training ship for the RFC, transferred for training and patrol work with the RNAS in 1914. Five crew
in two cockpits separated by the engines, no armament. Built by Royal Aircraft Factory.
In service 1913 at Farnborough until 1914, RNAS.
Powered by two 80hp Canton-Unne in-line pushers driving vertically swivelling propellors.
Serial: HMA 20.
Diameter: 33ft 6in/10.21m   Length: 188ft/57.3m   Ceiling: n/k   Range: 500 miles/805km
Speed: 42mph/68kmph.
Total 1; 1 (100%) accidental loss.

13. Astra-Torres Class

A French-designed patrol and training non-rigid for the RNAS, unarmed. It had three lobes, a biplane
tailplane under the rear of the envelope and one ventral fin/rudder mounted on the envelope. There was
an enclosed car for the eight crew.

Eta airship, Farnborough. (Peter
Green Collection)

In service 1913 at Farnborough RFC, also used at RN Air Station Kingsnorth until 1916.
Action: home waters and northern Europe.
Powered by two 210hp Chenu in-lines, one each side of the car.
Serials: HMA 3, HMA 8.

	Diameter	Length	Ceiling	Endurance	Speed
HMA 3	58ft/	248ft/75.59m	n/k	12 hrs	48mph/
HMA 8	46ft 5in/14.15m	"	"	"	51mph/82kmph

Total 2 but it is likely HMA 3 was never rigged; no losses.

14. Parseval Class

A German-designed patrol and training ship for the RNAS, with one Lewis mg on the envelope above
the nose and HMA 5 having one in a nose 'pulpit'. It had a more streamlined nose than the previous
ships and a pointed tailcone, with two tailplanes and a ventral fin/rudder on the envelope. The nine crew
were in an enclosed car. No.4 built in Germany, 5, 6 & 7 by Vickers.
In service 1913 at RFC Farnborough, used by four RN Air Stations (Cranwell, Howden, Kingsnorth,
Pulham) until 1919, Howden.
Action: home waters.
Powered by two 180hp Maybach or Wolseley-Maybach pushers, one each side of the car.
Serials: HMA 4–7 (4).
Diameter: 51-57ft/15.54–17.37m   Length: 276-301ft/84.12-91.74m   Ceiling and endurance: n/k
Speed: 53mph/85kmph.
Total 4. No losses.

15. Sea or Submarine Scout Class

The first really successful ship, used by the RNAS/RAF for patrol and training, with Armstrong-
Whitworth FK 3, R.A.F BE 2c or Farman fuselages as the car for two or three crew, the car also carrying
112lb/50kg of bombs externally.
In service 1915 at RN Air Station Kingsnorth, used by 13 Stations (Anglesey, Caldale, Capel-le-Ferne,
Cranwell, Howden, Imbros, Kingsnorth, Laira, Luce Bay, Marquise, Mudros, Pembroke, Polegate) until
1919, Pulham.
Action: home waters and Mediterranean.
Powered by one 70hp Renault WB/WC, 120hp Green E6, or 75hp RR Hawk I in-lines – pushers on
the Farman cars, tractors on the others.
Serials: SS1–50 (50).
Diameter: 27ft 9in–32ft/8.46–9.75m (depending on the car)   Length: 143ft 3in/43.67m
Ceiling: n/k   Endurance: 16–24 hrs   Speed: 47mph/76kmph.
Total 50; 9 (18%) accidental losses.

Sea Scout airship, RNAS
Cranwell. (Author's
Collection)

Coastal Class airship. (Peter
Green Collection)

16. Coastal Class

A patrol and training ship, with four or five crew and armed with a Lewis mg in the car and another on top of the envelope, plus 460lb/210kg of bombs carried on the car externally.

In service 1916 at Kingsnorth RNAS, used by 10 Stations (Capel-le-Ferne, Cranwell, East Fortune, Howden, Kingsnorth, Longside, Mullion, Pembroke, Polegate, Pulham) until 1919, Howden.

Action: home waters.

Powered by one 160hp Sunbeam Amazon, 100hp Berliet, or 120hp Green E6 in-line tractor and one 220hp Renault 12FE in-line pusher.

Serials: C1-27 (27).

Total 27; 14 accidental and 4 hostile losses.

16a. Coastal Star Class

As the above but with two Lewis in the car and none on the envelope, and able to carry 660lb/300kg of bombs.

In service 1918 at Howden RNAS, used by seven Stations (Cranwell, East Fortune, Howden, Kingsnorth, Longside, Mullion, Pulham) until 1919, Kingsnorth.

Action: home waters.

Powered by one 100hp Berliet in-line tractor and one 220hp Renault 12FE or 240hp Fiat in-line pusher.

Serials: C★1-10 (10).

Total 10; 1 accidental loss.

	Diameter	Length	Ceiling	Endurance	Speed
Coastal	37ft/11.28m	195ft 9in/59.44m	n/k	12hrs	47mph/76kmph
Coastal Star	47ft/14.33m	207-217ft/63.09-66.14m	"	"	56mph/90kmph

Total Coastal 37; in service 1916–19; 19 (51%) losses inc. 4 hostile.

17. HMA 9r

The first rigid ship for the RNAS/RAF, used for patrol work with 15 crew in two cars and armed with one Lewis mg on the envelope and one in the tail position plus 100lb/45kg of bombs. The structure was 17-sided and there was an external keel containing the crew quarters and the wireless cabin. Two tailplanes/elevators and a dorsal fin/rudder. Built by Vickers.

In service 1917 at East Fortune RNAS, used by four Stations (Cranwell, East Fortune, Howden, Pulham) until 1918, Pulham.

Action: home waters.

Powered by four 180hp Wolseley-Maybach in-line pushers, two in each car driving two propellers, later replaced in the rear car by one 240hp Maybach in-line pusher driving one propeller and two 180hp Wolseley-Maybach in-line pushers in the forward car.

Serial: HMA 9r.

Diameter: 53ft/16.15m   Length: 526ft/160.32m   Ceiling: n/k   Endurance: 26 hrs   Speed: n/k.

Total 1; no losses.

18. 23r Class

A rigid patrol and training ship for the RNAS/RAF, with 16 crew and armed with three Lewis mg and one 2 pdr gun. The external keel contained quarters, wireless cabin and bomb bay; there were three cars. Built by Armstrong-Whitworth, Beardmore and Vickers.

In service 1917 to 1919 at Pulham RNAS/RAF.

Action: home waters.

Powered by four 250hp RR Eagle II in-line pushers – one in the front car driving two vertically swivelling props, two in the middle car and one in the rear car driving two vertically-swivelling propellers; HMA 26r had only one propeller on the aft car.

Serial: HMA 23r–26r (4).

Diameter: 53ft/16.15m   Length: 535ft/163.06m   Ceiling: n/k   Endurance: 40 hrs Speed: 55mph/89kmph.

Total 23r Class 4; in service 1917–19; no losses.

23r airship, RNAS Howden. (Peter Green Collection)

Sea Scout Zero SSZ 36, RNAS
Godmersham Park. (Peter Green
Collection)

19. Sea or Submarine Scout Pusher Class

A development of the SS class, a non-rigid used for patrol and training by the RNAS/RAF; three crew
and armed with 112lb/50kg of bombs on the car externally.
In service 1917 at Capel-le-Ferne RNAS, used by four Stations (Anglesey, Caldale, Capel-le-Ferne,
Cranwell) until 1919, Cranwell.
Action: home waters.
Powered by one 120hp Green E6 or 75hp RR Hawk I in-line pusher.
Serials: SSP 1–6 (6).
Total 6; 3 accidental losses.

19a. Sea or Submarine Scout Zero Class

Similar to the above but able to carry 250lb/113kg of bombs, plus one Lewis mg in an improved boat-
shaped metal car. Nicknamed Zero.
In service 1917 at Capel-le-Ferne RNAS, used by 10 Stations (Anglesey, Capel-le-Ferne, Chathill, East
Fortune, Howden, Luce Bay, Mudros, Mullion, Pembroke, Polegate) until 1918, Polegate.
Action: home waters and Mediterranean.
Powered by one 75hp RR Hawk I in-line pusher.
Serials: SSZ1–76 (74).
Total 74; 17 accidental losses.

	Diameter	Length	Ceiling	Endurance	Speed
SSP	30ft/9.14m	143ft 4in/43.69m	n/k	50hrs	56mph/90kmph
SSZ	"	"	"	n/k	52mph/84kmph

Total SSP/SSZ classes 80; in service 1917–19; 20 accidental losses (25%).

20. North Sea Class

As the name suggests, this was an improved non-rigid for operations over the North Sea, with the
10 crew housed in a covered car and armed with two Lewis mg in the car and one on the envelope;
1,380lb/625kg of bombs on the car.
In service 1917 at East Fortune RNAS, used by five Stations (Cranwell, East Fortune, Howden, Longside,
Pulham) until 1921, Howden.
Action: home waters.
Powered by two 225hp RR Eagle I, 350hp Eagle VIII or 240hp Fiat in-line pushers.
Serials: NS1–16 (14).
Diameter: 56ft 9in/17.3m   Length: 262ft/79.86m   Ceiling: n/k   Endurance: 24hrs
Speed: 57mph/92kmph.
Total 15; 6 (42%) accidental losses.

North Sea
airship NS
11, RNAS
Longside.
(Peter Green
Collection)

21. Sea or Submarine Scout Twin Class

A patrol and training non-rigid for the RNAS/RAF, with three or four crew in a streamlined car armed with a Lewis mg and 250lb/113kg of bombs carried on the car sides.
In service 1918 at Mullion, used by four Stations (Capel-le-Ferne, Howden, Mullion, Pulham) until 1919, Howden.
Action: home waters.
Powered by two 100hp Sunbeam or 75hp RR Hawk I in-line pushers.
Serials: SST 1–14 (13).
Diameter: 35ft/10.67m   Length: 165ft/50.29m   Ceiling: n/k   Endurance: 16–24hrs
Speed: 57mph/92kmph.
Total 13; 2 (15%) accidental losses.

22. SR 1

An Italian semi-rigid ship for patrol and training work, with eight crew in an enclosed car and armed with one mg above the envelope nose; saw little use. Had a ventral fin with biplane elevators attached to its rear, the elevators having a rudder at each end.
In service at Pulham from 1918 to 1919.
Powered by two 180hp Itala in-line pushers.
Serial: SR1.
Diameter: 55ft/16.46m   Length: 270ft/82.3m   Ceiling: n/k   Endurance: n/k
Speed: 46mph/74kmph.
Total 1; no losses.

23. R 27 Class

A rigid patrol and training ship for the RNAS/RAF, as the 23r class but it had three cars and no external keel; armed with three Lewis mg and bombs. Built by Armstrong-Whitworth and Beardmore.
In service 1918 at Howden, used by two Stations (East Fortune, Howden) until 1919, East Fortune.
Action: home waters.
Powered by four 250hp RR Eagle II or 350hp RR Eagle VIII in-line pushers, one in the forward car and one in the rear each driving two swivelling propellers, and two in the mid car driving one propeller each.
Serials: R 27, R 29–30 (2).
Diameter: 53ft/16.15m   Length: 539ft/164.29m   Ceiling: n/k   Endurance: 30hrs
Speed: 56mph/90kmph.
Total 3; 1 (50%) accidental loss.

R 31 airship, Howden.
(Peter Green collection)

24. R 31 Class

A rigid wooden-framed patrol and training ship for the RAF with three cars. Built by Short Bros.
In service 1918 at Howden, used by two stations (East Fortune, Howden) until 1920, Howden.
Powered by five 250hp RR Eagle III in-line pushers, one in each forward car, one each in the two mid-ships side-by-side cars, and one in the rear car.
Serials: R 31–32 (2).
Diameter: 65ft 5in/19.94m   Length: 614ft/187.15m   Ceiling: n/k   Endurance: 20hrs   Speed: 65mph/105kmph.
Total 2; no losses.

25. R 33 Class

Another rigid patrol and training ship for the RAF, having a metal frame with four cars. Built by Armstrong-Whitworth.
In service 1919 at Howden and used by two Stations (Howden, Pulham) until 1920, Howden.
Powered by five 260hp Sunbeam Maori IV in-line pushers, arranged as on the R 31 above.
Serials: R 33–34 (2).
Diameter: 78ft 9in/24m   Length: 643ft/195.99m   Ceiling and Endurance: n/k
Speed: 62mph/100kmph.
Total 2; 1 (50%) accidental loss.

26. R 80 Class

The last rigid airship for the RAF before its use of airships finished. It carried a streamlined control car (forward) and had two engine pods side-by-side towards the tail. Built by Vickers.
Used for training at Howden during 1921.
Powered by four 230hp Wolseley-Maybach in-line pushers, two in the control car and one in each pod.
Serial: R 80.
Diameter: 70ft/21.34m   Length: 535ft/163.1m   Ceiling and endurance: n/k   Speed: 70mph/113kmph.
Total 1; no losses.

AIRSPEED (Portsmouth, Hants, UK)

A company formed in 1932 in York, moving to Portsmouth a year later. It produced, in the main, small airliners until the Second World War when, during 1940, it became part of de Havilland and in 1951 its name became that of the parent company. Supplied 8,844 examples of six types (Oxford and Queen Wasp see Vol. 1) and also manufactured DH Mosquito and GAL Hotspur.

27. Envoy III
A light airliner, advanced for its time, used by the RAF and FAA as a transport, with two crew and six passengers. It was a low-wing monoplane with a single, pointed fin/rudder and three large and one small fuselage windows each side; it had a retractable undercarriage.
In service 1938 with Delhi SFlt, used by 2xEWS, 2xFTS, 8x RAF and one FAA comms. units and 1xmisc. unit until 1945, Defford SFlt.
Based overseas in India and Far East.
Powered by two 310hp A-S Cheetah IX radials with cylinder head fairings around the cowlings.
Serials: L7270, N9107–08 (2), P5625–29 (5), P5778 plus two impressed X9370, DG663.
Span: 53ft 4in/16.25m   Length: 34ft 6in/10.51m   Ceiling: 22,000ft/6,600m   Endurance: 5hrs
Speed: 182mph/293kmph.
Total 9 plus 2 impressed, making a total of 11 (1 FAA); 2 (20%) losses inc. 1 hostile.

28. Courier
A light low-wing cabin monoplane impressed for communications work with the RAF, carrying a pilot and five passengers under extensive cabin glazing. It had a pointed fin/rudder and was the first British design to have a retractable undercarriage.
In service 1939 with the ATA, used by 1xOTU and 1xmisc. unit until 1944, 25 OTU. Couriers were built in several versions and the data below relates to the most common.
Powered by one 225hp A-S Lynx IVc radial.
Serials: X9342–47 (6), X9394, X9437.
Span: 47ft/14.33m   Length: 28ft 6in/8.68m   Ceiling: 13,500ft/4,050m   Range: 400 miles/644km
Speed: 134mph/216kmph.
Total 8 impressed; 2 (30%) losses inc. one hostile.

29. Ferry
A small biplane airliner carrying the pilot and nine passengers, impressed for communications work with the RAF.
In service 1940 to 1941 with Halton SFlt.
Powered by one 110hp DH Gipsy III (central on the upper-wing) and two 108hp Gipsy II in-lines (on the lower-wing).
Serial: AV968.
Span: 55ft/16.46m   Length: 39ft 8in/12.09m   Ceiling: 13,000ft/3,900m   Range: 320 miles/515km
Speed: 112mph/180kmph.
Total 1 impressed; no losses.

30. Horsa I
The most successful Second World War assault glider, carrying two crew and 25 passengers or 7,000lb/3,180kg of freight, loaded through a door in the front port fuselage; it had a single nose wheel and two towing eyes in the wing leading edges.
In service 1942, used by six GPR sqns, 2xPAFU, 2xCU, 4xHGCU, ORTU, 3xOTU, 1xPara&GTS, ECFS, 1xGTS and 3xmisc. units, until 1950, GPR.
Action: northern and southern Europe and North Africa.
No engines.
Serials: DP279–841 (400), HG736–989 (200), HS101–150 (49), LG511–LJ334 (856), PF690–817 (100), RJ111–359 (198), RN523–941 (319), RX595–717 (99).
Total 2,221; 193 accidental and 985 hostile losses; many to the USAAF.

30a. Horsa II
As the Mk I but unloading was made easier by fitting a detachable nose and tail; it had twin nose-wheels and one towing eye in the nose.
In service 1943, used by six GPR sqns, 3xCU, 4xHGCU, ORTU, 2xOTU, 1xParaTS, TSPC, 1xAGS and 4xmisc. units to 1950, GPR.

Airspeed Horsa
II. (Peter Green
Collection)

Action: northern Europe and Far East, also based overseas in Germany.

Serials: LF886–963 (65), PW637–897 (196), RN309–520 (175), RX534–583 (50), RX718–RZ408 (450), TK828–TL735 (600), TT353–367 (15).

Total 1,551;. 35 accidental and 283 hostile losses; some to USAAF.

	Span	Length
Mk I	88ft/26.82m	67ft/20.42m
Mk II	"	67ft 11in/20.7m

Total Horsas 3,772; in service 1942–50; 1,496 (40%) losses inc. 1,268 hostile; built by Airspeed, Austin and Harris Lebus.

ALBATROS (Germany)

A company which produced many types for the German military during the First World War. Supplied one example of one type.

31. BII

A unarmed two-seat reconnaissance two-bay biplane for the RNAS, purchased before the First World War commenced. It had a triangular fin and rudder.

In service 1914 at Killingholme, used by two units until 1917, Grain.

Powered by one 100hp Mercedes D 1 in-line.

Serial: 890.

Span: 42ft/12.8m   Length: 26ft 3in/8m   Ceiling: 10,000ft/3,000m   Endurance and speed: n/k.

Total 1; no losses.

ALLIANCE (London, UK)

Assembled Airco DH 9.

ARMSTRONG-WHITWORTH (Gosforth, Northumberland, later Coventry, Warks, UK)

A famous company, formed in 1897 from the merger of two engineering and shipbuilding companies; it started to build aircraft in 1914. In 1919 the aircraft side of the business moved to Coventry where it remained until becoming part of Hawker-Siddeley Aviation in 1965. Supplied 5,798 examples of seven types (FK2/3, FK8, Siskin, Atlas and Meteor NF see Vol. 1) and also assembled Bristol F2B, RAF BE 2c, Hawker Hart, Hart Trainer, Seahawk and Hunter, Avro Lancaster and Lincoln, and Gloster Meteor and Javelin.

A-W Whitley II, K7229,
97 Sqn. (*MAP*)

32. Whitley I
The RAF's first modern night-bomber, with five crew and a defensive armament of one Lewis or Vickers mg in a A-W 13 or FN 13 nose turret and one Vickers mg in a A-W 12, 15 or 38 tail turret, plus 3,365lb/1,530kg of bombs internally. Early production aircraft had no wing dihedral.
In service 1937 with 10 Sqn, used by four sqns (10, 58, 78, 166) until 1940, 166 Sqn, also served with 1xOAFU, 1xAAS, 3xAGS, 3xB&GS, CLE, 1xAOS and 1xParaTS to 1942. For paratroop training the rear turret was removed so that the opening could be used by the jump trainees.
Powered by two 810hp A-S Tiger IX radials.
Serials: K4586–87 (2), K7184–7216 (32).
Total 34; 9 accidental losses.

32a. Whitley II
As the Mk I but had wing dihedral as standard and was able to carry 3,500lb/1,590kg of bombs.
In service 1937 with 58 Sqn, used by four sqns (7, 51, 58, 97) until 1940, 97 Sqn. Also served with 1xOAFU, 1xAAS, 1xAGS, 3xB&GS, CLE, 1xOTU, 2xParaTS, 1xSS, 1xAOS and 5xmisc. units until 1943.
Powered by two 860hp Tiger VIII.
Serials: K7217–7262 (46).
Total 46; 16 accidental losses.

32b. Whitley III
The first Whitley to go to war – as the Mk II but with increased dihedral, one Vickers mg in a FN 16 powered nose turret, two Browning mg in a FN17 retractable ventral turret, and one Vickers in an A-W 38 tail turret, plus 5,500lb/2,500kg of bombs in fuselage and wing cells. The ventral turret was removed to make an exit when paratroop training.
In service 1938 with 51 Sqn, used by seven sqns (7, 51, 58, 77, 97, 102, 166) until 1940, 10 Sqn, also served with 1xOAFU, 2xAGS, 3xAOS, 2xB&GS, 1xATS, CLE, 2xBATFlt, 2xOTU, 1xParaTS and 2xmisc. units until 1943.
Action: northern Europe.
Powered by two 920hp Tiger VIII (supercharged).
Serials: K8936–9015 (80).
Total 80; 29 accidental and 2 hostile losses.

32c. Whitley IV
As the Mk III but re-engined and later fitted with four Browning mg in a FN4 tail turret and a chin bomb-aimers position (which was also fitted retrospectively to earlier Mks).
In service 1939 with 10 Sqn, used by two sqns (10, 51) until 1940, 10 Sqn; also served with 1xAAS, 1xAGS, 1xB&GS, ECFS, 2xOTU, 1xParaTS and 2xmisc. units until 1943.
Action: northern Europe.
Powered by two 1,030hp RR Merlin IV in-lines.
Serials: K9016–9048 (33).
Total 33; 15 accidental and 3 hostile losses.

32d. Whitley IVA

As the above but for the engines.

In service 1939 to 1940 with 78 Sqn, also used by the second-line units as the Mk IV until 1943.

Action: northern Europe.

Powered by two 1,145hp Merlin X.

Serials: K9049–55 (7).

Total 7; 1 accidental loss.

32e. Whitley V

The main variant of the Whitley, similar to the Mk IVA but with the ventral turret deleted, an FN4 tail turret in a lengthened tail section to improve the field of fire, a straight leading-edge to the fins, de-icing boots, and a faired DF loop; the bomb load was increased to 7,000lb/3,180kg and the crew to seven (as a transport it had four crew and 10 passengers).

In service 1939 with 58 Sqn, used by six sqns (10, 51, 58, 77, 78, 102), two GR sqns (502, 612), two SD sqns (138, 161), four transport sqns (295, 296, 297, 298), one RCM sqn (109) and one SD flt until 1942, 58 Sqn. It also served with 3xAGS, 3xB&GS, CGS, CLE, 1xBATFlt, 4xTTU, 2xHGCU, ORTU, 7xOTU, 2xParaTS, 1xcomms. unit and 14xmisc. units to 1945.

Action: northern and southern Europe, North Atlantic, and North Africa.

Serials: N1354–1528 (148), P4930–5112 (164), T4130–4339 (150), Z6461–6959 (291), Z6970–6980 (11), Z9119, Z9125–9134 (10), Z9140–9189 (31), Z9200–9363 (86), Z9384–9575 (179), AD665–714 (50), BD189–422 (157), BD626–674 (49), BD435–560 (62), EB283–313 (31), EB337–391 (39), EB402–10 (9), LA763–793 (31).

Total 1,499 (1 FAA); 551 accidental and 323 hostile losses.

32f. Whitley VII

A dedicated GR version of the Mk V, with six crew and carrying four DC; an astrodome was fitted and it had ASV-II radar with external aerials.

In service 1941 with 612 Sqn, used by four sqns (53, 58, 502, 612) until 1943, 612 Sqn; also served with 2xOTU and 1xFAA PTU until 1946.

Action: North Atlantic.

Serials: Z6960–6969 (10), Z9120–24 (5), Z9135–39 (5), Z9190–9199 (10), Z9364–9383 (20), Z9516–9529 (14), BD423–434 (12), BD561–625 (20), BD675–693 (19), EB282, EB327–336 (20), EB392–401 (10), LA794–817 (10).

Total 156 (15 FAA); 38 accidental and 14 hostile losses.

A-W Whitley V, N1390, 102 Sqn. (Author's Collection)

	Span	Length	Ceiling	Range	Speed
Mk I	84ft	69ft 3in	16,800ft	1,370 miles	192mph
	/25.6m	/21.11m	/5,040m	/2,206km	/309kmph
Mk II	"	"	23,000ft/6,900m	1,315 miles/	215mph/
				2,117km	346kmph
Mk IV	"	71ft 3in/	25,000ft/	1,800 miles/	245mph/
		21.72m	7,500m	2,898km	395kmph
Mk IVA	"	"	26,000ft/7,800m	1,500 miles/2,415km	230mph/370kmph
Mk V	"	72ft 6in	"	1,600 miles	"
		/22.1m		/2,576km	
Mk VII	"	"	"	2,300 miles	215mph/
				/3,703km	346kmph

Total Whitleys 1,855; in service 1937–46; 1,001 (54%) losses inc. 342 hostile; nicknamed Flying Barndoor, Wombat and Flying Coffin.

33. Albemarle ST I Series I

Designed as a bomber but overtaken by the new four-engine types, the Albemarle was found a niche as a special transport and glider tug; the differences between Mks and Series appear to have been slight and inconsistent. The ST I Srs I was a transport with four crew and able to carry 10 passengers, in some discomfort, or 5,000lb/2,270kg of freight loaded through a side door; armed with two Vickers mg in a dorsal position.
In service 1942 with 511 Sqn, used by one sqn (511) and one SD sqn (161) until 1944, 511 Sqn, also served with 1xOTU.
Action: northern Europe and North Africa.
Powered by two 1,590hp Bristol Hercules XI radials.
Serials: P1370-71 (2), P1377.
Total 3; no losses.

33a. Albemarle ST I Series II

As the above but with a new wiring system.
In service 1943 to 1944 with 511 Sqn and 1xParaTS.
Action: northern Europe and North Africa.
Serials: P1374, P1379, P1385, P1397, P1403, P1433, P1447–48 (2), P1452, P1454, P1472–73 (2), P1475.
Total 13; 2 accidental and 1 hostile loss.

A-W Albemarle GT I.
(Newark Air Museum)

33b. Albemarle ST I Series III
As the above but with minor internal modifications.
In service 1943 with the OAPU and 511 Sqn, and second-line with the ATA AFS, 1xAPS and 1xFTU until 1944, 511 Sqn.
Action: northern Europe.
Serials: P1479–80 (2), P1502–10 (9), P1519–20 (2), P1554–56 (3), P1558–1569 (12), P1590–1609 (20), P1630–1659 (30),V1598.
Total 79; 13 accidental and 1 hostile loss.

33c. Albemarle GT I Series I
As the above but with glider-towing equipment under the rear fuselage, and armed with four Browning mg in a BP-A dorsal turret.
In service 1943 with 296 Sqn, used by four sqns (295, 296, 297, 570) until 1944, 297 Sqn, also by the ORTU.
Action: northern Europe and North Africa.
Serials: P1363–69 (7), P1372–73 (2), P1375–76 (2), P1378, P1380–84 (5), P1386–94 (9), P1396, P1398–1401 (4).
Total 31; 3 accidental losses.

33d. Albemarle GT I Series II
As the above but able to carry 10 passengers, with paratroop doors under the rear fuselage.
In service 1943 with 296 Sqn, used by two sqns (296, 297) until 1944, 297 Sqn; also served with CGS, 2xHGCU, and 2xOTU.
Action: northern Europe and North Africa.
Serials: P1402, P1404–05 (2), P1407–09 (3), P1430–32 (3), P1434–1446 (13), P1449–51 (3), P1453, P1455–1471 (17), P1474, P1476–78 (3), P1501, P1511–18 (8).
Total 56; 14 accidental and 5 hostile losses.

33e. Albemarle GT I Series III
As the above with minor modifications.
In service 1943 with 296 Sqn, used by two sqns (296, 297) until 1944, 297 Sqn.
Action: northern Europe and North Africa.
Serials: P1521–29 (9), P1550-53 (4), P1557.
Total 14; 4 accidental and 2 hostile losses.

33f. Albemarle ST II Series I
As the above with four Browning mg in a BP-A dorsal turret, towing gear, anti-strop fouling gear, and parachute doors.
In service 1943 with 295 Sqn, used by four sqns (295, 296, 297, 570) until 1944, 297 Sqn; also served with 2xHGCU and 1xOTU.
Action: northern Europe.
Serials:V1598–1647 (48),V1694–1725 (30),V1738–1759 (22).
Total 100; 15 accidental and 5 hostile losses.

33g. Albemarle ST V Series I
As the above but with internal modifications and a fuel jettison system.
In service 1944 with 295 Sqn, used by four sqns (295, 296, 297, 570) until 1944, 297 Sqn; also served with 4xHGCU and 1xGTS.
Action: northern Europe.
Serials:V1761–1787 (27),V1809–1828 (20),V1841–42 (2).
Total 49; 4 accidental and 5 hostile losses.

33h. Albemarle ST VI Series I
A pure transport, with turret deleted, four crew, and 10 passengers or 5,000lb of freight loaded through a large freight door in the fuselage side.

In service 1944 with 297 Sqn, used by two sqns (296, 297) until 1944, 297 Sqn; also served with 1xHGCU.
Action: northern Europe.
Serials:V1843–1885 (45),V1917–1941 (25),V1962–2011 (50),V2025–2039 (15).
Total 135;. 15 accidental losses.

33j. Albemarle GT VI Series I

Retained the freight door but did not carry passengers and had the dorsal turret restored, with glider tug
gear under the rear fuselage.
In service during 1944 with 297 Sqn, and 1xGTS and 1xGIFlt.
Action: northern Europe.
Serials:V2040–2054 (15),V2067–68 (2).
Total 17; 2 accidental losses.

33k. Albemarle GT VI Series II

Not used operationally but as a glider and tug trainer, with armament deleted and the turret space faired over.
In service 1944 with 22 HGCU, used by 2xHGCU until 1946, 21 HGCU.
Serials: LV482–623 (100).
Total 100; 4 accidental losses.
All Mks: Span: 77ft/23.45m   Length: 59ft 11in/18.26m   Ceiling: 18,000ft/5,400m   Range: 1300
miles/2,093 km   Speed: 265mph/427kmph.
Total Albemarles 597; in service 1942–46; 95 (16%) losses inc. 19 hostile.

AUSTIN MOTORS (Birmingham, UK)

Assembled Airspeed Horsa, Avro Lancaster, Fairey Battle and Short Stirling.

AVRO (Manchester, Lancs, UK)

Founded by the pioneer airman Alliot Verdon Roe in 1910 and was a famous company, especially known
for its Second World War and post-war bombers; Roe left the company in 1928 and in 1935 it became
part of the Hawker-Siddeley Group whilst keeping its own name. However, in 1963 the historic name
disappeared and the company became part of the new Hawker-Siddeley Aviation. It supplied 22,994
examples of 21 types (500,501,502,503,504A-N, Tutor, Athena, see Vol. 1) and also assembled Bristol
Blenheim, Fairey Battle, Short Stirling and E.E. Canberra.

34. 504

Although largely remembered as a trainer (see Vol. 1) the 504 was initially a bomber for the RFC and
RNAS with one or two crew and able to carry 80lb/35kg of bombs underwing. It gained fame by carry-
ing out the first long-range bombing raid by British forces, on 21 November 1914, when four machines
bombed the Zeppelin sheds at Friedrichshafen, a return trip of 240 miles, causing severe damage. On
these raids the biplanes were flown as single-seaters but there were two cockpits.
In service 1914, 3N Sqn, used by two RFC sqns (1, 5) and one RNAS sqns (1N) until 1915, plus 13xR/
TSqns and 3xRNAS PTU until 1917.
Action: northern Europe.
Powered by one 80hp Gnome 7z Lambda rotary.
Serials: 179, 390, 397–98 (2), 637–38 (2), 652, 665, 683, 692, 715–16 (2), 750–793 (44), 873–78 (6).
Span: 36ft/10.97m   Length: 29ft 5in/8.97m   Ceiling: n/k   Range: n/k   Speed: 82mph/132kmph.
**Total 62 plus 1 rebuild making a total of 63 (7 RNAS; in service 1914–15); 6 accidental and 1
hostile RNAS losses.**

35. 510

A reconnaissance two-bay biplane seaplane for the RNAS, with a longer-span upper wing braced by
two triangular kingposts; the wings were un-staggered and had a pronounced dihedral. There were two
floats underwing and one under tail; two crew and no armament.

Avro 504.
(Scott
Collection)

In service 1914 at Killingholme, used by three units (Dundee, Killingholme, Newlyn) and 1xPTU until 1917, Calshot.
Action: home waters.
Powered by one 150hp Sunbeam Nubian in-line with a radiator above the cowling.
Serials: 130–34 (5), 881.
Span: 63ft/19.2m   Length: 38ft/11.58m   Ceiling: n/k   Endurance: 4.5hrs   Speed: 70mph/113kmph.
Total 6; no losses.

36. Bison I

A carrier-borne reconnaissance and spotter type for the FAA, with a crew of three/four and armed with a Vickers mg in the fuselage and a Lewis mg in the rear position. The upper-wing had dihedral and was flush with the fuselage top and it had a short fin plus two auxiliary fins on the tailplanes.
In service 1923 with 3 Sqn, RAF, used by one sqn (3) and two flts (421, 423), plus TB Leuchars, until 1926, 421 Flt. Embarked on three carriers.
Powered by one 500hp Napier Lion II in-line driving a 4xblade propeller.
Serials: N153–55 (2), N9591–9602 (12).
Total 14; 3 accidental losses.

36a. Bison IA

As the above but the upper-wing had no dihedral and was clear of, but strutted to, the fuselage; it had a long dorsal fin, with the auxiliary fins deleted. Some had portholes in the forward cabin.
In service 1927 with 423 Flt, used by three flts (421, 423, 445) until 1929, 423 Flt. Embarked on three carriers.
Total 7 conversions of the Mk I; 3 accidental losses.

36b. Bison II

As the Mk IA but with the wing raised further above the fuselage and the arrester gear deleted.
In service 1925 with 423 Flt, used by two flts (421, 423) until 1929, 421 Flt; embarked on four carriers.
Powered by one 470hp Lion V.
Serials: N9836–9853 (18), N9966–9977 (12), S1109–14 (6), S1163–67 (5).
Total 41; 11 accidental losses.

	Span	Length	Ceiling	Range	Speed
Mk I	46ft/14.02m	36ft/10.98m	14,000ft/4,200m	340 miles/547km	110mph/177kmph
Mk II	"	"	12,000ft/3,600m	360 miles/580km	108mph/174kmph

Total Bisons 55; in service 1923–29; 17 (31%) losses.

37. Andover I

A large biplane ambulance and transport for the RAF, with two crew and up to 12 passengers in an oval-shaped cabin with five windows each side. Two fuel tanks over the upper wing centre section.
In service 1924 to 1925 at Halton.
Powered by one 670hp RR Condor III in-line.
Serials: J7262–64 (3).
Span: 68ft/20.73m   Length: 51ft 3in/15.62m   Ceiling: n/k   Range: 652 miles/1050km   Speed: 110mph/177kmph.
Total 3; no losses.

Above: Avro Bison II, 423 Flt. (Newark Air Museum)

Left: Avro Aldershot III. (Newark Air Museum)

Avro Anson I, K6309, 61 Sqn. (Peter Green collection)

38. Aldershot III

A heavy-bomber version of the Andover (qv above), with three crew and armed with a Lewis mg in the rear cockpit and 2,000lb/908kg of bombs under fuselage.

In service 1924 with 99 Sqn, used by one sqn and 1xmisc. unit until 1925, 99 Sqn.

Powered by one 670hp RR Condor III in-line.

Serials: J6943–6956 (14).

Span: 68ft/20.73m   Length: 45ft/13.72m   Ceiling: 11,500ft/3,450m   Range: 650 miles/1046km
Speed: 110mph/177kmph.

Total 14; no losses.

39. Anson I

Developed from the Avro 652 airliner, this was the RAF's first modern land-based general reconnaissance type; it had a crew of three and was armed with one Vickers mg in the port fuselage side and a Lewis mg in an A-W dorsal turret, plus 360lb/165kg of bombs internally. It was being replaced in this role by the start of the Second World War and many were subsequently used for training (minus the turret), although these were not the true-trainer version (see below); many went to the BCATP.

In service 1936 with 48 Sqn, used by 13 sqns (48, 206, 217, 220, 224, 233, 269, 320, 321, 500, 502, 608, 612), two flts, one fighter flt, one PR flt, two met. sqns (251, 516) and six ASR sqns (275, 276, 278, 280, 281, 282) until 1941, 48 Sqn; also used by AB&GS ME, 1xAFS, 1 (India) AFU, 9xOAFU, 14xPAFU, ACS, 1xAG&BS, 2xAN&BS, 8xANS, 10xAONS, 10xAOS, SoASR, ASRTU, ATA AFTS, 1xSoACo-op, BAS, 2xB&GS, CFS, CNS, 10xCANS, CC Landplane Pilot's S., 1xCArtCo-opS, 1x AOS RATG, 8xCU, 8xEFTS, 6xBATFlt, 26xERFTS, ECFS, ERS, 1xFPTU, 5xFTU, 3xTTFlt, 1xShip. Recc.Flt., 1xBDTFlt, SoFC, 4xFIS, 23xFTS, 1xGTS, 1xGp Pl, 1xHGCU, ME C&CU, Nav. Staff Pilot's TFlt, 1xNavS, OATS, 2xOCU, 51xOTU, 1xPara&GTS, 1xParaTS, 1xSoP, 23xRFS, Pre-OTU S., 1xPT&RPl, 7xRS, RAFC, Staff PTU, SARTU, 12xFAA CU, 2xFAA ObsTU, 10xFAA ATU, 4xFAA RTU, 73xRAF and 6xFAA comms. units, and 98xRAF and 6xFAA misc. units, until 1955, 771 Sqn FAA.

Action: North Atlantic, also based overseas in northern and southern Europe, Middle East, East and South Africa, BWI, North America, Far East, Germany, Denmark, Greece, Malta, Palestine, Egypt, Rhodesia and Australia.

Powered by two 310hp A-S Cheetah IX or 395hp Cheetah XIX radials.

Serials: K6151–6325 (175), K8703–8865 (143), L7046–7073 (28), L7903–7994 (67), L9145–9165 (18), N1337–39 (3), N4856–5385 (451), N9526–9999 (283), R3304–3587 (78), R9567–9968 (172), W1651–2665 (62).

Total 1,480; 417 accidental and 82 hostile losses.

39a. Anson I

The true-trainer version for the RAF and FAA, as the above but with turret deleted, flaps, and later production had smooth engine cowlings (no fairings for the cylinder heads); many went to the BCATP. Post-war 51 MK Is were converted to MK I 'Classroom' standard for FAA observer training, some with ASH radar in a radome pod beneath the nose.

In service 1941 with 70 OTU, used by second-line units as above (MK I), based overseas as above (MK I), out of service 1955.

Serials: AW443–AX752 (181), DG700–DJ700 (409), EF805–EG704 (419), LS978–LV332 (466), MG102–MH237 (492), NK139–NL251 (592) plus seven impressed Avro 652–AX748-52 (5), DG655–56 (2)

Total 2,559 plus 7 impressed making a total of 2,566 (148 FAA); 480 accidental and 68 hostile losses.

39b. Anson I

A gunnery trainer variant with a Browning mg in a smaller (than the Mk I's) Bristol B-VI dorsal turret. In service 1942 with 3AGS, used by 12xAGS until 1945.

Total 313 conversions of the above, losses in the above.

39c. Anson X Series I

A light-transport version of the Mk I trainer, with two crew and six to eight passengers or three stretchers, two passengers and a nurse; it had a strengthened floor for freight (1,500–1,700lb/680–770kg) and was used by the RAF and FAA . Smooth cowlings as standard.

In service 1943 with 2 TAF Comms.Flt, used by 19xRAF comms. units, EAAS, 1xBDTFlt, Staff PilotTU, OATS, 1xFAA CU and 12xmisc. units, until 1951 66 Gp CommsFlt.

Action: northern Europe, also based overseas in North Africa and Germany.

Serials: MH193, NK139–NL251 range (103).

Total 104; 17 accidental and 4 hostile losses.

39d. Anson X Series II

As the Series I except that it had an hydraulically operated undercarriage.

Powered by two 395hp Cheetah XIX as standard.

Total, losses and units as the above.

39e. Anson C XI

A light transport and ambulance for the RAF, as the Mk X Series II but with a raised cabin roof and rectangular cabin windows replacing the familiar greenhouse of the earlier Mks.

In service 1944 with 84 Gp SU, used by 22xcomms. units, SoAS, 1xOCU, 1xRS, 1xSCR584 TU and 11xmisc. units until 1951, 66 Gp Comms.Flt.

Action: northern Europe and Far East, also based overseas in Germany.

Serials: NK139–NL251 range (90).

Total 90; 10 accidental and 6 hostile losses.

39f. Anson C XII Series I

As the above but re-engined, with spinners on the propellers.

In service 1944 with 147 Sqn, used by four sqns (31, 147, 167, 187), one cal. sqn (116), 81xRAF and 2xFAA comms. units, SoMR, 4xOCU, 1xRS, RAFFC, 3xANS, 1xASS, 1xAPC, CNCS, 1xCU, EAAS, EFS, ERS, FWS, 1xFTU, 1xFAA CU, 1xFAA ATU, and 7xRAF and 1xFAA misc. units, until 1957, 187 Sqn, and SFlts to 1958.

Action: northern and southern Europe, also based overseas in East and West Africa, Germany, Denmark, Greece, Malta, Egypt, Jordan, Iraq and Kenya.

Powered by two 420hp Cheetah XV.

Serials: NK139–NL251 range (15), PH528–839 (248).

Total 263 (5 FAA);. 79 accidental and 2 hostile losses.

Avro Anson C 19, PH814 converted from C 12. (Author's Collection)

39g. Anson C XII Series II

As the Series I but had metal-skinned wings – all other details as the Series I.

39h. Anson C 19 Series 1

As the C XII Series II but with wooden wings and tailplanes, oval cabin windows and soundproofing; two crew and nine passengers. The DF loop was offset to starboard behind the cockpit.

In service 1946 with 147 Sqn, used by five sqns (8, 31, 147, 173, 187), two cal. sqns (116, 527), two PR sqns (58, 81), 81xcomms. units, 1xAES, 1xANS, 2xASS, 1xCAACU, 1xEFTS, EAAS, ECFS, 1xBDT-Flt, 1xFTU, 3xFTS, 1xITS, SoLAW, SoMR, 4xOCU, SoP, 1xRS, RAFFC and 1xmisc. unit, until 1968, Southern Comms. Sqn.

Serials: PH840–865 (14), TX154–257 (81).

Total 95; 8 accidental losses.

39j. Anson C 19 Series 2

As the Series I but with metal-skinned wings of revised shape and metal tailplanes.

In service 1946 with AHQ India, used by units as above until 1968, Southern Comms. Sqn.

Series 1 and 2 based overseas in Germany, Greece, Malta, Cyprus, Egypt, Jordan, Iraq, Gulf, Aden, Sudan, Kenya, Rhodesia, India and Malaya.

Serials: TX range (6), VL285–363 (54), VM307–409 (84), VP509–538 (29).

Total 173 plus 7 conversions of the C XII and an unknown number of conversions of the C 19 Series 1; 75 accidental losses.

39k. Anson T 20

A bombing trainer version of the C19 Series 2, with a glazed nose, astrodome, DF loop further aft, a radio station behind the pilot, no external oil coolers on the cowlings and exhausts on the engine port sides; six crew and able to carry 16 light bombs internally.

In service 1948 with 3 ANS, used by 1xAFS, 3xANS, 3xFTS, 1xITS, 1xRFS, 11xcomms. units and 2xmisc. units, until 1957. Based overseas in Rhodesia.

Serials: VM410–18 (9), VS491–591 (48), VV866–67 (2).

Total 59; 12 accidental losses.

39l. Anson T 21

A navigation trainer, as the T 20 but with armament deleted and with a solid nose.

In service 1948 with 1 ANS, used by 2xOCU, 1xRS, 21xRFS, RAFC, RAFFC, 4xUASqns, 3xCFCS, 1xOCTU, 5xANS, 2xASS, 2xBANS, CNS, CNCS, 4xCAACU, EANS, 1xFTS, 1xITS, SoLAW and 8xmisc. units, until 1965, SFlts.

Serials: VS562–591 (30), VV239–333 (67), VV880–999 (90), WB446–465 (20), WD403–418 (17), WJ509–561 (28).

Total 252; 39 accidental losses.

39m. Anson C 21

As the above but adapted to light transport duties, with two crew and nine passengers. The astrodome was deleted and the DF loop was offset to the right just behind the cockpit making it almost indistinguishable from the C 19.

In service c.1950, used by 25xcomms. units until 1968, Southern Comms. Sqn.

Total 24 conversions of the T 21; losses in T 21.

39n. Anson T 22

The last Mk of Anson, a radio-trainer version of the T 21 with the astrodome deleted and the DF loop set further forward, plus internal differences.

In service 1949 with 4 RS, used by AES, ERS, 2xRS, ASS and 1xOCU until 1960, AES.

Serials: VS592–603 (12), VV358–370 (13), WD419–436 (8).

Total 33; 6 accidental losses.

	Span	Length	Ceiling	Range	Speed
Mk I	56ft 6in/	42ft 3in/	19,000ft/	790 miles/	188mph/
	17.22m	12.88m	5,700m	1,272km	303kmph
Mk X	"	"	"	"	175mph/282kmph
Mk XI	"	42ft 6in	15,000ft/	610 miles/	"
		/12.95m	4,500m	982km	
C XII	"	42ft 3in/	16,000ft/	660 miles/	149mph/
		12.88m	4,800m	1,063km	240kmph
C 19 Series 2	57ft 6in/17.52m	"	"	"	"

Total Ansons 5,115; in service 1936–68; 1,305 (25%) losses inc. 162 hostile; nicknamed Faithful Annie.

40. 642/4m

A high-wing monoplane airliner used for transport duties with the RAF, carrying two crew and seven passengers. It had a spatted main undercarriage and a single fin/rudder.

In service 1938 with AHQ India, used by 1xcomms. unit and 1xmisc. unit, until 1940, AHQ India.

Based overseas in India, not based in UK.

Powered by four 225hp A-S Lynx IVc radials.

Serial: L9166.

Span: 71ft 3in/21.72m   Length: 54ft 6in/16.46m   Ceiling: 15,000ft/4500m   Range: 560 miles/902km   Speed: 150mph/241kmph.

Total 1; no losses.

41. Manchester I

A heavy bomber for the RAF which did not, because of engine problems, live up to expectations and saw only limited service; seven crew, with an armament of two Browning mg in an FN5 nose turret and FN7 dorsal turret (sometimes deleted), and four in an FN4 tail turret, plus 10,350lb/4,700kg of bombs internally. It had three fins and the first 20 had shorter-span tailplanes.

In service 1940 with 207 Sqn, used by seven sqns (49, 50, 61, 83, 97, 106, 207) until 1942, 49 Sqn; also served with 4xAGS, 1xAOS, 13xCFlts and 1xTTFlt, until 1944.

Avro Manchester
I, L7284, 207 Sqn.
(Peter Green
Collection)

Action: northern Europe.
Powered by two 1,760hp RR Vulture II in-lines.
Serials: L7276–7482 (129), R5768–5841 (43).
Total 172.

41a. Manchester IA

As the Mk I but with the central fin deleted and larger outer fins, the longer-span tailplanes as standard,
and some with the dorsal turret deleted.
In service 1941 with 207 Sqn, used by seven sqns (49, 50, 61, 83, 97, 106, 207) until 1942, 49 Sqn; also
served with 1xACS, 6xCFlts, 1xOTU and 1xLancaster FinS, until 1944.
Action: northern Europe.
Serials: L7483–7526 (27).
Total 27; Mks I and IA had 74 accidental and 58 hostile losses.
Span: 90ft 1in/27.46m   Length: 70ft/21.34m   Ceiling: 19,200ft/5,760m   Range: 1,630
miles/2,624km   Speed: 275mph/443kmph.
Total Manchesters 199; in service 1940–44; 132 (66%) losses inc. 58 hostile.

42. Commodore

A staggered single-bay biplane cabin monoplane impressed for RAF communications work, with a pilot
and four passengers. It had a spatted undercarriage and a single fin/rudder.
In service 1941 with ATA TFP, used by ATA TFP and 1xOTU, until 1942, 51 OTU.
Powered by one 225hp A-S Lynx IVc radial.
Serials: DJ710, HH979.
Span: 37ft 4in/11.38m   Length: 27ft 3in/8.31m   Ceiling: 11,500ft/3,450m   Range: 500
miles/805km   Speed: 130mph/209kmph.
Total 2 impressed; 1 (50%) accidental loss.

43. Lancaster I

Developed from the Avro Manchester (qv), sharing its fuselage and Mk IA tail unit, the Lancaster was
arguably the best bomber of the Second World War. It had seven crew and was armed with two Browning
mg in a FN5 nose turret and FN50 dorsal turret, four Brownings in a FN20, FN120, or FN121 tail turret,
and some, c.1945, had two 0.5in in a Rose-Rice rear turret, others having two 0.5in Browning mg in
a FN64 ventral turret; bomb load was 14,000lb/6,350kg and some had a H2S radome just behind the
bomb bay, the doors of which were sometimes bulged.

In service 1942 with 44 Sqn, used by 54 sqns (7, 9, 12, 35, 44, 49, 50, 57, 61, 75, 83, 90, 97, 100, 101, 103, 106, 109, 115, 138, 149, 150, 153, 156, 166, 170, 186, 189, 195, 207, 214, 218, 227, 300, 405, 424, 427, 429, 433, 434, 460, 463, 467, 514, 550, 576, 582, 617, 619, 622, 625, 626, 630, 635) until 1950, 49 Sqn, and served with BCIS, CNS, 25xCFlt, EAAS, EANS, ECFS, 1xFTU, GCA OpS, 4xLancaster FinS, PNTU, 2xOCU, Gee H TFlt, 1xFAA CU, 1xFAA TU and 7xmisc. units.

Action: northern Europe.

Powered by four 1,390hp RR Merlin 20, or Merlin 22 in-lines.

Serials: L7527–7584 (39), R5482–5763 (200), R5842–5917 (57), W4102–4700 (207), W4761–9182 (170), DV155–407 range (91), ED303–451 range (135), HK535–806 (200), LL740–LM294 (350), LM301–750 range (10), ME295–551 range (44), ME554–868 (250), NF906–NG503 (400), NN694–816 (100), NX548–610 (65), PA158–509 (229), PB643–961 range (211), PB981–994 (14), PB962 (14), PD198–444 (200), PP663–792 (97), RA500–806 (99), RF120–197 (65), SW296–279 (37), TW858–929 (59).

Total 3,343 (3 FAA); 480 accidental and 1,425 hostile losses.

43a. Lancaster I (Special)

As the above but converted to carry the 22,000lb/9,990kg Grand Slam bomb, with cut-away bomb bay doors, strengthened undercarriage, and the nose and dorsal turrets deleted and faired over, reducing the crew to six; armament was thus four Browning mg in a FN120 tail turret and the H2S was also removed.

In service 1944 with 617 Sqn, used by three sqns (15, 44, 617) until 1947, 617 Sqn.

Action: northern Europe.

Powered by four 1,610hp Merlin 24.

Serials: PB966–PD139 (31).

Total 31; 1 accidental and 1 hostile loss.

43b. Lancaster B 1 (FE)

The standard Mk I was modified for service with the Tiger Force against Japan, with the FN121 tail turret as standard, internal modifications, improved navigational aids and an extra fuel tank in the bomb bay, reducing the bomb load.

In service 1945 with 7 Sqn, used by five sqns (7, 70, 115, 148, 214) and 1xcomms. unit until 1950, 214 Sqn.

Based overseas in Egypt.

Powered by four 1,610hp Merlin 24.

Serials: TW647–895 (22).

Total 22 plus an unknown number of conversions of the Mk I; 3 accidental losses from these Serials.

43c. Lancaster PR 1

A long-range photo-reconnaissance version of the Mk I, with all armament deleted and the turret spaces faired over, cameras in the fuselage and five crew; the rear of the canopy glazing was painted over.

Avro Lancaster I, W4103, 5 Lancaster Finishing School. (Scott Collection)

In service 1946 with 541 Sqn, used by three sqns (82, 541, 683) and one flt until 1953, 82 Sqn.
Based overseas in Gold Coast, Kenya and Egypt.
Total 20 conversions of the Mk I; 2 accidental losses.

43d. Lancaster II

A re-engined version of the Mk I, in case of a Merlin shortage; seven or eight crew and armed with two
Browning mg in a FN5 nose turret, FN50 dorsal turret and FN64 ventral turret (behind a bulged bomb
bay), four Brownings in a FN20 tail turret, and 14,000lb/6,350kg of bombs.
In service 1943 with 61 Sqn, used by six sqns (61, 115, 408, 426, 432, 514) until 1944, 408 Sqn; also served
with 8xCU and 1xLancaster FinS until 1945.
Action: northern Europe.
Powered by four 1,615hp Bristol Hercules XVI radials.
Serials: DS601–852 (199), LL617–739 (99).
Total 298; 48 accidental and 194 hostile losses.

43e. Lancaster III

The Mk I re-engined with American-built Merlins, otherwise identical except that some, late in the war,
had two 0.5in Browning mg in a Rose-Rice tail turret and some had a modified bomb-aimer's nose
blister. 23 had a cut-away bomb bay for the Dambuster mine, with the dorsal turret deleted.
In service 1943 with 460 Sqn, used by 54 sqns (7, 9, 12, 35, 37, 44, 49, 50, 57, 61, 75, 83, 90, 97, 100, 101, 103,
106, 115, 138, 149, 150, 153, 156, 166, 170, 178, 186, 189, 195, 207, 218, 227, 300, 405, 424, 427, 429, 433,
434, 460, 463, 467, 514, 550, 576, 582, 617, 619, 622, 625, 626, 630, 635), until 1950, 49 Sqn; also served with
11xCU, 3xLancaster FinS, PNTU, BCIS, EFS, GCAOpsS, 1xTFlt, 1xRadarTFlt, 1xSoTT and 4xmisc. units.
Action: northern Europe, also based in Far East.
Powered by four 1,390hp RR-Packard Merlin 28, 1,480hp Merlin 38, or 1,610hp Merlin 224 in-lines.
Serials: W4988–5012 (30), DV155–407 range (109), ED303–451 range (38), ED452–EE202 (444), JA672–
JB748 (550), LM311–756 (340), ME295–551 (156), ND324–NE181 (600), PA964–PB642 (539), PB648–961
range (37), RE115–226 (87), RF198–326 (105), SW283–296 (13), SW319–377 (47), TX263–273 (11).
Total 3,106; 390 accidental and 1,782 hostile losses.

43f. Lancaster III (FE)

As the Mk III but with the same modifications as the Mk I (FE) to prepare it for the Far East war.
Units and service n/k.
Unknown number of conversions of the Mk III.

43g. Lancaster ASR 3

A long-range air-sea-rescue version of the Mk III with bombs deleted, the bomb bay being used to carry
a partially enclosed Airborne Lifeboat Mk IIA or ASR gear; it had H2S radar.
In service 1945 with 279 Sqn, used by three sqns (179, 279, 621) until 1946, 179 Sqn; also served with
1xOTU and the JASS.
Based overseas in the Far East, Malta and Palestine.
Powered by four 1,610hp Merlin 224.
Total 24 conversions of the Mk III; 4 accidental losses.

43h. Lancaster GR/MR 3

A stop-gap anti-submarine and reconnaissance variant, as the Mk III but with the dorsal turret deleted,
an enlarged astrodome, ASV-10 radar in a belly radome, a FN82 tail turret, 14,000lb/6,350kg of stores
internally, extra fuselage windows, an air intake on the starboard fuselage side, and a large camera fairing
beneath the rear turret.
In service 1946 with 210 Sqn, used by eight sqns (18, 37, 38, 120, 160, 203, 210, 224) until 1954, 38 Sqn;
also served with the SoMR, 2xOCU and 1xOTU until 1956.
Based overseas in Malta, Palestine, Egypt and India.
Total 91 conversions of the Mk III; 33 accidental losses.

Avro Lancaster GR 3,
RF210, 203 Sqn. (Peter
Green Collection)

43j. Lancaster VI

A re-engined Mk III, with nose and dorsal turrets deleted and faired over, four Browning mg in a FN20
tail turret, 14,000lb/6,350kg of bombs internally, and H2S.
In service during 1944 with 635 Sqn.
Action: northern Europe.
Powered by four 1,635hp Merlin 85 with rounded cowlings and driving 4xbladed propellers.
Total 5 conversions of the Mk III; 1 accidental and 1 hostile loss.

43k. Lancaster VII (interim)

As the Mk I but had an unfaired FN50 mid-upper turret moved forward to the same position as in the
B 7, and possibly 1,610hp Merlin 24s.
In service 1945 with 100 and 460 Sqns, until 1945.
Action: northern Europe.
Serials: Possibly NX548–610 (50) – if not these were B 7s.
Total 50; 2 accidental and 4 hostile losses.

43l. Lancaster B 7

Too late to see war service, the B7 was similar to the Mk I but was armed with two Browning mg in a
FN5 nose turret, two 0.5in Brownings in a Martin 250 dorsal turret (which had a lower profile and was
set further forward), and two 0.5in Brownings in a FN82 tail turret; bomb load was 14,000lb/6,350kg
and it had H2S.
In service 1945 with 9 Sqn, used by three sqns (9, 37, 40) until 1948, 37 and 40 Sqns; also served with the
CGS, CNS, CNCS, EAAS, EFS, RAFFC and EANS.
Powered by four 1,610hp Merlin 24.
Serials: NX548–610 (50 but see VII interim above), NX611–794 (150), RT670–699 (29).
Total 179 plus possible 50 as above; 11 accidental losses.

43m. Lancaster B 7 (FE)

Another version for the Far East war and thankfully not required, with the same modifications as the
Mk I (FE).
In service 1946 with 617 Sqn, used by two sqns (104, 617) until 1947, 104 Sqn.
Based overseas in Egypt and India.
Unknown number of conversions of the B 7.

43n. Lancaster X

A Canadian-built Mk III (by Victory Aircraft), with the same armament, although some had the Martin 250 dorsal turret with 0.5in Brownings; there was some US equipment internally, a deepened bomb bay and it had H2S.

In service 1944 with 419 Sqn, used by eight sqns (405, 408, 419, 420, 425, 428, 431, 434) until 1946, s6 Group sqns; also served with 3xCU and 1xFTU.

Action: northern Europe, also based overseas in North America.

Powered by four 1,390hp RR-Packard Merlin 28 or 1,480hp Merlin 38.

Serials: FM104–229 (12), KB700–999 (296).

Total 308; 40 accidental and 70 hostile losses.

	Span	Length	Ceiling	Range	Speed
Mk I/III	102ft/	69ft 6in/	24,500ft/	1,660 miles/	287mph/
	31.09m	21.18m	7,350m	2,673km	462kmph
Mk II	"	"	18,000ft/	2,530 miles/	270mph/
			5,400m	4,073km	434kmph
B 7	"	70ft 5in/	24,500ft/	1660 miles/	287mph/
		21.47m	7,350m	2673km	462kmph
Mk X	"	69ft 6in/21.18m	"	"	"

Total Lancasters 7,337; built by Avro, Armstrong-Whitworth, Austin, Metropolitan-Vickers, Vickers and Victory; in service 1942–56; 4,592 (62%) losses inc. 3,477 hostile.

44. York C 1

The wings and tail unit of the Avro Lancaster (qv) were married to a capacious new fuselage, resulting in the York airliner and RAF transport; with the RAF it carried five crew, and 24 passengers or 9,000lb/4,085kg of freight. Nicknamed Yorkie.

In service 1943 with 24 Sqn, used by nine sqns (24, 40, 51, 59, 99, 206, 242, 246, 511) and 7xcomms. units until 1957, FEAF CFlt; also used by 2xCU, 1xOCU, EANS and 4xmisc. units.

Action: Berlin airlift, also based overseas in India and Singapore.

Powered by four 1,610hp RR Merlin 24 in-lines.

Serials: FM400, LV626–639 (4), MW100–333 (193), PE101–108 (8).

Span: 102ft/31.09m   Length: 78ft 6in/23.92m   Ceiling: 24,000ft/7,200m   Range: 2,700 miles/4,347km   Speed: 298mph/480kmph.

Total 206; 53 (26%) accidental losses.

Avro York C 1, MW100.
(*MAP*)

45. Lincoln B 1

A replacement heavy bomber for the Lancaster, the B 1 saw little use; it had a crew of seven and was armed with two 0.5in Browning mg in a BP-F nose turret, two in a B17 dorsal turret and two in a BP-D tail turret, plus 14,000lb/6,350kg of bombs and H2S in a radome behind the bomb bay.

In service 1945, used by one sqn (57), BCIS, BCInstR&E.Flt and 2xmisc. units, until 1947.

Powered by four 1,635hp RR Merlin 85 in-lines, driving 3, later 4xbladed propellers.

Serials: RA628–655 (23), RE228–257 (42), RF333, SS713–14 (2).

Total 68 but some not issued; 6 accidental losses.

45a. Lincoln B 2

The production version, as the B 1 but with different engines and the dorsal turret, deleted later in service, now carrying two 20mm cannon; the designations B 2/3G and B 2/4a indicated different H2S, the B 2/4a having a larger radome. Some were given faired noses and tailcones to replace the turrets and were used for navigation flights, being unofficially called 'Lincolnians'.

In service 1945 with 57 Sqn, used by 22 sqns (7, 9, 12, 35, 44, 49, 50, 57, 61, 75, 83, 90, 97, 100, 101, 115, 138, 148, 149, 207, 214, 617), three flts, three ECM sqns (151, 192, 199) and two cal. sqns (116, 527), until 1956, 7 Sqn; also served with BCBS, BCIS, CGS, CCGS, CNCS, EAAS, EANS, ERS, 2xFTU, Lincoln CFlt, 1xOCU, RAFFC, RAFTC, Radar TFlt and 8xmisc. units, until 1963.

Action: Malaya, Kenya and Aden, also based overseas in Egypt and Singapore.

Powered by four 1,315hp Merlin 68 or 1,635hp Merlin 85 driving 4xbladed propellers.

Serials: RA656–724 (52), RE289–424 (109), RF330–577 (192), SS715–18 (4), SX923–SZ493 (57), WD122–154 (18).

Total 432; 64 accidental and 1 hostile loss.

45b. Lincoln B 2 (FE)

As the B 2 but with modifications for tropical service.

Unknown number of conversions of the B 2.

Avro Lincoln B 2, RF345, 1426 Flt. (Author's Collection)

45c. Lincoln PR 2

A B 2 equipped with H2S radar to radar map entry points for the V-bombers and used for reconnaissance flights over the USSR; in service 1950 with 58 Sqn and used by one sqn and 1x misc. unit until 1956, RRFlt. Two conversions of the B 2.

Span: 120ft/36.58m   Length: 78ft 3in/23.85m   Ceiling: 22,000ft/6,600m   Range: 2,930 miles/4,717km Speed: 295mph/475kmph.

Total Lincolns 500.

Built by Avro, Armstrong-Whitworth and Metropolitan-Vickers.

In service 1945–63.

65 (14%) losses inc. 1 hostile.

46. Lancastrian C 2

A passenger-transport version of the Avro Lancaster bomber (qv), with nose and tail turrets replaced by streamlined fairings and the dorsal turret deleted; five crew and nine passengers, who were provided with some fuselage windows.

In service 1945 with 511 Sqn, used by four sqns (24, 231, 232, 511) and one flt until 1949, 24 Sqn; also served with 1xCU, EAAS, EANS, ECFS, EFS and 3xmisc. units, until 1950. Based overseas in India.

Powered by four 1,610hp RR Merlin 24 in-lines.

Serials: VL967–986 (14), VM701–738 (18).

Span: 102ft/31.09m   Length: 76ft 10in/23.41m   Ceiling: 23,000ft/6,900m   Range: 4,150 miles/6,681km   Speed: 310mph/499kmph.

Total 32; 2 (6%) accidental losses.

47. Shackleton MR 1

Based on the Avro Lincoln (qv) but extensively modified for maritime reconnaissance and anti-submarine work, with a new fuselage holding 10 crew; armed with two 20mm cannon in a B17 dorsal turret, able to carry 20,000lb/9,080kg of stores internally, and with ASV-13 in an under-nose radome.

In service 1951 with 120 Sqn, used by 10 sqns (42, 120, 203, 204, 205, 206, 220, 224, 240, 269) until 1951, also served with MOTU, 1xOCU and 1x misc. unit.

Based overseas in Gibraltar and Singapore.

Powered by two 2,500hp RR Griffon 57 and two 57a in-lines.

Serials: VP254-294 (29), WG507-29 (10).

Total 39; 2 accidental losses.

47a. Shackleton MR 1A

As the MR 1 except for the engines.

In service 1951 with 220 Sqn, used by eight sqns (120, 204, 205, 206, 220, 224, 240, 269) until 1962, 205 Sqn; also served with JASS, MOTU and 1xOCU.

Based overseas in Gibraltar and Singapore.

Powered by four 2,500hp Griffon 57a, with widened outer nacelles.

Serials: WB818-862 (36).

Total 36 plus 29 conversions of the MR 1 making a total of 65; 7 accidental losses.

47b. Shackleton MR 2

A redesign, with a lookout/gunner's position in a more streamlined nose above two remotely-controlled 20mm cannon in a BP-N mounting, plus two 20mm in a B17 dorsal turret (later deleted), 15,000lb/6,810kg of stores and ASV-21 in a retractable radome behind the bomb bay. It had twin tail wheels and a long, glazed tailcone and could carry 33 passengers if required.

In service 1953 with 42 Sqn, used by 14 sqns (37, 38, 42, 120, 203, 204, 205, 206, 210, 220, 224, 228, 240, 269) until 1960, also served with JASS and MOTU.

Action: Aden and Oman, based overseas in Gibraltar, Malta, the Gulf and Singapore.

Serials: WB833, WG530–558 (10), WL737–801 (40), WR951–969 (19).

Total 70; 9 accidental losses of all the MR 2 variants listed below.

Avro Shackleton MR 1A, VP255, 269 Sqn. (Author's Collection)

47c. Shackleton MR 2 Series 1

As the above but with improved electronics, two whip aerials on top of the fuselage and the dorsal turret deleted.

In service 1959 with 210 Sqn, units as above until 1963, 204 Sqn.

Action: Aden and Borneo.

Fifty-two conversions of the MR 2.

47d. Shackleton MR 2 Series 2

As above but with the electronics further improved, UHF, active sonobuoys, TACAN, an ECM 'lighthouse' aerial on the fuselage top, and long exhausts.

In service 1961 with 42 Sqn, units as the MR 2 until 1967.

Action: Aden and Borneo.

Fifty-seven conversions of the MR 2 and MR 2/1.

47e. Shackleton MR 2 Series 3, or MR 2C

As the above but with a revised internal layout reducing the passenger numbers to 11–16, strengthened wings, increased tankage, improved heating, a stronger undercarriage for the extra weight, and could carry US 34/60 nuclear DC.

In service 1966 with 205 Sqn, used by MR 2 units until 1972, 204 Sqn.

Powered by four 2,500hp Griffon 58.

Thirty-seven conversions of the MR2/2.

47f. Shackleton T 2

A crew-conversion trainer version of the MR 2, with extra radar equipment and a rear crew of one instructor and two students; the guns were deleted but it still carried 15,000lb/6,810kg of stores and ASV-21 radar.

In service 1968–70 with MOTU.

Ten conversions of the MR 2.

47g. Shackleton AEW 2

The RAF's first airborne radar station, adapted from the MR 2C and with a crew of nine; all guns and ASV radar were deleted and APS-20f/1 radar was fitted in a large radome under the front fuselage, together with internal modifications and improved avionics. Nicknamed Bear Hunter.

In service from 1972 to 1991 with 8 Sqn.

Twelve conversions of the MR 2C. 1 accidental loss.

47h. Shackleton MR 3

A modernised MR 2, with a twin nose-wheel tricycle undercarriage, the main undercarriage also having twin wheels, wingtip tanks, and a retractable radome behind the bomb bay for ASV-21; armed with two 20mm cannon in the nose, 15,000lb/6,810kg of stores internally including nuclear DCs, and operated by 10 crew who benefited from increased soundproofing and entered via a door in the bomb bay. The exhausts routed under the wings.

In service 1957 with 220 Sqn, used by six sqns (42, 120, 201, 203, 206, 220) until 1960.

Based overseas in Malta.

Serials: WR971–990 (19), XF700–706 (7).

Total 26; no losses.

47j. Shackleton MR3 Series 1

As the above but with internal modifications, improved electronics and two whip aerials on the roof. In service 1961 with 201 Sqn, units as MR 3, until 1963.

Serials: XF707–711 (5).

Total 5 plus 26 conversions of the MR 3 making a total of 31.

47k. Shackleton MR 3 Series 2

As the above but with internal modifications, improved electronics, UHF, TACAN, active sonobuoys and an ECM aerial on the cabin roof.

In service 1961 with 201 Sqn, used by units as MR 3 until 1968.

Thirty-one conversions of the MR 3/1; 2 accidental losses.

Avro Shackleton AEW 2, 8 Sqn. (Author's Collection)

Avro
Shackleton
MR 3, XF707,
206 Sqn.
(Air–Britain
Archives)

47l. Shackleton MR 3 Series 3

A more extensive modification, with a revised internal layout, strengthened wings, and able to carry homing torpedos though the stores weight was reduced to 12,000lb/5,448kg; it had auxiliary jet engines fitted in the deeper outboard nacelles to cope with the increased auw.

In service 1966 with 206 Sqn, used by units as MR 3 until 1972, 203 Sqn.

Powered by four 2,500hp Griffon 58 and two 2,500 lb st B–S Viper 203 jets in each outer nacelle.

Twenty-five conversions of the MR 3/2; 2 accidental losses.

47m. Shackleton T 4

A crew trainer conversion of the MR 1A, with the guns deleted, 15,000lb/6,810kg of stores, ASV-13 in a nose radome, and an ECM aerial.

In service 1957–61 with 236 OCU.

Powered by four 2,500hp Griffon 57a.

Ten conversions of the MR 1A; 1 accidental loss.

47n. Shackleton T 4 Series 1

As the above but with ASV-21 radar, internal modifications and improved electronics.

In service 1960–68 with MOTU.

Nine conversions of the T 4 and seven of the MR 1A; total 16; 1 accidental loss.

	Span	Length	Ceiling	Range	Speed
MR 1	120ft/ 36.58m	77ft 6in/ 23.6m	20,700ft/ 6,210m	2,160 miles/ 3,478km	284mph/ 457kmph
MR 2	"	87ft 6in/ 26.67m	18,800ft/ 5,640m	3,660 miles/ 5,893km	286mph/ 460kmph
MR 2C	"	"	20,200ft/ 6,060m	1,980 miles/ 3,188km	299mph/ 481kmph
AEW 2	"	"	"	"	262mph/422kmph
MR 3	119ft 10in/ 36.52m	"	18,600ft/ 5,580m	2,300 miles/ 3703km	297mph/ 478kmph

T 4   120ft/36.58m   77ft 6in/23.6m   20,700 ft/6,210m 2,160 miles/3,478km 272mph/438kmph

Total Shackletons 176; in service 1951–91; 23 (13%) losses; nicknamed Shack.

48. Vulcan B 1

The second of the RAF's V-bombers, a delta-wing design with five crew (the two pilots on MB-3k ejector seats) and no defensive armament; bomb load was 21,000lb/9,535kg and could include Blue Danube, Violet Club, US Mk5 and Yellow Sun MK I & 2 nuclear weapons. H2S Mk 9a radar in the nose radome.
In service 1956 with 230 OCU and 1957 with 83 Sqn, used by five sqns (44, 50, 83, 101, 617) until 1963, 101 Sqn, and 1xOCU.
Powered by four 9,750lb st Olympus 100, 11,000lb st B-S Olympus 101, or 12,000lb st Olympus 104 jets.
Serials: XA895–913 (18), XH475–532 (20).
Total 38; 3 accidental losses.

48a. Vulcan B 1A

As the B I but with improved ECM in a larger tailcone and a plate aerial under the two starboard engines.
In service 1960 with 617 Sqn, used by five sqns (44, 50, 83, 101, 617) until 1968, Waddington Wing, and by 1xOCU.
Twenty-eight conversions of the B I; 3 accidental losses.

48b. Vulcan B 2

As the B 1A but with a wider-span reshaped wing , AC electrics, MB-4 ejector seats and a shorter nose wheel; able to carry Yellow Sun Mk 2 and WE177A nuclear weapons and, for the Falklands war, some were modified to carry four Shrike anti-radar missiles on two wing pylons.
In service 1960 with 83 Sqn, used by nine sqns (9, 12, 27, 35, 44, 50, 83, 101, 617) until 1984, 50 Sqn; also served with 1xOCU.
Action: Falklands, also based overseas in Cyprus.
Powered by four 16,000lb st Olympus 200, 17,000lb st Olympus 201 or 20,000lb st Olympus 301.
Serials: XH533–563 (14), XJ780–825 (8), XL317–446 (24), XM569–657 (40).
Total 86; 11 accidental losses.

Avro Vulcan B 1, XH481, Waddington. (Charles Parker)

Avro Vulcan B 2, XL446, 35 Sqn. (Peter Green Collection)

48c. Vulcan B 2A

As the B 2 but modified to carry the Blue Steel stand-off nuclear missile, with cut-away bomb bay doors and internal modifications.
In service 1962 with 617 Sqn, used by three sqns (83, 27, 617) until 1970, Scampton Wing, then reverted to normal B 2s.
Powered by four 20,000lb st Olympus 301.
Twenty-four conversions of the B 2.

48d. Vulcan B 2 (MRR)

A strategic-reconnaissance version, without armament but with extra reconnaissance radar, Loran and, sometimes, a 'sniffer' pod under each wing for high-altitude air sampling; the TFR was deleted.
In service 1973–82 with 27 Sqn.
Four conversions of the B 2.

48e. Vulcan B 2 (K) or K 2

The Falkland war saw the RAF short of much-needed tankers and this Vulcan conversion was a short-term solution; the ECM was removed from the tailcone and an HDU fitted in the space, with the drogue housing beneath. Extra fuel tanks were carried in the bomb bay.
In service 1982–84 with 50 Sqn.
Six conversions of the B 2.

	Span	Length	Ceiling	Range	Speed
B 1	99ft/30.18m	92ft 9in/28.27m	55,000ft/16,500m	3,000 miles/4,830km	640mph/1,030kmph
B 1A	"	99ft 11in/30.46m	"	"	"
B 2	111ft/33.83m	"	60,000ft/18,000m	4,600 miles/7,406km	645mph/1,038kmph

Total Vulcans 124; in service 1956–84; 17 (14%) losses; nicknamed Aluminium Overcast and Tin Triangle.

BAE SYSTEMS – see British Aerospace

BARCLAY-CURLE (Glasgow, Scotland)

Assembled Fairey Campania.

BEAGLE (British Executive and General Light Aviation) (Shoreham, Sussex, UK)

Formed from Auster and Miles in 1960 to build a new range of light aircraft but hit financial problems and went out of business in 1969 despite having some successful designs; supplied 21 examples of two types (Husky see Vol. 1).

49. Bassett CC 1

Ordered as a ferry for V-bomber crews but had weight problems and was used instead for general communications work, with two crew and six passengers.
In service 1965 with the Northern Comms. Sqn, used by three sqns (26, 32, 207), 5xcomms. units and 2xmisc. units, until 1974, 26, 32 and 207 Sqns.
Powered by two 310hp RR-Continental G10-470a in-lines.
Serials: XS765–784 (20).
Span: 45ft 9in/13.95m   Length: 33ft 9in/10.29m   Ceiling: 19,000ft/5,700m   Range: 750 miles/1,207km   Speed: 220mph/354kmph.
Total 20; 1 (5%) accidental loss.

BEECH (USA)

Formed 1932 and famous for its light aircraft and small airliners to the present day but known as Raytheon from 1994. Supplied 453 examples of three types.

Beagle Bassett CC 1.
(Charles Parker)

Beech Traveller I, PB-1,
preserved example.
(Author's Collection)

50. Traveller I (UC-43)

A communications type for the RAF and FAA, with a pilot and four passengers. Nicknamed Staggerwing.
In service 1942 with various Comms.Flts, used by 6xRAF and 6xFAA comms. units, 2xFAA ATU and
one FAA misc. unit, until 1946, Aden Comms.Flt.
Based overseas in North Africa, Middle East, Aden, Palestine and India.
Powered by one 450hp P&W Wasp Junior R985-an-60 radial.
Serials: FL653–670 (18), FT461–535 (75), FZ428–439 (11), FZ442–43 (2) plus two impressed Beech 17s
– DR628, DS180.
Span: 32ft/9.75m   Length: 26ft 9in/8.15m   Ceiling: 20,000ft/6,000m   Range: 500
miles/305km   Speed: 212mph/341kmph.
Total 106, plus 2 impressed making a total of 108 (75 FAA); 22 (10%) losses inc. 13 hostile.

51. Navigator I (AT-7B)

Although this was supplied as a navigation trainer, as used by the USAAF and evidenced by an astro-
dome, the FAA used it for communications, carrying two crew and six passengers.
In service 1943 in the USA, used by 1xcomms. unit until 1946, 742 Sqn.
Based overseas in the Far East and Dutch East Indies.
Powered by two 450hp Wasp Junior R985-25.
Serials: FR879–83 (5).
Total 5; no losses.

51a. Expediter I (C-45B)

As the above but designed as a light airliner so had no astrodome; used by the RAF and FAA for communications work. In service 1944 with 782 Sqn, used by one RAF CU, 18xRAF and 4xFAA comms. units, and 2xRAF misc. units until 1947, 782 Sqn.

Based overseas in North America, North Africa, Far East, Egypt and India.

Powered by two 450hp Wasp Junior R985-an-1.

Serials: FT975–79 (5), HB128-206 (53).

Total 58 (6 FAA); 9 accidental losses.

51b. Expediter II (C-45F)

As the Mk I but had a longer nose for baggage stowage and room for seven passengers; also had longer engine nacelles.

In service 1944 with 742 Sqn, used by 6xFAA and 35xRAF comms. units, 1xRAF CU, 4xFAA ATU, and 8xRAF and 1xFAA misc. units, until 1955, 781 Sqn.

Based overseas in North Africa, southern Europe, Far East, Malta, Egypt, India, Ceylon, Singapore and Dutch East Indies.

Serials: FT980–996 (17), HB208–229 (73), HD752–776 (25), KJ468–560 (93), KN100–199 (50), KP100–123 (24).

Total 282 (67 FAA); 17 accidental losses.

Span: 47ft 8in/14.53m   Length: 34ft 2in/10.41m (34ft 8in/10.4m Mk II)   Ceiling: 25,000ft/7,500m   Range: 900 miles/1,449km   Speed: 230mph/370kmph.

Total Expediter variants 345; in service 1943–55; 26 (7%) losses.

BELL (USA)

A company formed in 1935 which did not have many successful Second World War designs but became a major helicopter manufacturer post-war. Supplied 52 examples of three types (Airacobra, 212 AH 1, Griffin HT 1 see Vol. 1).

52. Griffin HAR 2

A transport and SAR helicopter for the RAF in Cyprus, carrying three crew and nine passengers; has weather radar in a small radome on the nose.

In service 2003 with 84 Sqn, used by one sqn (84) and 1xCU until the present 2010.

Based overseas in Cyprus.

Powered by two P&W Canada PT6T-3b turborops in Twin-Pac configuration giving 1,800 shp.

Serials: ZJ703–706 (4).

Rotor diameter: 46ft/14.02m   Length: 42ft 5in/12.93m   Ceiling: 17,000ft/5,100m   Range: 311 miles/501km   Speed: 161mph/259kmph.

Total 4; no losses to date.

Beech Expediter II. (Newark Air Museum)

Bell Griffin HAR
2, 60 R Sqn – note
nose radome.
(Author's Collection)

BELLANCA (USA)

A well-known pre-war builder of light airliners and light aircraft, existing from 1927–55; supplied one example of one type.

53. Pacemaker

A high-wing cabin monoplane, the wing braced by four struts and with a single fin/rudder, impressed for communications work with the FAA, carrying a pilot and five passengers.
In service 1941–45.
Powered by one 300hp Wright Whirlwind R975 radial which was uncowled.
Serial: DZ209.
Span: 46ft 4in/14.12m   Length: 27ft/8.23m   Ceiling: n/k   Range: 670 miles/1,079km   Speed: 145mph/233kmph.
Total 1 impressed. No losses.

BERWICK (London, UK)

Assembled Airco DH 4, 9 and 9A.

BIRMINGHAM RAILWAY CARRIAGE & WAGON Co. (Smethwick, Staffs, UK)

Assembled Airco DH 10, HP 0/400 and GAL Hamilcar.

BLACKBURN (Leeds, later Brough, Yorks, UK)

A pioneer company founded by Robert Blackburn in 1914 and which concentrated on naval aircraft as its military market. Probably its most successful design was its last, the Buccaneer, after which the company was taken over by Hawker-Siddeley Aviation in 1960 and renamed in 1965. Supplied 1,824 examples of 15 types (B2, Skua, Roc, Firebrand and Buccaneer see Vol. 1), also assembled Sopwith Baby and Cuckoo, A-W Siskin, Fairey Swordfish and Barracuda, Short Sunderland, Percival Prentice, RAF BE2C, and B-P Balliol.

54. Kangaroo

An anti-submarine patrol bomber for the fledgling RAF, with two or three crew and armed with a Lewis mg in nose and dorsal positions, plus 920lb/420kg of bombs internally and underwing. Nicknamed Hopper.
In service 1918 with 246 Sqn, used by three sqns (246, 252, 256) until 1918, 246 Sqn; also served with 1xSASIObs, 1xFS and 2xMObsS.

Blackburn Kangaroo,
246 Sqn. (G. Stuart
Leslie)

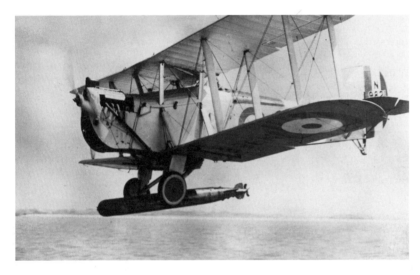

Blackburn Dart I,
N9821, Gosport
Base. (Newark Air
Museum)

Action: home waters. Powered by two 250hp RR Falcon II in-lines.
Serials: B8837–40 (4), B9970–989 (20).
Span: 74ft 10in/22.81m   Length: 44ft 2in/13.46m   Ceiling: 10,500ft/3,150m   Range: 250 miles/402
km   Speed: 98mph/158kmph.
Total 24; losses not known.

55. Dart I

The FAA's first post-First World War torpedo-bomber, a single-seater able to carry one torpedo under
the fuselage or 1,040lb/470kg of bombs underwing, but with no defensive armament; it could be fitted
with floats.
In service 1922 with 210 Sqn, used by one RAF sqn (210), one FAA sqn (810) and five FAA flts (460,
461, 462, 463, 464) until 1934, 810 Sqn; also served with SoACo-op ,1xFTS and 1xmisc. unit. Embarked
on three carriers.
Powered by one 480hp Napier Lion IIb or 470hp Lion V in-line.
Serials: N9536–9561 (26), N9620–9629 (10), N9687–9696 (10), N9714–9723 (10), N9792–9823 (32),
N9990–9999 (10), S1115–20 (6), S1129–1138 (10).
Span: 45ft 6in/13.87m   Length: 35ft 5in/10.8m   Ceiling: 12,700ft/3,810m   Range: 285 miles/459
km   Speed: 107mph/172kmph.
Total 114; 26 (19%) accidental losses.

56. Blackburn I

An ugly FAA spotter and reconnaissance type, with three or four crew and armed with a Vickers mg in the port fuselage side and a Lewis mg in the rear cockpit. The Mk I's upper wing was integral to the fuselage and it had split undercarriage legs and overwing fuel tanks.

In service 1926 with 422 Flt, used by two flts (420, 422) until 1926, 422 Flt, also used by TB Leuchars. Embarked on three carriers.

Powered by one 480hp Napier Lion IIb in-line.

Serials: N9579–9590 (11), N9681–86 (6), N9824–9835 (12).

Total 29; 6 accidental losses.

56a. Blackburn II

As the above but the upper wing was above, and strutted to, the fuselage, the wing tanks were deleted and it had an axle undercarriage.

In service 1926 with 420 Flt, used by four flts (420, 422, 448, 450) until 1931, 449 Flt; also served with TB Leuchars and 1xmisc. unit. Embarked on four carriers.

Powered by one 470hp Lion V.

Serials: N9978–9988 (10), S1046–1057 (13), S1153–57 (5).

Total 28 plus 11 conversions of the Mk I making a total of 39; 14 accidental losses.

56b. Blackburn Trainer

As the Mk II but with side-by-side seats in the front cockpit and dual controls in a wider fuselage. Two fuel tanks on the upper wing top surface. Nicknamed Bull.

In service 1926–31 at 1 FTS. Serials: N9589, N9982, N9989.

Total 3; no losses.

All Marks: Span: 45ft 6in/13.87m   Length: 36ft 2in/11.03m   Ceiling: 12,900ft/3,870m   Range: 440 miles/708 km   Speed: 122mph/196kmph.

Total Blackburns 60; in service 1926–31; 20 (32%) losses.

Blackburn Blackburn II, N9686 converted from Mk I, Leuchars TB. (Newark Air Museum)

Blackburn
Ripon
IIA, S1564,
811 Sqn.
(Newark Air
Museum)

57. Ripon II

A two-seat torpedo-bomber for the FAA, armed with a Vickers mg in the port fuselage and a Lewis mg
in the rear cockpit and able to carry one torpedo under the fuselage or 1,650lb/743kg of bombs under-
wing and fuselage. The Mk II was of composite wood/metal construction.
In service 1929 with 462 Flt, used by three flts (460, 461, 462) and one sqn (812) until 1933, 812 Sqn; also
served with 1xRAF TTFlt and two misc. units. Embarked on two carriers.
Powered by one 540hp Napier Lion XI in-line.
Serials: S1265–72 (7), S1357–1369 (13).
Total 20; 5 accidental losses.

57a. Ripon IIA

As the Mk II but had a cropped top to the fin, HP slots on the upper wing leading-edges and detail
modifications.
In service 1930 with 460 Flt, used by three flts (460, 461, 462) and one sqn (811) until 1934, 811 Sqn, also
used by TB Leuchars, 1xATU and 1xmisc. unit. Embarked on four carriers.
Powered by one 460hp Lion X or 530hp Lion XIa.
Serials: S1424–32 (9), S1465–73 (9), S1553–1574 (22), K2884–87 (4).
Total 44; 9 accidental losses.

57b. Ripon IIC

As the Mk IIA but with an all-metal frame and increased wing-sweep.
In service 1932 with 462 Flt, used by three flts (460, 461, 466) and three sqns (810, 811, 812) until 1935,
811 Sqn; also served with 1xATU and 1xmisc. unit. Embarked on three carriers.
Powered by one 530hp Lion XIa.
Serials: S1649–1674 (26).
Total 26 plus 11 conversions of the Mk II and Mk IIA making a total of 37; 4 accidental losses.
All Marks: Span: 44ft 10in/13.66m   Length: 36ft 9in/11.21m   Ceiling: 10,000ft/3,000m   Range: 815
miles/1,312km   Speed: 126mph/203kmph.
Total Ripons 90; in service 1929–35; 18 (21%) losses.

58. Iris III

A large general-reconnaissance flying boat for the RAF, with a crew of five and armed with a Lewis mg in nose and dorsal positions and a bomb load of 2,000lb/908kg carried underwing. It had an open pilot's cockpit with side-by-side seats and a slab-sided fuel tank under the upper wing above each engine.

In service from 1930–32 with 209 Sqn.

Powered by three 650hp RR Condor IIIb in-lines supported on fairings to the lower wing containing the radiators.

Serials: N238, S1263-64 (2), S1593.

Total 4; 1 accidental loss.

58a. Iris V

As the Mk III but with different engines.

In service 1932–34 with 209 Sqn.

Powered by three 825hp RR Buzzard IIms in-lines with large intakes on the rear of the cowlings and supported by struts.

Three conversions of the Mk III. 2 accidental losses.

	Span	Length	Ceiling	Range	Speed
Mk III	97ft/29.57m	67ft 5in/20.55m	10,000ft/3,000m	470 miles/757 km	118mph/190kmph
Mk V	"	"	"	"	129mph/208kmph

Total Irises 4; in service 1930–34; 3 (75%) losses.

59. Perth I

A development of the Iris V (above), with a redesigned hull and armed with a 37mm cannon and Lewis mg in the nose position and a Lewis mg in the dorsal and tail positions, plus 2,000lb/908kg of bombs underwing. It had a cockpit canopy and the three fuel tanks were wider than those on the Iris.

In service 1935–37 with 209 Sqn.

Powered by three 825hp RR Buzzard IIms in-lines.

Serials: K3580–82 (3).

Span: 97ft/29.57m   Length: 70ft/21.34m   Ceiling: 11,500ft/3,450m   Range: 780 miles/1,256 km   Speed: 132mph/213kmph.

Total 3; 1 (33%) accidental loss.

Blackburn Iris V, S1593, 209 Sqn. (Newark Air Museum)

Blackburn Baffin I,
S1671 converted from
Ripon, Gosport Base.
(Charles Parker)

60. Baffin I

A two-seat torpedo-bomber developed from the Blackburn Ripon IIC (qv), armed with a Vickers mg
in the port fuselage and a Lewis mg in the rear cockpit; it carried a torpedo under the fuselage or
1,650lb/743kg of bombs underwing.
In service 1934 with 812 Sqn, used by four FAA sqns (810, 811, 812, 820) until 1938, 810 Sqn; also served
with 1xPTU, SoNCo-op and 1xmisc. unit. Embarked on three carriers.
Powered by one 590hp Bristol Pegasus Im3 or 620hp Pegasus IIm3 radial.
Serials: K3546–3559 (14), K3589–90 (2), K4071–4080 (10), K4776–78 (3).
Span: 45ft 6in/13.87m   Length: 38ft 4in/11.68   Ceiling: 15,000ft/4,500m   Range: 450 miles/
724 km   Speed: 136mph/218kmph.
Total 29 plus 60 conversions of the Ripon making a total of 89; 26 (38%) accidental losses.

61. Shark I

Yet another two-seat torpedo-bomber for the FAA, with a Vickers on the top port side of the fuselage,
a Lewis mg in the rear cockpit, a torpedo under the fuselage, or 1,650lb/743kg of bombs under-wing.
Notable for its cantilever struts, much reducing the rigging wires.
In service 1935 with 820 Sqn, used by one sqn and one flt until 1936, 820 Sqn; also served with 1xPTU,
SoNCo-op and 1xmisc. unit until 1937. Embarked on two carriers.
Powered by one 720hp A-S Tiger IV radial.
Serials: K4349–4364 (16).
Total 16; 3 accidental losses.

61a. Shark II

As the Mk I but with detail changes which seemed to have made a difference to the type as, unlike the
Mk I, it saw widespread service; could be fitted with floats.
In service 1936 with 821 Sqn, used by four sqns (810, 820, 821, 822) and three flts until 1937, 820 Sqn. In
second-line service with 3xPTU, 2xCU, 2xObsTU, 1x TAGTU, 3xATU, 1xRAF TorpTU, SoNCo-op,
and 1xmisc. unit until 1943. Embarked on two carriers, three battleships, one battle-cruiser, one seaplane
carrier and two cruisers.
Action: Far East, also served overseas in BWI.
Powered by one 760hp Tiger VIc.
Serials: K4881–82 (2), K5607–5659 (52), K8450–8519 (70).
Total 124; 28 accidental and 3 hostile losses.

61b. Shark III

As the Mk II but with a long, glazed canopy for the two crew and a 3xbladed propeller; it only saw brief service as a torpedo-bomber, being replaced by the Fairey Swordfish (qv), but was much used for training and as a target tug in which role, like the Mk II, a winch and winch operator were installed in the rear cockpit.

In service 1937 with 821 Sqn, used briefly by three sqns (701, 810, 821) until 1937, also served with 2xPTU, 1xCU, 3xObsTU, 1xTAGTU, 3xATU, SoNCo-op, SPTFlt, 1xRAF OTU, 2xAACU, 1xTorpTU and one FAA misc. unit until 1943. Embarked on one carrier.

Action: Far East, also based overseas in BWI.

Serials: K8891–8935 (45), L2337–2386 (50).

Total 95; 22 accidental and 3 hostile losses.

All Marks: Span: 46ft/14.02m   Length: 35ft 2in/10.72m   Ceiling: 16,400ft/4,920m Range: 790 miles/1,272 km   Speed: 152mph/245kmph.

Total Sharks 235; in service 1935–43; 59 (25%) losses inc. 6 hostile.

62. Botha I

Designed as a torpedo-bomber for the RAF but was underpowered and saw little service in this role, being mostly used as a crew trainer and even in this role it was unpopular; as a bomber it had four crew and carried a torpedo or 2,000lb/908kg of bombs internally, and had one Browning mg in the port lower front fuselage and two in a FN-7 dorsal turret. Nicknamed Why Bother.

Blackburn Shark II, K8468, 820 Sqn. (Charles Parker)

Blackburn Botha I, L6328, 3 School of GR. (Peter Green Collection)

Blackburn Beverley C 1,
XL149, 84 Sqn. (Newark Air
Museum)

In service 1940 with 608 Sqn, used by two sqns (502, 608) and one transport sqn (24) until 1940; also
served with 4xOAFU, 2xPAFU, AAS, 5xAGS, 2xAONS, 3xAOS, 4xBGS, EWS, 1xFTS, 2xGRS, 1xOTU,
RDFS, 2xRS, 2xTorpTU, CC Landplane Pilot's S, 1xmisc. unit, 5xFAA TU and 1xFAA ATU, until 1943.
Action: North Atlantic.
Powered by two 750hp Bristol Perseus X or 860hp Perseus Xa radials.
Serials: L6106–6345 (239), L6347–6590 (200), W5017–5169 (138).
Span: 59ft/17.98m   Length: 51ft 1in/15.57m   Ceiling; 17,500ft/5,250m   Range: 1,270 miles/
2,045 km   Speed: 220mph/354kmph.
Total 577; 126 (22%) accidental losses.

63. Beverley C 1

A General Aircraft Ltd (qv) design for a civil freighter, taken over by Blackburn and developed as a large
military transport for the RAF, with four crew and able to carry 94 passengers or 49,000lb/22,050kg of
freight. Nicknamed Barrack Block.
In service 1956 with 47 Sqn, used by six sqns (30, 34, 47, 48, 53, 84) until 1967, 34 Sqn; also served with
1xOCU, FEAF T Sqn and 1xParaTS.
Action: Aden and Borneo, also based overseas in the Gulf, Kenya and Singapore. Powered by four 2,625hp
Bristol Centaurus 173 or 175 radials.
Serials: XB260–291 (18), XH116–24 (9), XL130–52 (8), XM103–112 (10).
Span: 162ft/49.38m   Length: 99ft 5in/30.31m   Ceiling: 16,000ft/4,800m   Range: 1,300 miles/2,093
km   Speed: 238mph/383kmph.
Total 45; 8 (17%) losses inc. 2 hostile.

BLOCH (France)

A company formed in 1918 and well known between the wars, going out of business in 1936; supplied
one example of one type.

64. Type 81

A light cabin transport (two seats) or ambulance (pilot and patient), a low-wing monoplane with the
pilot in an open cockpit behind the cabin. Taken over by a Free-French unit under RAF command.
In service 1940 with 2 F-F Flt, used by 1xcomms. unit and 1xmisc. unit, until 1940, F-F Comms.Flt.
Based in North Africa, not in UK.
Powered by one 175hp Salmson 9nD radial.
Serial: AX677.
Span: 39ft/11.89m   Length: 26ft 5in/8.05m   Ceiling: 21,000ft/6,300m   Range: 406 miles/
654 km   Speed : 117mph/188kmph.
Total 1; 1 (100%) accidental loss.

Boeing Fortress I, AN531. (Air-Britain Archives)

BOEING (USA)

One of the world's most famous aircraft companies which formed in 1917 but, surprisingly, has only supplied 344 examples of five types to the British; also assembled Consolidated Catalina and Douglas Boston.

65. Fortress I (B-17C)

Supplied as a heavy day-bomber for the RAF which found it not suited for operational roles over Europe, so it was quickly transferred to general-reconnaissance work; it had seven crew and was armed with one Browning mg in nose and beam positions, and two in dorsal and ventral positions, plus 2,500lb/1,135kg of bombs internally.

In service 1941–42 with 90 Sqn, and with 220 GR Sqn until 1942, also served with 2xCU until 1943.
Action: northern Europe, North Atlantic and Mediterranean.
Powered by four 1,000hp Wright Cyclone R1820-G205a radials.
Serials: AN518–537 (20).
Total 20; 6 accidental and 4 hostile losses.

65a. Fortress II (B-17F)

A developed version more fitted to European operations, but was used by the RAF for general-reconnaissance and RCM work; it had a dorsal fin, the ventral pannier was deleted and the much improved armament consisted of two 0.5in Browning mg in the nose position, two in a Sperry A2 dorsal turret, two in a Sperry A2 ventral turret, and two in a tail position, plus 8,000lb/3,672kg of stores internally and ASV-II radar with external aerials (GR and Met).

In service 1942 with 206 Sqn, used by two sqns (206, 220), three met. sqns, (251, 519, 521) and one RCM sqn (214) until 1946, 220 Sqn, and for met. reconnaissance to 1947; also served with 1xCU and 1xmisc. unit.
Action: North and South Atlantic and northern Europe.
Powered by four 1,380hp Cyclone R1820–97 driving paddle-blade propellors.
Serials: FA695–713 (19), SR376–389 (14).
Total 33; 8 accidental and 4 hostile losses.

65b. Fortress IIA (B-17E)

As the Mk II but with a shorter nose-transparency and detail modifications.
In service 1942 with 220 Sqn, used by five sqns (53, 59, 206, 220, 224), three met. sqns (251, 519, 521), 2xCU and 1xOTU until 1945, 220 Sqn, met-reconnaissance to 1947.
Action: North and South Atlantic.
Powered by four 1,200hp Cyclone R1820–65.
Serials: FK184–213 (30), FL449–464 (14).
Total 44; 14 accidental and 3 hostile losses.

Boeing Fortress IIA, FK212, 220 Sqn. (Newark Air Museum)

65c. Fortress III (B-17G)

A developed version used by the RAF for RCM duties, as the Mk II but with the nose guns and the ventral turret deleted, and one 0.5in Browning in each beam position; many external aerials for the RCM equipment and H2S in a radome under the nose.

In service 1944 with 214 Sqn, used by two sqns (214, 223) and two met. sqns (RCM gear removed) (220, 251), 3xCU and 1xmisc unit until 1946, RWE.

Action: northern Europe and North Atlantic.

Powered by four 1,380hp Cyclone R1820–98.

Serials: HB763–820 (32), KH998–LJ127 (30), KL830–37 (8).

Total 70; 2 accidental and 10 hostile losses.

	Span	Length	Ceiling	Range	Speed
Mk I	103ft 9in/ 31.62m	67ft 9in/ 20.65m	37,000ft/ 11,100m	2,400 miles/ 3,864 km	323mph/5 20kmph
Mk II	"	74ft 9in/ 22.79m	37,500ft/ 11,250m	2,000 miles/ 3,220km	325mph/ 523kmph
Mk IIA	"	73ft 10in/22.5m	36,000ft/10,800m	"	317mph/510kmph
Mk III	"	74ft 9in/22.79m or 74ft 4in/22.66m	35,600ft/ 10,680m	1,900 miles/ 3,059 km	302mph/ 486kmph

Total Fortresses 167; in service 1941–47; 51 (31%) losses inc. 21 hostile; nicknamed Flying Fortress and Fort.

66. Washington B 1 (B-29 or B-29A)

Ordered as a stop-gap until the Canberra arrived in Bomber Command, the Washington was the RAF's name for the Superfortress; it had eight or nine crew and was armed with two 0.5in Brownings in a GE front dorsal turret, two in a GE rear dorsal turret, two in a GE front ventral turret, two in a GE rear ventral turret, and two in a GE tail turret, plus 17,000lb/7,720kg of bombs internally and APQ-13 radar in a radome between the two bomb bays. The last three Washingtons, WZ966–68, were RB–29As and were used for ELINT duties with 192 Sqn though without a new role designation; all armament except the tail guns was removed and the crew increased to 12 including six special operators.

Boeing Washington B 1, WW346, Central Signals Est. (Author's Collection)

In service 1950 with the Washington CU and 115 Sqn, used by eight sqns (15, 35, 44, 57, 90, 115, 149, 207) until 1954, 90, 115 and 207 Sqns, also used by 1xCU and one ECM sqn (192) until 1958, 192 Sqn. Powered by four 2,200hp Wright Turbo-Cyclone R3350-23 radials.
Serials: WF434–574 (70), WW342–355 (10), WZ966–68 (3).
Span: 141ft 3in/43.06m or 142ft 3in/43.37m   Length: 99ft/30.18m   Ceiling: 31,800ft/9,540m   Range: 4,100 miles/6,601 km   Speed: 360mph/580kmph.
Total 83; 4 (5%) accidental losses.

67. Chinook HC 1 (CH-47D modified)

This helicopter (designed by the Vertol company and taken over by Boeing in 1973) had been in US and other air forces' service for many years before the RAF finally ordered it for heavy lift and transport duties; with a crew of four, it can carry 44 passengers or 28,000lb/12,720kg of freight, internally or underslung. Armament was two 0.5in gpmg mg mounted in the doors or windows.
In service 1980 with 240 OCU, 1981 with 18 Sqn, used by three sqns (7, 18, 78), 1xOCU and 1xmisc. unit until 1994, 7 Sqn.
Action: Falklands, Northern Ireland and the Gulf, also based overseas in Germany.
Powered by two 3,750shp Avco-Lycoming T55-L11e or Textron-Lycoming 4,500shp T55-L-712 turboprops.
Serials: ZA670–721 (33), ZD574–76 (3), ZD980–84 (5).
Total 41; 6 accidental and 3 hostile losses.

67a. Chinook HC 1B

A special forces version for the Gulf war, with special equipment, extra defensive aids, extra fuel tanks in the cabin, and glass-fibre rotor blades.
In service during the war, 1992.
Unknown number of conversions of the HC 1, as far as is known converted back to HC 1s.

67b. Chinook HC 2 (CH-47D)

As the HC 1 but with improved avionics, uprated transmission and two M134 7.62mm miniguns mounted in the windows plus an M60 0.5in mg on the ramp when required; externally it has an intake in the front of the rear rotor pylon.

Boeing Chinook HC 2. (Author's Collection)

In service 1994 with 27 (R) Sqn, used by four sqns (7, 18, 27, 78), 1xRSqn, one flt and 1xmisc. unit until the present, 2010. Embarked on one aircraft carrier and one helicopter ship.
Action: Bosnia, Kosovo, Sierra Leone, Afghanistan and Iraq, also based overseas in Germany and the Falklands.
Powered by two Textron-Lycoming 4,500shp T55-L-712.
Thirty-two conversions of the HC 1; 1 accidental and 3 hostile losses to date.

67c. Chinook HC 2A
As the HC 2 but are new-build aircraft incorporating detail improvements and with reduced vibration.
In service 2001 with 18 Sqn, used by two sqns (18, 27) until the present, 2010. Embarked on one aircraft carrier and one helicopter ship.
Action: Iraq and Afghanistan, also based overseas in the Falklands.
Serials: ZH775–77 (3), ZH891–96 (6).
Total 9; no losses to date.

67d. Chinook HC 3 (MH-47E)
Ordered as a special forces transport with much special equipment but without the vital avionics and software required so was put into storage; in 2007 it was announced that they will be converted into normal heavy lift transports to be in service by 2010 and will be very similar to the HC 2.
Powered by two T55-L-714.
Serials: ZH897–904 (8). Total 8.
All Marks: Rotor diameter: 60ft/18.29m   Length: 51ft/15.54m   Ceiling: 15,000ft/4,500m   Range: 242 miles/390 km   Speed: 183mph/295kmph.
Total Chinooks 58; in service 1980–present day; 10 (19%) losses inc. 5 hostile; nicknamed Hook, Wokka–Wokka. [22 new Chinooks were ordered as this book went to press.]

68. Sentry AEW 1 (E-3D)
After an ill-fated attempt to convert the Hawker-Siddeley Nimrod (qv) into an airborne radar station for the RAF the Sentry was ordered, albeit with more advanced features over the NATO E-3A which had been rejected by the MoD originally; it has a crew of 17/18 and is unarmed, with AN/APY-2 radar

in a very large circular radome above and strutted to the fuselage. Nicknamed (by the public) AWACS.
In service 1991 with 8 Sqn, used by two sqns (8, 23), one RSqn and one TSqn until the present, 2010.
Action: Kosovo, Iraq and Afghanistan.
Powered by four 24,000lb st CFM Int.56-2a-3 turbofans.
Serials: ZH101–07 (7).
Span: 145ft 9in/44.43m   Length: 152ft 11in/46.61m   Ceiling: 40,000ft/12,000m   Range: 4,500
miles/7,245 km   Speed: 530mph/853kmph.
Total 7; no losses to date.

69. Globemaster III C 1

The Kosovo campaign showed that the RAF sorely needed a heavy lift transport and it was decided
to lease four Globemasters from Boeing, keeping their USAF designation of C-17 because they were
leased but becoming the C 1 when purchased; the aircraft carries four crew, and 144 passengers or
172,200lb/78,179kg of freight. The type has proved so useful that the four leased aircraft have been pur-
chased together with an extra three.
In service 2001 with 99 Sqn, used by one sqn (99), still in service 2010.
Action: Afghanistan, Iraq.
Powered by four 41,700lb st P&W F117-p-100 turbofans.
Serials: ZZ171-77 (7).
Span: 165ft/50.3m   Length: 174ft/53.04m   Ceiling: 45,000ft/13,500m   Range: 3,225 miles/
5,192 km   Speed: 515mph/829kmph.
**Total 7; no losses to date. [As this book went to press an order was announced for 3 ex-USAF
Boeing Stratotanker KC135s which will be modified to replace the Nimrod R 1s in the
surveillance role.]**

Boeing Sentry AEW
1, ZH102, 8 Sqn.
(Author's Collection)

Boeing Globemaster
C 1, ZZ172, 99 Sqn.
(Andrew Nowland)

BOREL (France)

A little-known company which existed from 1909 to 1919; supplied eight examples of one type.

70. Seaplane

A shoulder-wing monoplane, braced by 'pyramid' kingposts above and below the fuselage, with two main floats and one tail; used for reconnaissance work with the RNAS as an unarmed two-seater, also as a landplane. In service 1913 at Calshot RNAS, used by six units (Calshot, Eastchurch, Dundee, Grain, Hendon, Leven) until 1914, Eastchurch RNAS. Embarked on one cruiser.
Powered by one 80hp Gnome 7z Lambda rotary.
Serials: 37, 48, 83–88 (6).
Dimensions and performance: n/k.
Total 8; 1 (12%) accidental loss.

BOULTON & PAUL (Norwich, Norfolk, later Wolverhampton, Staffs, UK)

A Norwich engineering company which started to build aircraft in 1915, often other companies' designs, but which also supplied 1,348 examples of five of its own types (Defiant, Balliol & Sea Balliol see Vol. 1). Also assembled RAF FE 2 and Fairey Barracuda.

71. Sidestrand II

A manoeuvrable day-bomber for the RAF, with three or four crew and armed with one Lewis mg in nose, dorsal and ventral positions, plus 1,050lb/480kg of bombs internally.
In service 1928 to 1931 with 101 Sqn.
Powered by two 440hp Bristol Jupiter VIII radials.
Serials: J9176–81 (6).
Total 6; 1 accidental loss.

71a. Sidestrand III

As the Mk II but with a bomb-aimer's window, intercom and internal changes.
In service 1930–36 with 101 Sqn.
Powered by two 460hp Jupiter VIIIf.
Serials: J9185–89 (5), J9767–70 (4), K1992–94 (3).
Total 12 plus 1 conversion of the Mk II making a total of 13; 3 accidental losses.

	Span	Length	Ceiling	Range	Speed
Mk I	71ft 11in/21.92m	46ft/14.02m	21,500ft/6,450m	500 miles/805km	129mph/208kmph
Mk II	"	"	24,000ft/7,200m	"	144mph/232kmph

Total Sidestrands 18; in service 1928–36; 4 (23%) losses.

Boulton & Paul Sidestrand II, 101 Sqn. (Newark Air Museum)

Boulton & Paul
Overstrand I, J9185
converted from
Sidestrand, 101 Sqn.
(Alastair Goodrum
Collection)

72. Overstrand I

A development of the Sidestrand (above), and the first RAF type to have a powered turret, a BP-1 in the nose carrying a Lewis mg; there was also one Lewis in the dorsal and ventral positions and the bomb load was 1,500lb/681kg carried internally and under the centre-section. Five crew.

In service 1935 with 101 Sqn, used by two sqns (101, 144) until 1938, 101 Sqn, also served with the AAS, 2xAOS, 1xB&GS, CLE and 1xmisc. unit until 1941.

Powered by two 620hp Bristol Pegasus IIm3 radials.

Serials: K4546–64 (19), K8173–77 (5).

Span: 71ft 11in/21.92m   Length: 46ft 2in/14.07m   Ceiling: 22,500ft/6,750m   Range: 545 miles/ 877 km   Speed: 153mph/246kmph.

Total 24 plus 5 conversions of the Sidestrand making a total of 29; 5 (17%) accidental losses.

BREGUET (France)

An early aviation company formed in 1911 which lasted until 1971; supplied 53 examples of three types (L 1, G 3 and L 2, see Vol. 1).

73. Biplane

A two-seat bomber for the RFC and RNAS, able to carry light bombs underwing but with no defensive armament. It had a very narrow circular fuselage, two-bay single strut wings and a cruciform tail; the undercarriage had four main wheels with a skid behind. Nicknamed Tin-Whistle.

In service 1912 at Eastchurch RNAS, used by one RNAS unit and two RFC sqns (2, 4) until 1914, 4 Sqn.

Powered by one 80hp Chenu or 110hp Canton-Unne/Salmson radial with a large propeller spinner.

Serials: 6, 310, 312 (3).

Dimensions and performance n/k.

Total 3 (1 RNAS).

74. Type II de Chasse

A bomber biplane for the RNAS, with two crew and armed with a Lewis mg in the front cockpit and 160lb/75kg of bombs underwing.

In service 1915 with 3 (N) Sqn, used by four units (1W, 3W, 5W, 3Nsqn) until 1916, Dover RNAS.

Action: northern and southern Europe.

Powered by one 200hp Canton-Unne/Salmson 2m7, 220hp Renault 12FE, or 200hp Sunbeam Mohawk in-line.

Serials: 1390–94 (5), 3209–13 (5), 3883–87 (5).

Total 15; 2 accidental losses.

Breguet V Concours, 9196, 3 Wing RNAS.
(S. Taylor via G. Stuart Leslie)

74a. Type V Concours

As the above with two crew, one Lewis mg in the front cockpit, and 112lb/50kg of bombs underwing; it had two fuel tanks under the upper wing. Built by Breguet and Grahame-White.

In service 1916 with 5 (N) Wing, used by two units (3 W, 5 W) until 1916, 5 Wing.

Action: northern Europe.

Powered by one 250hp RR Eagle II, 220hp Renault 12FE, or 200hp Sunbeam Mohawk in-line pusher.

Serials: 1398–99 (2), 9175–9200 (26), 9426.

Total 29; 4 accidental and 4 hostile losses.

74b. De Bombe

An RNAS bomber, a two-seater with a Lewis in the rear cockpit and bombs.

In service during 1916 with 5 (N) Wing.

Action: northern Europe.

Powered by one 200hp Sunbeam Mohawk.

Serial: 3888.

Total 1; no losses.

	Span	Length	Ceiling	Range	Speed
Type II de Chasse	61ft 9in/	32ft 6in/	12,800ft/	420 miles/	84mph/
	18.82m	9.9m	3,840m	676 km	135kmph
Type V	57ft 9in	"	14,000ft/	425 miles/	
	/17.6m		4,200m	684 km	"

Total Type II/Vs 45; in service 1915–16; 10 (22%) losses inc. 4 hostile.

BRISTOL (Bristol, Somerset, UK)

Formed as the British and Colonial Aircraft Co. in 1910, changing its name to Bristol in 1920; it built many famous types, including many civil, until 1963 when it merged into the British Aircraft Corporation (qv) having already lost its helicopter side to Westland in 1960. Supplied 18,193 examples of 18 types (Boxkite, Prieur, Coanda, Scout, S2A, F2A & B, M1, Bulldog, Beaufighter and Buckmaster, see Vol. 1).

75. TB 8

A bomber and reconnaissance type for the RNAS, with two crew and able to carry 120lb/55kg of bombs underbelly.

In service 1913 at Eastchurch RNAS, used by six units (Eastchurch Sqn, 1N, 2N, 3N, 4N, 5N) until 1916, Yarmouth, and 8xPTU until 1917.

Action: northern Europe.

Powered by one 80hp Gnome 7z Lambda, or 80hp Le Rhone 9c rotary.

Serials: 15, 43, 153, 916–917 (2), 948, 1216–1227 (12).

Span: 37ft 8in/11.48m   Length: 20ft 8in/6.3m   Ceiling: n/k   Endurance: 5 hrs   Speed: 75mph/121kmph.

Total 18; 11 losses (61%) inc. 2 hostile.

76. Blenheim I

An advanced light bomber when it entered service with the RAF but obsolescent by 1939; it had three crew and was armed with one Browning mg in the port wing and a Lewis mg in a B-1 dorsal turret, plus 1,000lb/454kg of bombs internally and light bombs externally behind the bomb bay.

In service 1937 with 114 Sqn, used by 33 sqns (8, 11, 18, 21, 30, 34, 39, 44, 45, 55, 57, 60, 61, 62, 82, 84, 88, 90, 101, 104, 107, 108, 110, 113, 114, 139, 144, 203, 211, 223, 242, 604, 608), six flts, four PR flts, one transport sqn (267) and one cal. sqn (285) until 1942, 62 Sqn; also served with 4xBATFlts, 3xFTS, 1xSoGR, 2xTTFlts, 1xGpTFlt, METS, 19xOTU, PT&RPl, RDFS, 1xRS, RAFC, 2xOAFU, 1xPAFU, 1xAAS, 1xAGS, 4xAOS, ATA S., 5xAACU, 2xSoACo-op, 2xB&GS, ECFS, 3xFTU, CGS, 1xTorpTU, 1xFAA CU, 3xFAA ATU and 9xcomms. units, until 1945.

Based overseas in Iraq, Egypt, India; action in southern Europe, Middle East, North Africa and Far East, also based overseas in East Africa.

Powered by two 825hp Bristol Mercury VIII radials.

Serials: K7035–7182 (148), L1097–1546 (450), L4817–4934 range (34), L6595–6843 (249), L8362–8731 (250).

Total 1,131 (16 FAA); 551 accidental and 91 hostile losses.

Bristol TB 8, 1216,
RNAS Eastchurch.
(A.A. Southeran via
G. Stuart Leslie)

Bristol Blenheim I.
(Peter Green Collection)

Blenheim If – see Volume 1

76a. Blenheim IV
A light bomber and army-co-operation type for the RAF, as the Mk I but with an extended, asymmetrical glazed nose for the navigator and a stepped windscreen. One Browning mg in the port wing, and a Vickers mg in a B-1E dorsal turret, plus 1,000lb/454kg of bombs internally.
In service 1939 with 53 Sqn, used by four sqns (53, 59, 90, 101) until 1939, 101 Sqn.
Action: northern Europe.
Powered by two 825hp Mercury XV.
Serials: L4823–4906 (84).
Total 84; losses in Mk IVL below.

76b. Blenheim IVL
Normally referred to as the Mk IV but differed from the above by having increased fuel and the armament improved to one Browning mg in the port wing, one Vickers mg in the B-1E or -II dorsal turret or two Brownings in a B-IV turret, and one/two Brownings in a FN-64 mounting under the nose, firing to the rear; some had rear firing Brownings in the nacelles and a few had a local Middle East modification of one 20mm cannon in the nose. 1,000lb/454kg of bombs were carried internally and 320lb/150kg externally behind the bomb bay, and some had 1xPR camera in the rear fuselage, with a port in the belly. The type suffered heavy losses in the early years of the Second World War.
In service 1939 with 90 Sqn, used by 37 sqns (6, 8, 11, 13, 14, 15, 18, 21, 34, 35, 39, 40, 45, 52, 53, 55, 57, 59, 60, 82, 84, 88, 90, 101, 104, 105, 107, 108, 110, 113, 114, 139, 203, 211, 218, 226, 13[Greek]), two flts, five army co-op sqns (18, 53, 57, 59, 614), four PR sqns (53, 59, 140, 212), three PR flts, six cal. sqns (287, 288, 289, 526, 527, 528), 11 GR sqns (53, 59, 86, 203, 233, 244, 407, 459, 489, 500, 608), one GR flt, one met. sqn (521), six met. flts, one RCM sqn (162), one transport sqn (173), and one SD flt until 1943, 11 Sqn; also served with Aden Comms&TFlt, AFTU, Blenheim RefU, 17xOTU, 2xRS, SS (India), CGS, CArtCo-opFlt, 1xCU, 3xFTU, SoGR, 5xAACU, 1xTFlt, ME C&CU, 2xMETS, 2xOAFU, 1xPAFU, 1xAASU, 1xAIS, 1xAGS, 2xAOS, ATA TFP, 2xSoACo-op, 2xB&GS, 3xFAA CU, 7xFAA ATU, 21 comms. units and 27 misc. units until 1944.
Action: northern and southern Europe, Middle East, North and East Africa and Far East, also based overseas in West Africa.
Serials: L8732–9044 (130), L9170–9482 (220), N3522–3631 (100), N6140–6242 (100), P4825–4927 (64), P6885–6961 (56), R2770–2799 (30), R3590–3919 (250), T1793–2444 (400), V5370–6529 (800), Z5721–6455 (420), Z7271–8323 (430), Z9533–9978 (200).
Total 3,200 (72 FAA); 1,280 accidental and 1,007 hostile losses.

Blenheim IVf – see Volume 1

Bristol Blenheim IV, R3743, 40 Sqn. (Alastair Goodrum Collection)

Bristol Blenheim VA, DJ702.
(Peter Green Collection)

76c. Blenheim VA

As the Mk IV but had a longer, more-asymmetrical nose with a pannier beneath, and a larger B-X
dorsal turret, slightly recessed into the fuselage; the undercarriage doors were of the standard type. The
Mk VA was an intruder bomber, sometimes known as the Bisley, and had three crew, with an armament
of two Brownings in a FN-60 mount in the rear of the pannier, two Vickers in the dorsal turret, and
1,000lb/454kg of bombs internally.
In service during 1942 to with 139 Sqn; also served with 1xAGS and 4xFTU.
Action: northern Europe.
Powered by two 825hp Mercury XXV or 810hp Mercury XXX.
Serials: AD658, AZ861 to BB184 range (50 approx.), DJ702.
Total 52 approx.; losses in Mk VD.

76d. Blenheim VC

An advanced trainer, as the Mk VA but with armament deleted and dual-controls.
In service 1942, served with 1xPAFU, 1xAACU, 1xCU, 12xOTU, ECFS, Fighter Pilot Practice Flt, 6xcal.
flts, Mosquito CU, 16 comms. units and 15 misc. units, until 1945, 12 PAFU.
160 (approx.) conversions of the Mk V; losses in the Mk VD total.

76e. Blenheim VD

A light bomber which proved vulnerable and had a poor performance, so was soon withdrawn from
front-line service; as the Mk VA but with tropical equipment and modifications.
In service 1942 with 18 Sqn, used by nine sqns (13, 18, 34, 42, 113, 114, 203, 454, 13[Greek]), two PR
flts, two GR sqns (8, 244) and one RCM sqn (162), until 1944, 244 Sqn; also served with ME C&CU,
2xMETS, AFTU, 1xTTFlt and 1xGGFlt until 1945.
Action: North Africa, Middle East, western Indian Ocean and Far East.
Serials: AZ861–BB184 range (569 approx.), EH310–872 (160).
Total 729 approx.; 378 accidental and 50 hostile losses (all Mk V variants).

	Span	Length	Ceiling	Range	Speed
Mk I	56ft 4in/	39ft 9in/	27,300ft/	1,125 miles/	265mph/
	17.17m	12.12m	8,190m	1,811km	427kmph
Mk IV	"	42ft 7in/	22,000ft/	1,100 miles/	260mph/
		12.98m	6,600m	1,771km	419kmph
Mk IVL	"	"	"	1,500 miles/	"
				2,415km	
Mk V	56ft 1in/17.1m	44ft 11in/13.69m	31,000ft/9,300m	1,600 miles/2,567km	"

**Total Blenheims 5,196; built by Bristol, Avro and Rootes; in service 1937–45; 3,357 (64%)
losses inc. 1,148 hostile.**

Above left: Bristol Bombay I, K3583 prototype. (Charles Parker)

Above right: Bristol Beaufort I, 22 Sqn. (Newark Air Museum)

77. Bombay I

A bomber-transport monoplane for the RAF, with four crew as a bomber or three as a transport and armed with one Vickers mg in a B-II nose turret, one in each beam position and one in a B-III tail turret; able to carry 2,000lb/908kg of bombs on underbelly racks. As a transport it could carry 24 passengers or 3,000lb/1,360kg of freight.

In service 1939 with 216 Sqn, used by three sqns (117, 216, 271), 3xcomms. units, 1xSoACo-op, CLE, 1xFTS, 1xOTU, and one misc. unit until 1944, 1 Air Ambulance Unit.

Action: northern Europe, Middle East, and North and East Africa.

Powered by two 835hp Bristol Pegasus XXII radials.

Serials: L580–5887 (49).

Span: 95ft 9in/29.19m   Length: 69ft 3in/21.11m   Ceiling: 25,000ft/7,500m Range: 880 miles/1,417km   Speed: 192mph/309kmph

Total 49; 35 (70%) losses inc. 11 hostile.

78. Beaufort I

The RAF's first monoplane torpedo-bomber, which had initial troubles but afterwards saw extensive service; it had a crew of four and was armed with one/two Browning mg in the wings, some with two Vickers in the nose position, one Vickers mg in a B-IV (later two in a B-IVa) dorsal turret, and one/two Brownings in a rear-firing mounting under the nose. A torpedo or 1,500lb/681kg of bombs could be carried in or beneath the bomb-bay and some had ASV-II with aerials on fuselage and wings.

In service 1939 with 22 Sqn, used by 10 sqns (22, 39, 42, 47, 48, 86, 100, 217, 415, 489) until 1944, 217 Sqn; also served with CGS, 6xFTU, ME C&CU, 1xMETS, 10xOTU, 1xSLAIS, 3xTorpTU, Aden Comms & TFlt, 4xcomms. units and 5x misc. units.

Action: North Atlantic, Mediterranean and Indian Ocean, also based overseas in East Africa, Far East and North America.

Powered by two 1,060hp Bristol Taurus II/VI or 985hp Taurus XII/XVI radials.

Serials: L4441–4518 (74), L9790–9972 (128), N1000–1186 (128), W6467–6543 (66), X8916–8939 (24), AW187–243 (45).

Total 465; 219 accidental and 110 hostile losses.

78a. Beaufort IA

As the Mk I but with a strengthened airframe, the B-V dorsal turret having cut-away sides to its fairing and two Vickers as standard, plus two Vickers in the nose and some had a Vickers mg in each beam position; the bomb load was increased to 2,000lb/908kg and some had ASV-II.

In service 1942 with 39 Sqn, used by seven sqns (22, 39, 42, 47, 217, 455, 489) until 1944, 217 Sqn; also served with 11xCU, 1xFAA CU and 3xFAA ATU.

Action: North Atlantic, Mediterranean and Indian Ocean.

Powered by two 985hp Taurus XII.

Serials: DD945–999 (60), DW802–DX157 (200), EK969–EL141 (50), JM431–593 (110), LR885–LS128 (108).

Total 528 (64 FAA); 116 accidental and 35 hostile losses.

78b. Beaufort II

As the Mk I but with different engines, the DF loop streamlined, two Vickers in the nose, and the trailing-edge fillets deleted; some had ASV-II with external aerials. Retractable tail wheel fitted but seemingly not always used.

In service 1941 with 217 Sqn, used by four sqns (39, 42, 86, 217) until 1943, 39 Sqn. Also served with 2xFTU, ME C&CU, 1xMETS and 7xOTU until 1944.

Action: North Atlantic, Mediterranean and Indian Ocean.

Powered by two 1,200hp P&W Twin Wasp R1830-S3C-4 radials.

Serials: AW244–253 (10), AW271–315 (45).

Total 55; 22 accidental and 19 hostile losses.

78c. Beaufort IIA

As the Mk II but with a strengthened airframe and the same armament and modifications as the Mk IA.

In service 1941 with 86 Sqn, used by four sqns (39, 42, 86, 217) until 1944, 39 Sqn. Also served with 9xCU, 1xFIS and CC FIS.

Action: North Atlantic, Mediterranean and Indian Ocean, also based overseas in North America.

Serials: AW335–384 (49), DD870–944 (60), LS129–149 (21).

Total 130 (1 FAA); 38 accidental and 26 hostile losses.

78d. Beaufort T II

An advanced trainer version of the Mk II for the RAF and FAA, with the armament removed and turrets faired over and dual controls.

In service 1944 with 17 SFTS, used by 1xPAFU, 1xFTS, 1xFIS and 2xFAA CU until 1946.

Serials: ML430–722 (226).

Total 226 (39 FAA); 19 accidental losses.

78e. Beaufort V

An Australian-built version, used in small numbers by the RAF for PR work. As the Mk II but with all armament removed and carrying one camera in the fuselage.

Action: Far East, not based in the UK.

In service 1941–42 with 4 PRU.

Total 6; 1 hostile loss.

	Span	Length	Ceiling	Range	Speed
MK I	57ft 10in/	44ft 2in/	16,500ft/	1,600 miles	260mph/
	17.62m	13.46m	4,950m	/2,576km	419kmph
Mk II	"	"	18,000ft/5,400m	1,450 miles/2,334km	265mph/427kmph

Total Beauforts 1,410; in service 1939–46; 605 (43%) losses inc. 191 hostile.

79. Buckingham C 1

Designed as a light-bomber but saw no service in this role; with armament deleted it saw limited service as a high-speed transport, with three crew and four passengers. It was a bulky looking aircraft, with twin, egg-shaped fin/rudders on the high set tailplane and a ventral pannier set behind the wings; the wings had no dihedral and a swept leading edge with rounded tips.

In service 1945 with TCDU, used by TCDU and ECFS until 1946.

Powered by two 2,400hp Bristol Centaurus VII radials.

Serials: KV301–479 range (5).

Span: 71ft 10in/21.89m   Length: 46ft 10in/14.27m   Ceiling: 25,000ft/7,500m   Range: 3,000
miles/4,830km   Speed: 352mph/567kmph.
Total 5; no losses.

80. Brigand TF 1

Intended as a replacement for the Bristol Beaufighter TF 10 (qv), but the torpedo-fighter role disappeared
after the Second World War so the TF Mk served only with second-line units. It had three crew and was armed
with four 20mm cannon in the nose, a 0.5in Browning mg in the rear of the canopy, one torpedo underbelly
or 2,000lb/908kg of bombs or eight RP underwing, and AI-VIII (modified as ASV) in a nose radome.
In service 1946–48 with the ASWDU and ECFS.
Powered by two 2,470hp Bristol Centaurus 57 radials.
Serials: RH742–34 (6).
Total 6; 3 accidental losses (50%).

80a. Brigand B 1

Adapted as a light bomber for overseas use, as the TF 1 but modified for overland operations, with the
dorsal gun, torpedo and radar deleted, and did not have a good reputation.
In service 1949 with 84 Sqn, used by three sqns (8, 45, 84) until 1953, 84 Sqn, also used by FEAF TSqn,
1xOCU, 1xcomms. unit and 1xmisc. unit.
Action: Aden and Malaya, also based overseas in Iraq and Singapore, not operational in UK.
Serials: RH755–852 (67), VS812–16 (5), VS833–877 (23), WA560, WB228, WB236.
Total 98; 28 accidental losses.

80b. Brigand MET 3

As the B 1 but used for meteorological reconnaissance, with armament deleted and specialist met. equip-
ment fitted, long-range tanks and de-icing equipment.
In service 1949 to 1954 with 1301 Met. Flt.
Based overseas in Ceylon, not in UK.
Serials: VS817–832 (15).
Total 15 plus 1 conversion of the B 1 making a total of 16; no losses.

80c. Brigand T 4

A radar-trainer version of the B 1, with AI-10 in a nose radome, a blanked-out rear canopy and the DF
loop deleted.
In service 1951 with 228 OCU, used by AIS and 2xOCU until 1957, 238 OCU.
Serials: WA561–69 (9).
Total 9 plus 31 conversions of the B 1 making a total of 40; 3 accidental losses.

80d. Brigand T 5

As the T 4 but with AI-21 in a slightly longer nose radome.
In service 1957 with 238 OCU, used by 1xOCU and 1xmisc. unit until 1958, 238 OCU.
11 conversions of the T 4. One accidental loss.
All Marks: Span: 72ft 4in/22.05m   Length: 46ft 5in/14.15m   Ceiling: 26,000ft/7,800m   Range: 2,800
miles/4,508km   Speed: 358mph/576kmph.
Total Brigands 128; in service 1946–58; 35 (27%) losses; nicknamed Tram.

81. Sycamore HC 10

The first successful British helicopter design, used as an ambulance with two crew and two stretchers, no
armament.
In service from 1951–56 by the JHTU.
Powered by one 520hp Alvis Leonides 524/1 radial.
Serial: WA578.
Total 1; no losses.

Above left: Bristol Brigand T 5, RH832, 238 OCU. (John Fletcher via Charles Parker)

Above right: Bristol Sycamore HR 14, XJ918. (Alastair Goodrum Collection)

81a. Sycamore HC 11
As the HC 10 but carried three passengers and had no ambulance equipment.
In service 1951 with 657 Sqn, used by two sqns, 1xcomms. unit and 1xmisc. unit until 1962, MCommsSqn.
Serials: WT923–26 (4).
Total 4; 1 accidental loss.

81b. Sycamore HR 12
A development for anti-submarine and ASR duties, as the HC 11 but with an experimental winch.
In service 1952 with ASWDU, used by one sqn, 1xCU and 1xmisc. unit, until 1954, 275 Sqn.
Serials: WV781–84 (4).
Total 4; 1 accidental loss.

81c. Sycamore HR 13
A further development, as the HR 12 but with a standard winch and a longer-stroke undercarriage.
In service 1953 to 1955 with 275 Sqn.
Serials: XD196–97 (2).
Total 2; 2 accidental losses.

81d. Sycamore HR or HC 14
The major production version, for SAR or transport duties, with two crew and three passengers. As the HR 13 but the captain's seat on the right in a redesigned cockpit and four cabin doors; a winch was fitted for SAR.
In service 1954 with 275 Sqn (SAR) and 194 Sqn (transport), used by seven transport sqns (32, 84, 103, 110, 118, 194, 225), four ASR sqns (22, 228, 275, 284), four SAR flts, 4xcomms. units, 1xAPS and 2xmisc. units, until 1972, 32 Sqn.
Action: Malaya, Cyprus, Suez and Borneo, also based overseas in Germany, Aden, Iraq, the Gulf and Libya.
Serials: XE306–322 (16), XF265–69 (5), XG500–549 (36), XJ361–385 (10), XJ895–919 (9), XL820–829 (10).
Total 86; 62 accidental losses.

	Rotor diameter	Length	Ceiling	Range	Speed
HC 10	48ft 7in/14.81m	42ft/12.8m	15,500ft/4,650m	260 miles/419km	132mph/213kmph
HR 14	"	"	"	150 miles/241km	127mph/204kmph

Total Sycamores 97; in service 1951–72; 66 (69%) losses; nicknamed Sickly Icarus.

82. Britannia C 1
The RAF ordered this airliner due to its shortage of transports and it gave sterling service until retirement due to defence cuts; it carried four crew, and 118 passengers or 37,000lb/16,800kg of freight.
In service 1959 with 99 Sqn, used by two sqns (99, 511) until 1976, 99 Sqn.
Powered by four 4,445shp Bristol Proteus 255 turboprops.
Serials: XL635–660 (10), XM489–520 (10).
Total 20; 1 accidental loss.

Bristol Britannia C 1, XL635,
Lyneham Transport Wing. (Charles
Parker)

82a. Britannia C 2

As the C 1 but with minor differences and used mainly for training and passenger flights as much of the
cabin floor was not strengthened.
In service 1959 with 99 Sqn, used by two sqns (99, 511) until 1976, 99 Sqn.
Serials: XN392–404 (3).
Total 3; no losses.
Span: 142ft 3in/43.37m   Length: 126ft 3in/38.48m   Ceiling: 25,000ft/7,500m   Range: 4,200
miles/6,762km   Speed: 360mph/580kmph.
**Total Britannias 23; built by Bristols and Shorts; in service 1959–76; 1 (4%) loss; nicknamed
Whistling Giant.**

BRITISH AEROSPACE (BAe) (Warton, Lancs, UK)

Formed in 1977 from the merger of the British Aircraft Corporation and Hawker-Siddeley Aviation, at
first a publicly owned company but then privatised in 1985; in 1999 it was renamed BAE Systems and has
moved into all areas of defence supply, the civil aircraft side having been abandoned and military-type
design being in co-operation with other countries and companies. Supplied 194 examples of three types
(Sea Harrier, Harrier GR5-T12, see Vol. 1).

83. 146 CC 1

An airliner ordered for trials to assess its suitability for the Queen's Flight; it carried three crew and up
to 20 passengers.
In service 1983–84 with 241 OCU.
Powered by four 6,970lb st Avco-Lycoming ALF502-R3 turbofans.
Serials: ZD695–96 (2).
Total 2; no losses.

83a. 146 CC 2

A VIP version of the above.
In service 1986 with the Queen's Flt, used by one flt and one sqn (32) to the present, 2010.
Powered by four ALF502-R5.
Serials: ZE700–02 (3).
Total 3; no losses to date.

	Span	Length	Ceiling	Range	Speed
CC 1	86ft/26.21m	85ft 11in/26.18m	30,000ft/9,000m	1,128 miles/1,816km	440mph/708kmph
CC 2	"	"	"	1,900 miles/3,059km	"

Total 146s 5; in service 1983–present 2010; no losses to date.

BRITISH AIRCRAFT CORPORATION (Bristol, Somerset, UK)

Formed from several famous companies in 1960, became part of British Aerospace in 1977. Supplied 28 examples of one type.

84. VC 10 C 1

A Vickers design for a very successful long-range airliner, ordered by the RAF for transport duties with eight crew, and 150 passengers or 54,000lb/24,515kg of freight. Nicknamed Skoda, Shiny Swish.
In service 1966 to 1996 with 10 Sqn.
Powered by four 22,500lb st RR Conway 301-550b jets.
Serials: XR806–10 (5), XV101–14 (9).
Total 14; no losses.

84a. VC 10 C 1 (K)

To increase the number of available tankers all the surviving VC 10 C1s were converted into transport-tankers, with a HDU under each wing, a CCTV camera underbelly, and tanker lighting and instruments; passenger/freight capacity remained the same as the C 1.
In service 1994 with 10 Sqn, used by two sqns (10, 101) to the present, 2010.
Twelve conversions of the C 1; 1 accidental loss to date.

BAe 146 CC 2, ZE702, 32 Sqn. (Author's Collection)

BAC VC 10 C 1 (K), XV109, 10 Sqn. (Author's Collection)

BAC VC 10 K 3, ZA148, 101 Sqn.
(Author's Collection)

84b. VC 10 K 2

A tanker-transport for the RAF carrying four crew and 18 passengers, with 25.2 tons/25 tonnes of fuel in fuselage tanks, meaning fewer cabin windows, and a HDU under each wing and in the rear belly. There were thrust reversers on the outboard engines.

In service 1983 with 241 OCU, 1984 with 101 Sqn, used by one sqn and one flt until 2001, 101 Sqn.

Action: Gulf and Bosnia, also based overseas in the Falklands.

Serials: ZA140–44 (5).

Total 5; no losses.

84c. VC 10 K 3

A tanker-transport with 17 passengers and 35.6 tons/35 tonnes of fuel in fuselage and fin tanks; it has a longer fuselage than the K 2, being based on the Super VC 10. Thrust reversers on all engines.

In service 1985 with 101 Sqn, used by one sqn and one flt until the present 2010.

Action: in the Gulf, Iraq and Afghanistan, also based overseas in the Falklands.

Serials: ZA147–50 (4).

Total 4; no losses to date.

84d. VC 10 K 4

The ultimate VC 10, another tanker-transport which can carry 30 passengers or freight, with 25.2 tons/25 tonnes of fuel in the fin tank but no fuselage tanks.

In service 1994 with 101 Sqn, used by one sqn and one flt until the present 2010.

Action: Iraq and Afghanistan, also based overseas in the Falklands.

Serials: ZD230–43 (5).

Total 5; no losses to date.

	Span	Length	Ceiling	Range	Speed
C 1	146ft 2in/ 44.56m	158ft 8in/ 48.36m	38,000ft/ 11,400m	5,370 miles/ 8,646km	580mph/ 934kmph
K 2	"	166ft 2in/ 50.65m	"	3,900 miles/ 11,700m	568mph/ 914kmph
K 3 & 4	"	179ft 1in/54.59m	"	"	"

Total VC 10s 28; in service 1966–present 2010; 1 (4%) loss to date; nicknamed Vicky Ten, Iron Duck.

BRITISH AIRCRAFT MANUFACTURING COMPANY
(Hanworth, Middlesex, UK)

Formed in 1933 as British Klemm Aeroplane Co. to build German Klemm designs under licence, became BAMC in 1935, into GAL 1939. Supplied 18 examples of two types.

B A M Swallow II, G-AFCL,
preserved example.
(Author's Collection)

B A M Eagle II, G-AFAX,
preserved example.
(Author's Collection)

85. Swallow II

An open-cockpit, two-seat, light low-wing monoplane, impressed for communications and training work with the RAF and FAA.

In service 1940 with 5 EFTS, used by the CLE and 2xGTS until 1943, GTS.

Powered by one 82hp Blackburn Cirrus Minor I in-line.

Serials: X5010, BJ575, BK893–97 (5), ES952, NP491.

Span: 42ft 8in/13m   Length: 27ft/8.23m   Ceiling: 17,000ft/5,100m   Range: 420 miles/676km   Speed: 112mph/180kmph.

Total 9 (1 FAA) impressed; 1 (10%) accidental loss.

86. Eagle II

A low-wing cabin monoplane, carrying the pilot and two passengers, impressed for communications duties by the RAF.

In service 1940, India, used by one PR flt, 1xCU, SoGR, and 5xcomms. units until 1943, India.

Based overseas in the Far East.

Powered by one 130hp DH Gipsy Major I in-line.

Serials: AW143, AW182, DP847, DR609 (2), ES944, ES948, HM506, MA945.

Span: 39ft 3in/11.97m   Length: 26ft/7.92m   Ceiling: 16,000ft/4,800m   Range: 650 miles/1,046km   Speed: 148mph/238kmph.

Total 9 impressed; 6 (66%) accidental losses.

BRITISH CAUDRON (London and Alloa, Scotland UK)

See Caudron.

BRITISH & COLONIAL AEROPLANE CO.

See Bristol.

BRUSH COACHWORKS (Loughborough, Leics, UK)

Assembled DH Dominie.

BRUSH ELECTRICAL ENGINEERING CO. (Loughborough, Leics, UK)

Assembled Farman F27 and Short 827 and 184.

CANADIAN CAR AND FOUNDRY (Canada)

Assembled HP Hampden.

CANADIAN VICKERS (Canada)

Assembled Consolidated Catalina.

CAPRONI (Italy)

A well-known company between the wars, founded in 1907 and out of business by 1983; supplied six examples of one type.

87. CA 42

A five-bay tri-plane bomber for the RNAS/RAF with twin rudders mounted on the tailplane which bridged the gap between the two fuselage booms; carried four crew and was armed with two Lewis guns in the nose position and in dorsal positions on each fuselage boom plus 1,000lb/454kg of bombs in a pod mounted centrally on the lower wing. It had an eight-wheel main undercarriage.

In service 1918 with the Caproni Flt, RNAS, used by one unit (6W) and one RAF sqn (227) until 1918, 227 Sqn.

Action: southern Europe, not based in UK.

Powered by three 400hp Liberty 12A in-lines, one a pusher.

Serials: N526–31 (6).

Span: 98ft/29.87m   Length: 49ft 6in/15.09m   Ceiling: 10,000ft/3,000m   Endurance: 7hrs   Speed: 87mph/140kmph.

Total 6; no losses.

CAUDRON (France)

A pioneer company which lasted from 1910 until 1947 and supplied 402 examples of five types (G II and G III, see Vol. 1); also assembled HP 0/400.

Caudron G IV.
(G. Stuart Leslie)

88. G IV

A twin-engined version of the GIII (Vol. 1), used by the RNAS as a bomber, with two crew and armed with one Lewis mg in the front cockpit plus 250lb/113kg of bombs underwing. Nicknamed Twin-Caudron.
In service 1916 with 5 Wing, used by five units (1W, 2W, 4W, 5W, 7NSqn) until 1917, 7 (N) Sqn.
Action: northern and southern Europe.
Powered by two 80hp Le Rhone 9c rotaries or 100hp Anzani radials.
Serials: 3289–3300 (12), 3333–39 (7), 3894–99 (6), 9101–9131 (31).
Span: 55ft 5in/16.56m   Length: 23ft 6in/7.16m   Ceiling: 14,000ft/4,200m   Range: 140 miles/225km   Speed: 82mph/132kmph.
Total 56; 15 losses (20%) inc. 4 hostile

89. Goeland

An impressed communications type, a low-wing cabin monoplane, unarmed and with two crew and eight passengers. It had a retractable undercarriage and tapered wings with curved tips.
In service from 1940 to 1942 with 1 (F-F) ME.
Based overseas in Middle East and North Africa, not in UK.
Powered by two 220hp Renault Bengali 6q in-lines.
Serials: AX775–76 (2).
Span: 57ft 7in/17.55m   Length: 44ft 9in/13.64m   Ceiling: 18,300ft/5,490m   Range: 1,056 miles/1,700m   Speed: 191mph/308kmph.
Total 2; 1 (50%) accidental loss.

90. Simoun

Another type from the French Air Force, a low-wing cabin monoplane used for communications by the Free French; carried the pilot and three passengers and was unarmed. It had a tall curved fin/rudder and a fixed undercarriage.
In service 1940 with 1 (F-F) ME, used by one sqn and 1xcomms. unit until 1942, 267 Sqn.
Based overseas in North Africa and the Middle East, not in UK.
Powered by one 220hp Renault Bengali 6q-09 in-line.
Serials: AX676, AX777, HK943.
Span: 34ft 1in/10.39m   Length: 28ft 6in/8.68m   Ceiling: 19,700ft/5,910m   Range: 560 miles/902km   Speed: 186mph/299kmph.
Total 3; no losses.

CESSNA. (USA).

Formed in 1927 and a famous maker of light aircraft but only supplied two examples of two types.

91. Airmaster

An impressed communications type, an unbraced high-wing cabin monoplane carrying the pilot and three passengers and unarmed. It had a single fin/rudder and a fixed undercarriage.
In service from 1941 to 1942 with Hucknall SFlt.
Powered by one 145hp Warner Scarab 40 radial.
Serial: HM502.
Span: 34ft 2in/10.41m   Length: 24ft 8in/7.52m   Ceiling: 18,000ft/5,400m   Range: 785 miles/1,264km   Speed: 165mph/267kmph.
Total 1 impressed; no losses.

92. Bird Dog L-19

A single-strut braced high-wing cabin monoplane lent to the RAF in Korea for communications work, to supplement the Auster AOP 6s (Vol. 1); two crew in tandem in a Perspex cabin with the wing mounted above, and no armament. Single fin/rudder with a dorsal fin and a single-strut undercarriage.
In service 1952 with 1913 Flt, used by 1x AOPFlt and 2xmisc. units until 1954, 1913 Flt.
Action: Korea, not based in UK.

Powered by one 213hp Continental 0-470-1 in-line.
Span: 36ft/10.98m   Length: 25ft 10in/7.87m   Ceiling: 21,200ft/6,360m   Range: 620
miles/998km   Speed: 135mph/217kmph.
Total 1; no losses.

CLAYTON & SHUTTLEWORTH (Lincoln, UK)

Assembled HP 0/400 and Vickers Vimy.

CONSOLIDATED (USA)

A successful company formed in 1923 and which became Consolidated-Vultee in 1944, supplying 2,778
examples of three types.

93. Catalina Model 28 (PBY-4)

The RAF ordered one of these early production Catalinas for evaluation; it did not have the prominent
gunner's Perspex blisters on the fuselage or any military equipment and the fin was a slightly different
shape from the Mk I (below) with a fabric-covered rudder. It was unarmed.
In service 1939, used by 210, 228 and 240 Sqns until 1940.
Powered by two 1,050hp P&W Twin Wasp R1830-72 radials.
Serial: P9630.
Total 1; 1 accidental loss.

93a. Catalina I (PBY-5)

A developed version of the above ordered to cover the shortage of RAF flying boats at the start of the
Second World War, this was a modern monoplane used for general-reconnaissance. It had a crew of eight
or nine and was armed with one Vickers mg in the nose turret, one in a ventral position and one or
two Vickers, later 0.5in Brownings, in each beam position, plus 2,000lb/908kg of bombs or four depth
charges underwing; radar was ASV-II with external aerials. The rudder was one-piece and the elevators
were cut-away to allow rudder movement.
In service 1941 with 240 Sqn, used by five sqns (205, 209, 210, 240, 413) and one flt until 1945, 240 Sqn,
also served with 2xOTU, 1xFTU, SoASR and 1xmisc. unit until 1947.
Based overseas in Singapore, action North and South Atlantic and Indian Ocean.
Powered by two 1,050hp P&W Twin-Wasp R1830-82 radials.
Serials: W8405–434 (30), Z2135–2153 (20), AH530–569 (40), AJ154–62 (9), SM706 (renumbered).
Total 99; 42 accidental and 23 hostile losses.

93bB. Catalina IB (PBY-5b)

As the Mk I but was supplied under Lend-lease so had American equipment.
In service 1941 with 202 Sqn, used by 14 sqns (119, 190, 191, 202, 210, 212, 259, 262, 265, 270, 333, 422,
490, 628) and one flt until 1945, 212 Sqn.
Action: North and South Atlantic and Indian Ocean.
Powered by two 1,200hp Twin-Wasp R1830-S13g.
Serials: FP100–325 (141).
Total 141; 68 accidental and 6 hostile losses.

93c. Catalina II (PBY-5)

As the Mk IB but built by Naval Aircraft Factory, with a cut-away rudder and straight-edged elevators,
and ice armour on the hull.
In service 1942 with 210 Sqn, used by two sqns (210, 321), 1xFTU and 1xOTU until 1945, 321 Sqn.
Action: North Atlantic and Indian Ocean.
Powered by two 1,050hp Twin-Wasp R1830-82.
Serials: AM264–69 (7).
Total 7; 3 accidental losses.

Consolidated Catalina I,
AH550, 210 Sqn. (Newark
Air Museum)

93d. Catalina IIA (PBY-5)

As the Mk I but built by Canadian-Vickers.

In service 1942 with 240 Sqn, used by three sqns (209, 333, 240), 1xOTU and 1xmisc. unit, until 1945, 333 Sqn.

Action: North Atlantic and western Indian Ocean.

Serials: VA703–732 (18).

Total 18; 11 accidental and 2 hostile losses.

93e. Catalina III (PBY-5a)

The amphibian version, with the undercarriage main wheels folding into the fuselage sides, the extra weight meaning it carried less fuel and armament.

In service 1942 with 330 Sqn, used by three sqns (119, 321, 330) and 1xOTU until 1946, 45 Gp.

Action: North Atlantic and Indian Ocean.

Powered by two 1,050hp R1830-92.

Serials: FP52–536 (12), FT998–99 (2 built by Boeing Vancouver).

Total 14; 2 accidental and 2 hostile losses.

93f. Catalina IVA (PBY-5b)

Similar to the Mk IB but with equipment changes.

In service 1943 with 190 Sqn, used by six sqns (190, 202, 210, 240, 413, 628) and one SD sqn (357) until 1945, 240 Sqn, also served with 1xFTU, 2xOTU and the Survival & Rescue School to 1947.

Action: North and South Atlantic and Indian Ocean, also based overseas in Norway.

Powered by two 1,200hp R1830-S13g.

Serials: JV925–935 (11), JX200–269 (54), JX570–585 (12).

Total 77; 15 accidental and 4 hostile losses.

93g. Catalina IVB (PB2B-1)

A Boeing built Mk IVA with ASV-V in a radome pod above the cockpit and detail changes, including a raised roof to the nose turret which carried two mg. The engine exhausts were faired in over the cowlings. Built by Boeing.

In service 1943 with 205 Sqn, used by five sqns (191, 205, 212, 262, 321), CC FIS, 1xFIS, 1xOTU and 1xFTU, until 1945, 321 Sqn.

Action: South Atlantic and Indian Ocean.

Serials: JX270–437 (168), JX586–617 (25).

Total 193; 17 accidental and 2 hostile losses.

93h. Catalina GR VI (PB2B-2)

As the Mk IVB but with a taller fin; used for ferry duties rather than general reconnaissance and was Boeing-built.

In service with 45 Gp during 1945.
Based overseas in Canada, not in UK.
Serials: JX628–35 (4).
Total 4; 1 accidental loss.

	Span	Length	Ceiling	Range	Speed
Mk I	104ft/	63ft 6in/	22,000ft/	2,115 miles/	90mph/
	31.39m	19.35m	6,600m	3,405km	1306kmph
Mk IB	"	65ft 2in/	14,700ft/	2,545 miles/	"
		19.86m	4,410m	4,097km	
Mk III	"	"	"	n/k	179mph/288kmph
Mk IVA	"	"	20,000ft/	2,545 miles/	190mph/
			6,000m	4,097km	306kmph
Mk IVB	"	63ft 10in/	15,800ft/	2,690 miles/	187mph/
		19.45m	4,740m	4,331km	301kmph
GR VI	"	64ft 8in/	14,100ft/	2,485 miles/	165mph/
		19.7m	4,230m	4,580km	266kmph

Total Catalinas 554; in service 194–47; 198 (36%) losses inc. 39 hostile; nicknamed Cat.

94. Liberator LB 30A

An early version of the B-24 used by the RAF as an unarmed ferry transport over the Atlantic, with four
crew and 24 passengers.
In service 1941 with Ferry Command, used by one sqn until 1944, 511 Sqn.
Powered by four 1,200hp P&W Twin-Wasp R1830-S3g-4c radials in circular cowlings.
Serials: AM260–63 (4).
Total 4; 3 accidental losses.

94a. Liberator I

A general-reconnaissance version, much needed to fill the 'Atlantic gap', and later used as a transport
like the LB 30A (above); for its GR role it had eight crew and was armed with four 20mm cannon in an
under-nose pod, one 0.5in Browning in the nose position, each beam position, ventral position and tail
position, plus eight DC carried internally and ASV-I or II with external aerials. It had self-sealing tanks.
In service 1941 to 1943 with 120 Sqn, also used by two transport sqns (231, 511) and one misc. unit, until
1945, 231 Sqn.
Action: North Atlantic and Indian Ocean, also based overseas in North America.
Powered by four 1,200hp R1830-33.
Serials: AM910–929 (19).
Total 19; 11 accidental and 1 hostile loss.

Consolidated Liberator I,
AM910, 120 Sqn. (Newark
Air Museum)

Consolidated Liberator II, AL566,
159 Sqn. (G. Stuart Leslie)

94b. Liberator II

A heavy-bomber version but also used for general-reconnaissance, transport and special duties; as the Mk I but with one Browning mg in the nose position, four in a BP-A dorsal turret, and two in the tail position (four in a BP-E tail turret in late-production aircraft), plus 12,000lb/5,448kg of bombs, the GR version carrying eight DC, and the transport 24 passengers. One aircraft was modified to a VIP transport, with a large single fin and turrets deleted and faired over.

In service 1941 with 108 Sqn, used by four sqns (108, 159, 160, 178), two GR sqns (120, 224), two transport sqns (231, 511), one SD sqn (148) and one SD flt until 1943, 178 Sqn, transport to 1945; also served with 3xCU, 3xFTU, 1xOTU, 1xCFlt, 3xcomms. units and 3xmisc. units.

Action: northern and southern Europe, North Africa, North Atlantic, also based overseas in Middle East and BWI.

Powered by four 1,200hp R1830-61.

Serials: AL504–667 (80).

Total 80; 43 accidental and 13 hostile losses.

94c. Liberator III (B-24D)

A further development for general-reconnaissance, heavy bomber and transport duties with the RAF; as the Mk II but with a 0.5in Browning in the nose position, two in a Martin 250CE dorsal turret moved forward to just behind the cockpit, and two Browning in a BP-E tail turret or four in a BP-A tail turret. Carried eight DC or 12,000lb/5,448kg of bombs, and for GR had ASV-II radar with external aerials.

In service 1942 with 120 Sqn, used by three GR sqns (59, 120, 311), five bomber sqns (159, 160, 178, 223, 355), one SD sqn (357), one PR sqn (160), three transport sqns (231, 232, 246), one GR flt, and two SD flts until 1945, 160 Sqn, and 1946 for transport, 231 Sqn; also served with 7xCU, 2xOTU, 1xCFlt, 1xC&CFlt and 1xmisc. unit.

Action: North Atlantic, Indian Ocean, North Africa and Far East, also based overseas in southern Europe, Middle East and BWI.

Powered by four 1,200hp R1830-43 with oval cowlings.

Serials: BZ711–999 range (80), FK214–245 (32), FL906–995 range (40), LV337–346 (9).

Total 161; 46 accidental and 16 hostile losses.

94d. Liberator IIIA (B-24D)

A Lend-lease Mk III for general reconnaissance with the RAF, with American equipment and increased fuel; armament as the Mk III with 0.5in Brownings in all positions, the rear turret now being a Consolidated A6A, and ASV-III with external aerials.

In service 1942 with 86 Sqn, used by three sqns (86, 224, 354), and one PR sqn (160), until 1945 86 Sqn, also served with 1xOTU until 1945.

Action: North Atlantic and Indian Ocean.

Total, serials, and losses in the Mk III statistics.

94e. Liberator IV (B-24E)

It is uncertain if the Mk IV was an official designation (it was probably counted as Mk V in RAF service) but it was sometimes applied to Willow Run factory-built B-24Es, which had different propellers.

94f. Liberator V (B-24D)

A general reconnaissance and transport (at war's end) for the RAF, as the Mk IIIA but built at the Willow Run factory with some detail changes; armament as the Mk IIIA but some had eight RP on stub wings on the forward fuselage, some had a Leigh Light under the outer starboard wing, and all had ASV-VI in a chin radome.

In service 1943 with 224 Sqn, used by eight sqns (53, 59, 120, 200, 224, 311, 354, 547) and one flt, two bomber sqns (159, 160), and one ASR flt until 1945, 160 Sqn, transport to 1946; also served with 3xCU, 2xOTU, 1xCFlt and 1xmisc. unit.

Action: North and South Atlantic, Indian Ocean and Far East, also based overseas in North Africa, Middle East, and BWI.

Powered by four 1,200hp R1830-43 or 1,300hp R1830-65.

Serials: BZ711–999 range (169), FL906–995 range (50).

Total 219; 50 accidental and 30 hostile losses.

94g. Liberator GR VI (B-24H or J)

A general reconnaissance and transport, as the Mk V but with a lengthened nose to house two 0.5in Brownings in an Emerson A15 or Consolidated A6a nose turret with a bomb aimers position beneath, two 0.5in in a Martin 250 dorsal turret and a Consolidated A6a tail turret, plus eight DC internally and ASV-IV/AN/APS radar in a retractable belly radome. The nose wheel doors opened outwards.

In service 1944 with 160 Sqn, used by 15 sqns (8, 37, 53, 86, 160, 200, 203, 206, 220, 224, 311, 321, 354, 422, 547), one flt, one ASR sqn (292), four ASR flts, one met. flt, and eight transport sqns, (52, 59, 102, 232, 246, 311, 423, 426) until 1946, 59 Sqn (GR), and 232 Sqn, (transport); also served with 1xOTU, 2xCU and 1xTSTU. For transport duties some aircraft had turrets deleted and faired over.

Action: North and South Atlantic, Mediterranean and Indian Ocean, also based overseas in BWI and Czechoslovakia.

Serials: BZ711–999 range (30), EV812–EW322 range (115), KG821–KH420 range (86), KK221–378 range (23), KL348–689 range (34), TW758–769 (12).

Total 300; 45 accidental and 16 hostile losses.

94h. Liberator B VI (B-24H or J)

A bomber version of the above, with the addition of two 0.5in Brownings in a Sperry A13 ventral turret (not always fitted) replacing the radome, and 12,800lb/5,810kg of bombs; nine crew.

In service 1944 with 178 and 356 Sqns, used by 11 sqns (40, 70, 99, 104, 159, 160, 178, 215, 355, 356, 358), one RCM sqn (214), and four SD sqns (148, 160, 301, 357) until 1946, 203 Sqn; also served with 1xAGS (India), 5xCU, ME C&CU, AFTU, TSTU (India), C&CFlt, 1xCFlt and 8xmisc. units.

Consolidated Liberator GR VI,
220 Sqn. (Scott Collection)

Action: northern and southern Europe and Far East, also based overseas in Egypt and Palestine.
Serials: BZ711–999 range (8), EV812–EW322 range (296), KG821–KH420 range (295), KK221–378 range (88), KL348–689 range (247), KN702–836 range (15), TS519–539 (21), TT336–43 (3), VB852, VB904, VD245–46 (2).
Total 97; 149 accidental and 99 hostile losses.

94j. Liberator C VII (C-87)

A dedicated transport variant, with all turrets deleted and faired over, a freight door in the port rear fuse-lage and cabin windows; carried five crew, and 27 passengers or 10,000lb/4,540kg of freight.
In service 1945 with 511 Sqn, used by three sqns (232, 246, 511) and 1xCU until 1946, 232 Sqn.
Action: northern and southern Europe, and Far East.
Serials: EW611–634 (24).
Total 24; 8 accidental losses.

94k. Liberator GR VIII (B-24L)

A general reconnaissance development of the GR VI, built at Fort Worth with detail differences including a bomb-aimer's window with a slightly different shape; eight crew and armed with two 0.5in Brownings in a Emerson A15 nose turret, Martin 250CE dorsal turret and Emerson A15 tail turret, plus eight DC and ASV in a retractable belly radome.
In service 1944 with 53 Sqn, used by nine sqns (53, 59, 86, 120, 203, 206, 224, 228, 422), one met. flt, 2xCU, 1xOTU, CCIS and 1xmisc. unit, until 1947, 120 Sqn.
Action: North Atlantic and Indian Ocean, also based overseas in BWI.
Serials: KG821–KH420 range (82), KK221–378 range (47), KL348–689 range (46), KN702–836 range (57), KP125–196 range (2).
Total 234; 19 accidental and 5 hostile losses.

94l. Liberator B VIII (B-24L)

As above but a bomber and transport (at war's end, some with turrets deleted and faired over), with a Sperry A13 ventral turret (not always fitted) replacing the radome, and 12,800lb/5,810kg of bombs.
In service 1944 with 614 Sqn, used by three sqns (159, 355, 614), one RCM sqn (214) with 11 or 12 crew, 2xCU, TSCU (India) and 1xmisc. unit, until 1946, 159 Sqn.
Action: southern Europe and Far East, also based overseas in Egypt and India.
Serials: KG range (37), KL range (48), KN range (63), KP range (20).
Total 168; 16 accidental and 1 hostile loss.

94m. Liberator C IX (RY-3)

A complete redesign, a transport version of the Privateer patrol bomber serving with the US Navy, sup-plied to the RAF for trans-Atlantic ferry work; it had a tall single-fin and was unarmed, with streamlined nose and tail, cabin windows and a freight door. Four crew, and 28 passengers or 16,640 lb/7,555kg of freight.
In service 1945 with 231 Sqn, used by one sqn and 1xCU until 1946, 231 Sqn. Based overseas in Canada, not in UK.
Powered by four 1,300hp R1830-65.
Serials: JT973–999 (27), JV936.
Total 28. 3 accidental losses.

	Span	Length	Ceiling	Range	Speed
LB 30A	110ft/ 33.53m	63ft 9in/ 19.43m	28,000ft/ 8,400m	2,200 miles/ 3,542km	n/k
Mk I	"	66ft 9in/ 20.35m	30,500ft/ 9,150m	"	292mph/ 470kmph
Mk II	"	66ft 4in/ 20.22m	34,000ft/ 10,200m	2,100 miles/ 3,381km	313mph/ 504kmph

Mk III	"	"	30,000ft/ 9,000m	1,800 miles/ 2,898km	303mph/ 488kmph
Mk IIIA	"	"	28,000ft/ 8,400m	3,500 miles/ 5,635km	290mph/ 467kmph
MkV	"	"	"	"	"
MkVI	"	67ft 7in/20.6m	"	"	"
CVII	"	66ft 4in/ 20.22m	31,000ft/ 9,300m	2,900 miles/ 4,669km	306mph/ 493kmph
MkVIII	"	67ft 2in/ 20.47m	28,000ft/ 8,400m	1,700 miles/ 2,737km	290mph/ 467kmph
C IX	"	75ft 5in/ 22.99m	21,300ft/ 6,390m	3,700 miles/ 5,957km	264mph/ 425kmph

Total Liberators 2,214; in service 1941–47; 574 (26%) losses inc. 181 hostile; nicknamed Lib.

95. Coronado I (PB2Y-3B)

A large high-wing monoplane flying boat with two fins, designed for general reconnaissance but used by the RAF for trans-Atlantic transport duties; four crew and unarmed, able to carry 44 passengers or 16,000lb/7,264kg of freight. It had retractable wingtip floats.
In service 1944 with 45 Gp, used by one sqn (231) until 1946, 231 Sqn.
Based overseas in Canada & BWI.
Powered by four 1,200hp P&W Twin-Wasp R1830-65 radials driving four-bladed props on the inboard engines and three-bladed on the outboard.
Serials: JX470-501 (10).
Span: 115ft/35.05m   Length: 79ft 3in/24.16m   Ceiling: 20,000ft/6,000m   Range: 3,000 miles/4,830km   Speed: 264mph/425kmph.
Total 10; 1 (10%) accidental loss.

CO-OPERATIVE WHOLESALE (Salford, Lancs, UK)

Assembled GAL Hamilcar.

CUBITT (Croydon, Surrey, UK)

Assembled Airco DH 9.

CURTISS (USA)

The only large American company to supply the British forces during both world wars, with 3,671 examples of 13 types (JN1-4, Mohawk, Tomahawk and Kittyhawk, see Vol. 1); a pioneer company formed in 1910 which went out of aircraft production during 1956.

96. H-1

A reconnaissance flying boat for the RNAS, with two crew and armed with one Lewis mg in the nose position and eight small bombs underwing.
In service 1914 to 1916 at Felixstowe.
Action: home waters.
Powered by two 90hp or 100hp Curtiss OX5 in-lines.
Serials: 950-51 (2).
Total 2; no losses.

96a. H-4

Developed from the H-1, a reconnaissance flying boat for the RNAS, with four crew and armed with one Lewis mg in the nose position and eight small bombs underwing. Built by Airco and Saunders.
In service 1915 at Felixstowe, used by five units (Calafrana, Calshot, Felixstowe, Gibraltar, Yarmouth) until 1917, Calafrana, training with 3xCU to 1918, Killingholme.

Action: home waters and Mediterranean.

Powered by two 100hp Curtiss OX5 in-lines or 100hp Anzani radials.

Serials: 1228–1239 (12), 3545–3594 (50).

Total 62; 6 accidental losses.

Both Marks: Span: 72ft/21.95m   Length: 36ft/10.98m   Ceiling: n/k   Range: n/k   Speed: 70mph/113kmph.

Total H-1 & 4s 64; in service 1914–18; 6 (8%) losses; nicknamed Small America.

97. R-2

A reconnaissance type and trainer for the RNAS, which saw little use; two crew and armed with a Lewis mg in the rear cockpit and 100lb/45kg of bombs underwing.

In service 1916 at Hendon, used by one unit (3W) until 1917, Prawle Point and by 2xATU until 1918.

Powered by one 160hp Curtiss VX, 150hp Sunbeam Nubian, or 200hp Sunbeam Arab in-line.

Serials: 3446–3544 (84).

Span: 45ft 11in/14m   Length: 24ft 5in/7.45m   Ceiling: n/k   Endurance: 6–7 hrs   Speed: 86mph/138kmph.

Total 84 but many not issued; no losses.

98. H-12

A reconnaissance biplane flying boat for the RNAS/RAF, originally the H 8 with Curtiss engines but re-engined before entering service; four crew and armed with one Lewis mg in the nose and each beam position and 460lb/210kg of bombs underwing.

In service 1916 at Felixstowe, used by five units (Calshot, Felixstowe, Killingholme, Tresco, Yarmouth), three RAF sqns (228, 234, 240) and 1xCU until 1919, 234 Sqn.

Action: home waters.

Powered by two 225hp RR Eagle I in-lines.

Serials: 8650–8699 (50).

Total 50; 19 accidental and 2 hostile losses.

98a. H-12B or Convert

A development of the H-12, with W/T, a nose cockpit, and revised fuselage decking.

In service 1916 at Tresco, used by seven units (Calshot, Felixstowe, Houton Bay, Killingholme, Port Said, Tresco, Yarmouth) and three flts until 1919, 249 Sqn.

Action: home waters and Mediterranean.

Powered by two 350hp Eagle VIII.

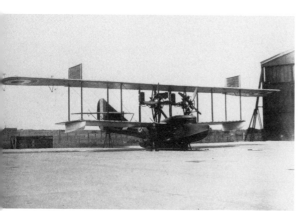

Above left: Curtiss H 4, 1234, RNAS Killingholme. (G. Stuart Leslie)

Above right: Curtiss R 2, RNAS Cranwell. (Graham Pitchfork via Peter Green)

Serials: N4330–4353 (21).

Total 21 plus 10 conversions of the H-12 making a total of 31; 7 accidental and 4 hostile losses.

Span: 92ft 8in/28.24m   Length: 46ft 4in/14.12m   Ceiling: 10,800ft/3,240m   Endurance: 6hrs   Speed: 85mph/137kmph.

Total H-12s 71; in service 1916–19; 32 (45%) losses inc. 6 hostile; nicknamed Large America.

99. H-16

Another reconnaissance flying boat for the RNAS/RAF, as the H 12 but with a Porte-designed hull for better seaworthiness, making it very similar to the Felixstowe F 2A (qv); four crew and armed with two Lewis mg in the nose and dorsal positions and one Lewis in each beam position, plus 460lb/210kg of bombs underwing. Nicknamed Large America.

In service 1918 at Killingholme, used by five units (Cattewater, Dundee, Houton Bay, Killingholme, 19N), four RAF sqns (228, 230, 238, 257) and four flts until 1919, 249 Sqn.

Action: home waters.

Powered by two 350hp RR Eagle VIII in-lines.

Curtiss H 12b,
8651, RNAS
Calshot.
(G. Stuart Leslie)

Curtiss Seamew I,
JW554, 755 Sqn.
(Newark Air
Museum)

Serials: N4060–4074 (15), N4890–4999 (60).
Span: 95ft/28.96m   Length: 46ft 1in/14.05m   Ceiling: 12,500ft/3,750m   Endurance: 6hrs   Speed: 98mph/158kmph.
Total 75; 4 accidental losses (5%).

100. Cleveland I (SBC-4)

Designed as a US Navy dive-bomber but taken over by the RAF from a French contract, serving in the communications role, unarmed, with a pilot and one passenger in tandem under a long canopy. It was a single-bay single-strut biplane with an undercarriage retracting into the fuselage sides and had a single fin/rudder.
In service 1940 with 24 Sqn, used by one sqn, 2xOTU, 3xcomms. units and 1xSoTT, until 1944, 9 Gp CF.
Powered by one 875hp Wright Cyclone R1820 radial.
Serials: AS467–471 (5).
Span: 34ft/10.36m   Length: 27ft 6in/8.38m   Ceiling: 24,500ft/7,350m   Range: 855 miles/1,377km   Speed: 235mph/378kmph.
Total 5; 1 (20%) hostile loss.

101. Seamew I (SO3C-2C)

A crew trainer for the FAA which wasn't much liked; it was a two-seater, armed with one Browning mg in the fuselage and one in the rear cockpit, and could be fitted with one main float under the fuselage and one smaller under each wing.
In service 1943 with 744 Sqn, used by 2xATU and 1xRTU, until 1945, 745 Sqn.
Based overseas in North America.
Powered by one 520hp Ranger V770-8 or 9 in-line.
Serials: FN450–499 (50), FN600–649 (50), JW554–649 (54 approx.).
Span: 38ft/11.58m   Length: 34ft 2in/10.41m   Ceiling: 16,500ft/4,950m   Range: 640 miles/1,030km   Speed: 190mph/306kmph.
Total 154 approx. but some not issued; 5 (5%) accidental losses.

102. Helldiver I (SBW-1B)

A dive-bomber for the FAA, with two crew and armed with two 0.5in Browning mg in the wings, one or two in the rear cockpit, and able to carry 1,000lb/454kg of bombs underbelly; despite widespread service with the US Navy, the FAA didn't like it and it was not operational although it served on one carrier. Its low-set wings had a wide chord, the tailplane was set high on the fuselage and the pilot's cockpit was separated by a metal fairing from the gunner's glazed cockpit.
Based overseas in North America.
In service during 1944 with 1820 Sqn and 1xmisc. unit.
Powered by one 1,650hp Wright Double-Row Cyclone R2600-8 radial.
Serials: JW100–125 (26).
Span: 47ft/14.33m   Length: 39ft 2in/11.94m   Ceiling: 23,000ft/6,900m   Range: 695 miles/1,119km   Speed: 284mph/457kmph
Total 26; 9 (35%) accidental losses.

DAIMLER (Coventry, UK)

Assembled Airco DH 10.

DE HAVILLAND (London, later Hatfield, Herts, UK)

Geoffrey de Havilland set up his own company in 1920, having previously designed all the types for the Airco company (qv) which had gone bankrupt after the First World War. Concentrating on civil aircraft DH designed the first really affordable British light aircraft, the Moth, and had no proper warplane designs until the superlative Mosquito. The company was taken over by Hawker-Siddeley Aviation in 1960, having supplied 15,924 examples of 25 types (Genet-Moth, Cirrus-Moth, Gipsy Moth, Tiger Moth, Queen Bee, Mosquito fighters, trainers and PR, Hornet, Sea Hornet, Vampire, Sea Vampire, Venom, Sea Venom and Sea Vixen see, Vol. 1). Also assembled Airco DH 9A.

103. Humming Bird

A single-seat, open-cockpit, ultra-light low-wing monoplane used by the RAF for communications. In service 1924 to 1927 with the CFS. The low wings were braced by V-style struts to the fuselage. Powered by one 26hp Blackburne Tomtit radial.

Serials: J7268–73 (6), J7325–26 (2).

Span: 30ft 1in/9.17m   Length: 19ft 8in/5.99m   Ceiling: 15,000ft/4,500m   Range: 150 miles/241km   Speed: 73mph/118kmph.

Total 8; 1 (12%) accidental loss.

104. Puss Moth

A high-wing cabin monoplane for communications work with the RAF and FAA, carrying the pilot and two passengers; during the Second World War many were impressed. The wing was braced by a tri-angular strut from the top of the undercarriage leg.

In service 1930 with Inland Area, used by 15xcomms. units, 1xCU, 1xPAFU, ATA TFP, 1xEFTS, 1xOTU, SoP and 4xmisc. units, until 1946, Doncaster SFlt.

Based overseas in North Africa, Middle East, Far East and India.

Powered by one 130hp DH Gipsy Major I in-line.

Serials: K1824 (1) plus 47 impressed – X5044, X9378, X9400–02 (3), X9439, AX868–70 (3), AX872, BD181, BK846, BK870, DD820–21 (2), DG661–62 (2), DJ711–12 (2), DP846, DP849–50 (2), DP853–54 (2), DR607–08 (2), DR755, EM995–96 (2), ES916–21 (6), ES953–54 (2), HH981, HK861, HK866, HL537, W9369 HM534, LV765–67 (3), MA946.

Span: 36ft 9in/11.21m   Length: 25ft/7.62m   Ceiling: 17,500ft/5,250m   Range: 300 miles/483km   Speed: 128mph/206kmph.

Total 1 plus 47 impressed, making a total of 48 (1 FAA); 14 (30%) accidental losses.

105. DH 89 Dragon Rapide

The RAF purchased one of these airliners as a light transport, carrying the pilot and six passengers. In service 1935 to 1946 with 24 Sqn and with 1xCU, 1xANS, 1xFU and 3xCFlts.

Powered by two 200hp DH Gipsy Six I in-lines.

Serials K5070 (1) plus two impressed – V4724–25 (2).

Total 1 plus 2 impressed making a total of 3; no losses.

105a. DH 89A Dragon Rapide

A light transport, as the above but fitted with flaps, increased area tailplane and elevators, and modified cockpit glazing with an emergency exit in the roof.

In service 1938 with 24 Sqn, used by one sqn, 1xCU, 1xAACU, 1xAPS, 1xAPC, 1xB&GS, EWS, 1xAOS and 4xcomms. units until 1947, RAF Nice.

Based overseas in southern Europe, Middle East and Far East.

Powered by two 205hp Gipsy Six II.

Serials: P1764–65 (2), P9588–89 (2), R2485–87 (3) plus 48 impressed – W6423–28 (6), W9365, X8505–11 (7), X9320, X9386–88 (3), X9448–51 (4), X9457, Z7253–7266 (14), AW115–19 (2), AW155, AX806, BD143, HK862, HK864, HK915–17 (3), MA961.

Total 7 plus 48 impressed, making a total of 55; 10 accidental and 5 hostile losses.

105b. Dominie I

A fully militarised version of the above, used by the RAF for radio training (seven crew and a DF loop above the cabin), by the RAF and FAA for communications, carrying the pilot and eight passengers, and by the RAF as an ambulance, with four stretchers. Built by Brush Coachworks.

In service 1939 with 2 EWS, used by 3xRS, 3xSS, 3xOAFU, 1xPAFU, 2xAONS, 2xAOS, SoAS, ERS, FLS, SoFC, 2xSGR, SoLAW, 16xOTU, 1xPara&GS, 1xParaTS, 2xITS, 2xTEU, 1xFTU, 1xFIS, 1xFAA CU, 1xFAA ATU, 56 RAF and 5xFAA comms. units, and 37 RAF and 7xFAA misc. units; out of service as radio trainer 1948, 4 RS, and for communications 1955.

Based overseas in North and West Africa, Far East, Germany and Denmark.

Above left: DH Dominie I, NF875, preserved example. (Alastair Goodrum Collection)

Above right: DH Don I, L2393, Eastchurch. (Peter Green Collection)

Serials: R5921–5934 (14), R9545–9564 (20), X7320–7525 (143), HG653–732 (47), MA963–66 (4 renumbered), NF847–896 (50), NR669–853 (150), RL936–946 (11).
Total 435 (65 FAA); 47 accidental and 4 hostile losses.

105c. Dominie II
A straight communications version for the RAF and FAA, with a pilot and nine passengers.
In service 1946 with TTCComms.Flt, used until 1963, 781 Sqn – also used by other comms. units but it is difficult to separate the Mk I and II in these units. Built by Brush Coachworks.
Serials: RL947–986 (29).
Total 29; 2 accidental losses.

	Span	Length	Ceiling	Range	Speed
DH 89	48ft/14.63m	34ft 6in/10.51m	19,500ft/5,850m	578 miles/931km	157mph/253kmph
Dominie	"	"	16,700ft/5,010m	"	"

Total DH 89s 472 plus 50 impressed making a total of 522; built by DH and Brush Coachworks; in service 1935–63; 68 (13%) losses inc. 9 hostile.

106. Don I
A fast communications monoplane for the RAF, which was not a success; it carried a pilot and four passengers.
In service 1937 with Grantham SFlt, used by 1xEWS, 9xFTS and 1xOTU until 1940, 6 OTU.
Powered by one 425hp DH Gipsy King I in-line.
Serials: L2388–2636 (47).
Span: 47ft 6in/14.48m   Length: 37ft 4in/11.38m   Ceiling: 21,500ft/6,450m   Range: 790 miles/1,272km   Speed: 189mph/304kmph.
Total 47; 1 (2%) accidental loss.

107. DH86B
A small biplane airliner, carrying two crew and 10 passengers, and used by the RAF for communications and as a radio trainer (six crew); it had auxiliary fins on the tailplanes.
In service 1938 with EWS, used by 2 sqns (24, 117), EWS, 1xRAF and 2xFAA comms. units, and 1xmisc. unit until 1945, 782 Sqn.
Based overseas in North Africa.
Powered by four 205hp DH Gipsy Six II in-lines.
Serials: L8037, L8040, N6246 plus 8 impressed – X9441, AX760, AX762, AX795, AX842, HK830 (2), HK843.
Total 3 plus 8 impressed making a total of 11 (3 FAA); 4 accidental and 1 hostile loss.

DH 86B, Electrical & Wireless School. (Scott Collection)

DH Dragonfly, G-AEDU, preserved example. (Author's Collection)

107a. DH 86A

As the above but without the auxiliary fins, and used for communications work by the RAF and FAA.
In service 1940 with 782 Sqn, used by two sqns (24, 117), 1xFTS, 1xSS, 1xAONS, 2xAACU, 1xFAA RTU, and 1xFAA comms. unit, until 1944, 782 Sqn.
Based overseas in North Africa.
Serials: L7596 (1) plus 10 impressed – X9441-42 (2), AX800, AX840–41 (2), AX843–44 (2), HK829, HX789, HK844.
Total 1 plus 10 impressed making a total of 11 (3 FAA); 6 losses inc. 1 hostile.

	Span	Length	Ceiling	Range	Speed
DH 86	64ft 6in/	46ft 1in/	18,000ft/	750 miles/	150mph/
	19.65m	14.05m	5,400m	1,207km	241kmph
DH 86B	"	"	17,400ft/	800 miles/	166mph/
			5,220m	1,288km	267kmph

Total DH 86s 4 plus 18 impressed making a total of 22; in service 1937–45; 11 (50%) losses.

108. Dragonfly

The smallest of the DH twin-engined designs, this elegant biplane carried a pilot and four passengers for communications work with the RAF.
In service 1939 with Bengal SFlt, used by 7xcomms. units, 3xAACU, 1xSoGR and 3xmisc. units until 1944, 2TAF Comms.Flt.
Based overseas in Far East.
Powered by two 130hp DH Gipsy Major I in-lines.
Serials: V4734, X9327, X9337, X9389–90 (2), X9452, AV976, AV987, AV992–94 (3), AW164, AX797, AX855, BD149, DJ716.
Span: 43ft/13.11m   Length: 31ft 8in/9.65m   Ceiling: 18,100ft/5,430m   Range: 900 miles/1,449km   Speed: 144mph/232kmph.
Total 16 impressed 5 (31%) accidental losses.

109. Fox Moth

A large single-engined cabin biplane impressed for communications work with the RAF and FAA, carrying a pilot in an open-cockpit behind four passengers in the cabin.

In service 1939 with the ATA, used by two RAF and 1xFAA comms. units, 2xAACU and 4xmisc. units until 1944, Bengal SFlt.

Based overseas in the Far East.

Powered by one 130hp DH Gipsy Major I in-line.

Serials: X2865–67 (3), X9304–05 (2), AW124, AX859, DZ213, MA954–55 (2), MA959.

Span: 30ft 10in/9.39m   Length: 25ft 9in/7.85m   Ceiling: 15,000ft/4,500m   Range: 415 miles/668 km   Speed: 123mph/198kmph.

Total 11 impressed (1 FAA); 1 (31%) accidental loss.

110. Hornet Moth

A communications cabin biplane for the RAF, carrying a pilot and two passengers; also used for coastal patrol during 1940 but had no armament.

In service 1939 at Lee-on-Solent, used by six coastal patrol flts, two PR flts, 2xPAFU, 1xAONS, 2xEFTS, 2xFTS, 3xTTFlts, 6xOTU, SoP, 1xcal.flt, 1xFAA CU, 1xFAA ATU, 26xRAF and 1xFAA comms. units and 20xmisc. units, until 1946, 529 Sqn.

Based overseas in the Far East.

Powered by one 130hp DH Gipsy Major I in-line.

Serials: V4731, W5746–5782 (23), W5784, W5830, W6421–22 (2), W9372, W9379–9391 (13), X9310, X9319, X9321–26 (6), X9443–47 (5), X9458, AV951–52 (2), AV969, AV972, AW114, AW118, AX857, BK830, BK837, HM498, LR227, LV763.

Span: 32ft 6in or 31ft 11in/9.9m or 9.73m (some had square tips, some tapered)   Length: 25ft/7.62m   Ceiling: 17,800ft/5,340m   Range: 640 miles/1,030 km   Speed: 127mph/204kmph.

Total 68 impressed; 14 (21%) losses inc. 1 hostile.

111. Leopard Moth

An impressed high-wing communications monoplane for the RAF and FAA, carrying a pilot and two passengers.

In service 1939 with 1 SFTS (India), used by 18xcomms. units, 4xAACU, 1xEFTS, 1xFTU, 1xFTS, 2xOTU, 1xFAA CU, 1xFAA ATU and 4xmisc. units, until 1946, 70 Gp Comms.Flt.

Based overseas in Far East and India.

Powered by one 130hp DH Gipsy Major I in-line.

DH Hornet Moth,
preserved example.
(Author's Collection)

DH Leopard Moth, G-ACUS, preserved example. (Author's Collection)

DH Moth Minor, G-AFPN. (Tony Hancock)

Serials: T1775–76 (2), W5783, W9370–71 (2), X9294–95 (2), X9380–85 (6), AV975, AV983–86 (4), AV988–89 (2), AW117, AW120–23 (4), AW125, AW156, AW165–66 (2), AW168–69 (2), AX801–02 (2), AX804–05 (2), AX858, AX861–62 (2), AX865, AX873, BD140, BD144, BD146–48 (3), BD167, BD169, BD172–73 (2), BK867, DD818, ES945, MA922.
Span: 37ft 6in/11.43m   Length: 24ft 6in/7.45m   Ceiling: 21,500ft/6,450m   Range: 715 miles/1,151 km
Speed: 119mph/192kmph.
Total 53 impressed (2 FAA); 25 (47%) losses inc. 1 hostile.

112. Moth Minor

A two-seat open-cockpit low-wing monoplane, impressed for communications work with the RAF.
In service 1939 with 2 Sqn, used by 8xcomms. units, 1xOAFU, 2xPAFU, 1xAAS, 1xAGS, 1xAACU, 1xFTS, 1xGTS, 8xOTU, 1xRS, 1xTorpTU, 2xUASqns and EANS, until 1946, TTC Comms. Flt.
Based overseas in the Far East.
Powered by one 90hp DH Gipsy Minor I in-line.
Serials: W6458–60 (3), W7971–75 (5), X5115–17 (3), X5120–23 (4), X5133, X9297–98 (2), AV977, AW112–13 (2), AW151, AX790, BD182, BK831, BK838–40 (3), BK847, HM544, HM579, HM584–85 (2), HX795–97 (3), NP490.
Span: 36ft 7in/11.16m   Length: 24ft 5in/7.45m   Ceiling: 18,400ft/5,520m   Range: 300 miles/483 km   Speed: 118mph/190kmph.
Total 37 impressed; 7 (19%) losses.

113. Flamingo

A high-wing, twin-finned monoplane airliner for use by the RAF and FAA; three crew and up to 17 passengers.
In service 1940 with the King's Flt, used by two RAF and 1xFAA comms. units, and 1xOTU until 1945, 782 Sqn.
Powered by two 815hp Bristol Perseus XIIc radials.
Serials: R2764–66 (3), T5357 plus three impressed – X9317, AE444, BT312.
Total 4 plus 3 impressed making a total of 7 (2 FAA); 2 accidental losses.

113a. Hertfordshire I

A military version of the above, with circular cabin windows instead of rectangular and carrying 22 passengers. In service during 1940 with 24 Sqn.

Powered by two 745hp Perseus XVI.

Serial: R2510.

Total 1; 1 accidental loss.

Both versions: Span: 70ft/21.34m   Length: 51ft 7in/15.72m   Ceiling: 20,900ft/6,270m   Range: 1,210 miles/1,948 km   Speed: 239mph/385kmph.

Total Flamingo variants 5 plus 3 impressed making a total of 8; in service 1940–45; 3 (37%) losses.

114. Albatross

A very graceful low-wing monoplane airliner with twin fins, introduced just before the Second World War and impressed into the RAF, carrying four crew and 22 passengers.

In service 1940 to 1942 with 271 Sqn.

Powered by four 425hp DH Gipsy Twelve I in-lines.

Serials: AX903–04 (2).

Span: 105ft/32m   Length: 71ft 6in/21.79m   Ceiling: 17,900ft/5,370m   Range: 1,040 miles/1,674 km   Speed: 224mph/361kmph.

Total 2 impressed; 2 (100%) accidental losses.

115. Dragon

A small biplane airliner impressed by the RAF for communications, carrying the pilot and five passengers.

In service 1940 with 6 AACU, used by 3xAACU, 1xSoGR and 1xcomms. unit, until 1946.

Powered by two 130hp DH Gipsy Major I in-lines.

Serials: X9379, X9395–99 (5), X9440, AV982, AW154, AW163, AW170–73 (4), AX863, AX867, BS816, HM569.

Span: 47ft 4in/14.43m   Length: 34ft 6in/10.51m   Ceiling: 14,500ft/4,350m   Range: 545 miles/877 km   Speed: 134mph/216kmph.

Total 18 impressed; 9 (50%) accidental losses.

116. Moth Major

An open-cockpit tandem two-seater single-bay biplane impressed by the RAF for communications work. Its wings were unswept and it had a strutted undercarriage.

In service from 1940 with St Andrews UASqn, used by 1xUASqn and 1xAAS until 1944, India.

Based overseas in North Africa and Far East.

Powered by one 130hp DH Gipsy Major I in-line.

Serials: W7976, AW161–62 (2), BK833, DG531, DG534, HK839.

Span: 30ft/9.14m   Length: 23ft 11in/7.29m   Ceiling: 20,000ft/6,000m   Range: 300 miles/483 km   Speed: 112mph/180kmph.

Total 7 impressed; 1 (14%) accidental loss.

DH Dragon, EI-ABI, preserved Irish example. (Author's Collection)

DH Mosquito IV, DZ353, 105 Sqn. (Scott Collection)

117. Mosquito B IV series I

A light bomber with two crew and, like all Mosquito bomber versions, having a V-shaped windscreen, glazed nose and no defensive armament; carried 2,000lb/908kg of bombs internally, and could have underwing drop tanks. One of the Second World War's best types.

In service 1941 to 1942 with 105 Sqn, also served with the Mosquito CU, until 1943.

Action: northern Europe.

Powered by two 1,390hp Merlin 21.

Serials: W4057, W4064–72 (8).

Total 9; 4 accidental and 4 hostile losses.

117a. Mosquito B IV series II

As the above but had longer engine nacelles and some were later fitted with a bulged bomb bay to carry a 4,000lb/1,816kg bomb; a few were modified to carry the Highball anti-shipping mine.

In service 1942 with 105 Sqn, used by six sqns (105, 109, 139, 618, 627, 692), one RCM sqn (192) and one met. sqn (521) until 1945, 627 Sqn; also served with 1xCU, 1xFTU, 1xMosquito CU, 3xOTU, PNTU, 2xcomms. units and 5xmisc. units.

Action: northern Europe, based overseas in Australia.

Powered by two 1,390hp Merlin 21 or 23.

Serials: DK284–339 (49), DZ311–652 (250).

Total 299; 98 accidental and 107 hostile losses.

117b. Mosquito B IX

A bomber version of the PR IX (Vol. 1), carrying 2,000lb/910kg of bombs internally or some a 4,000lb/1,816kg bomb in a bulged bomb bay, these having a solid nose carrying H2S radar.

In service 1943 with 109 Sqn, used by three sqns (105, 109, 139) and one met. flt until 1945, 109 Sqn.

Action: northern Europe.

Powered by two 1,280hp Merlin 72 or 1,250hp Merlin 76/77.

Serials: LR475–77 (3), LR495–513 (19), ML896–924 (29), MM237–38 (2), MM246.

Total 54; 26 accidental and 10 hostile losses.

117c. Mosquito B XVI/B 16

A bomber version of this Mk (for PR 16, see Vol. 1), carrying 4,000lb/1,816kg of bombs in a bulged bomb bay and some with H2S radar in a solid nose. The cockpit was pressurised.

In service 1944 with 105 Sqn, used by 14 sqns (4, 14, 69, 98, 105, 109, 128, 139, 163, 176, 180, 256, 571, 608) until 1948, 109 Sqn; also served with CNS, 1xCU, EANS, 3xOTU, 1xOCU, 1xTFlt, 2xcomms. units, and 9xRAF and 2xFAA misc. units.

Action: northern Europe and Far East, also based overseas in Germany, Egypt and Cyprus.

Powered by two 1,280hp Merlin 72/73 or 1,280hp Merlin 76/77 with intakes beneath the spinners.

Serials: ML925–MM258 (226), PF379–619 (192), RV295–363 (53).

Total 471 (4 FAA); 174 accidental and 71 hostile losses.

117d. Mosquito B XX/B 20

A Canadian-built B IV light bomber with Canadian or American equipment, carrying 2,000lb/908kg of bombs internally; no guns.

In service 1943 with 139 Sqn, used by five sqns (128, 139, 162, 608, 627) until 1946, 162 Sqn; also served with OAFU, PNTU, 1xOTU and 3xmisc. units.

Action: northern Europe, also based overseas in North America.

Powered by two 1,390hp RR-Packard Merlin 31 or 33.

Serials: KB100–299 (100), KB329–369 (31).

Total 131; 50 accidental and 28 hostile losses.

117e. Mosquito B XXV/B 25

A Canadian-built more powerful development of the above.

In service 1944 with 109 Sqn, used by nine sqns (128, 139, 142, 162, 163, 502, 608, 614, 627) until 1948, 502 Sqn. Also served with 1xCU, ECFS, 1xOTU, 2xFAA CU, 6xFAA ATU, and 2xRAF and 2xFAA misc. units.

Action: northern and southern Europe, also based overseas in North America, Malta and Ceylon.

Powered by two 1,610hp RR-Packard Merlin 225.

Serials: KA930–999 (30), KB370–699 (294).

Total 324 (73 FAA); 91 accidental and 10 hostile losses.

117f. Mosquito B 35

The last bomber Mk, with a bulged bomb bay to carry 4,000lb/1,816kg of bombs, but unpressurized.

In service 1947 with 14 and 98 Sqns, used by four sqns (14, 98, 109, 139) until 1953, 139 Sqn, and one cal. sqn (527) until 1954. Also served with EANS, ECFS, 3xOCU and 5xmisc. units.

Based overseas in Germany.

Powered by two 1,535hp RR Merlin 113a/114a.

Serials: RS699–723 (25), RV364–67 (7), TA617–724 (80), TH976–TJ158 (70), TK591–707 (54), VP178–202 (25), VR792–806 (15).

Total 276; 40 accidental losses.

	Span	Length	Ceiling	Range	Speed
B IV	54ft 2in/	40ft 10in/	34,000ft/	2,040 miles/	380mph/
	16.51m	12.44m	10,200m	3,284 km	612kmph
Mk IX	"	40ft 6in/	"	2,450 miles/	408mph/
		12.34m		3,944 km	657kmph
B XVI	"	44ft 6in/	43,500ft/	1,030 miles	412mph/
		13.56m	13,050m	/1,658 km	663kmph
B XX	"	40ft 10in/	28,800ft/	2,040 miles/	380mph/
		12.44m	8,640m	3,284km	612kmph
B XXV	"	"	32,200ft/9,660m	"	376mph/605kmph
B 35	"	41ft 6in/	45,000ft/	3,340 miles/	"
		12.65m	13,500m	5,377 km	

Total Mosquito bombers 1,510; in service 1941–54; 478 (37%) losses inc. 230 hostile; nicknamed Mossie.

118. Devon C 1

An RAF light transport based on the Dove feeder-liner, carrying two crew and seven passengers, and without armament.

In service 1948 with 31 Sqn, used by one sqn, 29xcomms. units, 1xOCU and 6xmisc. units, until 1970s.

Based overseas in Germany, Malta, Cyprus, Egypt, Iraq, Malaya and Singapore.

Powered by two 340hp DH Gipsy Queen 70 in-lines.

Serials: VP952–981 (28), WB530–35 (6), WX958 (Dove).

Total 35; 4 accidental and 1 hostile loss.

DH Mosquito B 35, TA686, 98 Sqn. (Ron Brittain via Peter Green)

DH Devon C 2 series 2, VP981 converted from C 1, 207 Sqn. (Author's Collection)

118a. Devon C 2

A re-engined C 1, with larger oil coolers and new exhausts.
In service 1965 and used by one sqn and 1xmisc. unit, until 1984, 207 Sqn.
Powered by two 400hp Gipsy Queen 175.
Twenty-six conversions of the C 1.

118b. Devon C 2 series 2

As the C 2 but with a raised cockpit roof and the port tailplane clipped to give an asymmetric shorter span.
In service from the 1970s with 207 Sqn, used by three sqns (21, 26, 207) and 1xFAA comms. unit until 1984, 207 Sqn.
Twenty-two (approx.) conversions of the C 2 (1 FAA).

	Span	Length	Ceiling	Range	Speed
C 1	57ft/17.37m	39ft 3in/11.97m	20,000ft/6,000m	1,000 miles/1,610km	210mph/338kmph
C 2	"	"	"	850 miles/1,368km	"

Total Devons 34 plus 1 Dove, making a total of 35. In service 1948–84. 5 (15%) losses inc. 1 hostile.

119. Sea Devon C 20

The FAA version of the Devon, as the C 1 but with naval avionics and used for communications and fishery patrol, with three crew and eight passengers.
In service 1955 with 781Sqn, used by 2xcomms. units, 1xATU, 1xPTU, 1xObsTU, 1xCU and 1xmisc. unit, until 1989, HMS Heron Ship's Flt.
Based overseas in Malta.
Powered by two 340hp DH Gipsy Queen 70 in-lines.
Serials: XJ319–350 (10), XK895–97 (3).
Span: 57ft/17.37m   Length: 39ft 3in/11.97m   Ceiling: 20,000ft.6,000m   Range: 1,000 miles/1,610km
Speed: 210mph/338kmph.
Total 13; no losses.

120. Heron C 2

A transport for the RAF, derived from the civil airliner and carrying two crew and eight passengers.
In service 1954 to 1968 with the UK Embassy in Washington, not operational in UK.
Powered by four 240hp DH Gipsy Queen 30 in-lines.
Serial: XG603.
Total 1; no losses.

120a. Heron C 3

A VIP transport for the RAF, as the C 2 but with a luxury interior.
In service 1955 to 1968 with the Queen's Flt.
Serials: XH375, XL961.
Total 2. No losses.

120B. Heron C 4 or CC 4

Used by the RAF and FAA, as the C 3 but with a different interior and detail improvements.
In service 1958 with the Queen's Flt, used by one sqn (60), 1xRAF and 1xFAA comms. units, 1xFAA
ATU and 1xmisc. unit until 1989, HMS Heron Ship's Flt.
Based overseas in Germany.
Serials: XM295–96 (2), XR391.
Total 3 (2 FAA); no losses.

	Span	Length	Ceiling	Range	Speed
C 2	71ft 6in/	48ft 6in/	18,500ft/	805 miles/	165mph/
	21.79m	14.78m	5,550m	1,296km	266kmph
C 3&4	"	"	"	915 miles/	183mph/
				1,473km	295kmph

Total Herons 6; in service 1954–89; no losses.

121. Sea Heron C 20, later C 1

An FAA version of the Heron for communications and, later, fishery patrol, with two crew and 14 pas-
sengers and naval equipment.
In service 1961 with 781 Sqn, used by 1xcomms. unit and 1xmisc. unit, until 1989, HMS Heron Ship's Flt.
Powered by four 240hp DH Gipsy Queen 30 in-lines.
Serials: XR441–45 (5).
Span: 71ft 6in/21.79m   Length: 48ft 6in/14.78m   Ceiling: 18,500ft/5,550m   Range: 915
miles/1,473km   Speed: 183mph/295kmph.
Total 5. 1 (20%) accidental loss.

DH Sea Heron C 1, XR443.
(Author's Collection)

122. Comet T 2

After the disasters with the Comet airliners, the RAF took over the Comet Mk 2s and thus, by accident, operated the world's first military jet transport, with five crew and 46 passengers. The T 2s were used to train crews and were also used as transports.

In service 1956–60 with 216 Sqn.

Powered by four 7,530lb st RR Avon 117 or 118 jets.

Serials: XK669–70 (2).

Total 2; no losses.

122a. Comet C 2

The pure passenger version, as the T 2 but without the training role.

In service 1956 to 1967 with 216 Sqn.

Serials: XK671, XK696–99 (4), XK715–16 (2).

Total 7 plus 2 conversions of the T 2 making a total of 9; no losses.

122b. Comet C 2 (RC)

Used for ECM work, with 16 crew and extra avionics which resulted in varying aerials and radomes, and wing pods; some had rectangular cabin windows.

In service 1957 with 192 Sqn, used by two sqns (51, 192) until 1975, 51 Sqn.

Powered by four 7,530lb st Avon 118.

Serials: XK655, XK659, XK663.

Total 3 plus 1 conversion of the C 2 making a total of 4; 1 accidental loss.

122c. Comet C 4

A transport, as the C 2 but longer, being the Mk 4C in its civil guise, and carrying 94 passengers; it had a fuel pod on each wing leading-edge.

In service 1962 to 1975 with 216 Sqn.

Powered by four 10,500lb st Avon RA29.

Serials: XR395–99 (5).

Total 5; no losses.

	Span	Length	Ceiling	Range	Speed
C 2	115ft/35.05m	95ft/28.96m	40,000ft/12,000m	2,500 miles/4,025km	480mph/773kmph
C 4	"	118ft/35.97m	"	2,650 miles/4,266km	542mph/873kmph

Total Comets 17; in service 1956–75; 1 (6%) loss.

DH Comet C 4, XR395, 216 Sqn. (Charles Parker)

DEPERDUSSIN (France)

A pre-First World War company which existed from 1910 to 1914 when it became SPAD (see Vol. 1); supplied 18 examples of one type.

123. Monoplane

A shoulder-wing reconnaissance and trainer type for the RE/RFC and RNAS, the wing braced by two triangular kingposts on the fuselage; two crew, unarmed and could be fitted with floats.
In service 1912 at Larkhill , used by four RNAS units (Chingford, Eastchurch, Felixstowe, Hendon) and one RFC sqn (3) until 1916, Felixstowe RNAS. Embarked on one cruiser.
Action: northern Europe
Powered by one 70hp Gnome 7 Gamma or 100hp Gnome-Monosoupape 9bz rotary, or 80hp Anzani radial.
Serials: 7, 22, 36, 252, 257–60 (4), 279–80 (2), 419, 436–37 (2), 1376–79 (4) plus one impressed – 885.
Span: 39ft 6in/12.04m   Length: 24ft 6in/7.47m   Ceiling: n/k   Endurance: 2.5 hrs   Speed: 71mph/114kmph.
Total 17 plus 1 impressed making a total of 18 (7 RNAS); 1 accidental RNAS loss, RFC n/k.

DESOUTTER (Croydon, Surrey, UK)

A short-lived company, formed in 1929 and out of business 1939; supplied three impressed examples of one type.

124. Desoutter I

A high-wing cabin monoplane impressed for communications work with the RAF, carrying a pilot and two passengers. The wing was braced by V-style struts and the fuselage legs went to the fuselage/wing junction.
In service 1941 with Turnhouse SFlt, used by 2xOTU and 1xcomms. unit until 1944, 81 OTU.
Powered by one 110hp Cirrus Hermes II with a long exhaust beneath the fuselage.
Serials: ES946, HM508.
Total 2 impressed; no losses.

124a. Desoutter II

As the above, but with a different engine.
In service 1941 with Swinderby SFlt, used by various SFlts until 1945, Tempsford SFlt.
Powered by one 110hp DH Gipsy III in-line.
Serial: HM507.
Total 1 impressed; no losses.

	Span	Length	Ceiling	Range	Speed
No. I	36ft/10.98m	27ft/8.23m	18,000ft/5,400m	400 miles/644km	115mph/185kmph
No. II	35ft 8in/10.87m	26ft/7.92m	17,000ft/5,100m	500 miles/805km	125mph/201kmph

Total Desoutters 3 impressed; in service 1941–45; no losses.

DFW (Germany)

A company established in 1910, which supplied two examples of two types.

125. Mars Arrow

A reconnaissance two-seater for the RNAS, an unarmed two-bay biplane with swept wings.
In service 1913 at Eastchurch, used by two units (Eastchurch, Killingholme) until 1914, Killingholme.
Action: home waters.
Powered by one 100hp Mercedes D I in-line.
Serial: 154.
Span: 54ft 10in/16.71m   Length: 30ft 3in/9.22m   Ceiling: n/k   Endurance: 2 hrs   Speed: 65mph/105kmph.
Total 1; no losses.

DFW Mars Arrow, 154,
RNAS Killingholme.
(Peter Green Collection)

126. B II

A reconnaissance and trainer three-bay biplane with curved, swept wings, impressed for use by the
RNAS; two crew and unarmed.
In service 1914 at Eastchurch, used by two units (Eastchurch, Killingholme) until 1915, Killingholme.
Powered by one 100hp Mercedes D I in-line.
Serial: 891.
Span: 41ft 4in/12.6m   Length and performance: n/k.
Total 1 impressed; 1 (100%) accidental loss.

DICK, KERR & CO. (Preston, Lancs)

Assembled Felixstowe F2A and F 3.

DONNET-LEVECQUE (France)

A very early company formed in 1912 and out of business in 1914, supplying one example of one type.

127. Flying Boat

A small three-bay biplane reconnaissance flying boat for the RNAS, unarmed and with a crew of two; it
formed the basis for the FBA (qv). Nicknamed Franco.
In service 1912 at Eastchurch, used by two units until 1913, Grain.
Powered by one 80hp Gnome 7z Lambda pusher rotary.
Serial: 18.
Span: 32ft 10in/10m   Length: 27ft 2in/8.28m   Performance: n/k.
Total 1; no losses.

DORNIER (Germany)

A famous company founded in 1914 and, apart from a period after the Second World War, still in existence. Supplied eight examples of one type .

128. Do. 22

An open-cockpit three-seat parasol-wing maritime patrol seaplane with two floats, operated by the
Yugoslav Navy when it came under RAF command. The monoplane wing was mounted above the
fuselage and joined to it by four struts connected to the float support struts. Armed with 1xmg in the
nose, 2xmg in the rear cockpit and 1xmg in the ventral position, plus one torpedo or bombs under belly.
In service with 2 (Yugoslav) Sqn from 1941 to 1942.
Action: Mediterranean, not based in UK.

Powered by one 860hp Hispano-Suiza 12 ybrs in-line with a large radiator under the forward fuselage.
Serials: AX708–715.
Span: 53ft 2in/16.2m   Length: 43ft/13.11m   Ceiling: 30,170ft/9,050m   Range: 1,430
miles/2,302m   Speed: 217mph/349kmph.
Total 8; 2 (25%) accidental losses.

DOUGLAS (USA)

A famous company formed in 1921 and which merged into McDonnell-Douglas in 1967; supplied
3,017 examples of seven types (Havoc and Boston fighters, see Vol. 1).

129. Boston I

Taken over from a Belgian contract, the Mk I was not used on operations but only for type conversion
training, with two crew and no armament.
In service 1940 with 85 Sqn, used by four fighter flts, ECFS, 1xBATFlt, 1xFTU, and 1xFAA ATU until
1944, 307 FTU.
Powered by two 1,050hp P&W Twin Wasp R1820-S3c-g radials.
Serials: AE457–472 (12), AX849–50 (2).
Total 14 (1 FAA); 5 accidental and 1 hostile loss.

Boston II and Turbinlites – see with Havoc I (Vol. 1)

129a. Boston III

A light bomber for the RAF, as the Mk I but with four crew and armed with two Browning mg on the
sides of the nose, two Vickers mg in a dorsal position, and 2,000lb/908kg of bombs internally; many went
to the SAAF.
In service 1941 with 88 Sqn, used by 10 sqns (18, 23, 88, 107, 114, 223, 226, 342, 418, 605) and two trans-
port sqns (173, 267) until 1944, 114 Sqn; also served with 1xCU, 2xFTU, 4xOTU, 1xRef.FU, 1xTTFlt,
2xFAA ATU, 3xcomms. units and 6xmisc. units, until 1946.
Action: northern and southern Europe, North Africa and Middle East; also based overseas in East Africa.
Powered by two 1,600hp Wright Double-Row Cyclone R2600 radials, with intakes above the nacelles.
Serials: W8252–8401 (150), Z2155–2304 (126), AH740, AL263–502 (56), AL668–907 (119).
Total 452 (1 FAA); 92 accidental and 128 hostile losses.

129d. Boston IIIA (A-20C)

A light bomber for the RAF, as the Mk III but Lend-lease with American equipment; armed with two
0.5in Brownings in the nose and two in the dorsal position, plus increased tankage.
In service 1943 with 88 Sqn, used by six sqns (18, 88, 107, 114, 226, 342) until 1945, 88 and 342 Sqns, also
served with 1xCU, 1xcomms. unit and 1xmisc. unit, until 1946.
Action: northern and southern Europe and North Africa.
Powered by two 1,600hp D-R Cyclone R2600-23asb, with stub exhausts and longer intakes above the
cowlings.
Serials: BZ196–399 (198).
Total 198 (1 FAA); 78 accidental and 49 hostile losses.

129e. Boston IV (A-20J)

As the Mk IIIA but with a clear, unframed, perspex nose; two 0.5in Browning mg in a Martin 250 dorsal
turret and two in the nose, plus 2,000lb/908kg of bombs internally.
In service 1944 with 88 Sqn, used by six sqns (13, 18, 55, 88, 114, 342), 1xOTU, 1xFTU and 1xcomms.
unit, until 1946, 55 Sqn.
Action: northern and southern Europe, also based overseas in Greece.
Powered by two 1,600hp D-R Cyclone R2600-23.
Serials: BZ400–568 (166).
Total 166; 34 accidental and 28 hostile losses.

Above left: Douglas Boston IV, BZ473, 88 Sqn. (Peter Green Collection)

Above right: Douglas DC 2, PH-AJU, preserved Dutch example. (Author's Collection)

129f. Boston V (A-20K)

As the Mk IV but with different engines.

In service 1944 with 55 Sqn, used by four sqns (13, 18, 55, 114) and 1xCU until 1946, 55 Sqn.

Action: southern Europe, also based overseas in Greece; not operational in the UK.

Powered by two 1,700hp D-R Cyclone R2600-29.

Serials: BZ580–669 (89).

Total 89; 13 accidental and 12 hostile losses.

	Span	Length	Ceiling	Range	Speed
Mk I	61ft 4in/	46ft 11in/	28,500ft/	630 miles/	n/k
	18.69m	14.3m	8,550m	1,014km	
Mk III	"	47ft 3in/	24,200ft/	1,020 miles/	304mph/
		14.41m	7,260m	1,642km	489kmph
Mk IIIA	"	48ft/	25,800ft/	1,090 miles/	320mph/5
		14.63m	7,740m	1,755km	15kmph
Mk IV	"	48ft 4in/	"	"	327mph/
		14.73m			526kmph
Mk V	"	"	25,100ft/	830 miles	333mph/
			7,530m	/1,336km	536kmph

Total Bostons 919; in service 1941–46; 502 (55%) losses inc. 250 hostile.

130. DC-2

An RAF transport version of the airliner, carrying three crew and 14 passengers.

In service 1941 with 31 Sqn, used by three sqns (31, 117, 267), 1xcomms. unit and 1xmisc. unit, until 1943, 117 Sqn.

Action: North and East Africa and Far East, not operational in the UK.

Powered by two 875hp Wright Cyclone SGR1820-F52 radials.

Serials: AX755, AX767–69 (3), HK820–21 (2), HK837, HK847 plus 12 impressed – DG468–79.

Span: 85ft/25.9m   Length: 61ft/18.59m   Ceiling: 22,450ft/6,735m   Range: 1,000 miles/ 1,610 km   Speed: 210mph/338kmph.

Total 8 plus 12 impressed making a total of 20; 9 (43%) losses inc. 3 hostile.

131. DC-3

A famous airliner, purchased by the RAF for transport duties, with three crew and 21 passengers.

In service 1942 with 31 Sqn, used by four sqns (24, 31, 117, 267), 1xCU, 1xME C&CU, 3xcomms. units and 1xmisc. unit, until 1945, FE VIP Flt.

Action: North Africa and Far East.

Powered by two 1,200hp P&W Twin Wasp R1830 radials.

Serials: HK867 (renumbered), HK983, LR230–35 (6) plus 4 impressed – MA925, MA928–29 (2), MA943.

Total 8 plus 4 impressed making a total of 12; 3 accidental and 2 hostile losses.

131a. Dakota I (C-47)

The military version of the DC-3, with four crew and able to carry 28 passengers or 7,500lb/3,405kg of freight on a strengthened floor, loaded through a large freight door on the port fuselage side.
In service 1943 with 31 Sqn, used by 10 sqns (24, 31, 52, 194, 216, 267, 271, 353, 511, 512), 3xCU, 1xME C&CU, 1xOTU, 1xParaTS, 6xcomms. units and 5xmisc. units, until 1947, 52 Sqn.
Action: North Africa and Far East, also based overseas in East and West Africa, Burma and Singapore.
Powered by two 1,200hp Twin Wasp R1830-92.
Serials: FD768–818 (45), FG857, HK983.
Total 47; 8 accidental and 2 hostile losses.

131b. Dakota II (C-53)

A passenger-only transport, without the floor and freight door of the Mk I and carrying 28 passengers.
In service 1942 with 117 Sqn, used by three sqns (24, 117, 216), 1xCU and 3xcomms. units, until 1947, 24 Sqn.
Action: North Africa and Far East,
Powered by two 1,200hp Twin-Wasp R1830-901 with 2xspeed blowers.
Serials: FJ709–12 (4), HK867, TJ167, TJ170.
Total 7; no losses.

131c. Dakota III (C-47A)

A passenger or freight version, as the Mk I but with equipment changes and 24 volt electrics; it could tow a glider and some in the Far East carried Browning mg in the door or windows. Short intakes over the cowlings.
In service 1943 with 194 Sqn, used by 27 sqns (10, 24, 31, 48, 52, 62, 77, 96, 110, 117, 167, 187, 194, 215, 216, 231, 233, 238, 267, 271, 353, 435, 436, 437, 511, 512, 575) until 1947, MCommsSqn; also served with 1xCFlt, 9xCU, 1xFTU, 1xLancaster FinS, 1xME C&CU, 1xMETS, ORTU, 5xOTU, 1xPara&GS, 2xParaTS, TSTU, Glider Pick-up TFlt, 24xRAF and 1xFAA CU, 1xFAA ATU and 21xmisc. units.
Action: northern and southern Europe, North Africa, Middle East and Far East, also based overseas in West Africa, North America, Germany, Palestine, Egypt, India, Burma, Malaya, Singapore, Hong Kong and Australia.
Serials: FD819–967 (132), FL503–652 (133), FZ548–698 (116), KG310–809 (459), TS422–436 (12).
Total 852; 162 accidental and 67 hostile losses.

131d. Dakota IV/C 4 (C-47B)

As the Mk III but had high-altitude blowers and increased tankage.
In service 1944 with 147 Sqn, used by 42 sqns (10, 18, 21, 24, 27, 30, 31, 46, 48, 52, 53, 62, 70, 76, 77, 78, 96, 110, 113, 114, 117, 147, 167, 187, 194, 204, 206, 209, 215, 216, 231, 233, 238, 243, 267, 271, 353, 435, 436, 437, 575, 620), one SD sqn (357), 5xCU, ECFS, EFS, 2xOCU, 4xOTU, 1xPara&GTU, 3xParaTS, TSTU (India), 1xFAA CU, 50xcomms. units and 14xmisc,units, until 1970, MECommsS.

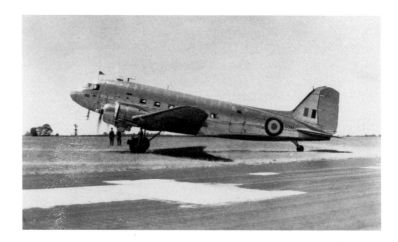

Douglas Dakota IV, KJ994,
SHAEF Comms. Sqn.
(Author's Collection)

Action: northern and southern Europe, Far East, DEI, Palestine, Malaya, Berlin Airlift, and Aden, also served overseas in West Africa, Germany, Iraq, Egypt, Kenya, India, Japan, Singapore, Hong Kong, Australia and Canada.

Powered by two 1,200hp Twin Wasp R1830-906 with long intakes over the nacelles.

Serials: KJ801–KK220 (276), KN202–701 (494), KP208–279 (72), TP181, TP187.

Total 844 (1 FAA); 184 accidental and 8 hostile losses.

	Span	Length	Ceiling	Range	Speed
DC-3	95ft/28.96m	64ft 6in/19.65m	24,000ft/7,200m	1,370 miles/2,206km	240mph/386kmph
Mk I	"	"	23,200ft/6,960m	1,500 miles/2,415km	230mph/370kmph
C 4	"	"	"	1,600 miles/2,576km	"

Total DC-3/Dakotas 1,758 plus 4 impressed making a total of 1,762; in service 1942–70; 436 (25%) losses inc. 79 hostile. Nicknamed Dak.

132. Skymaster I (C-54B or C)

A long-range transport which became the DC-4 in civilian service; used by the RAF with six crew and able to carry 42 passengers or 32,000lb/14,530kg of freight.

In service 1944 with 24 Sqn, used by three sqns (24, 232, 246), 1xCU, 1xcomms. unit and 1xmisc. unit, until 1946, 232 Sqn.

Based overseas in India.

Powered by four 1,380hp P&W Twin Wasp R2000 radials.

Serials: EW999, KL977–999 (10).

Span: 117ft 6in/35.81m   Length: 93ft 11in/28.63m   Ceiling: 26,600ft/7,980m   Range: 3,800 miles/6,118 km   Speed: 265mph/427kmph.

Total 11; no losses.

133. Dauntless I (SBD-5)

Designed as a low-wing monoplane dive-bomber for the USN but this role did not find favour with the FAA and the few aircraft supplied were used for communications, with armament deleted and carrying the pilot and one passenger in tandem under a long canopy.

In service 1944 with 787Sqn, used by 1xmisc. unit until 1946, Eastleigh (Hants) Ship's Flt.

Powered by one 1,200hp Wright Cyclone R1820-60 radial.

Serials: JS997–98 (2), JT923–26 (4).

Span: 41ft 6in/12.65m   Length: 33ft/10.06m   Ceiling: 25,200ft/7,560m   Range: 773 miles/1,245 km   Speed: 255mph/411kmph.

Total 6; 3 (50%) accidental losses.

Douglas Skymaster I, KL979, VIP Flt.
(Charles Parker)

Douglas Skyraider
AEW 1, WT949,
849 Sqn. (Newark
Air Museum)

134. Skyraider AEW 1 (AD-4W)

The FAA's first airborne radar station, unarmed, with three crew and AN/APS-20f radar in a large under-belly radome.

In service 1951 with 778 Sqn, 1952, 849 Sqn, used by one sqn and 1xCU until 1960, 849 Sqn; embarked on seven carriers.

Action: Suez.

Powered by one 2,700hp Wright Turbo-Cyclone R3350-26wa radial.

Serials: WT943–WV185 (50).

Span: 50ft/15.24m   Length: 38ft 11in/11.86m   Ceiling: 36,000ft/10,800m   Range: 3,000 miles/4,830 km   Speed: 330mph/531kmph.

Total 50; 8 (16%) accidental losses.

ENGLISH ELECTRIC (Preston, Lancs, UK)

Formed in 1918 from three companies which had assembled aircraft during the First World War, Pheonix Dynamo, Dick, Kerr & Co. and Coventry Ordnance Works, but did not manufacture aircraft of its own design on any scale until the 1940s, rather building other designs notably the Halifax. It was taken over by the new British Aircraft Corporation in 1960 and changed its name to the parent company in 1964. Supplied 959 examples of two types (Canberra PR, T and TT, and Lightning, see Vol. 1); also assembled H-P Halifax and Hampden.

135. Canberra B 2

The RAF's first, and very successful, jet bomber, carrying three crew on MB-1c, 1cn, or 2ca ejector-seats; it had no defensive armament but carried 6,000lb/2,725kg of bombs internally including the US Mk 7 nuclear weapon and, when used for photo-reconnaissance, one vertical camera.

In service 1951 with 101 Sqn, used by 31 sqns (6, 9, 10, 12, 15, 18, 21, 27, 32, 35, 40, 44, 45, 50, 57, 59, 61, 73, 76, 90, 100, 101, 102, 103, 104, 109, 139, 149, 207, 249, 617), one flt, one PR sqn (542), seven elint sqns (97, 98, 151, 192, 199, 245, 360), two cal. sqns (115, 527) and one nuclear-sampling sqn (76), until 1962, 45 Sqn, also served with BC JetCFlt, CAW, 1xFTU, 3xOCU, RAFFC, FC TFSqn, 3xcomms. units, and 8xRAF and 1xFAA misc. units to 1995.

Action: Malaya and Suez, also based overseas in Germany, Malta, Cyprus, Aden, Libya, Singapore and Australia.

Powered by two 6,500lb st RR Avon 101 jets.

Serials: WD934–WE122 (50), WF886–917 (15), WG789, WH637–742 (72), WH853–944 (59), WJ564–753 (93), WJ971–WK190 (70), WP514–15 (2), XA536, XK641.

Total 364; 59 accidental losses.

EE Canberra B 6,
WH968, 12 Sqn. (Peter
Green Collection)

135a. Canberra B 2 (T)

A conversion trainer adaptation of the B 2, with just two crew, dual-controls, improved avionics and no armament.

In service 1980 with 231 OCU, used by one sqn and 1xOCU until 1993, 360 Sqn.

One conversion of the B 2; no losses.

135b. Canberra B 6

An improved light-bomber version, with three crew on MB-1c, 1cn, or 2ca seats, larger wheels with anti-skid brakes, increased fuel, and carrying 6,000lb/2,725kg of bombs internally, including a Red Beard or US Mk 7 nuclear weapon.

In service 1954 with 101 Sqn, used by 10 sqns (6, 9, 12, 21, 100, 101, 109, 139, 249, 617), one nuclear sampling sqn (76), and one PR sqn (542) until 1963, 6 Sqn, also served with 1xOCU and 1xmisc. unit.

Action: Malaya and Suez, also based overseas in Malta, Cyprus, Christmas Island and Australia.

Powered by two 7,500lb st Avon 109, with longer central 'spinners'.

Serials: WH944–984 (39), WJ754–784 (28), WT205–13 (9), WT301–06 (6), WT369–74 (6), XH569–70 (2).

Total 90; 13 accidental and 2 hostile losses.

135c. Canberra B 6 (BS)

A bomber-support and elint version with improved avionics, including Blue Shadow radar, which gave rise to various and changing external aerials and radomes.

In service 1954 with 192 Sqn, used by three sqns (51, 192, 360) until 1974, 51 Sqn.

Twenty-five conversions of the B 6; losses included with B 6.

135d. Canberra B 6 (RC)

Used for radar calibration, with armament deleted, radomes at nose and tail, and extra aerials.

In service 1958 with 192 Sqn, used by two sqns (51, 192) until 1975, 51 Sqn.

Four conversions of the B 6; 1 accidental loss.

135e. Canberra B (I) 6

An intruder bomber, as the B 6 but with two crew on MB-1cn seats, four 20mm cannon in a belly-pack, and 3,000lb/1,360kg of bombs internally plus 2,000lb/908kg on two wing pylons, which could include US Mk 7 or 43 nuclear bombs.

In service 1956–69 with 213 Sqn.

Based overseas in Germany, not operational in UK.

Serials: WT307–325 (19), XG554, XJ249, XJ257.

Total 22; 8 accidental losses.

135f. Canberra B (I) 8

A dedicated intruder bomber, with the pilot's fighter-style canopy offset to port and the navigator in a non-glazed nose, both on MB-1c, 1cn, or 2ca seats. Armed with four 20mm cannon in a belly-pack, 5,000lb/2,270kg of bombs internally and on two wing pylons (including US Mk 7 or 43 nuclear bombs) or alternatively carried on the pylons were two AS-30 AGMs or SNEB rocket pods.
In service 1956 with 88 Sqn, used by five sqns (3, 14, 16, 59, 88) until 1972, 16 Sqn.
Based overseas in Germany, not operational in UK.
Serials: WT329–368 (22), XH204–244 (7), XK951–59 (2), XM244–279 (20), XM936.
Total 52; 13 accidental losses.

135g. Canberra T 11

A radar-trainer conversion of the B 2 for the RAF, with four crew (one on a jump-seat), no armament, but AI-17 in a lengthened nose radome.
In service 1959 with 228 OCU, used by 1xTFSqn (85), 1xOCU and FC TFSqn, until 1969, 85 Sqn.
Eight conversions of the B 2; 1 accidental loss.

135h. Canberra B 15

As the B 6 but with 6,000lb/2,725kg of bombs, including a Red Beard nuclear weapon internally and two AS-30 AGM or two SNEB pods on two wing pylons, plus a camera in the nose and extra radio and navigation aids.
In service 1962 with 32 Sqn, used by three sqns (32, 45, 73) until 1970, 45 Sqn.
Action: Borneo, also based overseas in Cyprus and Singapore; not operational in UK.
Powered by two 7,500lb st Avon 109.
Thirty-five conversions of the B 6; 3 accidental losses.

135j. Canberra E 15

A development of the B 15 for ECM training and calibration work; no armament but was fitted with TACAN and extra avionics with associated aerials.
In service 1970 with 98 Sqn, used by two sqns (98, 360) and 1xOCU until 1994, 360 Sqn.
Eight conversions of the B 15; 3 accidental losses.

135k. Canberra B 16

A light bomber based on the B 6, but with two crew on MB-1cn or 2ca seats, 6,000lb/2,725kg of bombs, including a Red Beard nuclear weapon, internally and two AS-30 AGM on two wing pylons; Blue Shadow radar and extra radio equipment.
In service 1962 with 6 Sqn, used by two sqns (6, 249) until 1969, 249 Sqn.
Based overseas in Cyprus, not operational in the UK.
Twenty conversions of the B 6 (BS); 5 accidental losses.

EE Canberra B (I) 8, XH234. (Peter Green Collection)

135l. Canberra T 17

An ECM trainer for the RAF and FAA, with a longer solid nose housing ECM equipment and with blister aerials on the nose, underwing and under fuselage plus extra blade aerials underwing.
In service 1967 with 360 Sqn, used by one joint RAF/FAA sqn until 1994, 360 Sqn.
Twenty-four conversions of the B 2; 4 accidental losses.

135m. Canberra T 17A

As the above but with extra avionics necessitating extra blade aerials under the wings.
In service from 1987–94 with 360 (Joint) Sqn.
Six conversions of the T 17; no losses.

135n. Canberra T 19

A target facilities version, converted from the T 11 but with the radar removed, leaving an empty radome in the long nose.
In service 1965 with 85 Sqn, used by two sqns (85, 100) until 1980, 100 Sqn.
Seven conversions of the T 11 and one of a B 6, making a total of eight; 1 accidental loss.

135p. Canberra T 22

An FAA radar trainer for Buccaneer crews, also used for target facilities work; based on the PR 7 but without cameras or ports and with a long pointed nose radome for Blue Parrot radar.
In service 1973 to 1985 with FRADU.
Seven conversions of the PR 7; no losses.

	Span	Length	Ceiling	Range	Speed
B 2	64–65ft 6in/ 19.5–19.96m	65ft 6in/ 19.96m	48,000ft/ 14,400m	2,660 miles/ 4,283km	570mph/ 918k
B 6	"	"	"	3,400 miles/ 5,474km	590mph/ 950k
B (I)	8 64ft/19.5m	65ft 6in/19.96m	"	"	560mph/902k
T 11	"	69ft 6in/ 21.18m	" 5,007km	3,110 miles/ "	
B 15	64ft/65ft 6in/ 19.5/19.96m	65ft 6in/ 19.96m	"	3,400 miles/ 5,474km	580mph/ 934k
T 17	"	"	"	3,110 miles/ 5,007km	570mph/ 918k
T 19	64ft/19.5m	69ft 6in/21.18m	"	"	"
T 22	"	n/k	"	3,350 miles/ 5,395km	560mph/ 902k

Total Canberras bombers and crew trainers 528; built by EE, Avro and Handley-Page; in service 1951–94; 113 (21%) losses inc. 2 hostile.

EUROCOPTER (International)

A Franco-German company, formed in 1992 from Aerospatiale and Messerschmidt-Bolkow-Blom. Supplied 45 examples of three types (Squirrel and AAC Dauphin, see Vol. 1).

136. Twin Squirrel HCC 1

A leased VIP transport helicopter for the RAF, with one or two crew and four or five passengers. It had an engine each side of the main rotor-hub fairing, giving a bulky appearance, and a swept fin beneath the swept tail rotor pylon.
In service 1996 with 32 (The Royal) Sqn, to 2006, 32 (The Royal) Sqn.
Powered by two 420shp Allison 250-C20f turbo-props.
Serials: ZJ139–40 (2), ZJ635.
Rotor diameter: 35ft 1in/10.7m   Length: 35ft 10in/10.92m   Ceiling: 6,500ft/1,950m

Range: 437 miles/704km   Speed: 137mph/221kmph.
Total 3; no losses.

137. Dauphin

Another leased helicopter, this one for communications work with the FAA; two crew and 10–14 passengers. It has a bulky 11xblade fenestron tail-rotor, a four-blade main rotor on a humped rotor mast with an engine each side, finned horizontal stabilisors and a tri-cycle undercarriage retracting into the fuselage.
In service 1996 at RN Plymouth, to the present, 2010.
Powered by two 724shp Turbomeca Arriel 1C1 turbo-props.
Serials: ZJ164–65 (2).
Rotor diameter: 39ft 2in/11.94m   Length: 38ft 9in/11.81m   Ceiling: 6,900ft/2,070m   Range: 530 miles/853km   Speed: 176mph/283kmph.
Total 2; no losses to date.

(For AAC Dauphin see Vol. 1).

FAIRCHILD (USA)

Formed 1924 and was a well-known company, particularly for its production of rugged small aircraft, from 1924 until the Second World War; out of business 1990. Supplied 847 examples of three types (Cornell, see Vol. 1).

138. 24W

A communications cabin monoplane for the RAF, with a pilot and three passengers.
In service 1937 at Washington DC, used by 1xmisc. unit until 1943, Halton SFlt.
Based overseas in the USA.
Powered by one 145hp Warner Scarab radial.
Serials: L7044 plus 3 impressed – BK869, BS817, EF523.
Total 1 plus 3 impressed making a total of 4; no losses.

138a. Argus I (C-61)

The military version of the 24, used by the RAF for communications work. In service 1941 with the ATA, used by the ATA, one met. flt, 2xOTU, 7xcomms. units and 1xmisc. unit, until 1945.
Based overseas in the Middle East, and North and West Africa.
Powered by one 165hp Super Scarab R500.
Serials: EV725–768 (24), FK313–361 (49), HK948–49 (2), HM164–188 (25).
Total 100; 17 accidental losses.

EE Canberra T
17, WK111, 360
Sqn. (Author's
Collection)

138b. Argus II (C-61A)

As the Mk I but with 24 volt electrics.

In service 1943 with the ATA, used by the ATA, one met. flt, AB&GS ME, AGS (India), AG&BS, 2xAACU, 1xCU, 1xBDTFlt, 4xOTU, 1xRef.FU, 47xcomms. units and 26xmisc. units, until 1947, FEAF. Based overseas in southern Europe, Middle East, North, West and East Africa, Far East, Germany, Greece, Palestine and India.

Powered by one 165hp Super Scarab R500-1.

Serials: EV769–811 (32), FS500–660 (160), FZ719–110 (110), HB551–643 (93).

Total 395; 52 accidental losses.

138c. Argus III (C-61K)

As the Mk II but with an in-line engine, giving a different nose shape.

In service 1944 with 232 Gp CommsSqn, used by AB&GS ME, AG&BS, 1xCU, 2xOTU, 12xcomms. units and 6xmisc. units, many going to the ATA, until 1947.

Based overseas in southern Europe, Middle East, North Africa, Far East, Germany, Greece and Palestine.

Powered by one 200hp Ranger L440-7 in-line.

Serials: HB644–758 (115), HB760, KK379–568 (190).

Total 306; 5 accidental losses but records not accurate.

	Span	Length	Ceiling	Range	Speed
Mk I	36ft 4in/	23ft 10in/	16,000ft/	530 miles/	123mph/
	11.08m	7.26m	4,800m	853km	198kmph
Mk II	"	"	15,700ft/	720 miles/	124mph/
			4,710m	1,159km	200kmph
Mk III	"	25ft 10in/		640 miles/	130mph/
		7.87m		1,030km	209kmph

Total Arguses 805; in service 1937–47; 74 (9%) losses.

139. 91

An amphibian high-wing monoplane which the RAF used for air-sea-rescue, carrying two crew and eight passengers; unarmed.

In service 1941 to 1943 with the Sea Rescue Flt.

Action: Mediterranean, not operational in UK.

Powered by one 800hp P&W Hornet radial mounted above the fuselage.

Serial: HK832.

Span: 56ft/17.07m   Length: 46ft 8in/14.22m   Ceiling: n/k   Range: 700 miles/1,127km   Speed: 170mph/274kmph.

Total 1; 1 accidental loss (100%).

Fairchild Argus III, KK549, Levant Comms. Sqn. (Newark Air Museum)

Above left: Fairey Campania, RNAS Newhaven. (Newark Air Museum)

Above right: Fairey Hamble Baby, N1190, RNAS Felixstowe. (G. Stuart Leslie)

FAIREY (Hamble, Hants, Hayes & Hounslow, Middlesex & Stockport, Cheshire)

Established in 1915 by C.R. Fairey, later to become Sir Richard, and famed for its naval aircraft. After the Second World War it started to design helicopters and this part of the company attracted the attention of Westland (qv) which took over Fairey in 1960. Supplied 11,703 examples of 16 types (Flycatcher, Fulmar and Firefly fighters see Vol. 1); also assembled Short 827, Sopwith 1& 1/2 Strutter and H-P Halifax.

140. Campania

A biplane seaplane used by the RNAS/RAF for reconnaissance, with a crew of three and armed with a Lewis mg in the rear cockpit and light bombs under belly. Nicknamed Fairey.
In service 1917 at Scapa, used by eight RNAS units (Bembridge, Calshot, Cherbourg, Houton Bay, Newhaven, Portland, Rosyth, Scapa), four RAF sqns (240, 241, 242, 253), 3xRNAS PTU and 1xRAF TDS, until 1919, HMS Nairana; embarked on three seaplane carriers.
Action: home waters and Russia.
Powered by one 284hp RR Eagle IV, 275hp Eagle VI, 350hp Eagle VIII, or 260hp Sunbeam Maori III in-line.
Serials: N1000–09 (10), N1840–89 (12), N2360–99 (40).
Span: 61ft 7in/18.77m   Length: 43ft 1in/13.14m   Ceiling: 6,000ft/1,800m   Endurance: 5hrs   Speed: 85mph/137kmph.
Total 62; 9 (15%) losses inc. 1 hostile.

141. Hamble Baby

A single-seat reconnaissance seaplane for the RNAS/RAF based on the Sopwith Baby (Vol. 1), armed with one Vickers mg on the cowling and 112lb/50kg of bombs under belly.
In service 1917 at Scapa, used by 19 RNAS units (Bembridge, Calafrana, Cattewater, Dover, Dundee, Felixstowe, Fishguard, Hornsea, Houton Bay, Killingholme, Mudros, Newlyn, Otranto, Port Said, St Maria de Leuca, South Shields, Suda Bay, Westgate, Yarmouth), 2xPTU, and five RAF sqns (219, 229, 249, 253, 263), until 1918, 219 Sqn; embarked on one seaplane carrier.
Action: home waters and Mediterranean.
Powered by one 110hp Clerget 9z, or 130hp Clerget 9b rotary.
Serials: N1190–219 (30), N1320–1339 (20), N1450–1479 (30), N1960–1985 (26).
Total 106; 31 accidental and 5 hostile losses.

141a. Hamble Baby Convert

A dual-control two-seat trainer for the RNAS/RAF; as the Hamble Baby but the armament was deleted and it had a wheeled undercarriage.

In service 1917 at Cranwell, used by one RNAS unit (6W), 4xRNAS PTU, one RAF sqn (225) and 2xRAF TDS, until 1918, Cranwell.

Based overseas in southern Europe.

Powered by one 130hp Clerget 9b.

Serials: N1986-2059 (74).

Total 74 plus one conversion of the Baby, making a total of 75, but many not issued. One accidental and three hostile losses.

Span: 27ft 9in/8.46m   Length: 23ft 4in/7.11m as seaplane   Ceiling: 7,600ft/2,280m   Endurance: 2hrs Speed: 90mph/145kmph.

Total Hamble Babies 181; in service 1917–18; 40 (22%) losses inc. 8 hostile.

142. IIIA

A bomber for the RAF/FAA, with two crew and armed with one Lewis mg in the rear cockpit and 60lb/25kg of bombs under wing or belly.

In service 1918 with 258 and 272 Sqns, used by those two sqns and one RNAS unit (Luce Bay) until 1919, 258 and 272 Sqns.

Powered by one 260hp Sunbeam Maori III in-line.

Serials: N2850–2899 (50).

Total 50 but little used; 1 accidental loss.

142a. IIIB

A development of the IIIA but was a seaplane with an extended-span upper-wing.

In service 1918 at Westgate, used by two RAF sqns (219, 230) until 1920, 219 Sqn, embarked on two seaplane-carriers.

Action: Russia.

Serials: N2230–2259 (28).

Total 28; 1 accidental and 1 hostile loss.

142b. IIIC

A general-purpose seaplane for the RAF and FAA, as the IIIB but with a reduced wing-span and a different engine.

In service 1918 with 230 Sqn, used by two sqns (229, 230) until 1921, 230 Sqn, embarked on two seaplane-carriers.

Action: Russia.

Powered by one 350hp RR Eagle VIII in-line.

Serials: N9230-9259 (30).

Total 30, plus 7 conversions of the IIIB, making a total of 37; 3 accidental and 1 hostile loss.

Fairey IIIC, N9236, Hamble. (Peter Green Collection)

	Span	Length	Ceiling	Endurance	Speed
IIIA	46ft 2in/14.07m	31ft/9.45m	15,000ft/4,500m	4.5hrs	109mph/175kmph
IIIB	62ft 9in/19.13m	37ft 1in/11.31m	10,300ft/3,090m	"	95mph/153kmph
IIIC	46ft 1in/14.05m	36ft/10.98m	15,000ft/4,500m	5.5hrs	110mph/177kmph

Total IIIA-Cs 108; in service 1918–21; 7 (6%) losses inc. 2 hostile.

143. IIID Mk I

Based on the above, this was a widely used general-purpose land or seaplane for the RAF and FAA; it had two crew (RAF), or three (FAA), and was armed with one Vickers mg on the port fuselage side and one Lewis mg in the rear cockpit. Some were converted into dual-control trainers.
In service 1922 with 441 and 444 Flts, FAA, used by five FAA flts (441, 442, 443, 444, 481) and two RAF sqns (202, 267), SoAN, A&GS, CDCo-opFlt, SoNCo-op, TB Leuchars, SPTFlt, SPTSqn, 1xcomms. unit and 1xmisc. unit, until 1930, 202 Sqn. Embarked on four carriers, two seaplane-carriers and two cruisers, Based overseas in Malta.
Powered by one 350hp RR Eagle VIII, 360hp Eagle IX, or 480hp Napier Lion IIb in-line.
Serials: N9450–9499 (43), N9630–9635 (6), N9730–9763 (34).
Total 83; 17 accidental losses.

143a. IIID (T)

A dual-control version, with two crew and with the armament deleted.
In service 1922 with the SPTSqn, used by one RAF sqn (267), SPTSqn, one FAA flt (481), and other units, until 1930. Embarked on one seaplane-carrier.
Based overseas in Malta,
Serials: N9467, N9478–9479 (2), N9485, N9491, N9497–9498 (2).
Total 7; 3 accidental losses.

143b. IIID Mk II

As the Mk I but with the Lion engine as standard.
In service 1923 with 267 Sqn, used by two RAF sqns (202, 267), eight FAA flts (422, 440, 441, 442, 443, 444, 445, 481), 1xFAA PTU, and units as the Mk I, until 1933, 202 Sqn.; embarked on six carriers and three cruisers.
Based overseas in Malta.
Powered by one 480hp Napier Lion IIb or 500hp Lion Va in-line.
Serials: N9567–9578 (12), N9636–9641 (6), N9764–9791 (28), S1000–1035 (36).
Total 82; 18 accidental losses.

143c. IIID Mk III

As the Mk II but had wooden floats and the Lion Va as standard.
In service 1926 with 440 Flt, used by one RAF sqn (202), six FAA flts (440, 441, 442, 443, 444, 481), and training units as the Mk I until 1932, Hal Far Ship's Flt. Embarked on three carriers, one battleship and two cruisers.
Based overseas in Malta,
Powered by one 500hp Lion Va.
Serials: S1074–1108 (34).
Total 34; 3 accidental losses.

All Marks: Span: 46ft 1in/14.05m   Length: 36ft 1in/11.01m   Ceiling: 16,500ft/4,950m   Range: 550 miles/885km   Speed: 120mph/193kmph.
Total IIIDs 206; in service 1922–33; 41 (20%) losses.

144. IIIF (Interim)

An improved IIID, delivered initially to the FAA but passed on to the RAF as a general-purpose type, with two crew and armed with a Vickers mg in the forward port fuselage side and a Lewis mg in the rear cockpit; it had the IIID-style rectangular fin.

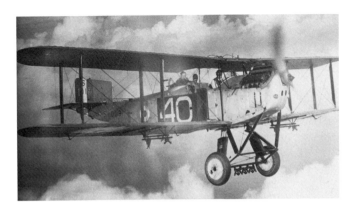

Fairey IIID Mk II, S1019, 440 Flt.
(Newark Air Museum)

In service 1924 with 47 Sqn, used by two RAF sqns (45, 47) and 1xmisc. unit, until 1931, Heliopolis SFlt. Based overseas in Sudan and Egypt, not operational in UK.

Powered by one 500hp Napier Lion Va in-line.

Serials: S1139–1148 (10).

Total 10; 2 accidental losses.

144a. IIIF Mk I

As above but a spotter-reconnaissance version for the FAA (three crew) and a general-purpose type for the RAF (two crew); could be fitted with floats. It had a metal fuselage, wooden folding-wings and the rectangular fin, but some were retro-fitted with a curved fin later.

In service 1928 with 440 Flt, used by four FAA flts (445, 443, 446, 440) and five RAF sqns (14, 35, 45, 47, 207) until 1937, SoNCo-op. Embarked on four carriers.

Based overseas in Sudan, Egypt and Jordan.

Serials: S1168–1207 (40).

Total 40; 8 accidental losses.

144b. IIIF Mk II

As the Mk I but had the curved fin as standard and an increased load capacity.

In service 1928 with 442 Flt, used by seven FAA flts (440, 442, 443, 445, 446, 447, 450), three FAA sqns (701, 820, 822), and one RAF sqn (202) until 1936, Gibraltar; embarked on three carriers and one battleship.

Based overseas in Malta and Gibraltar.

Powered by one 540hp Lion XI or 530hp XIa.

Serials: S1208–1227 (20), S1250–1262 (13).

Total 33; 15 accidental losses.

144c. IIIF Mk IIIM

As the Mk II but had an all-metal frame and a spinner on the propeller.

In service 1929 with 440 Flt, used by 10 FAA flts (421, 423, 440, 441, 442, 443, 445, 446, 447, 448), six FAA sqns (820, 821, 822, 823, 824, 825), and one RAF sqn (202), until 1937, SoNCo-op. Embarked on six carriers, one battleship and four cruisers.

Based overseas in Malta.

Serials: S1303–1356 (53), S1370–1408 (39).

Total 92; 27 accidental losses.

144d. IIIF Mk IIIM (DC)

A dual-control two-seat trainer, with a Vickers in the port fuselage side and able to carry 500lb/227kg of bombs underwing; the wings didn't fold.

In service 1930 with 1 FTS, used by 1xFTS and SPTFlt, until 1937, SPTFlt.
Powered by one 530hp Lion XIa.
Serials: S1454–1463 (10).
Total 10; 1 accidental loss.

144e. IIIF Mk IIIB

As the IIIF Mk IIIM but with a strengthened fuselage and other detail changes – it had the Vickers and Lewis, and could carry 500lb/227kg of bombs underwing.
In service 1930 with 444 Flt, used by 13 FAA flts (440, 441, 442, 443, 444, 445, 446, 447, 448, 449, 450, 705, 708), four FAA sqns (701, 822, 823, 824), and one RAF sqn (202) until 1936, and on second-line duties to 1941 (see end of entry for training units). Embarked on six carriers, three battleships, two battle-cruisers and nine cruisers.
Based overseas in Malta.
Powered by one 530hp Lion XIa.
Serials: S1474–1552 (79), S1779–1844 (68), S1852–1865 (14).
Total 161 plus 4 conversions of the Mk IIIM, making a total of 165; 35 accidental losses.

144f. IIIF Mk IIIB Faerie Queen

A radio-controlled target for the FAA with the radio equipment in the rear cockpit, armament deleted, and increased wing-dihedral.
In service 1931–33.
Three conversions of the Mk IIIB.

144g. IIIF Mk IIIB (DC)

A two-seat dual-control trainer for the FAA, as the IIIB but with the rear cockpit Lewis deleted.
In service 1931 at TB Leuchars, used by 1xFTS and the SPTFlt, until 1937, SPTFlt.
Serials: S1845–1851 (7).
Total 7; 1 accidental loss.

144h. IIIF Mk IVC

An RAF general-purpose type, of composite construction, and which could be fitted with floats; two crew and the armament of the Mk IIIB.
In service 1927 with 47 Sqn, used by two sqns (47, 207) until 1935, 207 Sqn.
Based overseas in Malta, Egypt, Iraq, Jordan, Aden and Sudan.
Powered by one 530hp Lion XIa.
Serials: J9053–9077 (24).
Total 24; 4 accidental losses.

144j. IIIF Mk IVCM

As the above but with detail changes and more metal framing.
In service 1928 with 8 Sqn, used by three sqns (8, 47, 207) until 1933, 8 Sqn.
Based overseas in Aden and Sudan.
Serials: J9132–9154 (23).
Total 23; 9 accidental losses.

144k. IIIF Mk IVM

As the above but with an all-metal frame except for the tail-ribs.
In service 1928 with 47 Sqn, used by six sqns (8, 35, 45, 47, 48, 207) and one comms sqn (24) until 1934, 47 Sqn; training to 1935.
Based overseas in Aden and Sudan.
Serials: J9155–9174 (16).
Total 16 plus 1 conversion of the Mk IVCM, making a total of 17; 3 accidental losses.

Fairey IIIF Mk IVm,
J9166, 8 Sqn. (Peter
Green Collection)

144l. IIIF Mk IVMA

As the above but had an all-metal frame.
In service 1929 with 207 Sqn, used by seven sqns (6, 8, 14, 35, 45, 47, 207) and 3xmisc. units, until 1936, 8 Sqn, training to 1939.
Based overseas in Egypt, Iraq, Jordan, and Aden.
Serials: J9637–9685 (45), J9784–9831 (48), K1119–1121 (3), K1158–1170 (12).
Total 108; 16 accidental losses.

144m. IIIF Mk IVB

As the above but with detail changes and a strengthened fuselage.
In service 1930 with 207 Sqn, used by five sqns (8, 24[comms], 45, 47, 207) until 1937, 45 Sqn, training etc to 1941.
Based overseas in Jordan, Aden and Egypt.
Serials: K1697–1728 (32), K1750–1778 (29).
Total 61; 6 accidental losses.

144n. IIIF (Communications)

A version for communications work, with a modified rear cockpit to carry a passenger and armament deleted.
In service 1930–35 with 24 Sqn.
Serials: J9061, K1115–1118 (4), K1749.
Total 6; 1 accidental loss.

Second-line units. It is not possible to ascribe individual IIIF Mks to second-line units, but IIIFs of various Mks served with the following – 1xAACU, CDTFlt, CArtCo-opS, CDCo-opU, 2xFTS, SoNCo-op, SPTFlt, SPTSqn, 1xATC, A&GS, SoP and 1xAAS.

	Span	Length	Ceiling	Range/end	Speed
Mk I	45ft 9in/	33ft 10in/	20,000ft/	4hrs	150mph/
	13.95m	10.31m	6,000m		241kmph
Mk IIIM	"	34ft/10.36m	"	"	136mph/219kmph
Mk IVM	"	36ft 9in/11.21m	"	400 miles/644km	"

Total IIIFs 591; in service 1924–41; 128 (22%) losses.

145. Fawn I

A day-bomber for the RAF, with two crew and armed with one Vickers mg in the port forward fuselage, one Lewis mg in the rear cockpit, and 460lb/210kg of bombs underwing.
In service 1925 with 11 Sqn, used by two sqns (11, 602) until 1929, 602 Sqn.
Powered by one 500hp Napier Lion VA in-line with slab radiators mounted on the fuselage sides.
Serials: J7182–7183 (2).
Total 2; no losses.

145a. Fawn II

The main production version for the RAF, as the Mk I but with two fuel tanks over the upper-wing centre section, a chin radiator, and one or two Lewis in the rear cockpit.
In service 1924 with 12 Sqn, used by five sqns (11, 12, 100, 503, 602), 1xFTS, 1xA&GS and 1xParaTS, until 1929, 503 Sqn.
Powered by one 500hp Lion II or Lion VA.
Serials: J6990–6991 (2), J7184–7231 (47).
Total 49; 12 accidental losses.

145b. Fawn III

As the Mk II but re-engined.
In service 1926 with 11 Sqn, used by five sqns (11, 12, 100, 503, 602) until 1929, 503 Sqn.
Powered by one 525hp Lion VI.
Serials: J7768–7779 (11), J7978–7985 (8).
Total 19; no losses.
All Marks: Span: 49ft 11in/15.22m   Length: 32ft 1in/9.78m   Ceiling: 13,800ft/4,140m   Range: 650 miles/1,046km   Speed: 114mph/184kmph.
Total Fawns 70; in service 1924–29; 12 (17%) losses.

146. Fox I

A fast day-bomber for the RAF which out-performed its contemporary fighters; two crew and armed with one Vickers mg in the port fuselage side, a Lewis mg in the rear cockpit, and 460lb/210kg of bombs underwing.
In service 1926 with 12 Sqn, used by one sqn and the RAFC until 1931, 12 Sqn.
Powered by one 480hp Curtiss D12 in-line.
Serials: J7941–7958 (18), J8423–8427 (5).
Total 23; 4 accidental losses.

Fairey Fawn II,
J7191. (Peter Green
Collection)

Above left: Fairey Fox IA, J9026, 12 Sqn. (Newark Air Museum)

Above right: Fairey Gordon I, K1776 converted from IIIF Mk IVB, 35 Sqn. (Alastair Goodrum Collection)

146a. Fox IA
Due to the politics of buying an American engine a Rolls-Royce was used to power this sub-Mk.
In service 1929 to 1931 with 12 Sqn.
Powered by one 490hp RR Kestrel IIa in-line, in a smoother cowling without the cylinder-bank 'humps'
of the Mk I.
Serials: J9025–9028 (4).
Total 4 plus 5 conversions of the Mk I, making a total of 9.

	Span	Length	Ceiling	Range	Speed
Mk I	38ft/11.58m	31ft 2in/9.5m	17,000ft/5,100m	500 miles/805km	156mph/251kmph
Mk IA	"	"	"	"	160mph/258kmph

Total Foxes 27; in service 1926–31; 4 (15%) losses.

147. Gordon I
A general-purpose type for the RAF, owing much to the IIIF in its design; two crew and armed with
one Vickers mg externally mounted on the port fuselage side, a Lewis mg in the rear cockpit, and
460lb/210kg of bombs underwing. It had a rectangular fin originally but later production had a rounded
fin, and it could be fitted with floats. Widely used as a target-tug.
In service 1931 with 40 Sqn, used by nine sqns (6, 14, 29, 35, 40, 45, 47, 207, 223) until 1938, 14 Sqn, and
by 2xAAS, 2xAOS, 3xAACUs, 5xATC, EWS, 3xATS, 5xFTS, METS, PT&RPl, 4xTTFlts, 3xcomms.
units and 2xmisc. units, until 1943.
Action: Middle East, also based overseas in Egypt, Palestine, Jordan, Sudan, Kenya and North Africa.
Powered by one 605hp A-S Panther IIa radial.
Serials: K1729–1748 (19), K2603–2649 (47), K2683–2769 (86).
Total 152 plus 94 conversions of the IIIF, making a total of 246; 40 accidental losses.

147a. Gordon II
As the Mk I but with the taller, rounded fin as standard, a modified rear fuselage, and Frise ailerons; could
be fitted with floats.
In service 1934 with 14 Sqn, used by sqns as the Mk I until 1939, 47 Sqn, second-line to 1943.
Based overseas in Egypt, Jordan and Sudan, action Middle East, not operational in UK.
Serials: K3986–4009 (24).
Total 24; 2 accidental losses.

	Span	Length	Ceiling	Range	Speed
Mk I	45ft 9in/13.95m	36ft 9in/11.21m	22,000ft/6,600m	600 miles/966km	145mph/233kmph
Mk II	"	33ft 8in/10.26m	"	"	"

Total Gordons 176 plus 94 conversions of IIIF making a total of 270; in service 1931–43; 42 (16)% losses.

148. Seal I

The FAA version of the Gordon for spotter-reconnaissance duties, with three crew (two of them in a longer rear cockpit than the Gordon) and armed with one Vickers mg mounted externally on the port fuselage side, a Lewis mg in the rear cockpit, and 500lb/227kg of bombs underwing; could be fitted with floats.

In service 1934 with 820 Sqn, used by five FAA sqns (820, 821, 822, 823, 824) and three flts (444, 701, 702), until 1937, 824 Sqn, also used by 2xCU, 1xPTU, 12xATU, 1xObsTU, 1xRTU, 1xcomms. unit, 3xmisc. units, one RAF sqn (273), 2xAOS, 4xAACUs, 1xATC, 3xATS, 1xB&GS, CArtCo-opFlt, 1xFTS, SoNCo-op, TB Leuchars, SPTSqn, 2xTTFlts and 1xcomms. unit, until 1942. Embarked on four carriers and five battleships.

Based overseas in Malta, India, Singapore and Far East.

Powered by one 605hp A-S Panther IIa radial.

Serials: K3477–3487 (11), K3514–3545 (32), K3575–3579 (5), K4201–4225 (25), K4779–4795 (17).

Span: 45ft 9in/13.95m   Length: 33ft 8in/10.26m   Ceiling: 17,000ft/5,100m   Endurance: 4.5 hrs   Speed: 139mph/224kmph.

Total 90; 15 accidental losses (17%).

149. Hendon II

The RAF's first monoplane night bomber, with a crew of five and armed with one Lewis mg in nose, dorsal and tail positions, plus 2,500lb/1,135kg of bombs internally.

In service 1936 with 38 Sqn, used by two sqns (38, 115) until 1939, 38 Sqn.

Powered by two 695hp RR Kestrel VI in-lines.

Serials: K5085–5098 (14).

Span: 101ft 9in/31.01m   Length: 60ft 9in/18.52m   Ceiling: 21,500ft/6,450m   Range: 1,360 miles/2,190km   Speed: 155mph/250kmph.

Total 14; 2 accidental losses (14%).

Fairey Seal I, K4201, 824 Sqn. (Peter Green Collection)

Fairey Hendon II, K5095, 38
Sqn. (Newark Air Museum)

Fairey Swordfish I, K8861, 820
Sqn. (Charles Parker)

150. Swordfish I

One of the FAA's most famous types, designed as a torpedo-bomber spotter-reconnaissance type with
three crew; it was armed with one Vickers mg in the port fuselage side, a Lewis mg in the rear cockpit,
and was able to carry one torpedo or mine underbelly, or 1,000lb/454kg of bombs or four depth-charges
underwing, and late in its service some had ASV-IIn radar with external aerials. Could be fitted with
floats, and the dual-control trainer had a revised rear cockpit with headrest.

In service 1936 with 825 Sqn, used by 34 sqns (700, 701, 702, 703, 705, 710, 810, 811, 812, 813, 814, 815,
816, 818, 819, 820, 821, 822, 823, 824, 825, 826, 828, 829, 830, 833, 834, 835, 836, 838, 840, 841, 848, 860)
until 1943, 860 Sqn, and by 9xCU, 6xPTU, 17xATU, 2xObsTU, 2xRTU, 4xcomms. unit, 3xmisc. units,
plus two RAF sqns (8,202), 1xPAFU, 3xAACUs, CArtCo-opFlt, METS, SoNCo-op, 1xOTU, SPTSqn,
1xTorpTU, 1xcomms. unit and 6xmisc. units, until 1945. Embarked on 10 carriers, seven escort-carriers
and seven battleships.

Based overseas in Malta and Singapore, action North and South Atlantic, Mediterranean and Indian
Ocean, also based overseas in West, East & South Africa, Far East, North America and BWI.

Powered by one 620hp Bristol Pegasus IIIM3 radial.

Serials: K4190, K5660–5662 (3), K5926–6011 (86), K8346–8449 (104), K8860–8886 (27), L2718–2866
(149), L7632–7701 (62), L9714–9785 (60), P3991–4279 (200), V4288–4719 (300), W5836–5995 (100).

Total 1,092; 365 accidental and 103 hostile losses.

150a. Swordfish II

An anti-submarine and reconnaissance version, as the Mk I but with strengthened lower-wings with metal skinning beneath; the Vickers mg was deleted and it could carry 1,000lb/454kg of bombs, four depth-charges or eight RP underwing, and the radar was ASV-X with external aerials. Wheeled under-carriage only. Built by Blackburn and nicknamed Blackfish.

In service 1943 with 822 Sqn, used by 23 sqns (810, 811, 812, 813, 815, 816, 818, 819, 822, 824, 825, 829, 833, 834, 835, 836, 837, 838, 840, 841, 842, 860, 886) until 1945, 836 Sqn; also served with 9xCU, 5xPTU, 17xATU, 1xObsTU, 4xRTU, 3xcomms. units, 14xmisc. units, and 1xRAF PAFU. Embarked on four car-riers, 12 escort-carriers and 19 MAC-ships.

Action: North and South Atlantic, Mediterranean, Indian Ocean and Northern Europe, also based over-seas in southern Europe, North, West and South Africa, Far East, Ceylon and North America.

Powered by one 620hp Pegasus IIIM3 or 775hp Pegasus 30.

Serials: DK670–792 (100), HS154–678 (400), LS151–461 (250), NE858–NF250 (230).

Total 980; 238 accidental and 11 hostile losses.

150b. Swordfish III

As the Mk II but with two crew, the rear cockpit having its forward-half sheltered, and the radar changed to ASV-XI in a radome between the undercarriage legs; it was RATOG equipped.

In service 1944 with 838 Sqn, used by eight sqns (811, 813, 819, 825, 835, 836, 838, 860) and one RAF sqn (119), until 1945, 860 Sqn, also served with 3xCU, 1xPTU, 1xRTU, 2xcomms. units and 3xmisc. units, and until 1951 for torpedo trials. Embarked on three escort-carriers and 19 MAC-ships.

Action: North and South Atlantic and northern Europe.

Powered by one 775hp Pegasus 30.

Serials: NF251–414 (120), NR857–NS204 (200).

Total 320; 33 accidental and 2 hostile losses.

150c. Swordfish IV

Possibly an unofficial Mk number, but it was applied to the Mk IIs modified to train TAGs in Canada, with a glazed cockpit for the three crew; guns and radar were deleted but it could carry the underwing armament.

In service 1944 to 1946 with 745 Sqn.

Based overseas in North America, not operational in the UK.

Unknown number of conversions of the Mk II. Losses included with the Mk II.

All Marks: Span: 45ft 6in/13.87m   Length: 36ft 4in/11.08m   Ceiling: 12,400ft/3,720m   Range: 1,030 miles/1,658km   Speed: 132mph/213kmph.

Total Swordfish 2,392; in service 1936–51; 752 (31%) losses inc. 116 hostile; nicknamed Stringbag.

151. Seafox I

A reconnaissance seaplane for the FAA, with two crew and armed with a Lewis mg in the rear cockpit plus 20lb/10kg of bombs underwing. Nicknamed Trout.

In service 1937 with 702 Flt, used by seven flts/sqns (700, 702, 703, 713, 714, 716, 718), 1xCU, 1xPTU, 1xATU, 1xObsTU, SoNCo-op and SPTSqn, until 1943, 702 Sqn. Embarked on one carrier, eight cruis-ers and nine AMCs.

Action: South Atlantic and Indian Ocean, also based overseas in the Mediterranean and BWI.

Powered by one 365hp Napier Rapier VI in-line.

Serials: K4305, K8569–8617 (49), L4519–4533 (15).

Span: 40ft/12.19m   Length: 33ft 5in/10.19m   Ceiling: 9,700ft/2,910m   Range: 333 miles/536km   Speed: 124mph/200kmph.

Total 65; 8 (12%) losses inc. 1 hostile.

152. Battle I

A light bomber for the RAF which, by the outbreak of the Second World War, was obsolescent and suf-fered heavy losses during the Battle of France; it was relegated to night bombing and then training and target-towing (many going to the BCATP). As a bomber it had three crew and was armed with a fixed Browning mg in the starboard wing, a Vickers in the rear of the canopy, and 1,000lb/454kg of bombs in wing-cells. Nicknamed Greenhouse.

In service 1937 with 63 Sqn, used by 20 sqns (12, 15, 35, 40, 52, 63, 88, 103, 105, 106, 142, 150, 185, 207, 218, 226, 300, 301, 304, 305), one GR sqn (98), seven interim fighter sqns (234, 235, 242, 245, 253, 266, 616) and one fighter flt until 1941, 88 Sqn; it also served with 2xPAFU, 1xAAS, 3xAGS, 9xAOS, 12xAACUs, ATA S, 8xB&GS, CGS, EWS, 19xOTU, 14xERFTS, RTFlt, 1xSoGR, 1xGp Pl, Polish Grading & Test Flt, 3xcomms. units and 16xmisc. units, until 1944.

Action: northern Europe and North Atlantic, also based overseas in Middle East and East Africa.

Powered by one 1,030hp RR Merlin I, II or III in-line; aircraft were supposedly given the Mk number of the engine fitted, but this was not commonly used.

Serials: K7559–7712 (154), K9176–9675 (311), L4935–5797 (662), N2020–2258 (152), P2155–2369 (116), P5229–5294 (20), P6482–6615 (16).

Total 1,431 (3 FAA); 243 accidental and 219 hostile losses.

152a. Battle TT I

A target-tug conversion with the armament replaced by a winch on the port side and drogue stowage under the rear fuselage; two crew. Many went to the BCATP.

In service 1940, used by 1xOAFU, 4xAACUs, 1xAOS RATG, 7xTTFlts, 3xOTU and 2xmisc. units, until 1944, Collyweston.

Based overseas in Far East.

Serials: L5624–5797 (128), V1202–1594 (59), HK931–2 (2), HK958.

Total 190; 23 accidental and 2 hostile losses.

Fairey Seafox I, L4533, 702 Sqn. (*MAP*)

Fairey Battle I, K7650, 63 Sqn. (Newark Air Museum)

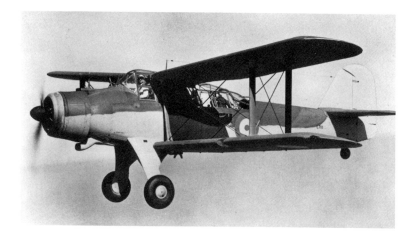

Fairey Albacore I, L7111.
(Newark Air Museum)

152b. Battle Trainer

An advanced trainer, with the long greenhouse canopy replaced by two separate cockpit canopies and dual control; armament was deleted.

In service 1940 with 11 & 12 FTSs, used by 1xEFTS, 7xFTS and the Polish TU, until 1944, 16 (Pol) SFTS. Serials: P6616–6769 (100), R7356–7480 (40).

Total 140; 19 accidental and 2 hostile losses.

All Marks: Span: 54ft/16.46m   Length: 42ft 5in/12.93m   Ceiling: 23,500ft/7,050m   Range: 1,050miles/1,690km   Speed: 241mph/388kmph.

Total Battles 1,761; in service 1937–44; 508 (29%) losses inc. 223 hostile.

153. Albacore I

Intended to replace the Swordfish but, in fact, outlived by it, this was a torpedo-bomber, reconnaissance and anti-submarine type for the FAA; it had a crew of three and was armed with one Browning mg in the starboard lower-wing and one/two Vickers mg in the rear of the canopy, plus a torpedo underbelly, or 1,500lb/681kg of bombs or four depth-charges underwing. Nicknamed Applecore.

In service 1940 with 826 Sqn, used by 16 sqns (810, 815, 817, 818, 820, 821, 822, 823, 826, 827, 828, 829, 830, 831, 832, 841) until 1943, 820 Sqn, and also served with 7xCU, 5xPTU, 8xATU, 3xObsTU, 1xRTU, 2xFAA & 1xRAF comms. units, 1xRAF PAFU, and 1xmisc. unit, until 1946, Aden Comms Flt. Embarked on six carriers.

Action: North and South Atlantic, Mediterranean, western Indian Ocean and North Africa; also based overseas in Middle East, Far East and Aden.

Powered by one 1,060hp Bristol Taurus II, or 985hp Taurus XII radial.

Serials: L7074–7173 (98), N4152–4425 (200), T9131–9260 (100), X8940–9290 (250), BF584–777 (150). Span: 50ft/15.24m   Length: 39ft 9in/12.12m   Ceiling: 17,000ft/5,100m   Range: 930 miles/1,497 km   Speed: 169mph/272kmph.

Total 798; 270 (34%) losses inc. 75 hostile.

154. Barracuda I

A torpedo and dive bomber for the FAA which, despite its unattractive appearance, was quite good in these roles. It had a crew of three, was armed with two Vickers mg in the rear cockpit and could carry a torpedo or mine under belly, or 2,000lb/908kg of bombs under belly or under wing. The Mk I was underpowered.

In service 1942 with 831 Sqn, used by two sqns (827, 831), 3xCU, 2xPTU and 1xRAF PAFU, until 1943, 827 Sqn.

Action: North Atlantic, embarked on one carrier.

Powered by one 1,300hp RR Merlin XXX in-line driving a three-bladed propeller.

Serials: P9646–9666 (18), BV660–664 (5), DN625–629 (5).

Total 28; 8 accidental losses.

Fairey Barracuda
AS 3, RJ796, 796
Sqn. (Newark Air
Museum)

154a. Barracuda II

A much more powerful engine made this the major production version, which was also used for anti-submarine patrols, some having ASV-IIn radar with aerials on the wings and some with ASH radar in a wing pod. Its limited range saw it replaced by the Grumman Avenger (qv) in the Pacific.

In service 1943 with 827 Sqn, used by 20 sqns (810, 812, 814, 815, 816, 817, 818, 820, 821, 822, 823, 824, 826, 827, 828, 830, 831, 837, 841, 847) until 1946, 827 Sqn; also served with 11xCU, 4xPTU, 6xATU, 3xObsTU, 3xRTU, 1xcomms. unit, 4xmisc. units, 1xRAF PAFU and 4xRAF AACU. Embarked on 11 carriers and two escort-carriers.

Action: North Atlantic, Mediterranean, Indian Ocean and Pacific, also based overseas in BWI and Australia.

Powered by one 1,620hp Merlin 32 driving a four-bladed propeller.

Serials: P9666–9986 (224), BV665–981 (245), DN630–642 (13), DP856–DR317 (277), DT813–887 (50), LS464–974 (400), MD612–807 (150), MX535–907 (300), PM682–PN164 (300), RK328–481 (125).

Total 2,084; 400 accidental and 8 hostile losses.

154b. Barracuda III or AS 3

A dedicated anti-submarine version of the Mk II with the torpedo capability deleted, so was armed with two Vickers mg in the rear cockpit, 1,600lb/720kg of bombs or four depth-charges under wing, and ASV-XI radar in a radome beneath the rear fuselage.

In service 1945 with 815 Sqn, used by five sqns (810, 815, 821, 822, 860) until 1953, 815 Sqn, also served with 8xCU, 2xPTU, 2xATU, 1xObsTU, 3xRTU and 2xmisc. units. Embarked on two carriers and three escort-carriers.

Action: North Atlantic.

Serials: DR319–335 (17), MD811–ME293 (300), RJ759–966 (91).

Total 408; 81 accidental and 4 hostile losses.

154c. Barracuda BR 5

A much-modified version which overcame the earlier Mark's handling shortcomings but was too late for war service; the wingtips were squared-off and later production had a taller, pointed fin, with dorsal fillet. Two crew, and was armed with one 0.5in Browning in the starboard wing, 2,000lb/908kg of bombs under belly or wings, and ASV-9 or AI-5 radar in a radome on the port wing.

In service 1947 with 783 Sqn, used by 1xRTU until 1948, 783 Sqn.

Powered by one 2,020hp RR Griffon 37 in-line.

Serials: RK532–574 (27).

Total 27 but some not issued; 2 accidental losses.

	Span	Length	Ceiling	Range	Speed
Mk I	49ft 2in/14.99m	39ft 9in/12.12m	18,400ft/5,520m	853 miles/1,373km	235mph/378kmph
Mk II	"	"	15,000ft/4,500m	686 miles/1,104km	228mph/367kmph
Mk III	"	"	20,000ft/6,000m	"	239mph/385kmph
BR 5	53ft/16.15m	41ft 1in/12.53m	26,800ft/8,040m	600 miles/966km	270mph/435kmph

Total Barracudas 2,547; in service 1943–53; 503 (20%) losses inc. 12 hostile; built by Fairey, Blackburn, Boulton-Paul and Westland.

Firefly Mks 1–4 and FR 5, see Vol. 1.

155. Firefly AS 5

A two-seat anti-submarine variant of the good fighter-reconnaissance type (see Vol. 1), with power-folding wings, internal changes, and able to carry American sonobuoys. ASV-9 radar in a port-wing pod and four 20mm cannon in the wings, plus 2,000lb/908kg of bombs or eight rp under wing.
In service 1948 with 812 Sqn, used by five sqns (810, 812, 814, 820, 825) until 1951, 820 Sqn. Also served with 1xObsTU. Embarked on two carriers.
Powered by one 2,245hp RR Griffon 74 in-line.
Serials: VT362–499 (105), VX378–438 (30), WB243–421 (149).
Total 284 but this included the FR 5 too; 58 accidental losses, including the FR 5.

155a. Firefly AS 6

Another anti-submarine variant, as the AS 5 but with guns deleted and able to carry AS stores, including British sonobuoys, under wing and with ASV-9 in the port-wing pod.
In service 1950 with 817 Sqn, used by 10 sqns (812, 814, 820, 821, 824, 826, 1830, 1840, 1841, 1844) until 1956, 1844 Sqn; also served with 2xCU, 1xATU, 1xObsTU, 1xRTU, 1xcomms. unit and 3xmisc. units. Embarked on six carriers.
Action: Korea.
Serials: WB423–440 (18), WD841–923 (73), WH627–632 (6), WJ104–121 (18).
Total 115 plus 40 conversions of the FR 5, making a total of 155; 19 accidental losses.

Fairey Firefly AS 6, WD849. (Air-Britain Archives)

Fairey Firefly
T 7, WJ216.
(Peter Green
Collection)

155b. Firefly T 7

An extensive redesign, intended for anti-submarine use but only used for training as the Fairey Gannet (qv) had become available. It had a taller fin, a larger, bulged, rear cockpit canopy to carry two observers, rounded wingtips, and the radiator was under the spinner. Arrester hook not fitted. No armament but had ASV-9 in the wing pod.

In service 1953 with 719 Sqn, used by 1xATU, 2xObsTU and 1xmisc. unit, until 1957, 796 Sqn.

Powered by one 2,500hp Griffon 59.

Serials: WJ154–216 (47), WK348–373 (26), WM761–85509 (71).

Total 144 but some not issued; 6 accidental losses.

	Span	Length	Ceiling	Range	Speed
AS 5	41ft 2in/12.55m	38ft 9in/11.81m	29,200ft/8,760m	1,300 miles/2,093km	386mph/621kmph
T 7	44ft 6in/13.56m	38ft 3in/11.66m	25,500ft/7.650m	860 miles/1,385km	300mph/483kmph

Total Firefly AS5-T7s 543; in service 1948–57; 83 (15%) losses; built by Fairey and General Aircraft Ltd.

156. Gannet AS 1

The FAA's last fixed-wing anti-submarine type, with a unique engine arrangement which meant half of it could be shut down when on patrol; it had three crew and could carry two torpedos, mines, or depth-charges internally, and 16 RPs under wing, with ASV-19b radar in a retractable radome behind the weapons bay.

In service 1954 with 703X Sqn, 1955 with 826 Sqn, used by 12 sqns (812, 814, 815, 816, 817, 820, 824, 825, 826, 831, 847, 1840) until 1958, 847 Sqn, also served with 2xCU, 1xObsTU and 3xmisc. units. Embarked on three carriers.

Powered by one 2,950shp A-S Double-Mamba 100 turboprop, driving two propellers.

Serials: WN342–464 (87), XA319–411 (56).

Total 143; 16 accidental losses.

156a. Gannet T 2

A conversion trainer with armament and radar deleted and a periscope between the two forward cockpits, which had dual-controls.

In service 1955 with 737 Sqn, used by the sqns, 2xCU, 1xATU, 1xObsTU and 1xmisc. unit, until 1965, 849 Sqn.

Based overseas in Malta.

Serials: XA508–531 (20), XG869–890 (12), XT752.

Total 33; 2 accidental losses.

156b. Gannet AEW 3

A very useful addition to the FAA, this extensively modified Mk was an airborne radar station with only a pilot's canopy, the two observers being enclosed within the fuselage with a small, bulged window each side; the fin was squared off and there were no fillets on the wing leading-edges, under which were the engine exhausts. No armament but had APS-20f radar in a large radome under the forward fuselage. It was sorely missed during the Falklands War.

In service 1959 with 700G Flt, 1960 with 849 Sqn, used by one sqn, and 1x misc. unit, until 1978, 849 Sqn. Embarked on five carriers.

Powered by one 3,875shp Double-Mamba 112.

Serials: XL449–503 (31), XP197–229 (9), XR431–433 (3).

Total 43; 21 accidental losses.

Fairey Gannet
AS 1, WN420,
825 Sqn.
(Newark Air
Museum)

Fairey Gannet
AEW 3, XL500,
849B Sqn.
(Peter Green
Collection)

156c. Gannet AS 4

As the AS 1 but with internal changes.

In service 1956 with 824 Sqn, used by seven sqns (810, 814, 815, 824, 825, 847, 849) and one ECM sqn (831) until 1960, 810 Sqn. Also served with 1x comms. unit and 1x misc. unit, to 1966. Embarked on five carriers. Powered by one 3,035shp Double-Mamba 101.

Serials: XA412–473 (42), XG783–855 range (12).

Total 54; 7 accidental losses.

156d. Gannet COD 4

A conversion of the AS 4 for ship-to-shore transport, with armament and radar deleted and under wing tanks for greater range; carried the pilot and two passengers plus freight in the weapons bay.

In service 1961 to 1974 with 849 Sqn, embarked on two carriers.

Five conversions of the AS 4.

156e. Gannet T 5

The conversion trainer for the AEW 3, with armament and radar deleted and a periscope between the two forward cockpits, which had dual-controls.

In service 1961–76 with 849 Sqn.

Serials: XG882–889 (7).

Total 7 plus one conversion of a T 2, making a total of 8; 1 accidental loss.

156f. Gannet AS 6 (ECM)

As the AS 4 but with extra avionics and aerials for ECM work.

In service 1960 to 1966 with 831 Sqn, embarked on two carriers.

Seven conversions of the AS 4; two accidental losses.

156g. Gannet AS 7

As the above but with different avionics for ECM work.

In service 1960 with 831 Sqn, used by two sqns until 1971, 849 Sqn.

Unknown number of conversions of the AS 4.

	Span	Length	Ceiling	Range	Speed
AS 1	54ft 4in/16.56m	43ft/13.11m	25,000ft/7,500m	943 miles/1,518km	310mph/499kmph
AEW 3	"	44ft/13.4m	"	700 miles/1,127km	250mph/402kmph
AS 4	"	43ft/13.11m	"	662 miles/1,066km	299mph/481kmph

Total Gannets 280; in service 1954–78; nicknamed Dammit; 49 (17%) losses.

FAIRFIELD ENGINEERING (Glasgow)

Assembled Sopwith Cuckoo.

FARMAN (HENRI) (France)

One of two English brothers born and domiciled in France who became great names in early French aviation, sharing a factory; formed 1912 until went out of business 1940. Supplied approximately 527 examples of six types (Seaplane, Biplane and F20, see Vol. 1).

157. F 22H

A two-bay reconnaissance and bomber biplane for the RNAS, with two crew and able to carry light bombs under the fuselage; could be fitted with floats. The upper wings had a longer span braced by triangular kingposts and the tailplane was set on top of the upper boom, with a curved, elongated rudder mounted on the stern post; twin-wheel undercarriage.

In service 1914 at Felixstowe, used by four units (Calshot, Felixstowe, Grain, Yarmouth) until 1915, Yarmouth.

Action: home waters.

Powered by one 80hp Gnome 7z Lambda or 120 hp Gnome rotary pusher.
Serials: 139–144 (6), 156.
Span: 51ft/15.54m   Length: 28ft 10in/8.78m   Ceiling: n/k   Endurance: 5.5hrs   Speed: 62mph/100kmph.
Total 7; 6 (86%) accidental losses.

158. F 27

A bomber and reconnaissance landplane for the RFC and RNAS, with a metal frame and four-wheeled undercarriage; a two-seater armed with a Lewis mg in the front cockpit and 560lb/255kg of bombs under the fuselage. Built by Farman and Brush.
In service 1915 with 5 Sqn, RFC, used by five RFC (5, 26, 30, 31, 114) and seven RNAS units (1, 3, 4, and 7NSqns, 1W, 2W, 3W) until 1918, 31 Sqn, RFC; also served with 2xRNAS PTU.
Action: northern and southern Europe, Middle East, East Africa, and based overseas in India.
Powered by one Canton-Unne 140hp B9 or 160 hp R 9 in-line pusher.
Serials: 3617–3636 (20), 3900–3919 (20), 7746–49 (4), 7752–55 (4), 8238–8249 (12), 9134–9153 (20), 9251, A387–410 (24), A1806, A8974–8998 (25), N3000–3049 (25).
Span: 53ft/16.15m   Length: 30ft 3in/9.22m   Ceiling: n/k   Endurance: 2.5hrs   Speed: 90mph/145kmph.
Total 156 (98 RNAS); 10 accidental and 6 hostile RNAS losses, RFC n/k.

159. F 40/56

An RNAS bomber, with two crew and armed with a Lewis mg in the front cockpit and 560lb/255kg of bombs under the fuselage; the F56 had a shorter nacelle and wingspan but the RNAS did not differentiate between the two, giving the type the designation as above. The nacelle was streamlined and set between the three-bay wings, joined to them by struts; the upper wing had a longer span braced by triangular kingposts. The tailplane was mounted on the top boom with a curved and elongated rudder and it had a twin-wheel undercarriage. Nicknamed Horace.
In service 1916 at Yarmouth, used by eight units (2NSqn, 1W, 2W, 4W, 5W, Bacton, Burgh Castle, Yarmouth), 4xPTU, 1xObsTU and 1xATU until 1917, Burgh Castle.
Action: northern Europe.
Powered by one 160hp Renault in-line pusher with a radiator each side.
Serials: 9155–9174 (20), N3210–3239 (30).
Span: 57ft 10in/17.93m   Length: 30ft 4in/9.24m   Ceiling: 16,000ft/4,800m   Endurance: 2.5 hrs   Speed: 83mph/134kmph.
Total 50; 6 (12%) accidental losses.

Henri Farman F 27,
2 Wing RNAS.
(G. Stuart Leslie)

FARMAN (MAURICE) (France)

The other Farman brother, whose designs rather overshadowed those of Henri. Supplied 1,526 examples of three types (S7 Longhorn and S11 Shorthorn, see Vol. 1).

160. F 37

A two-seat reconnaissance three-bay biplane for the RNAS, able to carry light bombs under the fuselage. In service during 1916 with 2 Wing.
Action: southern Europe.
Powered by one 110hp Renault in-line pusher.
Serial: 9133.
Dimensions and performance n/k but similar to the Farman S11 (Vol. 1).
Total 1; 1 accidental loss (100%).

FBA – see Franco-British Aviation.

FELIXSTOWE (Felixstowe, Suffolk, UK)

A company formed in 1917 to build the modified Curtiss flying-boats designed by John Porte, an RN officer; out of business 1919. Supplied 335 examples of three types.

161. F 2A

A very successful fighter-reconnaissance flying-boat for the RNAS/RAF, with four crew and armed with one/two Lewis mg in nose, dorsal and each beam position and able to carry 460lb/210kg of bombs under wing. Built by Felixstowe, Airco, May Harden & May, and Saunders.
In service 1917 at Felixstowe, used by seven RNAS units (Calshot, Dundee, Felixstowe, Killingholme, Newhaven, Westgate, Yarmouth), nine RAF sqns (228, 230, 231, 232, 238, 240, 247, 257, 267), one RAF flt, 1xTDS, and 3xRNAS PTU, until 1923, 230 Sqn.
Action: home waters, also based overseas in Malta.
Powered by two 350hp RR Eagle VIII in-lines.
Serials: N4080–4099 (20), N4280–4309 (30), N4430–4479 (40), N4510–4519 (10), N4530–4554 (25), N4564–4572 (10).
Total 135; 27 accidental and 5 hostile losses.

Felixstowe F2A, N4465, RNAS Killingholme. (Peter Green Collection)

Felixstowe F 3,
N4404, Houton Bay.
(G. Stuart Leslie)

161a. F 2C

As the F 2A but with a modified bow and hull.
In service 1917 at Felixstowe, used by two RNAS/RAF units until 1919, Grain.
Action: home waters.
Serials: N64–5 (2).
Total 2; no losses.
Span: 95ft 7in/29.14m   Length: 46ft 3in/14.1m   Ceiling: 9,600ft/2,880m   Endurance: 6hrs   Speed: 96mph/155kmph.
Total F 2s 137; in service 1917–23; 32 (23%) losses inc. 5 hostile; nicknamed Baby Porte.

162. F 3

A larger flying-boat than the F 2A but not so well liked; it had four crew and was armed with a Lewis mg in nose, dorsal and each beam position and 460lb/210kg of bombs under wing. Built by Dick, Kerr & Co., Malta Dockyard, Pheonix and Shorts.
In service 1918 at Felixstowe, used by seven RNAS units (Alexandria, Calafrana, Cattewater, Houton Bay, Stenness, Taranto, Tresco), 10 RAF sqns (230, 231, 232, 234, 238, 247, 263, 267, 270, 271) and one RAF flt, until 1921, 267 Sqn.
Action: home waters and Mediterranean, also based overseas in Malta and Egypt.
Powered by two 350hp RR Eagle VIII in-lines.
Serials: N4000–4037 (25), N4160–4179 (18), N4230–4279 (48), N4310–4321 (12), N4360–4397 (18), N4400–4429 (30).
Span: 102ft/31.09   Length: 49ft 2in/14.99m   Ceiling: 8,000ft/2,400m   Endurance: 6hrs   Speed: 91mph/147kmph.
Total 151; 12 (8%) accidental losses

163. F 5

A general-reconnaissance flying-boat for the post-First World War RAF, on the lines of the F 2 and F 3 with four crew and armed with a Lewis mg in the dorsal and each beam position plus 920lb/420kg of bombs underwing. Built by Dick, Kerr & Co., Gosport Av., and Shorts.
In service 1918 with 231 Sqn, used by two sqns (230, 231), SoNCo-op, Air Pilotage S, SoNCo-op&AN and 4xmisc. units, until 1925, 480 Flt.
Powered by two 350hp RR Eagle VIII in-lines.
Serials: N4038–4049 (12), N4112–4118 (7), N4192–4199 (8), N4630–4679 (10), N4830–4839 (10).
Span: 103ft 8in/31.59m   Length: 49ft 3in/15.02m   Ceiling: 6,800ft/2,040m   Endurance: 7hrs   Speed: 88mph/142kmph.
Total 47 plus 2 conversions of the F 2A, making a total of 49; 16 (33%) accidental losses.

Felixstowe F 5, N4041, 232 Sqn.
(G. Stuart Leslie)

FOKKER (Holland)

Famous for the First World War fighters he designed for Germany, the Dutchman set up his own company in 1912 and built many successful airliner types until 1995 when the company went out of business. Supplied 10 examples of two types.

164. T 8W

This was a mid-wing monoplane general-reconnaissance seaplane, with two floats, built for the Royal Dutch Navy, but taken over by the RAF when Holland was occupied; it carried three crew and was armed with one mg in nose, dorsal and ventral positions, plus 1,300lb/590kg of bombs internally.
In service during 1940 with 320 (Dutch) Sqn.
Action: North Atlantic.
Powered by two 450hp Wright Whirlwind R975-E3 radials.
Serials: AV958–965 (8).
Span: 65ft 7in/19.99m   Length: 49ft 10in/15.19m   Ceiling: 22,300ft/6,690m   Range: 1,305 miles/2,101km   Speed: 222mph/357kmph.
Total 8; 3 (37%) losses inc. 1 hostile.

165. XXII

A high-wing monoplane airliner with a bulky fixed undercarriage and a curved single fin/rudder; impressed for use by the RAF as a navigation trainer and transport, with two crew and up to 22 passengers and unarmed.
In service 1941 with 12 EFTS, used by one sqn, 1xOTU, 1xEFTS and 1xAONS until 1943, 24 Sqn.
Powered by four 525hp P&W Wasp T181 radials.
Serials: HM159–160 (2).
Span: 98ft 5in/30m   Length: 70ft 7in/21.52m   Ceiling: 16,070ft/4,820m   Range: 835 miles/1,344 km   Speed: 177mph/285kmph.
Total 2 impressed; 1 (50%) accidental loss.

FORD (USA)

The famous car company, which supplied one example of one type.

166. 5 AT

A useful between-the-wars high-wing monoplane airliner impressed for use as a transport by the RAF, carrying two crew and 14 passengers. Had a single angular fin/rudder. Nicknamed Tri-motor.
In service during 1940 with 271 Sqn.
Powered by three 420hp P&W Wasp radials, one in the nose.
Serial: X5000.
Span: 77ft 10in/23.7m   Length: 50ft 3in/15.32m   Ceiling: 20,000ft/6,000m   Range: 540 miles/869 km   Speed: 115mph/185kmph.
Total 1; 1 (100%) accidental loss.

FOSTER-WICKNER (London, UK)

A company formed in 1935 to build light aircraft, going out of business in 1939, and supplying seven examples of one type.

167. Warferry

A rare example of the RAF renaming an impressed type, as this high-wing cabin monoplane with two bracing struts was called the Wicko in civil use; it carried the pilot and one passenger and was used for communications by the RAF. Spatted undercarriage and curved fin/rudder.

In service 1941 with the ATA, used by 1xOTU and 3xcomms. units, until 1945, 81 OTU.

Powered by one 130hp DH Gipsy Major I in-line.

Serials: DR613, ES913, ES924, ES943, ES947, HM497, HM499.

Span: 34ft 6in/10.51m   Length: 23ft 3in/7.09m   Ceiling: 20,000ft/6,000m   Range: 480 miles/ 773 km   Speed: 140mph/225kmph.

Total 7 impressed; 2 (29%) accidental losses.

FRANCO-BRITISH AVIATION (FBA) (France)

Despite its name this was a wholly French First World War company, in existence from 1913–18, which supplied 130 examples of two types (FBA Type A and B, see Vol. 1).

168. Flying-Boat Type H

A three-bay biplane reconnaissance boat for the RNAS, with two crew and able to carry 65lb/30kg of bombs underwing. The lower wing was mounted above and strutted to the fuselage as was the tailplane and there was a single rudder (no fin) above the tailplane. The upper wing had a longer span with angled outer support struts.

In service 1917 at Otranto, used by two units until 1918, 66 and 67 Wings.

Action: Mediterranean, not operational in UK.

Powered by one 160hp Isotta-Fraschini pusher in-line between the wings with a large radiator in front.

Serials: N1075–1078 (4).

Span: 47ft 7in/14.51m   Length: 33ft 2in/10.11m   Ceiling and endurance: n/k   Speed: 90mph/145kmph.

Total 4; 2 (50%) hostile losses.

G.A.L – see General Aircraft.

GENERAL AIRCRAFT LTD (GAL) (Hanworth, Middlesex, UK)

Formed in 1931 to build general-aviation types and was an innovative company, building the Monospar series of tourers and other light aircraft; during the Second World War it specialised in glider design culminating in the very large Hamilcar – this led to the post-war Universal Freighter but after a merger with Blackburn in 1949 the General Aircraft name disappeared and the Freighter became the Beverley. Supplied 1,370 examples of six types (Cygnet, Owlet and Hotspur, see Vol. 1).

169. Monospar ST 25

The Monospar was an advanced low-wing cabin monoplane built in several different versions; the ST 25 carried a pilot and five passengers, had twin fin/rudders and a three-strut undercarriage. Ordered by the RAF for communications work.

In service 1939 with 19 GpCommsFlt, used by 2xAACU, 1xOTU, 3xcomms. units and 2xmisc. units, until 1944.

Powered by two 85hp Pobjoy Niagara III or 98hp Niagara IV radials.

Serials: K8308, N1531 plus 12 impressed – T9264, X9330–31 (2), X9333–35 (3), X9348 (renumbered DR848), X9365, X9369, X9372–73 (2), X9377.

Span: 40ft 2in/12.24m   Length: 25ft 4in/7.72m   Ceiling: 15,300ft/4,590m   Range: 419 miles/675km   Speed: 131mph/211kmph.

Total 2 plus 12 impressed making a total of 14; 2 (14%) accidental losses.

170a. Monospar ST 4

Impressed for communications work with the RAF, carrying the pilot and three passengers; had a single fin/rudder and a spatted undercarriage.

In service 1940 with 110 Wing, used by 2xAACU and 1xcomms. unit until 1942, 2 FPP ATA.

Powered by two 85hp Pobjoy R radials.

Serials: X9367, X9376 (renumbered DR849), X9434.

Total 3 impressed; 2 accidental losses.

170b. Monospar ST 6

As the ST 4 but had a retractable undercarriage, different cowlings and a redesigned nose which gave a slightly larger cabin carrying the pilot and three passengers; impressed by the RAF for communications work.

In service 1940 with 6 AACU, used by 2xAACU until 1940, 8 AACU.

Serial: AV979.

Total 1 impressed; no losses.

170c. Monospar ST 10

As the ST 6 but with different engines, a roomier cabin, dual controls and more fuel.

In service 1940 with 6 AACU, used by 2xAACU and 1xmisc. unit, until 1943.

Powered by two 84hp Niagara I.

Serial: X9453.

Total 1 impressed; no losses.

170d. Monospar ST 12

As the ST 10 but with more powerful engines.

In service 1940 with 6 AACU, used by 2xAACU, CFS and 1xcomms. unit, until 1943, Honiley SFlt.

Powered by two 130hp DH Gipsy Major I in-lines.

Serials: X9341, BD150.

Total 2 impressed; no losses.

	Span	Length	Ceiling	Range	Speed
ST 4	"	26ft 4in/8.02m	18,000ft/5,400m	540 miles/869km	130mph/209kmph
ST 6	"	"	"	550 miles/885km	135mph/217kmph
ST 10	"	"	"	585 miles/942km	142mph/229kmph
ST 12	"	"	21,000ft/6,300m	410 miles/660km	158mph/254kmph.

Total Monospars ST 4-12s 7; in service 1940–43. 2 (29%) losses.

171. Hamilcar I

A large transport glider for the RAF and GPR, with two crew and able to carry 17,000lb/7,720kg of freight loaded through clamshell nose-doors; it was towed by H-P Halifaxes (qv). Built by GAL, AC Motors, Birmingham Carriage Co., and Co-Operative.

In service 1943 with the GPR, used by one GPR sqn, TSPC and 3xmisc. units, until 1949, GPR.

Action: northern Europe, also based overseas in Germany.

Serials: DR851–854 (4), HH921–975 (34), LA632–750 (94), NX805–876 (60), RR923–995 (55), RZ410–431 (19), TK714–791 (66).

Span: 110ft/36.08m   Length: 68ft/22.3m.

Total 332; 105 (32%) losses inc. 63 hostile.

GENERAL MOTORS (USA)

Assembled Grumman Avenger.

GLENDOWER (London, UK)

Assembled Airco DH 4.

G.A.L. Hamilcar I. (*MAP*)

GOSPORT AVIATION (Gosport, Hants, UK)

Assembled Felixstowe F 5.

GRAIN (Isle of Grain, Kent, UK)

An RNAS experimental station, which supplied seven examples of one type during the First World War.

172. Griffin

A two-seat bomber for the RNAS/ RAF, armed with a Lewis mg in the rear cockpit and light bombs under-belly; it was developed from the Sopwith B 1 (qv) and was a two-bay, un-staggered biplane.
In service 1918, HMS Vindictive, used by two units (Donisbristle, Turnhouse) until 1920, Donisbristle; embarked on one cruiser.
Action: Estonia and Russia.
Powered by one 200hp Sunbeam Arab II in-line or 200hp Bentley BR 2 rotary.
Serials: N100–106 (7).
Span: 42ft 6in/12.95m   Length: 27ft 3in or 27ft 6in/8.31m or 8.38m   Ceiling: 9,000ft/2,700m   Endurance: 3hrs   Speed: 116mph/187kmph.
Total 7; 2 (29%) accidental losses.

GRUMMAN (USA)

A company formed in 1929 and noted for its naval aircraft, becoming Northrop-Grumman in 1994. Supplied 3,387 examples of five types (Wildcat and Hellcat, see Vol. 1).

173. Goose I (JRF-5)

A light transport amphibian for the FAA carrying a pilot and six or seven passengers.
In service 1944 at Piarco, used by one unit and 1xRAF OTU until 1945.
Based overseas in BWI and North Africa, not operational in the UK.
Powered by two 450hp P&W Wasp Junior R985-AN6 radials.
Serials: FP470–474 (5), FP738–739 (2), HK822, MV993.
Total 9 (4 RAF); no losses.

173a. Goose IA (JRF-6B)

An observer trainer version of the above, with a crew of five and different radio, electrics and equipment.
In service 1942 with 749 Sqn, used by one ASR flt, 1xObsTU and 2xcomms. units, until 1945, 749 Sqn.
Based overseas in BWI and North Africa, not operational in the UK.
Serials: FP475–524 (42).
Total 42; 7 accidental losses.
Span: 49ft/14.94m   Length: 38ft 4in/11.68m   Ceiling: 21,000ft/6,300m   Range: 640 miles/ 1,030 km   Speed: 200mph/322kmph.
Total Goose 51; in service 1942–45; 7 (14%) losses.

Grumman
Goose I,
MV993.
(Air-Britain
Archives)

174. Widgeon I (J4F-2)
A small communications amphibian for the FAA and RAF, originally called the Gosling; carried the pilot and four passengers. It had a long nose, the engines were mounted on the top surface of the high wing and the braced tailplanes were mounted half-way up the fin; the wheels retracted into recesses in the fuselage sides and there was a strutted float beneath each wing.
In service 1943 with 111 OTU, used by 1xOTU, 1xRAF and 1xFAA comms. unit and 1xFAA PTU, until 1945, Pensacola.
Based overseas in North America and BWI, not operational in the UK.
Powered by two 200hp Ranger L440-5 in-lines.
Serials: FP455–469 (15), FP474, JS996.
Span: 40ft/12.19m   Length: 31ft/9.45m   Ceiling: 15,500ft/4,650m   Range: 775 miles/ 1,248 km   Speed: 164mph/264kmph.
Total 17 (1 RAF); 2 (9%) accidental losses.

175. Avenger I (TBF-1)
A three-seat torpedo and strike bomber for the FAA, originally called the Tarpon; it was a very useful type, armed with two 0.5in Browning in the wings and one in a Grumman 150 dorsal turret plus one 0.3in Browning in the ventral position, and it carried one torpedo or 2,000lb/908kg of bombs internally.
In service 1943 with 832 Sqn, used by 12 sqns (820, 828, 832, 845, 846, 848, 849, 850, 851, 852, 854, 857) until 1945, 828 Sqn; also served with 4xCU, 3xPTU, 2xATU, 1xRTU, ECFS and 2xmisc. units. Embarked on five carriers and eight escort-carriers.
Action: North Atlantic, northern Europe, Indian Ocean and Pacific, also based overseas in North America and Australia.
Powered by one 1,750hp Wright Double-Row Cyclone R2600-8 radial.
Serials: USN (25), FN750–949 (200), JZ100–300 (201).
Total 426; 125 accidental and 13 hostile losses.

175a. Avenger II (TBM-1 or 1C)
A General Motors-built Mk I, with detail changes.
In service 1943 with 853 Sqn, used by 12 sqns (820, 828, 832, 846, 848, 849, 853, 852, 854, 855, 856, 857) until 1946, 820 Sqn, also served with 7xCU, 2xPTU, 3xATU, 1xRTU, 1xcomms. unit and 5xmisc. unit. Embarked on four carriers and four escort-carriers.
Action: North Atlantic, Indian Ocean and Pacific, also based overseas in North America and Australia.
Serials: JZ301–634 (334).
Total 334; 79 accidental and 22 hostile losses.

175b. Avenger III (TBM-3)

As the Mk II but had a strengthened wing to carry eight RP in addition to its other armament.
In service 1945 with 854 Sqn, used by two sqns (828, 854) until 1946, 828 Sqn; also served with 2xCU, 2xPTU, 1xATU, 1xRTU and 1xmisc. unit. Embarked on one carrier.
Action: Indian Ocean and Pacific, also based overseas in North America and Australia.
Powered by one 1,850hp D-R Cyclone R2600-20.
Serials: JZ635–720 (86), KE430–467 (22).
Total 108 but many not issued; 6 accidental losses.

175c. Avenger TBM-3E

In the early 1950s the FAA was short of an effective anti-submarine aircraft, pending the delivery of the delayed Fairey Gannet (qv), so the trusty Avenger was supplied by the USN; the first deliveries were unmodified American aircraft, as the Mk III but without provision for a torpedo.
In service 1953 with 815 Sqn, used by two sqns (815, 824) and 1xmisc. unit until 1954, 815 Sqn; embarked on one carrier.
Serials: XB296–449 range (21).
Total 21; 2 accidental losses.

175d. Avenger AS 4 (TBM-3E)

This Mk was modified to FAA standards and had ASH radar in a pod radome on the starboard wing.
In service 1954 with 815 Sqn, used by four sqns (814, 815, 820, 824) until 1955, 820 Sqn, also served with 1xCU, 1xRTU and 1xmisc. unit. Embarked on two carriers.
Serials: XB296–449 range (36).
Total 36; 2 accidental losses.

175e. Avenger AS 5 (TBM-3E)

A development of the AS 4 with ASV-19a radar in a larger wing-radome and underwing bomb racks.
In service 1954 with 814 Sqn, used by five sqns (814, 815, 1830, 1841, 1844) until 1957, RNVR sqns, embarked on three carriers.
Serials: XB296–449 range (46).
Total 46 plus 11 conversions of the TBM-3E, making a total of 57; 6 accidental losses.

Grumman Avenger
I, FN908, 846 Sqn.
(Alastair Goodrum)

175f. Avenger TS 5

As the AS 5 but for ECM work, having Orange Harvest equipment and extra aerials under the nose.
In service 1956 to 1957 with 745 Sqn.
Four conversions of the AS 5; 1 accidental loss.

175g. Avenger ECM 6A

As the AS 5 but another ECM version, with a radome under the bomb bay, extra aerials and the dorsal
turret deleted and glazed over.
In service 1958–59 with 831 Sqn. Nicknamed Chuffbox.
Six conversions of the AS 5.

175h. Avenger ECM 6B

As the above but with different equipment and the rear canopy blanked over.
In service 1958 to 1959 with 831 Sqn.
Three conversions of the ECM 6A; no losses.

	Span	Length	Ceiling	Range	Speed
Mk I	54ft 2in/16.51m	40ft/12.19m	23,000ft/6,900m	1,020 miles/1,642km	259mph/417kmph
Mk III	"	"	25,000ft/7,500m	1,000 miles/1,610km	262mph/422kmph
AS 4	"	41ft/12.5m	22,600ft/6,789m	"	261mph/420kmph

Total Avengers 971; in service 1943–46 and 1953–59; 264 (27%) losses inc. 35 hostile.

HANDLEY PAGE (Radlett, Herts, UK)

One of our pioneer companies, formed in 1909 by Frederick Handley Page (later Sir Frederick) and
specialising in large aircraft both military and civil. However, in the rationalization of the 1950s/'60s the
company refused to amalgate, to the Government's displeasure, with BAC or HSA and thus forfeited any
military orders. The development costs of the Jetstream light airliner (see Scottish Aviation) put the firm
into liquidation in 1970. Supplied 8,353 examples of 14 types, nearly all bombers (Type G, see Vol. 1); also
assembled EE Canberra.

176. 0/100

Designed to meet the RNAS's request for a 'bloody paralyser' of a bomber, this large biplane had a
crew of four, was armed with one Lewis mg in nose, ventral, and each beam position and could carry
1,792lb/815kg of bombs internally.
In service 1917 with 3 Wing, used by eight RNAS (7, 14, 15 and 16 NSqns, A Sqn, HP Sqn, 2W, 3W)
and four RAF sqns (207, 214, 215, 216) until 1918, 214 Sqn; also served with 3xRNAS NavTU and
1xSoN&BD.
Action: northern Europe.
Powered by two 225hp RR Eagle I or 320hp Sunbeam Cossack in-lines.
Serials: 1455–67 (12), 3115–142 (28).
Total 40; 32 losses inc. 14 hostile.

176a. 0/400

A development of the above, this was the second heavy bomber for the fledgling RAF, following the
0/100s taken over from the RNAS; it had four crew and was armed with one Lewis mg in nose, ven-
tral and each beam position and carried 1,650lb/743kg of bombs internally. Built by HP, Birmingham
Carriage, British Caudron, Clayton & Shuttleworth, Harris Lebus, Metropolitan Wagons, National A/C
Factory, and Royal Aircraft Factory. Nicknamed Handley Page.
In service 1918 with 16N and 97 Sqns, used by 10 RAF sqns (58, 70, 97, 100, 115, 116, 207, 214, 215, 216)
and one RNAS sqn (16) until 1921, 216 Sqn; also served with 2xSoN&BD, Air Pilotage S, 3xFS, Obs.
SoAG, 7xTDS, 2xcomms. units and 1xmisc. unit.
Action: northern Europe and Middle East, also based overseas in Egypt.
Powered by two 284hp RR Eagle IV, 350hp Eagle VIII, or 260hp Sunbeam Maori III in-lines.

Serials: B8802–8813 (12), B9446–9451 (6), C3487–3498 (12), C9636–9785 (150), D4561–4660 (100), D5401–5450 (50), D8301–8350 (50), D9681–9730 (46), F301–320 (20), F3748–3767 (7), F5349–5448 (14), J2242–2291 (23).

	Span	Length	Ceiling	Endurance	Speed
0/100	100ft 2in/30.53m	62ft 10in/19.15m	7,000ft/2,100m	n/k	76mph/122kmph
0/400	100ft/30.48m	"	10,000ft/3,000m	8hrs	97mph/156kmph

Total 490 approx. (probably not all delivered); 143 losses inc. 25 hostile.
Total 0/100s and 0/400s 530; in service 1917–21; total losses 175 (33%) inc. 39 hostile.

177. V/1500

A much larger aircraft, again a heavy bomber, designed to reach Berlin from France. It had five to seven crew, was armed with two Lewis mg in nose, dorsal and ventral positions and carried 2,000lb/908kg of bombs internally, but arrived to late to see active service in Europe. Built by HP, Beardmore, and Harland & Wolff. Nicknamed Super Handley.
In service 1918 with 166 Sqn, used by three sqns (166, 167, 274) until 1920, 274 Sqn.
Action: India.
Powered by four 350hp RR Eagle VIII, 500hp BHP/Galloway Atlantic, or 500hp Napier Lion II in-lines, arranged as two tractors and two pushers in the same nacelles.
Serials: E4304–4323 (5), E8287–8306 (9), F7134–7143 (10), F8201–8230 (10), F8281–8320 (10), J1936.
Span: 126ft/38.4m   Length: 64ft/19.5m   Ceiling: 11,000ft/3,300m   Range: 1,300 miles/ 2,093 km   Speed: 99mph/159kmph.
Total 45 but some not issued; losses not known.

HP 0/400, D9702.
(Charles Parker)

HP V/1500.
(Scott Collection)

HP Hyderabad I, J8815, 503 Sqn.
(Peter Green Collection)

178. Hyderabad I

An RAF heavy bomber, with four crew and armed with one Lewis mg in nose, dorsal and ventral
positions, able to carry 1,100lb/500kg of bombs under fuselage and wings. Early production had a long
fin and rounded rudder, later had a squared-off fin and rudder.
In service 1925 with 99 Sqn, used by four sqns (10, 99, 502, 503) and 1xmisc. unit, until 1934, 503 Sqn.
Powered by two 480hp Napier Lion IIb or 470hp Lion V in-lines.
Serials: J7738–7752 (15), J8317–8324 (8), J8805–8815 (11), J9031–9036 (5), J9293–9298 (5).
Span: 75ft/22.86m   Length: 59ft 2in/18.03m   Ceiling: 14,000ft/4,200m   Range: 500 miles/
805 km   Speed: 109mph/175kmph.
Total 44; 8 (18%) accidental losses.

179. Hinaidi I

Developed from the Hyderabad, differing mainly in its engines; it had a wooden structure and straight
wings. Four crew, and armed with one Lewis mg in nose, dorsal and ventral positions plus 1,448lb/655kg
of bombs under wings or fuselage.
In service 1929 with 99 Sqn, used by three sqns (10, 99, 503) and 1xmisc. unit, until 1934, 503 Sqn.
Powered by two 460hp Bristol Jupiter VIIIf radials.
Serials: J9033, J9298–9303 (6).
Total 7 plus 6 conversions of the Hyderabad, making a total of 13; 1 accidental loss.

179a. Hinaidi II

As the Mk I but with a metal frame and the outer wings slightly swept.
In service 1930 with 503 Sqn, used by three sqns (10, 99, 503) until 1935, 503 Sqn.
Serials: K1063–1078 (16), K1909–1925 (17).
Total 33; 1 accidental loss.
Both Marks: Span: 75ft/22.86m   Length: 59ft 3in/18.06m   Ceiling: 14,500ft/4,350m   Range: 850
miles/137km   Speed: 122mph/196kmph.
Total Hinaidis 40 plus 6 conversions, making a total of 46; in service 1929–34; 2 (5%) losses.

180. Clive II

A transport derived from the Hinaidi II, carrying two crew and 17 passengers and unarmed. There were
nine windows in the starboard fuselage side and eight in the port.
In service 1930 to 1934 with the Heavy Transport/Bomber Transport Flt.
Based overseas in India, not operational in the UK.
Powered by two 525hp Bristol Jupiter IX radials.
Serials: J9948–49 (2).
Total 2; 1 (50%) accidental loss.
Span: 75ft/22.86m   Length: 63ft/19.2m   Ceiling: 12,600ft/3,780m   Range: 765 miles/
1,232 km   Speed: 111mph/179kmph.

181. Heyford I

A night bomber for the RAF with a unique lower-wing arrangement; it had four crew and was armed with one Lewis mg in nose and dorsal positions and one in an HP ventral turret, plus 1,660lb/750kg of bombs in the bottom-wing centre-section.

In service 1933 with 99 Sqn, used by two sqns (97, 99) until 1939, 97 Sqn.

Powered by two 480hp RR Kestrel IIIs in-lines.

Serials: K3489–3503 (13).

Total 13; 4 accidental losses.

181a. Heyford IA

As the Mk I but with a power-generator, four-bladed propellers and able to carry 2,000lb/908kg of bombs.

In service 1934 with 10 Sqn, used by three sqns (10, 97, 149),until 1939, 149 Sqn; also served with 1xATC.

Serials: K4021–4043 (22).

Total 22; 7 accidental losses.

181b. Heyford II

As the Mk IA but with bomb load increased yet again to 3,500lb/1,587kg in extra lower-wing cells.

In service 1935 with 7 Sqn, used by two sqns (7, 102) until 1939, 102 Sqn, also served with 1xAOS.

Powered by two 695hp Kestrel VI (derated).

Serials: K4863–4878 (16).

Total 16 plus 4 conversions of the Mks I and IA, making a total of 20; 5 accidental losses.

HP Hinaidi II, K1075, 99 Sqn.
(Scott Collection)

HP Heyford II, 7 Sqn.
(Air-Britain Archives)

181c. Heyford III

The ultimate Heyford, as the Mk II but with V-type engine-intakes and steam condensers in the wing leading-edge.
In service 1935 with 38 Sqn, used by 12 sqns (7, 9, 10, 38, 58, 78, 97, 99, 102, 148, 149, 166) until 1939, 166 Sqn; also served with 2xAOS and 2xB&GS until 1941.
Serials: K5180–5199 (20), K6857–6906 (50).
Total 70 plus 2 conversions of earlier Mks, making a total of 72; 21 accidental losses.

	Span	Length	Ceiling	Range	Speed
Mk I	75ft/22.86m	58ft/17.68m	21,000ft/6,300m	920 miles/1,481km	138mph/222kmph
Mk IA	"	"	"	"	142mph/229kmph
Mk II	"	"	"	"	154mph/248kmph

Total Heyfords 121; in service 1933–41; 37 (31%) losses.

182. Harrow I

A monoplane night bomber and transport for the RAF, although short-lived as a bomber; it had five crew as a bomber and four crew and 20 passengers as a transport, and the bomber was armed with one Lewis or Vickers mg in a FN-14 nose turret and FN-5 dorsal turret and two Lewis or Vickers in a FN-15 tail turret plus 3,000lb/1,360kg of bombs internally.
In service 1937 with 214 Sqn, used by five sqns (37, 75, 115, 214, 215) until 1939, also served with 1xAAS, 1xAGS, 4xAOS, 4xB&GS, 1xOTU, 1xParaTS, 1xcomms. unit and 2xmisc. units.
Powered by two 980hp Bristol Pegasus X radials.
Serials: K6935–6970 (36).
Total 36; 1 accidental loss.

182a. Harrow II

As the Mk I but with different engines and the guns were all Brownings.
In service 1937 with 115 Sqn, used by five sqns (37, 75, 115, 214, 215) until 1939, 215 Sqn; also served with 2xAGS, 5xAOS, 3xB&GS, CLE, 1xcomms. unit and 5xmisc. units until 1943.
Powered by two 835hp Pegasus XX.
Serials: K6971–7032 (62).
Total 62 plus 35 conversions of the Mk I, making a total of 97; 14 accidental and 3 hostile losses.

182b. Harrow II (LAM)

One of the misguided attempts at stopping German night bombing, these Harrows carried 120 aerial parachute mines in the bomb bay to drop onto those bombers.
In service 1940 with 420 Flt, used by one sqn and one flt until 1941, 93 Sqn.
Action: northern Europe.
Five conversions of the Mk II; losses included in the above.

HP Harrow I, K6946, 37 Sqn.
(Scott Collection)

HP Hampden I, 49 Sqn.
(Author's Collection)

182c. Harrow Transport

A dedicated transport conversion with turrets deleted and faired-over giving a stream-lined appearance; a modified door and strengthened floor meant it could hold 20 passengers or 3,000lb/1,360kg of freight and it had three crew. Nicknamed Sparrow.
In service 1940 with 1680 Flt, used by one sqn (271), one flt and 1xFAA comms. unit, until 1945, 271 Sqn. Action: northern Europe.
Thirty-four conversions of the Mk II (9 FAA); 6 accidental and 8 hostile losses.

	Span	Length	Ceiling	Range	Speed
Mk I	88ft 5in/26.03m	82ft/24.99m	23,000ft/6,900m	1,250 miles/2,012km	190mph/306kmph
Mk II	"	"	22,800ft/6,840m	"	200mph/322kmph

Total Harrows 98; in service 1937–45; 32 (33)% losses inc. 11 hostile.

183. Hampden I

One of the three night bombers with which Bomber Command fought the first two years of the Second World War, this monoplane had four crew and was initially armed with one Browning in the port nose and one Vickers mg in the nose, dorsal and ventral positions, later increased to two Vickers in the dorsal and ventral; bomb load was 4,000lb/1,816kg carried internally and underwing, or one mine. Nicknamed Flying Panhandle.
In service 1938 with 49 Sqn, used by 14 sqns (7, 44, 49, 50, 61, 76, 83, 97, 106, 144, 185, 207, 408, 420) until 1942, 408 Sqn; also served with three met. sqns (517, 519, 521), seven met. flts, 1xAAS, 1xAOS, 2xB&GS, 2xBATFlts, 2xTTFlts, 4xOTU, CGS and 1xmisc. unit, until 1944.
Action: northern Europe, also based overseas in North America.
Powered by two 835hp Bristol Pegasus XXII radials.
Serials: L4034–4211 (178), P1145–1356 (200), P2062–2145 (75), P4285–4418 (119), P5298–5436 (80), X2893–3154 (150), AD719–AE422 (425), AT109–260 (120).
Total 1,347 plus 39 conversions of the HP Hereford (qv), making a total of 1,389; 604 accidental and 281 hostile losses.

183a. Hampden TB I

As the Mk I bomber but modified to carry a torpedo or 1,000lb/454kg of bombs in a bulged bomb bay with partly cut-away doors.
In service 1942 with 144 Sqn, used by four sqns (144, 415, 455, 489) until 1943, 455 Sqn, also served with 2xTorpTU.
Action: North Atlantic.
Serials: AN100–167 (25).
Total 25 plus 286 conversions of the Mk I, making a total of 327; 88 accidental and 40 hostile losses.

	Span	Length	Ceiling	Range	Speed
Mk I	69ft 2in/21.08m	53ft 7in/16.33m	19,000ft/5,700m	1,885 miles/3,035km	254mph/409kmph
TB I	"	"	"	1,960 miles/3,156km	"

Total Hampden 1,372 plus 39 Hereford conversions making a total of 1,411; built by HP, Canadian Car & Foundry, and English Electric; in service 1938–44; 1,013 (74%) losses inc. 321 hostile.

184. Hereford I

A re-engined Hampden which had problems with its new engines and was relegated to operational training, some of the survivors being converted to Hampdens (see above). Four crew and armed with a Browning in the port nose and one Vickers in nose, dorsal and ventral positions; 4,000lb/1,816kg of bombs internally and underwing. Built by Shorts.
In service 1940 with 185 Sqn, used by one sqn (185), 1xAAS, 2xAOS, 1xB&GS and 2xOTU until 1941.
Powered by two 955hp Napier Dagger VIII in-lines.
Serials: L6004–6101 (97), N9055–9106 (49).
Span: 69ft 2in/21.08m   Length: 53ft 7in/16.33m   Ceiling: 19,000ft/5,700m   Range: 1,885 miles/3,035km   Speed: 265mph/427kmph.
Total 146; 31 (21%) accidental losses.

185. HP 42

The famed 1930s airliner, a large biplane with cantilever struts and with the upper wing strutted to the lower wing which was mounted on the fuselage top; impressed by the RAF as a transport carrying four crew and 24 passengers.
In service 1940 with 271 Sqn, used by one RAF sqn until 1941.
Powered by four 500hp Bristol Jupiter XIf radials, two on the lower wing and two on the upper.
Serials: AS981–83 (3).
Span: 130ft/39.62m   Length: 89ft 9in/27.36m   Ceiling: n/k   Range: 500 miles/800 km   Speed: 120mph/193kmph.
Total 3 impressed; 2 (67%) accidental losses.

186. Halifax I Series I

The second of the RAF's four-engined bombers, the Mks I, II and V having several controllability problems resulting from the normal wartime urgency to get new types into service. The Mk I had six crew and was armed with two Browning mg in a BP-C nose turret and BP-R ventral turret, and four Brownings in a BP-E tail turret, plus 12,000lb/5,448kg of bombs internally and in wing-cells.
In service 1940 with 35 Sqn, used by three sqns (10, 35, 76) and 1xCU until 1942, 76 Sqn.
Action: northern Europe and Middle East.
Powered by four 1,145hp RR Merlin X in-lines.
Serials: L7244–45 (2), L9486–9534 (46).
Total 48; 17 accidental and 17 hostile losses.

186a. Halifax I Series II

As the Series I but with seven crew, the ventral turret deleted and replaced by one Vickers in each beam position, 13,000lb/5,902kg of bombs and increased auw.
In service 1941 with 76 Sqn, used by two sqns (10, 76) until 1942, 10 Sqn; also served with 11xCU until 1943.
Action: northern Europe.
Serials: L9560–9584 (25).
Total 25; 15 accidental and 5 hostile losses.

186b. Halifax I Series III

As the Series II except that it carried more fuel.
In service 1941 with 35 Sqn, used by two sqns (35, 76) until 1942, 76 Sqn; also served with 1xCU until 1943.

Action: northern Europe.

Powered by four 1,390hp Merlin XX

Serials: L9600–9608 (9).

Total 9; 2 accidental and 4 hostile losses.

186c. Halifax II Series I

As the Mk I Series III but had a BP-C dorsal turret with two Brownings to replace the beam guns, although this was sometimes deleted to improve the performance; bomb load reverted to 12,000lb/5,448kg and some were fitted with H2S radar in a radome under the rear fuselage. Different engine radiators.

In service 1941 with 76 Sqn, used by 18 sqns (10, 35, 51, 76, 77, 78, 102, 103, 158, 405, 408, 419, 428, 429, 460, 462, 614, 624) and one SD Flt until 1945, 614 Sqn; also served with 23xCU, 3xFTU, METS, PNTU, 1xBTFlt, 1xRef.FU, 1xRTFlt and 5xmisc. units.

Action: northern and southern Europe, North Africa and Middle East.

Serials: L9609–9624 (16), R9363–9533 (92), V9976–W1276 (181), W7650–7939 (199), BB189–446 (199), DG219–230 (12), DT481–808 (250), HR654–988 (248), HX147–225 (49), JB781–974 (127), JN882–JP338 (250).

Total 1,623; 623 accidental and 774 hostile losses.

186d. Halifax II Series I (Special)

As above but with the nose turret deleted and replaced by a metal fairing giving a more streamlined shape, the dorsal turret deleted, six crew, exhaust muffs and able to carry 13,000lb/5,902kg of bombs.

In service 1941 with 10 Sqn, used by units as above plus three SD sqns (148, 178, 301), until 1945, 301 Sqn.

Action: northern and southern Europe.

Total and losses included in the Series I above.

186e. Halifax II Series IA

In a further attempt to improve the Mk II's performance the Series IA had a streamlined Perspex nose with one Vickers mg, a BP-A dorsal turret and BP-E tail turret, each with four Brownings, 13,000lb/5,902kg of bombs and some had H2S. Late production had rectangular fins and a retractable tail wheel.

In service 1941 with 10 Sqn, served with units as the Mk II Series I until 1945, 192 (RCM) Sqn.

Action: northern and southern Europe, and North Africa.

Powered by four 1,390hp Merlin XXII in redesigned cowlings.

Serials: JD105–421 (223), LW223–345 (100).

Total 323; 44 accidental and 157 hostile losses.

HP Halifax I, L7245. (Author's Collection)

HP Halifax III, MZ660,
432 (Can) Sqn – note
ventral gun. (Ray Leach via
Peter Green)

186f. Halifax GR II Series IA

A successful general-reconnaissance and anti-shipping strike version, as the above but with one 0.5in Browning in the Perspex nose, rectangular fins as standard, more fuel, 13,000lb/5,902kg of stores internally, ASV-III in a rear fuselage radome and some with four-bladed propellers.

In service 1942 with 58 Sqn, used by two sqns (58, 502), one flt, one met. flt and 2xCU until 1945, 58 and 502 Sqns.

Action: North Atlantic.

Seventy conversions of the Mk II Series IA; losses included with the Mk II Series IA.

186g. Halifax III

A much improved Mk which rivaled the Avro Lancaster (qv) but by the time it entered service AC-M Harris had set his face against the Halifax. The Mk III had rectangular fins, new engines and most had rounded wingtips, all giving a much better performance and handling. Seven crew, armed with one 0.5in Browning in the Perspex nose, four Brownings in a BP-A dorsal and BP-E tail turret, and some had a manual 0.5in in a Preston-Green ventral mounting, plus 13,000lb/5,902kg of bombs and H2S.

In service 1943 with 35 Sqn, used by 26 sqns (10, 35, 51, 76, 77, 78, 102, 158, 346, 347, 408, 415, 420, 424, 425, 426, 427, 429, 431, 432, 433, 434, 462, 466, 578, 640), five transport sqns (96, 187, 190, 246, 511), one GR flt, and three RCM sqns carrying Mandrel and ABC, (171, 192, 199), until 1945, 4 Gp sqns; also served with BCIS, CGS, CNS, 7xCU, EANS, 1xOTU, 1xAGS and 5xmisc. units.

Action: northern Europe and North Africa, also based overseas in the Far East and BWI.

Powered by four 1,615hp Bristol Hercules XVI radials.

Serials: HX228–357 (96), LK747–887 (99), LL543–615 (60), LV771–LW210 (224), LW346–724 (260), MZ282–NA309 (714), NA492–704 (180), NP930–NR290 (200), PN167–207 (41), PN365–619 (80), RG345–446 (80).

Total 2,034; 385 accidental and 745 hostile losses.

186h. Halifax A III

An airborne forces transport and glider tug, as the Mk III but with the dorsal turret and H2S deleted, rounded wingtips as standard, a parachute exit under the rear fuselage and towing gear under the tail; six crew and nine to 11 passengers.

In service 1944 with 298 Sqn, used by three sqns (296, 297, 298), 2xCU, 1xHGCU, ORTU and 2xmisc. units, until 1946, 297 Sqn.

Action: northern Europe.

30 conversions of the Mk III; losses included with the Mk III.

186j. Halifax Met. III

A conversion of the Mk III for met. reconnaissance, with the bomber armament, ASV-III in the radome and specialist equipment.

In service 1945 with 517 and 518 Sqns, used by six sqns (502, 517, 518, 519, 520, 521) until 1946, 517 Sqn.
Action: North Atlantic.
Fifty conversions of the Mk III; losses included with the Mk III.

186k. Halifax V Series I

This was actually an earlier Mk than the Mk III and was the same as the Mk II except that it had a
lighter, strutted and thus weaker Messier-designed undercarriage (which gave rise to take-off and land-
ing weight problems) and a fixed tail wheel. The Series I had the old triangular fins, two Browning
mg in a BP-C nose turret, two or four in a BP-A dorsal turret, and four in a BP-E tail turret, with
13,000lb/5,902kg of bombs, seven crew and some with H2S.
In service 1942 with 408 Sqn, used by 11 sqns (76, 77, 346, 347, 408, 427, 428, 429, 431, 434, 624), four SD
sqns (138, 148, 161, 301), and two SD flts until 1944, 434 Sqn; also served with BCIS, 14xCU, EFS, RTFlt
and 1xmisc. unit, until 1945.
Action: northern and southern Europe and North Africa, also based overseas in North America and Far East.
Powered by four 1,390hp Merlin XXII in-lines.
Serials: DG231–424 (137), DJ980–DK271 (150), EB127–276 (100), LK626–746 (96), LK890–LL542 (420).
Total 903; 296 accidental and 271 hostile losses.

186l. Halifax V Series I (Special)

As the Mk V Series I but with a metal faired nose replacing the turret and the dorsal turret deleted.
In service 1942 with units as above, until 1945, 148 Sqn.
Action: northern and southern Europe.
Unknown number of conversions of the Mk V Series I; losses with the Mk V Series I.

186m. Halifax V Series IA

As the Mk V Series I but with a Perspex nose mounting a 0.5in Browning, the BP-A dorsal turret, some
with H2S and some with rectangular fins and a retractable tail wheel.
In service 1943, with units as the Mk V Series I, until 1944 operational and 1945 training.
Action: northern Europe.
Powered by four 1,390hp Merlin XXII in redesigned cowlings.
Unknown number of conversions on the Mk V Series I; losses included with the Mk V Series I.

186n. Halifax A V

An airborne forces transport and glider tug, with a Perspex nose, dorsal turret deleted, rectangular fins,
towing gear under the tail and a paratroop exit under the rear fuselage. Six crew and nine passengers.
In service 1943 with 295 Sqn, used by five sqns (295, 296, 297, 298, 644), 1xCU and 2xmisc. units, until
1945, 296 and 297 Sqns.
Action: northern Europe.
**One hundred and twenty-five (approx.) conversions of the Mk V Series I; losses included
with the Mk V Series I.**

186p. Halifax Met. V Series IA

As the Mk V Series IA but had eight crew, a 0.5in in the nose, ASV-III replacing the H2S, rectangular
fins, specialist met. equipment and some had four-bladed propellers.
In service 1943 with 1404 Met. Flt, used by three sqns (517, 518, 520), one flt and 1xCU until 1945, 517
and 518 Sqns.
Action: North Atlantic.
Seventy-one (approx.) conversions of the Mk V Series IA; losses in the Mk V Series I.

186q. Halifax B VI

A development of the Mk III, with increased fuel, tropical filters and a pressurized fuel system; armament
was one 0.5in Browning in the Perspex nose, four Brownings in a BP-A dorsal and BP-E tail turret,
13,000lb/5,902kg of bombs and H2S, with seven crew.

In service 1945 with 102 Sqn, used by nine sqns (76, 77, 78, 102, 158, 346, 347, 466, 649) until 1945, 346 and 347 Sqns; also served with EANS, ERS, 1xOTU, 1xRS, RAFFC and 4xmisc. units.
Action: northern Europe.
Powered by four 1,675hp Hercules 100 radials.
Serials: NP821–927 (77), PP165–216 (35), RG480–879 (298), ST794–818 (25).
Total 435; 24 accidental and 8 hostile losses.

186r. Halifax C VI

A transport version of the B VI, with the dorsal turret and H2S deleted and a paratroop exit under the rear fuselage; six crew and nine to 11 passengers.
In service during 1945.
Unknown number of conversions of the B VI.

186s. Halifax Met. 6

A version for met. reconnaissance, with eight crew and special met. equipment.
In service 1945 with 1361 Met. Flt, used by two sqns (202, 224), two flts and 1xCU until 1951, 224 Sqn.
Based overseas in Gibraltar.
Thirty-five conversions of the B VI; 17 accidental losses.

186t. Halifax GR 6

A post-war general-reconnaissance version, with nine crew and armament as the B VI but with ASV replacing the H2S and a low-level bombsight.
In service 1946 with 202 Sqn, used by two sqns (202, 224) until 1952, 224 Sqn.
Based overseas in Gibraltar.
Fourteen (approx.) conversions of the B VI; losses included in Met 6.

186u. Halifax B VII

The last heavy bomber Mk, similar to the B VI but with different engines, which all exhausted to port; some had 2x0.5in Browning in a BP-D rear turret. Seven crew and armament as the B VI.
In service 1944 with 426 Sqn, used by five sqns (408, 415, 426, 432, 644) and 1xmisc. unit until 1945, 6 Gp sqns, second-line to 1946.
Action: northern Europe.
Powered by four 1,615hp Hercules XVI.
Serials: LW197–210 (14), NP681–820 (111), PN208, PN223–242 (20), RG447–479 (20), TW774–796 (23)(renumbered).
Total 189; 33 accidental and 58 hostile losses.

HP Halifax C 8, PP331.
(Peter Green Collection)

186v. Halifax A 7

An airborne forces transport and glider tug, with dorsal turret and H2S deleted, four crew and nine passengers, 8,000lb/3,672kg of freight in a pannier beneath the bomb bay, towing gear and a paratroop exit under the fuselage.

In service 1945 with 644 Sqn, used by eight sqns, (47, 113, 190, 295, 296, 297, 298, 620) 6xCU, 1xHGCU, ORTU and 2xmisc. units until 1947, 113 Sqn.

Action: Far East and Palestine, also based overseas in Egypt and India.

Serials: NA310–468 (121), PN243–343 (69), PP339–389 (38), RT753–757 (4).

Total 232; 11 accidental and 15 hostile losses.

186w. Halifax C 8

A dedicated transport Mk, with all turrets deleted and faired over, cabin windows and a pannier below the bomb bay for 8,000lb/3,672kg of freight; five crew and 11 passengers.

In service 1946 with 301 Sqn, used by two sqns (301, 304) until 1946, 301 Sqn.

Powered by four 1,675hp Hercules 100.

Serials: PP217–388 (90).

Total 90; 3 accidental losses.

186x. Halifax A 9

The last Halifax Mk, a dedicated airborne forces transport and glider tug with two 0.5in Browning mg in a BP-D tail turret, five crew and 16 passengers, and 8,000lb/3,672kg of freight in the underbelly pannier; there were cabin portholes, and a paratroop exit and towing gear under the rear fuselage.

In service 1946 with 620 Sqn, used by six sqns (47, 113, 295, 297, 620, 644) until 1948, 295 and 297 Sqns, also served with one met. sqn (202), 2xCU, 1xParaTS, 1xOCU and 1xmisc. unit, until 1950.

Action: Palestine.

Powered by four 1,615hp Hercules XVI.

Serials: RT759–938 (144).

Total 144; 10 accidental losses.

	Span	Length	Ceiling	Range	Speed
Mk I/I	98ft 8in/ 30.07m	69ft 9in/ 21.26m	18,000ft/ 5,400m	1,552 miles/ 2,499km	262mph/ 422kmph
Mk I/III	"	"	"	1,900 miles /3,059km	"
Mk II/IA	"	71ft 7in/ 21.82m	21,000ft/ 6,300m	1,660 miles/ 2,673km	264mph/ 425kmph
Mk III	98ft 10in or 103ft 8in	30.12 or 31.59m	20,000ft/ 6,000m	1,770 miles/ 2,850km	282mph/ 454kmph
MkV	98ft 8in /30.07m	69ft 9in/ 21.26m	22,000ft/ 6,600m	1,900 miles/ 3,059km	250mph/ 402kmph
MkV/I (Sp)	"	71ft 7in/21.82m	"	"	"
MkV/IA	"	"	21,000ft/ 6,300m	"	241mph/ 388kmph
BVI	103ft 8in/ 31.59m	"	22,000ft/ 6,600m	1,260 miles/ 2,029km	312mph/ 502kmph
B 7	"	"	20,000ft/ 6,000m	2,225 miles/ 3,582km	281mph/ 452kmph
C 8	"	73ft 7in/ 22.43m	25,000ft/ 7,500m	2,420 miles/ 3,896km	289mph/ 465kmph
A 9	"	71ft 7in /21.82m	20,000ft/ 6,000m	2,050 miles/ 3,300km	"

Total Halifaxes 6,055; built by HP, English Electric, Fairey, London Transport and Rootes; in service 1940–52; 3,480 (57%) losses inc. 2,054 hostile; nicknamed Halibag.

HP Hastings C 1,
TG500, AAEE.
(Author's Collection)

187. Hastings C 1

A strategic transport for the RAF, post Second World War, with five crew and able to carry 50 passengers
or 35,000lb/15,890kg of freight.
In service 1948 with 47 Sqn, used by 11 sqns (24, 36, 47, 48, 53, 70, 99, 114, 242, 297, 511), two Elint sqns
(116, 151), EFS, SoMR, 2xOCU, 2xParaTS, RAFFC, 1xcomms. unit and 10xmisc. units, until 1968, 70 Sqn.
Action: Berlin Airlift, Malaya and Suez, also based overseas in Cyprus and Singapore.
Powered by four 1,615hp Bristol Hercules 101 radials.
Serials: TG503–755 (96).
Total 96; 21 accidental losses.

187a. Hastings C 1A

As the C 1 but with long-range tanks under the wingtips.
In service 1952 with sqns as above, 1xOCU and BCBS until 1967, 36 Sqn.
Action: Malaya and Suez, based overseas in Cyprus and Singapore.
Powered by four 1,675hp Hercules 106 or 216.
Fifty conversions of the C 1; 4 accidental losses.

187b. Hastings Met. 1

A conversion for met. reconnaissance fitted with specialised met. equipment.
In service 1950–64 with 202 Sqn.
Eighteen conversions of the C 1; 1 accidental loss.

187c. Hastings C 2

A development of the C 1 with increased fuel and longer-span, lower-set tailplanes.
In service 1951 with 24 Sqn, used by 10 sqns (24, 36, 47, 48, 53, 70, 97, 99, 114, 511), until 1968, 24 Sqn;
also used by two ECM sqns (115, 151), RAFFC, 1xcomms. unit and 5xmisc. units, ECM to 1969.
Action: Suez, also based overseas in Cyprus.
Powered by four 1,675hp Hercules 106 or 216.
Serials: WD475–499 (21), WJ327–343 (17).
Total 38; 9 accidental losses.

187d. Hastings C (VIP) 4

A VIP version of the C 2 with a luxury interior for 12 to 30 passengers and airstairs; no freight door.
In service 1951 with 24 Sqn, used by one sqn, 2xcomms. units and 1xmisc. unit, until 1968, 24 Sqn.
Based overseas in Aden and Singapore.
Powered by four 1,675hp Hercules 736.
Serials: WD500, WJ324–26 (3).
Total 4; no losses.

187e. Hastings T 5

A radar-bombing trainer for the V-Force, as the C 1A but with eight crew and H2S in a radome under the mid-fuselage; also used for fishery patrol during the 'Cod War'.
In service 1953 with BCBS, used by BCBS, SCBS and 1xOCU until 1977, 230 OCU.
Eight conversions of the C 1. No losses.

	Span	Length	Ceiling	Range	Speed
C 1	113ft/34.44m	82ft 8in/25.19m	26,700ft/8,010m	1,220 miles/1,964km	354mph/570kmph
C 1A	"	"	25,500ft/7,650m	1,690 miles/2,721km	348mph/560kmph
C 2	"	"	26,500ft/7,950m	"	"
C 4	"	"	"	4,250 miles/6,842km	"

Total Hastings 138; in service 1948–77; 35 (25%) losses.

188. Marathon T 11

A light airliner originally designed by Miles (qv) but this company's aircraft manufacturing side was taken over by HP and the Marathon was sold to the RAF as a navigation trainer, in which role it was not liked; five crew.
In service 1953 with the ANS, used by 2xANS and 1xFTS until 1958, 1 ANS.
Powered by four 330hp DH Gipsy Queen 71 in-lines.
Serials: XA250–278 (27).
Span: 65ft/19.81m   Length: 52ft 3in/15.93m   Ceiling: 15,000ft/4,500m   Range: 1,100 miles/1,771km   Speed: 200mph/322kmph.
Total 27; 8 (30%) accidental losses.

189. Victor B 1

The final, and most advanced, of the RAF's three V-bombers, the Victor had the so-called 'crescent wing'. It carried five crew, the pilots on MB-3L ejector seats, had no defensive armament but carried 35,000lb/15,890kg of bombs internally, including Blue Danube, Red Beard and Yellow Sun Mks 1 and 2 nuclear weapons, plus H2S in an integral radome under the nose.
In service 1957 with 232 OCU, 1958 with 10 Sqn, used by four sqns (10, 15, 55, 57), one flt, 1xOCU and Tanker TFlt until 1966, 57 Sqn.
Powered by four 10,500lb st A-S Sapphire 202 or 11,050lb st 207 jets.
Serials: XA917–941 (22), XH587–612 (8).
Total 30; 2 accidental losses.

HP Marathon
T 11, XA273, 1
Air Navigation
School. (John
Fletcher via
Charles Parker)

HP Victor
B 1, XA930.
(Peter Green
Collection)

189a. Victor B 1A

As the B 1 but had ECM blisters on the tailcone, a strengthened pressure cabin, revised internal equipment, drooped wing leading-edges and a FR probe above the cockpit.
In service 1960 with 15 Sqn, used by four sqns (10, 15, 55, 57), 2xOCU and Tanker TFlt until 1966, 57 Sqn.
Serials: XH613–651 (17).
Total 17 plus 8 conversions of the B 1, making a total of 25; 2 accidental losses.

189b. Victor B (K) 1A

When the Vickers Valiant tankers (qv) were retired early due to unexpected fatigue, Victors were hastily converted to take their place; the B (K) 1A was the first tanker variant, with a bomber dual-role, and had two HDU pods underwing.
In service 1965–67 with 55 Sqn.
Six conversions of the B 1A; no losses.

189c. Victor K 1

A dedicated tanker without the bomber role, having two HDU pods underwing and one under the rear fuselage, tanks in the bomb bay, and no ECM blisters.
In service 1966 with 57 Sqn, used by three sqns (55, 57, 214) until 1977, 57 Sqn.
Ten conversions of the B 1; no losses.

189d. Victor K 1A

As the K 1 but with ECM blisters on the tailcone and other B 1A improvements.
In service 1967 with 55 Sqn, used by three sqns (55, 57, 214) and Tanker TFlt until 1977, 57 Sqn.
Fourteen conversions of the B 1A and B (K) 1A; 2 accidental losses.

189e. Victor B 2

A much improved bomber, with extended wingspan, ECM tailcone, AC electrics, retractable air intakes on top of the rear fuselage and a further intake at the base of the fin. The pilots sat on MB-3ls seats and it could carry the Yellow Sun Mk 2 nuclear weapon.
In service 1961 with 232 OCU, 1962 with 139 Sqn, used by two sqns (100, 139), Victor TU and 1xmisc. unit until 1964, 232 OCU.
Powered by four 20,000lb st RR Conway 201 jets.
Serials: XH669–675 (6), XL158–233 (17), XL511–513 (3), XM714–718 (5).
Total 31; 1 accidental loss.

189f. Victor B 2R

As the B 2 but had cut-away bomb doors to carry the Blue Steel AGM in the bomb bay; it had internal modifications and a large trailing-edge wing pod on each wing.

In service 1963 with 139 Sqn, used by two sqns (100,139) until 1968, 139 Sqn.

Powered by four 20,000lb st Conway 210.

Twenty-one conversions of the B 2; no losses.

189g. Victor SR 2

A strategic-reconnaissance variant, with armament deleted and carrying Red Neck reconnaissance radar, with nine cameras in the bomb bay plus increased fuel.

In service 1965 to 1974 with 543 Sqn.

Four conversions of the B 2; 2 accidental losses.

189h. Victor K 2

A major redesign of the B 2 as a dedicated tanker, with shorter span wings, HDUs under each wing and the rear fuselage and with the ECM removed; also used for maritime reconnaissance during the Falklands war.

In service 1974 with 232 OCU, 1975 with 55 Sqn, used by two sqns (55, 57) and 1xOCU until 1993, 55 Sqn.

Action: Falklands and the Gulf.

Powered by four 20,000lb st Conway 201.

Twenty-two conversions of the B 2 and B 2R; 5 accidental losses.

	Span	Length	Ceiling	Range	Speed
B 1	110ft/33.53m	114ft 11in/35.03m	55,000ft/16,500m	2,700 miles/4,347km	645mph/1,038kmph
B 2	120ft/36.58m	"	60,000ft/18,000m	3,500 miles/5,635km	630mph/1,014kmph
K 2	113ft/34.44m	"	49,000ft/14,700m	4,000 miles/6,440km	610mph/982kmph

Total Victors 78; in service 1957–93; 14 (18%) losses.

HP Victor K 1A, XA936,
214 Sqn. (Charles Parker)

HP Victor K 2, 55 Sqn.
(Author's Collection)

HARLAND & WOLFF (Belfast, N.I.)

Assembled HP V/1500.

HARLOW (USA)

A small company which existed from 1938 to 1945 and supplied five examples of one type.

190. PC-5A

A modern-looking low-wing cabin monoplane, with retractable undercarriage and two crew under a large lightly framed Perspex canopy; one large fin/rudder. Used for communications by the RAF. Built by Hindustan Aircraft.
In service 1941 with 155 Sqn, used by 1xAACU, 1xGGFlt, 1xcomms. unit and 1xmisc. unit until 1945.
Based overseas in Far East, not operational in the UK.
Powered by one 165hp Warner Super Scarab radial.
Serials: DR423–427 (5).
Span: 35ft 7in/10.85m   Length: 23ft 7in/7.19m   Ceiling: 16,000ft/4,800m   Range: 425 miles/684km   Speed: 163mph/262kmph.
Total 5; 1 (20%) accidental loss.

HARRIS LEBUS (London)

Assembled Airspeed Horsa, GAL Hotspur, and HP 0/400.

HAWKER (Kingston, Surrey, UK)

Formed from the ashes of the defunct Sopwith Company in 1920 by Tom Sopwith (later Sir Tom) and Harry Hawker and became famous for its range of military aircraft, both fighters and bombers. Its success meant that it was able to purchase Gloster in 1933 to form Hawker-Siddeley Aircraft Ltd in 1934, (though keeping both individual names); this company formed the greater part of Hawker-Siddeley Aviation on its formation in 1963 and the Hawker title then disappeared. Supplied 21,987 examples of 19 types (Woodcock, Tomtit, Hart F, Hart T, Fury, Nimrod, Audax, Osprey, Demon, Hind T, Hector, Hurricane, Henley, Sea Hurricane, Typhoon, Tempest, Sea Fury, Seahawk and Hunter, see Vol. 1); also assembled Airco DH 9A.

191. Horsley I

This large biplane was a day-bomber for the RAF, with two crew and armed with a Vickers mg in the port fuselage, a Lewis mg in the rear cockpit and 1,500lb/681kg of bombs underwing.
In service 1926 with 100 Sqn, used by one sqn, 1xPTU and 2xmisc. units until 1931, 100 Sqn.
Based overseas in Singapore.
Powered by one 670hp RR Condor III in-line.
Serials: J7987–7996 (10).
Total 10; 2 accidental losses.

191a. Horsley II

A day-bomber and torpedo-bomber for the RAF, as the Mk I except it was of composite construction; carried one torpedo underbelly or 1,500lb of bombs/681kg underwing.
In service 1929 with 33 Sqn, used by six bomber sqns (11, 15, 22, 33, 100, 504), one TB sqn (36), 1xFTS, 2xAACU, TB Leuchars and 3xmisc. units, until 1934, 504 Sqn.
Powered by one 650hp Condor IIIb.
Serials: J7997–8026 (30), J8597–8621 (25), S1236–1247 (12).
Total 67; 14 accidental losses.

191b. Horsley III

A dedicated torpedo-bomber for the RAF, as the Mk II but with a metal frame.
In service 1930 to 1935 with 36 Sqn and 1xAACU until 1937.
Based overseas in Singapore, not operational in the UK.

Serials: S1436–1453 (18), S1597–1613 (18).
Total 36; 11 accidental losses.
All Marks: Span: 56ft 6in/17.22m   Length: 38ft 10in/11.83m   Ceiling: 11,200ft/3,360m   Endurance: 10hrs   Speed: 126mph/203kmph.
Total Horsleys 113; in service 1925–37; 27 (24%) losses.

192. Hart I

An advanced day-bomber for the RAF, outperforming its contemporary fighters; it was a two-seater armed with a Vickers mg in the port fuselage, a Lewis mg in the rear cockpit and 500lb/227kg of bombs underwing. Built by Hawker, Armstrong-Whitworth and Vickers.
In service 1930 with 33 Sqn, used by 21 bomber sqns (12, 15, 18, 33, 40, 45, 57, 142, 218, 500, 501, 503, 600, 601, 602, 603, 604, 605, 609, 610, 611) until 1938, 503 Sqn; also used by two comms. sqns (173, 510), one met. flt, 3xAAS, 1xAGS (India), 1xAOS, ATA TFP, ATA EFTS, ATA IFTS, ATA.S, 1xAACU, 3xATC, 1xATS, 2xCDTFlts, 1xCArtCo-opFlt, 1xEFTS, 28xERFTS, 13xFTS, RAFC, GDGS, SoNCo-op, 5xOTU, SoP, RDFS, 1xRS, 14xRAF and 1xFAA comms. units, and 3xmisc. units, until 1940.
Based overseas in Egypt, Palestine, Jordan, Aden, Malaya, Singapore, North Africa, Middle East and Far East.
Powered by one 480hp RR Kestrel Ib or 545hp Kestrel X in-line.
Serials: J9934–9947 (14), K1416–1447 (32), K2424–2475 (49), K2966–3054 (89), K3808–3904 (97), K3955–3972 (18), K4437–4495 (59).
Total 358; 56 accidental losses.

Hawker Horsley III, S1452.
(Air-Britain Archives)

Hawker Hart (India),
K2123, 27 Sqn.
(G. Stuart Leslie)

192a. Hart (C)

A communications variant, having a revised rear cockpit with headrest and the armament deleted.
In service 1934–40 with 24 Sqn.
Serials: K4297–98 (2).
Total 2; no losses.

192b. Hart (India)

A general-purpose version, as the Mk I but with detail and equipment changes for service in India.
In service 1931 with 39 Sqn, used by four sqns (5, 11, 27, 39) until 1941, 5 Sqn, 1xFTS (India) and
1xcomms. unit until 1943.
Action: India and Far East, not operational in the UK.
Powered by one 695hp Kestrel V.
Serials: K2083–2132 (50), K3921–22 (2), K8627–8631 (5).
Total 57; 32 accidental losses.

192c. Hart (Special)

As the Mk I bomber but was a general-purpose type with tropical radiator, heavy-duty tyres, brakes and
desert equipment. Built by Gloster.
In service 1935 with 6 Sqn, used by two sqns (6, 237) until 1940, 237 Sqn.
Based overseas in Egypt and Palestine, action East Africa; not operational in the UK apart from training.
Powered by one 520hp Kestrel X (derated).
Serials: K1999–2000 (2), K3128–3144 (18), K4365–4379 (16), K4407–4436 (30).
Total 66; 22 accidental losses.
All Marks: Span: 37ft 3in/11.36m   Length: 29ft 4in/8.94m   Ceiling: 21,300ft/6,390m   Range: 470
miles/757km   Speed: 184mph/296kmph.
Total Hart bombers and GPs 483; in service 1930–41; 290 (23%) losses; nicknamed 'Eavenly 'Arp.

Fighters and Trainers see Vol. 1

193. Hardy I

A general-purpose development of the Hart, with a message hook, long exhausts, tropical equipment
and heavy-duty tyres as required, for Middle East service; two crew and armed with a Vickers in the port
fuselage side, a Lewis in the rear cockpit and 250lb/113kg of bombs underwing.
In service 1935 with 30 Sqn, used by three sqns (6, 30, 237) and one comms. sqn (173) until 1941, 237
Sqn; also served with 1xOTU, PT&RPl, TU&ReservePl and 2xcomms. units until 1943.
Based overseas in Palestine, Iraq and North Africa, action East Africa; not operational in the UK.
Powered by one 480hp RR Kestrel Ib or 545hp Kestrel X in-line.
Serials: K4050–4070 (21), K4306–4321 (16), K5914–5923 (10).
Span: 37ft 3in/11.36m   Length: 29ft 7in/9.02m   Ceiling: 17,000ft/5,100m   Endurance: 3hrs   Speed:
161mph/259kmph.
Total 47; 14 (40%) losses inc. 6 hostile.

194. Hind I

A light bomber used in large numbers to prepare the 'expansion sqns' for their monoplane types; it had a
cut-away gunner's cockpit, stub exhausts and a tail wheel. A two-seater armed with a Vickers in the port
fuselage side, a Lewis in the rear cockpit and 500lb/227kg of bombs underwing.
In service 1935 with 21 Sqn, used by 44 sqns (12, 15, 18, 21, 34, 40, 44, 49, 50, 52, 57, 62, 63, 82, 83, 88, 90,
98, 103, 104, 106, 107, 108, 110, 113, 114, 139, 142, 185, 211, 500, 501, 502, 503, 504, 602, 603, 605, 609, 610,
611, 613, 614, 616) until 1940, 613 Sqn; also served with 1xcomms sqn (267), 1xPAFU, 3xAAS, 2xAOS,
ATA EFTS, 1xATC, 1xATS, 1xB&GS, SoACo-op, CLE, 3xEFTS, 43xERFTS, 1xFIS, 8xFTS, 1xGIS,
GPEU, 4xGTS (as tug), 3xOTU, PT&RPl. Practice FU, RAFC, 2xUASqns, TU&Reserve Pl, 7xcomms.
units and 4xmisc. units, until 1942.
Based overseas in Egypt, Palestine, Middle East, and North and East Africa.

Hawker Hind I, K6741, 50 Sqn. (50 Sqn)

Powered by one 695hp RR Kestrel V in-line.
Serials: K4636–4655 (20), K5368–5560 (193), K6613–6856 (244), L7174–7233 (50).
Span: 37ft 3in/11.36m   Length: 29ft 7in/9.02m   Ceiling: 26,400ft/7,920m   Range: 430
miles/692km   Speed: 186mph/299kmph.
Total 507; 188 (38%) losses inc. 10 hostile.

Hind Trainer see Vol. 1.

HAWKER BEECHCRAFT (USA)
Formed from the Raytheon Aircraft Company in 2007 and builds a wide range of executive and trainer aircraft.

195. King Air 350ER (T1?)
The FAA has ordered four of these twin-engined executive types to train its Observers. It will be
equipped with Telephonics RDR1700 radar in a radome under the centre section and carry a crew of
5/6. It is somewhat larger than the King Air 200 pilot trainer (see Vol. 1) and may well be ordered for the
RAF to replace its venearble H-S Dominies (qv).
Due in service 2011 with 750 Sqn.
Powered by two 1,050shp P&W PT6A-60A turboprops.
Serials: ZZ500–503 (4).
Span: 58ft 8in/17.65m   Length: 47ft 4in/14.22m   Ceiling: 35,560ft/10,668m   Range: 2,050
miles/3,280km   Speed: 364mph/583kmph.
Total 4.

HAWKER-SIDDELEY AVIATION (Kingston, Surrey, UK)
Formed by the merger of Armstrong-Whitworth, Avro, Blackburn, de Havilland, Folland, Gloster and
Hawker in 1963 as the Government tried to rationalise an aircraft industry in which too many firms
were chasing too few orders; most of its designs were already on the drawing boards or flying as prototypes with these companies. In 1977 the Government nationalised the again too large industry and HSA
merged with the British Aircraft Corporation (qv) to become the State-owned British Aerospace (qv).
Supplied 629 examples of nine types (Gnat, Kestrel, Harrier and Hawk, see Vol. 1).

196. Argosy C 1
An Armstrong-Whitworth design taken over at the merger, this was a tactical transport for the RAF, the
first with a straight-in rear loading ramp, covered by clamshell doors; it had four crew and carried 69
passengers or 29,000lb/13,165kg of freight.
In service 1961 with the Argosy CU, 1962 with 114 Sqn, used by five sqns (70, 105, 114, 215, 267) until
1975, 70 Sqn; also served with 1xParaTS, AE&AEngS, 1xOCU, Argosy CU and 1xmisc. unit.

148. HS Argosy C 1,
XP438, 267 Sqn.
(Charles Parker)

Action: Borneo, based overseas in Cyprus, Aden, the Gulf and Singapore.
Powered by four 2,680shp RR Dart 101 turboprops.
Serials: XN814–858 (20), XP408–450 (20), XR105–143 (16).
Total 56; 3 accidental losses.

196a. Argosy E 1
When retired as a transport some Argosies were used for radar and radio calibration by the RAF, with
eight crew and appropriate equipment in the hold.
In service 1968 to 1978 with 115 Sqn.
10 conversions of the C 1. No losses.
All Marks: Span: 115ft/35.05m   Length: 89ft 2in/27.18m   Ceiling: 25,000ft/7,500m   Range: 1,070
miles/1,723km   Speed: 268mph/431kmph.
**Total Argosies 56; in service 1961–78; 3 (5%) losses; nicknamed Whistling Wheelbarrow,
Screaming Nipple, Whistling Tit.**

197. Andover C 1
Based on the Avro 748 airliner but heavily modified in its C 1 form, this was a smallish tactical transport
designed for rough-field operations, with three crew and able to carry 44 passengers or 14,750lb/6,690kg of
freight, loaded via a rear ramp. Its main undercarriage could 'kneel' to give differing loading ramp heights.
In service 1966 with the Andover TS and 46 Sqn, used by five sqns (32, 46, 52, 60, 84) until 1994, 32 Sqn;
also served with Andover TSqn, 1xOCU, 1xcomms. unit and 2xmisc. units.
Based overseas in Germany, Aden, the Gulf and Singapore.
Powered by two 3,245 shp RR Dart 201 turboprops.
Serials: XS594–647 (31).
Total 31; 2 accidental losses.

197a. Andover C 1 (PR)
A photo-reconnaissance conversion, with one camera and its port in the fuselage and the freight door deleted.
In service 1990–94 with 60 Sqn, then transferred to QinetiQ.
Based overseas in Germany, not operational in the UK.
Two conversions of the C 1; no losses.

197b. Andover CC 2
A VIP and passenger transport, as the airliner, so did not have the various modifications of the C 1; it had
six crew and 29–44 passengers.
In service 1964 with the Queen's Flt, used by three sqns (21, 32, 60) and 4xcomms. units to 1995, 32 Sqn.
Based overseas in Germany, Norway, Aden, the Gulf and Singapore.
Powered by two 2,105 shp Dart 531s.
Serials: XS789–794 (6).
Total 6; 1 accidental loss.

197c. Andover CC 2A

As the C 2 but with detail changes.
In service with 32 Sqn until 1995.
One conversion of the CC 2.

197d. Andover E 3

A modified C 1 for radio and radar calibration, with internal modifications and appropriate equipment, a searchlight on the port side of the nose and five to six crew.
In service 1976 to 1993 with 115 Sqn.
Eight conversions of the C 1; no losses.

197e. Andover E 3A

As the E 3 but with internal modifications, also used as a transport.
In service 1981 to 1993 with 115 Sqn.
Three conversions of the E 3. No losses.

	Span	Length	Ceiling	Range	Speed
C 1	98ft 3in/29.95m	77ft 11in/23.73m	23,800ft/7,140m	704 miles/1,133km	302mph/486kmph
CC 2	"	67ft/20.42m	24,500ft/7,350m	965 miles/1,554km	312mph/502kmph

Total Andovers 37; in service 1964–95; 3 (8%) losses.

198. Dominie T 1

A navigation and non-pilot aircrew trainer for the RAF, with six crew, and based on the DH 125 business jet; 11 were given a new interior fit of Tornado-style work stations during the '90s but without a change in designation. Originally had Ekco E190 radar in a nose radome, replaced during the refit by Supersearcher radar in a longer nose radome.
In service 1965 with 1 ANS, used by 1xANS, 2xFTS, CAW and RAFC until the present, 2010.
Powered by two 3,120lb st BS Viper 300 or 3,310lb st Viper 520 jets.
Serials: XS709–739 (20).
Total 20; no losses to date.

198a. 125 CC 1

A straight purchase of the HS 125 business jet for VIP transport, with three crew and six passengers.
In service 1971–94 with 32 Sqn.
Powered by two 3,000lb st Viper 301 jets later replaced by 3,700lb st Garrett-Airresearch TFE 731 turbofans in larger pods.
Serials: XW788–91 (4), XX505–06 (2).
Total 6; no losses.

HS Andover C 1, 60 Sqn.
(Author's Collection)

HS Andover
CC 2, 32 Sqn.
(Author's
Collection)

HS Dominie
T 1, XS728,
55 R Sqn.
(Author's
Collection)

198b. 125 CC 2

As the above but able to carry eight passengers in a longer fuselage, with extra cabin windows; it would have been used for aero-medical duties in wartime.

In service 1973–98 with 32 Sqn.

Powered by two 3,750lb st Viper 601 jets later replaced by 3,700lb st TFE 731 turbofans, in larger pods.

Serials: XX507–08 (2).

Total 2; no losses.

198c. 125 CC 3

As the CC 2 but with turbofans from service entry and sometimes used for non-VIP work.

In service 1983 to the present, 2010, with 32 Sqn.

Action: Iraq and Afghanistan.

Powered by two 4,300lb st TFE 731-5r-1h turbofans.

Serials: ZD620–21 (2), ZD703–04 (2), ZE395–96 (2).

Total 6; no losses to date.

HS 125 CC
3, ZE396, 32
Sqn. (Author's
Collection)

	Span	Length	Ceiling	Range	Speed
Dominie	47ft/14.33m	47ft 5in or 48ft 11in /14.46 or 14.91m	40,000ft/ 12,000m	1,338 miles/ 2,154km	472mph/ 760kmph
CC 1	"	47ft 6in /14.48m	30,000 or 41,000ft/ 9,000 or 12,300m	1000 or 2000 miles/ 1,610 or 3,220km	470mph/ 757kmph
CC 2	"	50ft 6in/ 15.39m	40,000ft/ 12,000m	1,100 or 2000 miles/ 1,771 or 3,220km	518mph/ 834kmph
CC 3	"	50ft 8in/ 15.44m	41,000ft/ 12,300m	2,785 miles/ 4,484km	495mph/ 797kmph

Total Dominies and 125s 34; in service 1965–present 2010; no losses to date.

199. Nimrod MR 1

A maritime-reconnaissance type to replace the Shackleton, over which it was a quantum leap; it was derived from the Comet airliner, had a crew of 11 and was armed with 12,000lb/5,448kg of stores internally (including nuclear DC) plus two Martel, AS 12, or Stingray ASMs on two wing pylons, and ASV-21 radar in a nose radome.

In service 1969 with 236 OCU, 1970 with 201 Sqn, used by five sqns (42, 120, 201, 203, 206), MOTU and 1xOCU until 1984, 42 Sqn.

Action: Falklands, also based overseas in Malta and Italy.

Powered by four 12,160lb st RR Spey 250 jets.

Serials: XV226–263 (38), XZ280–84 (5).

Total 43; 1 accidental loss.

199a. Nimrod MR 1A

As the MR 1 but late build aircraft manufactured to make conversion to the MR 2 easier.

In service 1970s–84 with Kinloss Wing.

6 in the MR 1 total.

199b. Nimrod R 1

An electronic-intelligence gatherer, as the MR 1 but with 24-29 crew and different avionics and equipment entailing the provision of more aerials, including an extended port wing pod and small radomes on the pods and tailcone; the MAD tailcone was deleted and there are fewer cabin windows.

In service 1971–83 with 51 Sqn, and again from 1994 to the present, 2010, but due out of service in 2011.

Action: Iraq and Afghanistan.

Serials: XW664–66 (3).

Total 3 plus 1 conversion of a MR 2; 1 accidental loss to date.

HS Nimrod R 1, 51 Sqn.
(Author's Collection)

HS Nimrod MR 2, XV226,
Kinloss Wing. (Author's
Collection)

199c. Nimrod R 1P

As a result of the Falklands war the R 1s were given a refuelling probe above the cockpit countered by tailplane finlets and a strake under the rear fuselage, plus ECM wingtip pods.

In service 1983–94 with 51 Sqn, then reverted to R 1 designation, whilst retaining the modifications.

Action: Falklands and the Gulf.

Three conversions of the R 1.

199d. Nimrod MR 2

A development of the MR 1, with 13 crew, Searchwater radar, improved avionics and carrying 12,000lb/5,448kg of stores (including nuclear DC) internally plus two Harpoon or Sea Eagle ASMs on two wing pylons. Externally, there is a retractable air intake on top of the port rear fuselage. In later service (2000+) some aircraft were provided with extra surveillance equipment for anti-insurgent operations, including a flir turret under the starboard wing. The type was castigated by a Coroner during 2008 after a fatal crash in Afghanistan but its safety record is no worse than other types. It was prematurely retired in 2010.

In service 1979 with 236 OCU, 1980 with 206 Sqn, used by four sqns, (42, 120, 201, 206), 1xOCU and 1xRSqn until 1982, and again from 1994 to 2010, with three sqns (120, 201, 206) and 1xRSqn.

Action: Falklands, Iraq and Afghanistan.

Serials: XZ285–87 (3).

Total 3 plus 34 conversions of the MR 1, making a total of 37; 3 accidental losses.

199e. Nimrod MR 2P

Like the R 1P, the MR 2 was modified as a result of the Falklands war, with a refuelling probe over the cockpit, countered by tailplane finlets and a strake beneath the rear fuselage; it could carry four Sidewinder AAMs on the wing pylons.

In service 1982–94 with the Kinloss Wing, then reverted to MR 2 designation, retaining all the modifications.

Thirt-two conversions of the MR 2; no losses.

199f. Nimrod MRA 4

This is a heavily modified Nimrod, so much so that, although conversions, the aircraft have new serials; it will carry a crew of 10, Searchwater 2000 radar, six Harpoon, nine Stingray ASMs, four Sidewinder or ASRAAM AAMs on four wing pylons or internally, also ALARM, Maverick or Stormshadow AGMs. It has a 'glass' cockpit, FLIR turret under the nose, new wings, taller, lesser chord tailplane finlets, an air intake in the fin leading edge replacing the fuselage top retractable, a blister on the forward port-side fuselage, a centrally mounted FR probe and the wingtip pods have aerials on their topside. Unfortunately, the conversions have not proceeded smoothly and the MRA 4 is much delayed, hopefully entering service during 2011.

Powered by four 11,995lb st BMW-RR BR710-101 fanjets.

Serials: ZJ514–531 (9).

Total 9 conversions of the MR 2.

	Span	Length	Ceiling	Range	Speed
MR 1	114ft 10in /35m	126ft 9in/ 38.63m	42,800ft/ 12,750m	5,755 miles/ 9,266km	575mph/ 926kmph
R 1	"	117ft 11in/35.94m	"	"	"
R 1P	"	120ft 1in/36.61m	"	"	
MR 2	"	126ft 9in/38.63m	"	"	"
MR 2P	"	129ft 1in/39.35m	"	"	"
MRA 4	127ft/ 38.71m	126ft 7in/ 38.58m	42,000ft/ 12,600m	6,000 miles/ 9,660km	600mph/ 966kmph

Total Nimrods 49; in service 1969–to the present, 2010; 5 (10%) losses to date; nicknamed Nimjob, Happy Hunter.

HEINKEL (Germany)

A feared name in Second World War Britain, the company formed in 1935 and remained independent until 1964; it supplied four examples of one type.

200. 115A-2

These large shoulder-wing monoplane seaplanes, with two floats, were acquired via the Royal Norwegian Navy and were used for clandestine operations and training; it had four crew and some were armed with eight Browning mg in the wings (four backward firing), and two in the dorsal position.

In service 1941 at Calshot, until 1942, Wig Bay.

Action: northern Europe and Mediterranean.

Powered by two 900hp BMW-132n radials.

Serials: BV184–87 (4).

Span: 75ft 10in/23.11m   Length: 57ft/17.37m   Ceiling: 17,000ft/5,100m   Range: 1,305 miles/2,101km   Speed: 196mph/316kmph.

Total 4; 2 (50%) losses inc. 1 hostile.

HS Nimrod
MRA 4, XJ518.
(Charles Parker)

HESTON (Heston, Middlesex, UK)

Formed in 1934 from the Comper Company, went out of business 1948. Supplied three examples of one type.

201. Pheonix

This was an advanced high-wing cabin monoplane, carrying the pilot and four passengers, impressed for communications work with the RAF. The wings were braced by reverse V-style struts and the undercarriage retracted into small sponsons on the fuselage sides; it had a pointed fin and rudder.
In service 1940 with 24 Sqn, used by one sqn, 1xFTU and 1xmisc. unit until 1945, Abingdon SFlt.
Powered by one 205hp DH Gipsy Six II in-line.
Serials: X2891, X9338, X9393.
Span: 40ft 4in/12.29m   Length: 30ft 2in/9.19m   Ceiling: 15,500ft/4,650m   Range: 500 miles/805km   Speed: 150mph/241kmph.
Total 3 impressed; no losses.

HILLS & SON (Manchester, Lancs, UK)

Assembled Percival Proctor.

HINDUSTAN (India)

Assembled Harlow PC 5.

HUNTING (Luton, Beds, UK)

A short-lived manufacturer of aircraft, taking over Percival (qv) in 1954 to become Hunting-Percival and then Hunting three years later, in 1957. Hunting Aircraft Ltd then became part of the British Aircraft Corporation in 1965 as part of the Government's rationalization. It supplied 559 examples of two types (Jet Provost, see Vol. 1).

202. Pembroke C 1

The RAF's version of the Prince airliner, used as a light transport with two crew and eight passengers.
In service 1954 with Aden Protectorate Comms Flt, used by 9 sqns (21, 32, 60, 78, 84, 152, 207, 209, 267), 27xcomms. units and 1xmisc. unit, until 1990, 60 Sqn.
Based overseas in Germany, Malta, Cyprus, Egypt, Iraq, Aden, the Gulf and Singapore.
Powered by two 560hp Alvis Leonides 503/127 radials.
Serials: WV699–753 (36), XK859–885 (6), XL929–954 (5).
Total 47 plus 5 conversions of the C (PR) 1, making a total of 52; 10 accidental losses.

Hunting Pembroke C 1, WV741, Aden Protectorate Support Flt. (Author's Collection)

202a. Pembroke C (PR) 1

A transport as the C 1 but could also be used for photo-reconnaissance, with a camera in a glazed nose.
In service 1956 with 81 Sqn, used by two sqns (60, 81) until 1990, 60 Sqn, having been converted back to
C 1 standard.
Based overseas in Germany, the Gulf and Singapore.
Serials: WV754–55 (2), XF796 (4), XL955–56 (2).
Total 8; no losses.
Span: 64ft 6in/19.65m　Length: 46ft/14.02m　Ceiling: 22,000ft/6,600m　Range: 1,150 miles/
1,851 km　Speed: 224mph/361kmph.
Total Pembrokes 55; in service 1954–90; 10 (18%) losses.

KOOLHOVEN (Holland)

A well-known First World War designer, employed by Armstrong-Whitworth, who returned to Holland
and established his own company from 1934 to 1940. Supplied one example of one type.

203. FK 43

A high-wing cabin monoplane for communications taken over from Dutch army, carrying the pilot and
three passengers. The fixed undercarriage was strutted to the wing and it had a single fin/rudder.
In service 1942 with Martlesham Heath SFlt, used by one sqn and four comms. units until 1945, 510 Sqn.
Powered by one 115hp Cirrus Hermes III in-line.
Serial: MX459 but flew as FK-43.
Span: 35ft/10.67m　Length: 26ft/7.92m　Ceiling: n/k　Range: n/k　Speed: 108mph/174kmph.
Total 1; no losses.

LOCKHEED (USA)

One of the best known American companies, established 1926 and becoming Lockheed-Martin in 1995.
Supplied 2,507 examples of 10 types (Lightning, see Vol. 1).

204. Model 14 Super Electra

A low-wing twin-finned monoplane transport for the RAF, with three crew and 11 passengers.
In service 1940 with 267 Sqn, used by two sqns (117, 267) and 1xcomms. unit until 1945.
Action: North Africa and Middle East, not operational in the UK.
Powered by two 820hp Wright Cyclone GR1820-G3b radials.
Serials: AX681–82 (2) plus 2 impressed – HK982 (renumbered VF247), HK984 (renumbered VF251).
Total 2 plus 2 impressed – making a total of 4; 2 accidental losses.

204a. Hudson I

A general-reconnaissance type for the RAF, derived from the Super Electra airliner above, and much
needed at the beginning of the Second World War. It had a crew of four or five and was armed with two
fixed Browning mg above the nose, two in a BP-C dorsal turret, and carried 1,400lb/635kg of bombs
internally; later, some had ASV-I or II radar with external aerials.
In service 1939 with 224 Sqn, used by six sqns (206, 212, 224, 233, 269, 320), two transport sqns (24, 267)
and one SD sqn (161), until 1942, 320 and 233 Sqns; also served with 1xAAS, CGS, ECFS, 3xFTU, 5xOTU,
2xRS, ATA AFS, CC Landplane Pilot's S., 1xAACU, 6xcomms. units and 3xmisc. units, until 1945.
Action: North Atlantic and northern Europe.
Powered by two 1,100hp Wright Cyclone GR1820-G102a radials.
Serials: N7206–7404 (181), P5116–5165 (50), R4059, T9266–365 (100).
Total 332; 127 accidental and 64 hostile losses.

204b. Hudson I (PR)

A photo-reconnaissance version of the Mk I carrying one vertical camera in the fuselage.
In service during 1940 with the PDU. Action: northern Europe.
Total 3 conversions of the Mk I.

Lockheed Hudson I, 233
Sqn. (Author's Collection)

204c. Hudson II

As the Mk I but with a strengthened airframe, flush rivets and Hamilton-Standard constant-speed propellers.
In service 1941 with 320 Sqn, used by two sqns (206, 320), one transport sqn (24), one PR flt, 2xOTU
and 3xcomms. units to 1942, 206 Sqn.
Action: North Atlantic and Far East.
Serials: T9366–385 (17).
Total 17; 9 accidental and 4 hostile losses.

204d. Hudson III (LR)

As the Mk I but with ASV-II as standard and increased fuel; it could carry the Airborne Lifeboat Mk I
under the bomb bay for ASR.
In service 1940 with 220 Sqn, used by 15 sqns (48, 59, 139, 200, 203, 206, 220, 224, 233, 269, 320, 353, 407,
459, 608), one ASR sqn (278), one SD sqn (357), four met. sqns (251, 519, 520, 521), two transport sqns
(62, 267) and four cal. sqns (285, 287, 288, 289), until 1945, 269 Sqn; also served with AFTU, ALS (India),
1xANS, 4xFTU, ME C&CU, 1xMETS, 4xOTU, 2xPTS, 1xBATFlt, 11xcomms. units and 6xmisc. units.
Action: North and South Atlantic, northern Europe, Mediterranean and Indian Ocean, also based overseas in West Africa, Far East, North America and India.
Powered by two 1,200hp Cyclone GR1820-G205a, with larger intakes over the cowlings.
Serials: V9066–9254 (129), AE485–608 (124), AM931–953 (23).
Total 276 (1 FAA); 175 accidental and 62 hostile losses.

204e. Hudson III (SR)

As the Mk III (LR), but carried less fuel.
In service 1940 with 269 Sqn, used by 12 sqns (48, 53, 59, 203, 224, 233, 269, 320, 353, 459, 500, 608), one
ASR sqn (279), one SD sqn (161), four met. sqns (251, 519, 520, 521), three met. flts, one transport sqn
(24), 4xOTU, 1xMETS, 3xFTU, ATA and 1xcomms. unit until 1946, 1407 Flt.
Action: as the Mk III (LR)
Serials: T9386–9468 (78), V8975–9065 (68).
Total 146; 71 accidental and 14 hostile losses.

204f. Hudson IIIA (A-29)

As the Mk III (LR) but was Lend-lease with US equipment.
In service 1942 with 200 Sqn, used by five sqns (200, 217, 233, 269, 608), two transport sqns (163, 231),
one SD sqn (161), one SD flt, and two met. sqns (519, 521), until 1945, 251 Sqn; also served with 1xCU,
CNS, 3xFTU, ME C&CU, 2xMETS, 4xOTU, 18xcomms. units and 11xmisc. units, until 1946.

Action: South Atlantic, Mediterranean, Indian Ocean, northern Europe and North Africa, also based overseas in southern Europe, Middle East, Far East, North America, Canada and Iraq.
Powered by two 1,200hp Cyclone GR1820-27.
Serials: FH167–466 (223), FK731–813 (79).
Total 302; 150 accidental and 20 hostile losses.

204g. Hudson IV

As the Mk IIIA but not Lend-lease and with different engines.
In service 1941 with 200 Sqn, used by two sqns (200, 206), three transport sqns (24, 117, 267) and one met. flt until 1942, 200 Sqn; also served with SoAN, and 10xRAF and 2xFAA comms. units.
Action: North and South Atlantic and western Indian Ocean, also based overseas in the Middle East and West Africa.
Powered by two 1,050hp P&W Twin Wasp R1830-53c4g radials.
Serials: AE609–638 (30).
Total 30 (2 FAA); 8 accidental and 5 hostile losses.

204h. Hudson V (SR)

As the Mk IV but armed with two fixed Brownings above the nose, two in a BP-C dorsal turret and one in a ventral position; some had ASV-III with external aerials.
In service 1941 with 224 Sqn, used by 10 sqns, (48, 53, 59, 206, 224, 233, 320, 407, 500, 608), one ASR sqn (279), one SD sqn (161), two transport sqns (24, 271) and one met flt until 1944, 608 Sqn; also served with SoAN, CNS, ME C&CU, 4xOTU, 2xFTU, 1xFIS, 2xRAF and 1xFAA comms. units, and 1xmisc. unit, until 1945.
Action: North Atlantic, Indian Ocean, northern Europe, BWI and North America, also served overseas in Egypt.
Powered by two 1,200hp Twin Wasp R1830-S3c4g with cooling gills.
Serials: AM520–702 (183).
Total 183 (1 FAA); 72 accidental and 53 hostile losses.

204j. Hudson V (LR)

As the Mk V (SR) but carried more fuel.
In service 1942 with 233 Sqn, used by 11 sqns (48, 53, 59, 206, 220, 224, 233, 269, 407, 500, 608), two transport sqns (24, 271), one ASR sqn (279), and one SD flt until 1944, 608 Sqn; also served with other units, as above, until 1945.
Action: North and South Atlantic, northern Europe and Mediterranean.
Serials: AE639–657 (19), AM703-909 (207).
Total 226; 74 accidental and 52 hostile losses.

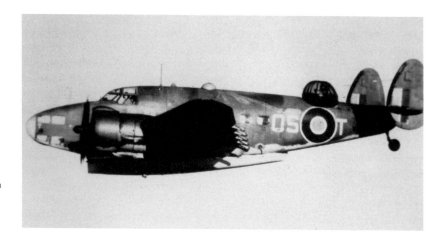

Lockheed Hudson
III carrying a
lifeboat, 279 Sqn.
(Scott Collection)

204k. Hudson VI (A-28A)

The ultimate GR Hudson, with armament as the Mk I (no ventral position), 1,000lb/454kg of bombs/ depth charges internally or a Mk I lifeboat beneath the bomb bay, and ASV-II with external aerials; it was Lend-lease with US equipment.

In service 1942 with 220 Sqn, used by 12 sqns (8, 48, 59, 62, 200, 217, 220, 320, 353, 459, 500, 608), two met. sqns (520, 521) and one ASR sqn (279), until 1945, 520 Sqn; also served with ALS (India), 1xCU, 2xFTU, 1xFIS, ME C&CU, 1xMETS, 3xOTU and 3xmisc. units.

Action: North and South Atlantic, Mediterranean and Indian Ocean, also based overseas in the Middle East, Far East and North America.

Powered by two 1,200hp Twin Wasp R1830-67 with long intakes over cowlings and nacelles.

Serials: EW875–972 (86), FK381–730 (225).

Total 311; 46 accidental and 13 hostile losses.

204l. Hudson C VI

A dedicated transport version of the Mk VI with armament deleted and the dorsal turret removed; able to carry four crew and 14 passengers or freight. In service 1942 with 117 Sqn, used by seven sqns (24, 117, 163, 194, 216, 231, 267) until 1945, 231 Sqn; also served with 1xParaTS, 11xcomms. units and 6xmisc. units, until 1946.

Action: North and East Africa and Far East, also based overseas in North America.

135 (approx.) conversions of the MK VI. Losses included with the Mk VI.

	Span	Length	Ceiling	Range	Speed
Super Electra	65ft 6in /19.96m	44ft 2in/ 13.46m	24,000ft/ 7,200m	1,705 miles/ 2,745m	257mph/ 414kmph
Mk I	"	44ft 4in/ 13.51m	25,000ft/ 7,500m	1,960 miles/ 3,157km	246mph/ 396kmph
Mk III (LR)	"	"	24,500ft/ 7,350m	2,800 miles/ 4,508km	255mph/ 411kmph
Mk III (SR)	"	"	"	2,160 miles/3,478km	"
Mk IIIA	"	"	26,500ft/7,950m	2,800 miles/4,508km	253mph/407kmph
Mk IV	"	"	27,000ft/8,100m	2,160 miles/3,478km	240mph/386kmph
Mk V (SR)	"	"	"	"	284mph/457kmph
Mk V (LR)	"	"	"	2,800 miles/4,508km	"

Total Hudsons 1,827 plus 2 impressed making a total of 1,829; in service 1939–46; 1,021 (56%) losses inc. 287 hostile.

205. Model 12A Electra Junior

A low-wing, twin-finned monoplane transport for the RAF with two crew and six passengers.

In service 1939 with AHQ India, used by one sqn (24), 8xcomms. units and 2xmisc. units, until 1945, MCommsSqn. X9316 was a photo-reconnaissance version with three vertical cameras and their ports in the fuselage, which entered service in 1939 with the Air Ministry Independent Flt, and was used by two flts. Based overseas in the Far East.

Powered by two 450hp P&W Wasp Junior 5b radials.

Serials: LA619–23 (5) plus 10 impressed – V4732, X9316, AX803, HM573, HX793, HX798, LV760–62 (3), NF753.

Span: 49ft 6in/15.09m   Length: 36ft 4in/11.08m   Ceiling: 22,300ft/6,690m   Range: 824 miles/1,327km   Speed: 225mph/362kmph.

Total 5 plus 10 impressed making a total of 15; 4 accidental losses (21%).

206. Model 18

A light transport for the RAF, carrying two crew and 14 passengers.

In service 1940 with 267 Sqn, used by three sqns (117, 173, 267), ME C&CU and 3xmisc. units until 1948, Iraq Comms Flt.

Lockheed Electra Junior,
F-AZLL, preserved
French example.
(Author's Collection)

Lockheed Lodestar II,
EW987, Middle East
Comms. Sqn.
(Air-Britain Archives)

Based overseas in North Africa, Middle East, Far East and Iraq.
Powered by two 1,200hp P&W Twin Wasp SC-3g radials.
Serials: AX685–87 (3), AX722–23 (2).
Total 5; 1 accidental loss.

206a. Lodestar IA (C-59)

A militarised version of the Model 18, used as a transport by the RAF.
In service 1942–1943 with 267 Sqn.
Based overseas in the Middle East, not in UK.
Powered by two 750hp P&W Hornet R1690-25 radials.
Serials: EW976–82 (6), HK852, HK855.
Total 8; 1 accidental loss.

206b. Lodestar II (C-60)

As the Mk IA but re-engined.
In service 1942 with 267 Sqn, used by three sqns (117, 173, 267), 1xCU and 5xcomms. units until 1947,
ME CommsSqn.
Based overseas in Middle East, East Africa, Far East and Egypt.
Powered by two 1,200hp Wright Cyclone R1820-87 radials.
Serials: EW983–997 (15), HK851, HK973, HK980–81 (2), HK990, RR997–98 (2)(renumbered).
Total 22; 2 accidental losses.

	Span	Length	Ceiling	Range	Speed
Model 18	65ft 6in/	49ft 10in/	20,000ft/	1,890 miles/	270mph/
	19.96m	15.19m	6,000m	3,043km	435kmph
Mk IA	"	"	20,400ft/	1,800 miles/	218mph/
			6,120m	2,898km	351kmph
Mk II	"	"	26,000ft/	1,890 miles/	253mph/
			7,800m	3,043km	407kmph

Total 18/Lodestars 35; in service 1940–48; 5 (14%) losses.

207. Model 10 Electra

A light low-wing twin-finned monoplane transport for the RAF, carrying two crew and six passengers.
In service 1941 with Takoradi SFlt, used by three sqns (24, 173, 267), one PR sqn (680), one PR flt and
6xcomms. units until 1944, Takoradi SFlt.
Based overseas in North and West Africa and Far East.
Powered by two 450hp P&W Wasp Junior SB-2 radials.
Serials: AX766 plus 6 impressed – W9104–06 (3), AX699–701 (3).
Span: 55ft/16.46m   Length: 38ft 7in/11.76m   Ceiling: 19,400ft/5,820m   Range: 713 miles/
1,148 km   Speed: 192mph/309kmph.
Total 1 plus 6 impressed making a total of 7; 4 (57%) losses inc. 1 hostile.

208. Ventura I

A light bomber for the RAF to replace the Bristol Blenheim (qv), but which proved nearly as vulnerable; it had five crew and was armed with two fixed Browning mg above the nose, two 0.5in Brownings
in the nose position, two Brownings in the BP-C dorsal turret and two in the ventral position, plus
2,500lb/1,135kg of bombs internally. Many were transferred to the SAAF.
In service 1942 with 21 Sqn, used by two sqns, (21, 464), one met sqn (251), one transport sqn (299), and
one PR sqn (140), until 1943, 464 Sqn, also served with 1xOTU, 1xTTFlt, 1xCU, 1xcomms. unit and
3xmisc. units.
Action: northern Europe and North Atlantic, also based overseas in North America.
Powered by two 1,850hp P&W Double Wasp R2800-5184g radials.
Serials: AE660–845 (95).
Total 95; 30 accidental and 21 hostile losses.

208a. Ventura II (B-34)

As the Mk I but with an armament of two Brownings above the nose, two 0.5in in the nose position, two
or four Brownings in a BP-A dorsal turret, two in the ventral position, and able to carry 3,000lb/1,360kg
of bombs internally.

Lockheed Ventura I, AE748. (Air-Britain Archives)

In service 1942 with 487 Sqn, used by three sqns (21, 464, 487), two transport sqns (299, 624), and one SD flt until 1943, 21 Sqn; also served with ECFS, 1xFTU, 2xOTU, 1xcomms. unit and 7xmisc. units, until 1945. Action: northern Europe and North Africa, also based overseas in North America and Egypt.

Powered by two 2,000hp Double Wasp R2800-31.

Serials: AE846–957 (46), AJ163–537 (41).

Total 87; 21 accidental and 19 hostile losses.

208b. Ventura V (PV-1)

A general-reconnaissance version for the RAF, with a glazed or solid nose and an armament of two fixed 0.5in mg in the solid nose, two in a Martin 250CE dorsal turret and two in a ventral position, with six depth-charges carried internally in a bulged bomb bay, plus ASD-1 radar in a nose radome, if carried. Many to the SAAF.

In service 1943 with 13 Sqn, used by three sqns (13, 459, 500) until 1944, 459 Sqn; also served with two met. sqns (519, 521), one met. flt, 1xCU, ECFS, ME C&CU, 2xOTU, Staff Navigators S. and 8xcomms. units until 1946.

Action: North Atlantic and Mediterranean, also based overseas in North Africa, Middle East, North America and Egypt.

Serials: FN956–999 (30), FP537–884 (99), JS889–984 (83), JT800–898 (77).

Total 289; 65 accidental and 15 hostile losses.

	Span	Length	Ceiling	Range	Speed
Mk I	65ft 6in/19.96m	51ft 5in/15.67m	25,000ft/7,500m	925 miles/1,489km	312mph/502kmph
Mk II	"	"	24,000ft/7,200m	950 miles/1,529km	315mph/507kmph
Mk V	"	51ft 9in/15.77m	26,300ft/7,890m	1,360 miles/2,190km	322mph/518kmph

Total Venturas 471; in service 1942–46; 171 (36%) losses inc. 55 hostile; nicknamed Pig.

209. Neptune MR 1 (P2V-5)

Supplied to Coastal Command to bridge the gap between the retirement of the Lancaster GR and the arrival of the Shackleton, this was a maritime patrol type, with nine crew and armed with two 20mm cannon in an Emerson nose turret (reportedly some had 30mm), two 0.5in Brownings in a Martin dorsal turret and two 20mm in an Emerson tail turret; 8,000lb/3,672kg of stores were carried internally and it could carry 8xRP underwing, with the APS-20 radar in a large underbelly radome. The last 27 had a glazed nose instead of the turret and a MAD tailcone replacing the tail turret.

In service 1952 with 217 Sqn, used by four sqns (36, 203, 210, 217) and 1xOCU until 1957, 217 Sqn.

Powered by two 3,250hp Wright Turbo-Cyclone R3350-30w radials.

Serials: WX493–691 (52).

Total 52; 6 accidental losses.

Lockheed
Neptune MR 1,
WX547, 36 Sqn.
(Newark Air
Museum)

Lockheed Hercules C 1,
Lyneham Wing. (N. Horsley)

209a. Neptune MR 1 (MOD)

The RAF's first attempt at an airborne radar station, this had a modified radar compared to the above and some detail differences.

In service 1952 with Vanguard Flt, used by two flts until 1956, 1453 Flt.

Four conversions of the MR 1; no losses.

Span: 104ft/32m   Length: 78ft 3in/23.85m or 91ft 8in/27.94m with MAD cone   Ceiling: 26,000ft/7,800m   Range: 4,200 miles/6,762km   Speed: 353mph/568kmph.

Total Neptunes 52; in service 1952–57; 6 (12%) losses

210. Hercules C 1 (C-130H)

The world's most popular military transport ordered as a tactical 'lifter' for the RAF; it has five crew and carries 92 passengers or 46,000lb/20,885kg of freight, loaded through a tail ramp. Some fitted with wingtip ECM pods for Special Forces duties, until 2003. The C 1s are getting very tired and will probably be out of service in 2010.

In service 1967 with 242 OCU and 36 Sqn, used by six sqns (24, 30, 36, 47, 48, 70), 1xParaTS, 1xOCU and 1xRSqn until 1982, then 1994 to the present, 2010.

Action: Aden, Bosnia, Gulf, Iraq and Afghanistan, also based overseas in Cyprus and Singapore.

Powered by four 4,050shp Allison T56a-7a, or 4,910shp T56-a-15 turboprops.

Serials: XV176–223 (48), XV290–307 (18).

Total 66; 6 accidental and 1 hostile loss to date.

210a. Hercules C 1P

As a result of the Falklands war the Herc was hastily fitted with a refuelling probe over the starboard side of the cockpit and extra navigational aids; later, some had ECM pods under the wingtips for SD operations.

In service 1982–94 with Lyneham Wing, reverted to C 1 designation 1994, keeping the modifications.

Action: the Falklands, Gulf and Bosnia.

Twenty-five conversions of the C 1.

210b. Hercules C 1P (LR2)

As the C 1P but with two extra fuel tanks in the forward cargo hold for flights to the Falklands, reducing the normal load.

In service 1982–85 with Lyneham Wing, then converted back to C 1P.

Sixteen conversions of the C 1P; no losses.

210c. Hercules C1P (LR4).

As the above but with four tanks in the forward hold.

In service 1982–85 with Lyneham Wing, then converted to C 1 (K).

Four conversions of the C 1P; no losses.

210d. Hercules C 1 (K)

A transport, tanker, maritime patrol and SAR version, with six crew, an HDU in the rear cargo door and fuel tanks in the hold.

In service 1982 with Lyneham Wing, used by one flt and 1xOCU until 1996, 1312 Flt.

Based overseas in the Falklands.

Six conversions of the C 1P (LR4) and C 1P; no losses.

210e. Hercules C 3

As the C 1 but incorporating two fuselage plugs to make a longer cabin capable of carrying 128 passengers or 63,000lb/28,600kg of freight.

In service 1980 with Lyneham Wing, used by four sqns (24, 30, 47, 70) 1xPTS, and 1xRSqn until 1982, then again from 1994 to the present, 2010.

Action: Bosnia, Iraq and Afghanistan.

Powered by four 4,910shp T56-a-15.

Thirty conversions of the C 1; 1 accidental loss to date.

210f. Hercules C 3A

A Special Forces version of the C 3 with ECM blisters on the sides of the rear fuselage.

In service 2003 with LTW to the present, 2010.

Six conversions of the C 3.

210g. Hercules C 3P

Just like the C 1, the C 3 was modified with a refuelling probe and extra navigational equipment for flights to the Falklands.

In service 1982–94 with Lyneham Wing, then reverted to C 3 designation, keeping the modifications.

Action: Gulf.

Thirty conversions of the C 3.

210h. Hercules C 4 (C-130J)

An updated Hercules, as the C 3 but with a glass cockpit reducing the crew to three or four, improved avionics and a revised, neater refuelling probe on the port side of the cockpit roof; it also has defensive countermeasures and light armour for the cockpit. Rarely carries underwing fuel tanks. Software problems meant that it operated under restrictions for some years. During 2009 some were seen with ECM fuselage blisters. In service 2000 with 57 (R) Sqn, 2001 with 24 Sqn, used by three sqns (24, 30, 47) and 1xRSqn until the present, 2010.

Action: Iraq and Afghanistan.

Powered by four 4,591shp RR-Allison AE2100d3 turboprops driving six-bladed curved propellers.

Serials: ZH865–879 (15).

Total 15; no losses to date.

Lockheed Hercules C 4, Lyneham Wing. (Author's Collection)

210j. Hercules C 5

As the C 4 but a shorter fuselage version as with the C1.
In service 2001 with Lyneham Wing, used by two sqns (24, 30) and 1xRSqn until the present, 2010.
Action: Iraq and Afghanistan.
Serials: ZH880–889 (10).
Total 10; no losses to date.

	Span	Length	Ceiling	Range	Speed
C 1	132ft 7in/40.42m	98ft 9in/30.1m	30,000ft/9,000m	4,780 miles/7,696km	384mph/618kmph
C 1P	"	99ft 9in/30.41m	"	"	"
C 3	"	112ft 9in/39.37m	"	"	"
C 3P	"	113ft 9in/34.67m	"	"	"
C 4	"	"	"	3,418 miles/5,503km	410mph/660kmph
C 5	"	99ft 9in/30.41m	"	3,262 miles/5,252km	400mph/644kmph

Total Hercules 91; in service 1967–present; 8 (8%) losses inc. 1 hostile to date; nicknamed Herc, Herky Bird, Fat Albert.

211. TriStar

The RAF found, as a result of the Falklands war, that it urgently needed a long-range transport and tanker so the TriStar was selected; the first were unconverted ex-British Airways aircraft, with eight or nine crew and carrying 300 passengers.
In service 1983 with 241 OCU, 1984 with 216 Sqn, used by one sqn and 1xCU until 1985, 216 Sqn.
Powered by three 50,000lb st RR RB-211-524b turbofans.
Serials: ZD948–49 (2).
Total 2; no losses.

211a. TriStar K 1

These were converted to tanker and transport duties, with 187 passengers, a refuelling probe over the cockpit, two HDU pods under the rear fuselage, a CCTV pod, and air intakes in the front fuselage. Fuel load totals 128 tons/140 tonnes.
In service 1986 to the present, 2010, with 216 Sqn.
Action: Gulf, Iraq and Afghanistan.
Serials: ZD951.
Total 1 plus 1 conversion of the above, making a total of 2; no losses to date.

Opposite: Lockheed Hercules C 5, Lyneham Wing. (Author's Collection)

Lockheed TriStar KC 1, ZD952, 216 Sqn. (Author's Collection)

211b. TriStar KC 1

As the K 1 but able to carry 187 passengers or 95,000lb/43,130kg of freight on a strengthened floor, loaded through a large freight door in the forward port fuselage. The FR probe is deleted.
In service 1985 to the present, 2010, with 216 Sqn.
Serials: ZD950, ZD952–53 (2).
Total 3 plus 1 conversion of the airliner TriStar, making a total of 4; no losses to date.

211c. TriStar C 2

These were ex-Pan American aircraft and thus slightly different, and are used as transports only, with 14 crew and 266 passengers; they have no freight door or FR probe and the fuel is reduced.
In service 1985 to the present, 2010, with 216 Sqn.
Serials: ZE704–05 (2).
Total 2; no losses.

211d. TriStar C 2A

As the C 2 but with updated avionics, a stronger undercarriage, and increased auw.
In service 1993 to the present, 2010, with 216 Sqn.
Serial: ZE706.
Total 1; no losses.
All Marks: Span: 164ft 4in/50.09m   Length: 164ft 2in/50.04m   Ceiling: 43,000ft/12,900m   Range: 7,013 miles/11,291km   Speed: 605mph/974kmph.
Total TriStars 9; in service 1983–present 2010; no losses to date.

LOIRE (France)

Formed 1925, merged into SNCAN 1936. Supplied one example of one type.

212. 130

A high-wing monoplane flying boat with its engine mounted above the fuselage, used by the Free-French for communications, with three or four crew and armed with a mg in the nose and dorsal positions and able to carry 330lb/150kg of bombs underwing.
In service 1940–1941 with 2 F-F Flt.
Based overseas in North Africa, not operational in the UK.
Powered by one 720hp Hispano-Suiza 12 in-line pusher.
Serial: AX694.
Span: 52ft 6in/16m   Length: 37ft 1in/11.31m   Ceiling: 19,600ft/5,880m   Endurance: 5hrs   Speed: 140mph/225kmph.
Total 1; no losses.

LONDON TRANSPORT (London, UK)

Assembled HP Halifax.

MALTA DOCKYARD (Malta)

Assembled Felixstowe F 3.

MANN-EGERTON (Norwich, Norfolk, UK)

A motor company which only ventured briefly into aircraft production, during the First World War. Supplied 10 examples of one type, also assembled Airco DH 9, DH 9A, DH 10, Short 184 and Bomber, and Sopwith 11/2 Strutter.

213. Type B

A two-bay biplane reconnaissance seaplane, with two main underwing floats and one tail, for the RNAS, very similar to the Short 184 (qv) but with new lower-wings without ailerons and an increased gap between the wings; it was a two-seater armed with a Lewis mg in the rear cockpit and 520lb/235kg of bombs under the fuselage.

In service 1916 at Felixstowe, used by seven units (Calshot, Felixstowe, Fishguard, Killingholme, Newlyn, Otranto, Westgate) until 1917, Otranto.

Action: home waters and Mediterranean.

Powered by one 200hp Sunbeam Mohawk in-line.

Serials: 9085–9094 (10).

Span: 72ft/21.95m   Length: 40ft 7in/12.37m   Ceiling: 9,000ft/2,700m   Endurance: 4.5hrs   Speed: 88mph/142kmph.

Total 10; 1 accidental loss (10%).

MARTIN (USA)

Formed in 1933, this company designed a series of bombers before, during, and after the Second World War, until 1966 when it turned to missile production and then merged with Lockheed in 1995. Supplied 2,219 examples of four types.

214. Maryland I

A light bomber and reconnaissance monoplane for the RAF and FAA (which used it for recc. only) with a crew of three, taken over from a French contract; armed with one Browning mg in the dorsal and ventral positions and four fixed Brownings in the wings and could carry 2,000lb/908kg of bombs internally plus cameras as required.

In service 1940 with 431 Flt, used by two sqns (8, 39), one flt, two PR sqns (69, 544), two PR flts, and two GR sqns (203, 223) until 1942, 223 Sqn; also served with 2xFTU, 2xOTU, 1xTTFlt, 1xFAA ATU and 1xcomms. unit, until 1943.

Action: southern Europe, Middle East, North Africa, North Atlantic and Mediterranean, also based overseas in East Africa.

Powered by two 1,200hp P&W Twin Wasp R1830-S3cg radials.

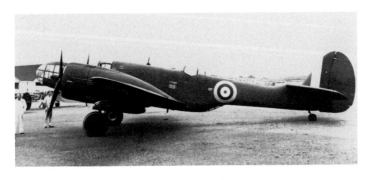

Martin Maryland I. (Newark Air Museum)

Serials: AR702–(50), AX670–71 (2), AX689–90 (2), AX692–93 (2), BJ421–28 (5), BS760–767 (18), HK836, HK845, HK865.
Total 82 (7 FAA); 27 accidental and 28 hostile losses.

214a. Maryland II

As the Mk I but with two Brownings in a A-W dorsal turret, one in the ventral position and four in the wings, plus 2,000lb/908kg of bombs; many went to the SAAF.
In service 1941 with 39 Sqn, used by one PR sqn (69), three GR sqns (39, 203, 223), and one PR flt until 1942, 223 Sqn; also served with 1xMETS and 1xOTU, until 1943.
Action: North Africa, also based overseas in the Middle East, not operational in the UK.
Powered by two 1,200hp Twin Wasp R1830-S3cg-4 with two-stage superchargers.
Serials: AH280–429 (68).
Total 68; 17 accidental and 20 hostile losses.

	Span	Length	Ceiling	Range	Speed
Mk I	61ft 4in/18.69m	46ft 8in/14.22m	29,500ft/8,850m	1,300 miles/2,093km	304mph/489kmph
Mk II	"	"	26,000ft/7,800m	1,210 miles/1,948km	316mph/509kmph

Total Marylands 150; in service 1940–43; 92 (61%) losses inc. 48 hostile.

215. Baltimore I

A light bomber for the RAF, with four crew and armed with one Vickers mg in a dorsal position, one Browning in a ventral position and four fixed Brownings in the wings; carried 2,000lb/908kg bombs internally and cameras as required.
In service 1942 with 223 Sqn, used by one sqn (223), one PR sqn (69), one GR sqn (203), one RCM sqn (162) and two PR flts, until 1943, 162 Sqn; also served with 1xAACU, ME C&CU, 1xMETS and 2xOTU.
Action: North Africa, southern Europe and Mediterranean, also based overseas in the Middle East, not operational in the UK.
Powered by two 1,600hp Wright Double-Row Cyclone R2600-19 radials.
Serials: AG685–734 (49).
Total 49; 15 accidental and 11 hostile losses.

215a. Baltimore II

As the Mk I but with two Vickers in the dorsal position and two in the ventral position, four Brownings in the wings and 2,000lb/908kg of bombs.
In service 1942 with 223 Sqn, used by four sqns (14, 55, 223, 454), one PR sqn (69), one GR sqn (203), one RCM sqn (162), and two PR flts until 1944, 162 Sqn; also served with 1xAACU, ME C&CU, 2xMETS, 2xOTU and 2xmisc. units.
Action: North Africa, southern Europe and Mediterranean, also based overseas in the Middle East, not operational in the UK.
Serials: AG735–834 (99).
Total 99; 44 accidental and 11 hostile losses.

215b. Baltimore III

As the Mk II but with two Brownings in a BP-A dorsal turret, four in the wings and 2,000lb/908kg of bombs internally.
In service 1942 with 223 Sqn, used by five sqns (52, 55, 223, 454, 13 s[Greek]), one PR sqn (69), one PR flt, one GR sqn (203) and one RCM sqn (162) until 1944, 162 Sqn; also served with AG&BS ME, ME CGS, 1xAACU, 1xCU, ME C&CU, 1xMETS, 3xOTU, AG&BS and 1xmisc. unit, until 1945.
Action: North Africa, southern Europe, Middle East and Mediterranean, also based overseas in East Africa, not operational in the UK.
Powered by two 1,650hp Double-Row Cyclone R2600-asb, with tropical filters.
Serials: AG835–AH184 (250).
Total 250;. 78 accidental and 45 hostile losses.

Martin Baltimore
IV. (Newark Air
Museum)

215c. Baltimore IIIA (A-30)

As the Mk III but lend-lease, with American equipment; some went to the SAAF.
In service 1943 with 55 Sqn, used by two sqns (52, 55) and one PR sqn (69) until 1944, 52 Sqn, also served
with AB&GS ME, ME CGS, ME C&CU, 1xMETS, AB&GS, 1xAACU, 1xFTU, 1xcal.flt, 2xcomms.
units and 1xmisc. unit, until 1945.
Action: North Africa and southern Europe, also based overseas in the Middle East, not operational in UK.
Serials: FA100–380 (259).
Total 259; 19 accidental and 14 hostile losses.

215d. Baltimore IV (A-30A)

As the Mk IIIA but with the BP dorsal turret replaced by a Martin 250CE mounting two 0.5in Brownings.
In service 1943 with 55 Sqn, used by six sqns (52, 55, 223, 454, 500, 13[Greek]), one flt, two GR sqns (13,
459), and one PR sqn (69) until 1945, 500 Sqn; also served with 1xAACU, 1xCU, ME CGS, ME C&CU,
4xOTU, GGFlt, 1xcal.flt, 9xcomms. units and 5xmisc. units.
Action: North Africa, southern Europe and Mediterranean, also based overseas in East Africa, Far East,
and Palestine; not operational in the UK.
Serials: FA382–674 (292).
Total 292; 72 accidental and 32 hostile losses.

215e. Baltimore V

As the Mk IV but with equipment and detail changes and more powerful engines.
In service 1943 with 454 Sqn, used by six sqns (52, 55, 223, 249, 454, 500), one flt, two GR sqns (13, 459),
two PR sqns (69, 680), and one PR flt, until 1946, 249 Sqn; also served with AB&GS ME, 1xAACU,
4xCU, ME CGS, 1xMETS, 2xOTU, 12xcomms. units and 3xmisc. units.
Action: southern Europe and Mediterranean, also based overseas in East Africa, Kenya, Egypt and Malta;
not operational in the UK.
Powered by two 1,700hp D-R Cyclone R2600-29.
Serials: FW281–705 (419), FW706–880 (174).
Total 593 (8 FAA); 110 accidental and 47 hostile losses.

	Span	Length	Ceiling	Range	Speed
Mk I	61ft 4in/18.69m	48ft 6in/14.78m	22,300ft/6,690m	1,082 miles/1,742km	308mph/496kmph
Mk III	"	"	24,000ft/7,200m	950 miles/1,529km	302mph/486kmph
Mk IV	"	"	23,300ft/6,690m	"	305mph/491kmph
Mk V	"	"	24,000ft/7,200m	980 miles/1,579km	320mph/515kmph

Total Baltimores 1,542; in service 1942–46; 498 (32%) losses inc. 160 hostile.

216. Marauder I (B-26A)

Used by the RAF as a medium, or torpedo, bomber, with five crew and armed with one 0.5in Browning in the nose position and two in a Martin 250CE dorsal turret, ventral position and Bell tail turret, plus 4,800lb/2,180kg of bombs or one /two torpedos internally.

In service 1942 with 14 Sqn, used by one sqn, 2xFTU, 1xMETS and 2xcomms. units, until 1944, 14 Sqn.

Action: North Africa, southern Europe and Mediterranean, not operational in the UK.

Powered by two 1,850hp P&W Double-Wasp R2800-5 or -9 radials.

Serials: FK109–160 (42).

Total 42; 29 accidental and 12 hostile losses.

216a. Marauder IA (B-26B)

As the Mk I but with no provision for torpedos, a revised rear gunner's position and more powerful engines.

In service 1942 with 14 Sqn, used by one sqn and 1xMETS, until 1944, 14 Sqn.

Action: North Africa and southern Europe, not operational in the UK.

Powered by two 2,000hp Double-Wasp R2800-41.

Serials: FK369–380 (16).

Total 16; 1 accidental and 7 hostile losses.

216b. Marauder II (B-26C)

As the Mk IA but had two 0.5in fixed Brownings in pods on the forward fuselage sides, carried 4,000lb/1,816kg of bombs and had longer span wings; it was used by the RAF as an operational trainer, not on front-line service, and many went to the SAAF.

In service 1943 with 70 OTU, used by 1xCU, ME C&CU, 1xMETS, 1xOTU and 1xcomms. unit until 1946, 70 OTU.

Based overseas in North and East Africa, not operational in the UK.

Serials: FB418–522 (99).

Total 99; 23 accidental losses.

216c. Marauder III (B-26F or G)

As the Mk II but with two 0.5in in the nose position, Martin 250 dorsal turret and Bell rear turret, one in each beam position, and four fixed in pods on the front fuselage, plus 4,000lb/1,816kg of bombs; it also had increased wing incidence and larger intakes above the cowlings. Many went to the SAAF.

In service 1944 with 14 Sqn, used by two sqns (14, 39) until 1946, 39 Sqn; also served with 1xCU, 1xFTU, ME C&CU, 1xOTU and 2xcomms. units.

Action: southern Europe, also based overseas in North and East Africa, and Sudan; not operational in the UK.

Serials: HD402–751 (347).

Total 347; 54 accidental and 13 hostile losses.

Martin Marauder IA, 14 Sqn.
(Peter Green Collection)

	Span	Length	Ceiling	Range	Speed
Mk I	65ft/19.81m	56ft/17.07m	25,000ft/7,500m	1,000 miles/3,000km	315mph/507kmph
Mk IA	"	58ft 3in/17.76m	23,500ft/7050m	1,150 miles/1,851km	317mph/510kmph
MK II	71ft/21.64m	"	21,700ft/6,510m	1,200 miles/1,932km	282mph/454kmph
Mk III	"	56ft 6in/17.22m	28,000ft/8,400m	"	305mph/491kmph

Total Marauders 504; in service 1942–46; 139 (28%) losses inc. 32 hostile.

217. Mariner I (PBM-3B)

A large general-reconnaissance flying boat, widely used by the US Navy but not by Coastal Command which was reluctant to take on a new type; it had seven crew, and was armed with two 0.5in Brownings in nose, dorsal and tail turrets, one in each beam position and 8,000lb/3,672kg of stores, including 8xDC, in the engine nacelles; ASV-V in a pod radome above the cockpit. It had a gull wing mounted high on the deep, slab-sided fuselage and there was dihedral on the tailplanes with two rounded fins/rudders which tilted inwards; the underwing floats were heavily strutted.

In service during 1943 with 524 Sqn.

Powered by two 1,700hp Wright Double-Row Cyclone R2600-12 radials.

Serials: JX100–132 (23).

Span: 118ft/35.97m   Length: 78ft/23.77m   Ceiling: 17,000ft/5,100m   Range: 3,200 miles/5,152km   Speed: 225mph/362kmph.

Total 23; 1 accidental loss (4%).

MAY, HARDEN & MAY (Felixstowe, Suffolk, UK)

Assembled Felixstowe F2A and F5, and Porte Baby.

MESSERSCHMITT (Germany)

A company formed in 1938 and a feared name in Britain during the Second World War. Supplied three examples of one type.

Messerschmitt Aldon, preserved German example. (Author's Collection)

218. Aldon

An impressed low-wing cabin monoplane, with retactable u/c, used as a communications type by the RAF; actually it was the Me 108, very similar in appearance to the Bf 109 but carrying the pilot and three passengers and, amazingly, was not shot down by friendly fire.
In service 1940 with 110 Wing, used by 6xcomms. units until 1945, MCommsSqn.
Based overseas in Germany.
Powered by one 270hp Argus AS10e in-line.
Serials: AW167, DK280, ES955.
Span: 34ft 5in/10.49m   Length: 27ft 2in/8.28m   Ceiling: 20,300ft/6,090m   Range: 620 miles/998km   Speed: 196mph/316kmph.
Total 3 impressed; 1 accidental loss (33%).

METROPOLITAN CARRIAGE & WAGON (Birmingham, Warwicks)

Assembled HP 0/400.

METROPOLITAN-VICKERS (Manchester, Lancs)

Assembled Avro Manchester, Lancaster and Lincoln.

MILES (Woodley, Berks, UK)

A revered name in British aviation of the 1930s; formed in 1931 as Phillips & Powis and becoming Miles in 1943 though the Miles name seems to have been used well before that date. It designed many advanced monoplane touring types and a large number of the RAF's Second World War trainers. Post-Second World War it had a turbulent time financially and was absorbed into Beagle (qv) in 1960. Supplied 5,872 examples of 12 types (Magister, Master and Martinet, see Vol. 1).

219. Nighthawk I

An RAF instrument trainer but more used for communications and based on the Miles Falcon Six (qv), with the pilot and two or three crew/passengers. As an instrument trainer the right-hand seat could be covered by a blind-flying hood. There was a small triangular cabin window behind the cockpit and it had a long fin.
In service 1937 with CFS, used by one sqn, CFS and 3xmisc. units until 1939, 24 Sqn.
Powered by one 200hp DH Gipsy Six I in-line.
Serial: L6846.
Span: 35ft/10.67m   Length: 25ft/7.62m   Ceiling: n/k   Range: n/k   Speed: 180mph/290kmph.
Total 1; no losses.

220. Mentor I

A communications type for the RAF based on the Nighthawk (above); originally ordered as a radio trainer, it carried the pilot and two passengers.
In service 1938 with CFS and 24 Sqn, used by one sqn, one PR flt, CFS, 1xPAFU, 1xAAS, EWS, 1xBAT-Flt, 1xFTS, 1xGp Pl, 4xOTU, 21xcomms. units and 1xmisc. unit, until 1944, Andover SFlt.
Powered by one 200hp DH Gipsy Six I in-line.
Serials: L4392–4436 (44).
Span: 34ft 10in/10.61m   Length: 26ft 2in/7.97m   Ceiling: 13,800ft/4,140m   Range: nk   Speed: 180mph/290kmph.
Total 44; 13 (30%) losses inc. 3 hostile.

221. Falcon Six

An impressed low-wing cabin monoplane for communications with the RAF and FAA, with a pilot and three passengers.
In service 1940, 781 Sqn, used by 2xRAF and 1xFAA comms. unit and 1xmisc. unit, until 1945, ADGB CommsSqn.
Based overseas in the Far East.

Powered by one 200hp DH Gipsy Six I in-line.

Serials: W9373, AV973, DG576.

Total 3 impressed (1 FAA); 1 accidental loss.

221a. Falcon Major

As the Falcon Six but with a less-powerful engine and a pilot and only two passengers.

In service 1940 with 81 Gp CommsFlt, used by 2xcomms. units until 1945, Northolt SFlt.

Powered by one 130hp DH Gipsy Major I in-line.

Serials: X9300–01 (2), HM496.

Total 3 impressed; no losses.

	Span	Length	Ceiling	Range	Speed
Six	35ft/10.67m	25ft/7.62m	15,000ft/4,500m	560 miles/902km	180mph/290kmph
Major	"	"	"	615 miles/990km	145mph/233kmph

Total Falcons 6 impressed; in service 1939–45; 1 (17%) loss.

222. Hawk Major

An open-cockpit two-seater low-wing monoplane impressed for communications work with the RAF.

In service 1939 with the ATA TFPl, used by 1xBAS, 1xEFTS, 2xcomms. units and 1xmisc. unit until 1946, Watchfield SFlt.

Based overseas in the Far East.

Powered by one 130hp DH Gipsy Major I in-line.

Serials: X5125, BD180, DG577, DG590, DP848, DP851, HK863, HL538, LV768, NF752.

Total 10 impressed; 2 accidental losses.

Miles Mentor I L4393. (Peter Green collection)

Miles Falcon Major, G-AEEG, preserved example. (Author's Collection)

222a. Hawk

As the Hawk Major but with a less powerful engine, impressed for communications work with the RAF.
In service 1941 with 5 MU, used by 2xcomms. units until 1943, Levant CommsFlt.
Based overseas in the Middle East.
Powered by 90hp ADC Cirrus IIIa in-line.
Serials: DG578, HK863.
Total 2 impressed; 1 accidental loss.

222b. Mohawk

The sole example of this variant (built for the American aviation pioneer Charles Lindbergh) was
impressed by the RAF for communications and had a canopy over the crew and a different engine.
In service 1941 with Turnhouse SFlt, used by 2xcomms. units until 1946, MCommsSqn.
Powered by one 200hp Menasco Buccaneer B6s in-line.
Serial: HM503.
Total 1 impressed; no losses.

	Span	Length	Ceiling	Range	Speed
Major	33ft/10.06m	24ft/7.32m	20,000ft/6,000m	560 miles/902km	150mph/241kmph
Hawk	"	"	16,000ft/4,800m	450 miles/724km	115mph/185kmph
Mohawk	35ft/10.67m	25ft 6in/7.77m	n/k	n/k	185mph/299kmph

Total Hawks 13 impressed; in service 1939–46; 3 (25%) losses.

223. Whitney Straight

A fast low-wing cabin monoplane impressed for communications with the RAF and FAA, carrying the
pilot and one passenger.
In service 1939 at Paris, used by 1xPAFU, 1xAONS, ATA TFPl, 1xFTS, 3xTTFlts, 1xOTU, 1xFAA CU,
1xFAA ATA and 14xcomms. units until 1947, FC CommsSqn.
Based overseas in Far East and India.
Powered by one 130hp DH Gipsy Major I in-line.
Serials: W7422, AV970–71 (2), BD145, BD168, BD183, BS755, BS814–15 (2), BS818, DJ713–14 (2),
DP237, DP845, DP855, DR611–12 (2), EM999, ES922, MA944, NF747, NF751.
Span: 35ft 8in/10.87m   Length: 25ft/7.62m   Ceiling: 17,400ft/5,220m   Range: 570
miles/918km   Speed: 145mph/233kmph.
Total 22 impressed (I FAA); 6 (27%) losses inc. 1 hostile.

Miles Whitney
Straight, G-AFGK.
(Tony Hancock)

Miles Messenger I, RH333, preserved example. (Author's Collection)

224. Monarch

An RAF impressed low-wing cabin monoplane used for communication, with the pilot and two passengers; an enlarged version of the Whitney Straight (see above).

In service 1939 with 13 EFTS, used by 1xEFTS, 1xFTU and 6xcomms. units until 1948, 91 Gp CommsFlt.

Powered by one 130hp DH Gipsy Major I in-line.

Serials: W6461–63 (3), X9306.

Span: 35ft 7in/10.85m   Length: 26ft/7.92m   Ceiling: 20,000ft/6,000m   Range: 600 miles/966km   Speed: 145mph/233kmph.

Total 4 impressed; 1 (25%) accidental loss.

225. Messenger I

A communications type for the RAF, carrying the pilot and three passengers.

In service 1943 with 2 TAF CommsSqn, used by 13xcomms. units, 1xEFTS and 7xmisc. units until 1948, various comms flts.

Powered by one 130hp DH Gipsy Major I in-line.

Serials: RG327, RG333, RH368–429 (19).

Span: 36ft 2in/11.03m   Length: 24ft/7.32m   Ceiling: 14,000ft/4,200m   Range: 260 miles/419km   Speed: 116mph/187kmph.

Total 21; 1 (5%) accidental loss.

MORGAN (Leighton Buzzard, Beds, UK)

Assembled Vickers Vimy.

NATIONAL AIRCRAFT FACTORY (NAF) (Various locations)

Assembled Airco DH 9, DH 10 and HP 0/400.

NORMAN-THOMPSON (Middleton-on-Sea, Sussex, UK)

A short-lived company, formed from White & Thompson (qv) in 1915 and out of business 1918. Supplied 46 examples of two types (NT 5, see Vol. 1); also assembled Short S38.

NT 2B. See White & Thompson.

226. NT 4

A small general-reconnaissance flying boat for the RNAS, with two crew in a glazed cockpit in the nose and armed with one Lewis mg on the top of the cockpit, plus 460lb/210kg of bombs underwing.

In service 1917 at Killingholme, used by three units (Calshot, Dundee, Killingholme) until 1918, Dundee.

Action: home waters.

Powered by two 150hp Hispano-Suiza 8aa in-line pushers mounted just under the upper wing.
Serials: 8338–43 (6).
Total 6; 2 accidental losses.

226a. NT 4A

As the above but with a modified hull and a fuel tank over the upper wing and the cockpit moved back
to above the nose; saw little use.
In service 1917 at Calshot, used by three units (Cattewater, Newhaven, Westgate) and 3xPTU until 1918,
Felixstowe.
Powered by two 200hp Hispano-Suiza 8bb in-line pushers.
Serials: 9061–64 (4), N2140–2159 (16).
Total 20; no losses.
Both Marks: Span: 77ft 10in/23.7m   Length: 40ft 9in/12.42m   Ceiling: 14,500ft/4,350m   Endurance:
6hrs   Speed: 96mph/155kmph.
Total NT 4s 26; in service 1917–18; 2 (8%) losses.

NORTH AMERICAN (USA)

Formed in 1928 this company owed much to the RAF for its specification for the famed Mustang
fighter, and for its orders for the Harvard trainer; became North American Rockwell in 1966 and
Rockwell Int. in 1973. Supplied 6,482 examples of five types (Harvard, Mustang, Mitchell PR, Tornado
and Sabre, see Vol. 1).

227. Mitchell I (B-25B)

This was the first Mk of Mitchell ordered for the RAF but was not up to operational standards and was
therefore used for conversion training, with armament deleted.
In service 1942–45 with 111 OTU.
Based overseas in North America and BWI, not operational in the UK.
Powered by two 1,700hp D-R Cyclone R2600-9.
Serials: FK161–183 (19).
Total 19; 3 accidental losses.

Mitchell B-25C PR, see Vol. 1.

Norman Thompson
NT 4, 8343, RNAS
Killingholme.
(G. Stuart Leslie)

North
American
Mitchell II,
FV905, 227
Sqn. (Alastair
Goodrum
Collection)

227a. Mitchell II (B-25C or D)

An operational light bomber for the RAF, with five crew and armed with one manual 0.5in Browning in the Perspex nose, two in a Bendix-A dorsal turret and two in a Bell-A ventral turret, plus 6,000lb/2,725kg of bombs internally.

In service 1942 with 98 and 180 Sqns, used by six sqns (98, 180, 226, 305, 320, 342) until 1945, 98 and 226 Sqns; also served with ECFS, EFS, 1xFTU, Mosquito CU, 1xGpTFlt, 2xOTU and 2xmisc. units.

Action: northern Europe, also based overseas in BWI.

Serials: FL164–218 (54), FL671–709 (39), FR141–209 (63), FR362–384 (21), FR393–97 (5), FV900–FW280 (268), HD302–345 (15).

Total 465; 120 accidental and 100 hostile losses.

227b. Mitchell II Series I

As the Mk II but with a rear fuselage similar to the Mk III, but without the tail guns.

In service 1943–45 with units as above. Number n/k but possibly those in the HD serial range above.

227c. Mitchell III (B-25J)

As the Mk II Series I but with six crew, the Bendix R dorsal turret moved forward to just behind the cockpit, a manual 0.5in in each beam position, and two 0.5in in a Bell rear turret with a Perspex bubble canopy for the gunner's head.

In service 1944 with 98 Sqn, used by five sqns (98, 180, 226, 320, 342) until 1945, 342 Sqn; also served with 1xOTU, 1xTTFlt, 4xcomms. units and 2xmisc. units, until 1947.

Action: northern Europe, also based overseas in BWI.

Powered by two 1,700hp D-R Cyclone R2600-29.

Serials: HD346–400 (51), KJ561–216 (216).

Total 267; 13 accidental and 10 hostile losses.

	Span	Length	Ceiling	Range	Speed
Mk I	67ft 7in/20.6m	54ft 1in/16.49m	27,000ft/8,100m	2,000 miles/3,220km	300mph/483kmph
Mk II	"	52ft 11in/16.13m	21,200ft/6,360m	1,635 miles/2,632km	292mph/470kmph
Mk III	"	"	24,200ft/7,260m	1,350 miles/2,173km	"

Total Mitchells 751; in service 1942–47; 246 (33%) losses inc. 111 hostile.

NORTHROP (USA)

Formed in 1930 but only supplied, by default, 24 examples of one type. Also assembled Vultee Vengeance. Became Northrop-Grumman in 1994.

228. N3P-B

A general-reconnaissance seaplane with two underwing floats, taken over by the RAF from the Royal Norwegian Navy; it had three crew under a long greenhouse canopy and was armed with four 0.5in Browning in the wings, and one 0.3in manual in a dorsal and a ventral position; it could carry 2,000lb/908kg of bombs underbelly.

In service 1941–43 with 330 Sqn.

Action: North Atlantic from Iceland, not operational in the UK.

Powered by one 1,100hp Wright Cyclone GR1820-G205A radial.

Serials: Norwegian.

Span: 48ft 11in/14.91m   Length: 36ft/10.98m   Ceiling: 24,000ft/7,200m   Range: 1,000 miles/1,610km   Speed: 228mph/367kmph.

Total 24; losses not known.

PALLADIUM AUTOCARS (London, UK)

Assembled Airco DH 4

PARNALL (Yate, Somerset, UK)

A wood-working firm which obtained contracts to assemble aircraft early in the First World War and went into design from 1917. It built military and civil aircraft in smallish numbers until 1939 when it abandoned aircraft production to concentrate on ancillary work, notably gun turrets. Supplied 142 examples of four types (Plover, see Vol. 1); also assembled Fairey Hamble Baby and Short 827 and Bomber.

229. Panther I

A spotter-reconnaissance biplane for the FAA, with two crew and armed with a Lewis mg in the rear cockpit. In service 1919 with 205 Sqn, used by one sqn and two flts (441, 442) until 1924, 442 Flt; embarked on two carriers.

Powered by one 200hp Bentley BR 2 rotary.

Serials: N92–93 (2), N7400–7549 (122).

Span: 29ft 6in/8.99m   Length: 24ft 11in/7.6m   Ceiling: 14,500ft/4,350m   Endurance: 4.5hrs   Speed: 108mph/174kmph.

Total 124; 30 (25%) accidental losses.

Parnall Panther I, N7511, 205 Sqn. (G. Stuart Leslie)

230. Peto I

The only British aircraft designed to operate from a submarine, this was a small, two-seat reconnaissance single-bay biplane seaplane for the FAA, with two floats and unarmed.
In service 1926–32 with HM Submarine M2.
Powered by one 140hp Bristol Lucifer IV or 155hp A-S Mongoose III radial.
Serials: N181–82 (2). One accidental loss but rebuilt as N225.
Span: 28ft 5in/8.66m   Length: 22ft 6in/6.86m   Ceiling: 9,500ft/2,850m   Endurance: 2hrs   Speed: 113mph/182kmph.
Total 2; 1 (50%) accidental loss.

231. Hendy Heck II

The RAF bought two examples of this three-seater cabin monoplane for communications work, and impressed another later. It had a low wing with retractable undercarriage and a pointed fin/rudder.
In service 1937, used by one sqn (24), 2xSFlts and 1xcomms. unit until 1944, 17Gp CommsFlt.
Powered by one 200hp DH Gipsy Six I in-line.
Serial: K8853, R9138 (Mk III) plus one impressed – NF749.
Span: 31ft 6in/9.6m   Length: 26ft 2in/7.97m   Ceiling: n/k   Range: 620 miles/998km   Speed: 150mph/241kmph.
Total 2 plus 1 impressed making a total of 3; no losses.

PEGLER (Doncaster, Yorks, UK)

Assembled Sopwith Cuckoo.

PERCIVAL (Luton, Beds, UK)

A company founded in 1934 which became famous for its luxurious cabin monoplanes pre-Second World War; in 1944 it became part of the Hunting Group and was renamed Hunting-Percival in 1954. Supplied 1,936 examples of five types (Prentice and Provost, see Vol. 1); also assembled DH Mosquito.

232. Vega Gull III

A communications monoplane for the RAF and FAA, carrying the pilot and three passengers.
In service 1938 with 24 Sqn, used by three sqns (24, 267, 510), 3xAACU, 2xEFTS, 1xFTS, 1xOTU, 1xMETS, 1xFAA CU, 2xFAA ObsTU and 22xRAF and 2xFAA comms. units, until 1945, 510 Sqn.
Based overseas in South America, the Middle East, North and East Africa and Far East.
Powered by one 205hp DH Gipsy Six II in-line.
Serials: L7272, P1749–54 (6), P5986–93 (8) plus 24 impressed – W6464, W9375–78 (4), X1032–34 (3), X1085–86 (2), X9315, X9332, X9339–40 (2), X9349, X9368, X9371, X9391–92 (2), X9435–36 (2), X9455, BK872, DR808.
Span: 39ft 6in/12.04m   Length: 25ft 4in/7.72m   Ceiling: 16,000ft/4,800m   Range: 660 miles/1,063km   Speed: 174mph/280kmph.
Total 15 plus 24 impressed making a total of 38 (7 FAA); 11 (29%) losses inc. 2 hostile.

Percival Vega Gull, G-AEZJ, preserved example. (Author's Collection)

233. Gull Six

A low-wing cabin monoplane for communications with the RAF, carrying a pilot and two passengers. It had undercarriage spats and a rounded fin/rudder.
In service 1940, Middle East, used by two sqns (24, 173), 1xPAFU, 1xGTS, 1xOTU, 4xcomms. units and 2xmisc. units, until 1945.
Based overseas in the Middle and Far East.
Powered by one 200hp DH Gipsy Six I in-line.
Serials: AX698, AX866, HX794, MA927, MA942, MA962.
Span: 36ft 2in/11.03m   Length: 25ft 9in/7.85m   Ceiling: 20,000ft/6,000m   Range: 640 miles/1,030km   Speed: 178mph/287kmph.
Total 6 impressed; 1 (17%) accidental loss.

234. Petrel I or Q6

A sleek-looking low-wing monoplane light transport and communications type for the RAF and FAA, carrying two crew and six passengers. The tailplane was set high on the fuselage and it had a curved fin/rudder, while the undercarriage legs were 'trousered' to the engines.
In service 1939 with 24 Sqn, used by three sqns (24, 267, 510), one PR flt, 1xANS, 1xAACU, 1xFTU, 1xOTU, 1xEFTS, 1xFAA ATU and 12xRAF and 3xFAA comms. units, until 1946, Northolt SF.
Based overseas in the Middle East, North and East Africa, and Far East.
Powered by two 205hp DH Gipsy Six II in-lines.
Serials: P5634–40 (7) plus 12 impressed Q6 – W6085, W9374, X9328–29 (2), X9336, X9363, X9406–07 (2), X9454, AX860, HK838, HK913.
Span: 48ft 8in/14.83m   Length: 32ft 3in/9.83m   Ceiling: 21,000ft/6,300m   Range: 700 miles/1,127km   Speed: 195mph/314kmph.
Total 8 plus 12 impressed making a total of 20 (4 FAA); 4 (20%) losses inc. 2 hostile.

235. Proctor I

Designed as a military derivative of the Vega Gull (qv) and used for communications and radio training by the RAF, with the pilot and two passengers or three crew; as a radio trainer the trainee operator sat in the rear of the cabin which sometimes had a Perspex faired DF loop above.
In service 1940 at Heliopolis, used by five sqns (24, 117, 173, 267, 510), EWS, 3xEFTS, 1xGTS, OATS, 2xOTU, SoP, 4xRS, 2xSS, ATA IFTS, 1xFTS, 40xcomms. units and 14xmisc. units, until 1946, 23 Gp CommsFlt.
Based overseas in southern Europe, Middle East, and North and East Africa.
Powered by one 210hp DH Gipsy Queen II in-line.
Serials: P5998, P6114–6332 range (140), R7485–7529 (25).
Total 166 plus 2 conversions of the Mk IIA, making a total of 168; 59 accidental and 6 hostile losses.

235a. Proctor IA

As the Mk I but a radio trainer and communications type for the FAA, with naval equipment and dual-controls.
In service 1939 with 755 and 756 Sqns, used by 5xCU, 1xPTU, 5xATU, 2xObsTU, 2xTAGTU and 2xcomms. units, until 1944, 780 Sqn.
Serials: P5999–6167 (99).
Total 99; 22 accidental losses.

235b. Proctor II

A radio trainer for the RAF and FAA, as the Mk IA but without the dual-controls so the trainee opera-tor sat beside the pilot.
In service 1940 with 2 SS, used by 1xPAFU, 2xOTU, 2xSS, 1xUASqn, 3xRS, 3xFAA ATU, 2xFAA ObsTU, 1xFAA TAGTU and 15xRAF and 1xFAA comms. units, until 1954, 66 Gp CommsFlt.
Based overseas in Far East and BWI.
Serials: Z7193–7252 (46), BT278–281 (4).
Total 50 (16 FAA); 11 accidental losses.

Percival Proctor III, HM415,
Middle East Comms. Sqn.
(Peter Green Collection)

235c. Proctor IIA

A radio trainer for the FAA, as the Mk II but with naval radio equipment.
In service 1940 with 754 Sqn, used by 1xCU, 2xATU, 2xTAGTU and 1xcomms. unit, until 1945.
Based overseas in BWI.
Serials: BV535–658 (100).
Total 100; 39 accidental losses.

235d. Proctor III

A radio trainer and communications type for the RAF, as the Mk IIA but with RAF radio equipment.
In service 1941 with 1 RS, used by one sqn (510), 1xPR flt, 2xOAFU, 2xPAFU, 1xAPS, 3xCU, 1xEFTS,
1xFPTU, 1xBDTFlt, 1xAACU, 1xHGCU, OATS, 12xOTU, 4xRS, 1xRFS, 2xSS, TSTU (India), 1xFAA
TAGTU, 100xcomms. units and 32xmisc. units, until 1951, 31 Sqn.
Based overseas in southern Europe, the Middle East, North and East Africa, Far East, Germany, Denmark,
Greece, Malta, Palestine and Egypt.
Serials: R7530–7573 (25), DX181–243 (50), HM279–485 (162), LZ556–804 (200).
**Total 437 plus 21 conversions of the Mk II, making a total of 458 (12 FAA); 55 accidental and
8 hostile losses.**

235e. Proctor IV/C 4

A radio trainer and communications type for the RAF, as the Mk III but had a larger, deeper fuselage
with an extra side-window, to carry the pilot and three passengers or four crew; some had dual-controls.
In service 1943 with the RSs, used by two sqns (24, 31), 1xASS, CGS, 1xCU, ERS, GCAOpsS, 1xGrading
S., OATS, 3xRS, 1xUASqn, 1xFAA TAGS, 39xcomms. units and 8xmisc. units, until 1955, HC CommsSqn.
Based overseas in southern Europe, Greece, Malta, Libya, Egypt, Iraq and Kenya.
Serials: LA586–87 (2), MX450–55 (6), NP156–403 (200), RM160–230 (49).
Total 257; 17 accidental losses.

235f. Proctor C 5

A VIP version of the C 4, carrying a pilot and three passengers in some luxury.
In service 1946, Rome, used by 1xcomms. unit until 1954, 83 Gp CommsFlt.
Serials: VN895–98 (4).
Total 4; 1 accidental loss.

	Span	Length	Ceiling	Range	Speed
Mk I	39ft 6in/12.04m	25ft 10in/7.87m	17,000ft/5,100m	600 miles/966km	160mph/258kmph
C 4	"	28ft 2in/8.58m	14,000ft/4,200m	500 miles/805km	157mph/253kmph

**Total Proctors 1,113; built by Percival and Miles; in service 1940–55; 218 (20%) losses inc. 14
hostile.**

236. Sea Prince C 1

A small transport for the FAA, based on the Percival Prince airliner; it carried two crew and eight passengers.
In service 1950–65 with 781 Sqn.
Powered by two 520hp Alvis Leonides 501 radials.
Serials: WF136–38 (3).
Total 3; no losses.

236a. Sea Prince T 1

The Sea Prince found favour with the FAA and this version was an observer trainer, with five crew; as the
C 1 but with ASV radar in a longer nose radome and twin-wheel undercarriage units with smaller wheels.
In service 1953 with 744 Sqn and 750 Sqns, used by 1xCU, 1xPTU, 1xObsTU, 1xcomms. unit and
2xmisc. units, until 1979, 750 Sqn.
Based overseas in Malta.
Powered by two 540hp Leonides 503/125 in longer nacelles.
Serials: WF118–133 (16), WF934, WF949, WM735–42 (8), WP307–321 (15).
Total 41; 3 accidental losses.

236b. Sea Prince C 2

As the T 1 but without radar in the radome, used for communications with two crew and eight passengers.
In service 1953 with 781 Sqn, used by 2xcomms. unit until 1973, Culdrose Ship's Flt.
Serials: WJ348–50 (3), WM756.
Total 4; no losses.

	Span	Length	Ceiling	Range	Speed
C 1	56ft/17.07m	42ft 10in/13.05m	20,000ft/6,000m	1,500 miles/2,415km	223mph/359kmph
T 1	"	46ft 4in/14.12m	"	"	"

Total Sea Princes 48; in service 1950–79; 3 (6%) losses.

Pembroke – see Hunting.

PHEONIX DYNAMO (Bradford, Yorks, UK)

Assembled Felixstowe F 3, Short 184 and Bomber.

PHILLIPS & POWIS SEE MILES.

Percival Sea Prince T
1, 750 Sqn. (Author's
Collection)

PIPER (USA)

Formed in 1936 from Taylorcraft and became famous for its many light and general-aviation types, supplying 27 examples of three types to the British forces.

237. Cub Coupe

This light V-style strut-braced high-wing cabin monoplane was similar to the Cub (see below) but the pilot and passenger, or two crew, sat side-by-side in a widened fuselage; it was impressed for artillery spotting and communications with the RAF. In service 1940 with D Flt, used by two AOP flts, 6xcomms. units and 3xmisc. units, until 1945, 10 Gp CommsFlt.
Powered by one 65hp Continental A65-1 in-line.
Serials: BT440–42 (3), BV180–81 (2), BV984–91 (8), DG667, DP852, ES923, HM565.
Span: 36ft 2in/11.03m   Length: 22ft 6in/6.86m   Ceiling: 12,000ft/3,600m   Range: 455 miles/733km   Speed: 83mph/134kmph.
Total 17 impressed; 9 (53%) accidental losses.

238. Cub (L-4B)

A high-wing braced by V-style struts, two-seat cabin monoplane with the pilot and passenger in tandem and used for communications.
In service 1943 with Western Desert CU, used by 1xBATFlt, 2xcomms. units and 1xmisc. unit, until 1946, MCommsSqn.
Based overseas in North Africa.
Powered by one 65hp Continental O-173-3 in-line with exposed cylinders.
Serials: HK936–39 (4) plus 4 impressed – HL530–31 (2), MA923, MA958.
Span: 35ft 3in/10.75m   Length: 22ft 5in/6.84m   Ceiling: 9,300ft/2,790m   Range: 216 miles/348km   Speed: 89mph/143kmph.
Total 4 plus 4 impressed making a total of 8; 4 (50%) accidental losses.

239. Cruiser

An impressed light high-wing cabin monoplane for RAF communications, with a pilot and two passengers side-by-side. V-style bracing struts for the wings and longer cabin windows than the Coupe (above).
In service 1942, used by 1xcomms. unit until 1944.
Based overseas in the Far East, not operational in the UK.
Powered by one 75hp Continental A75-8 in-line.
Serials: LV769, MA921.
Span: 35ft 5in/10.8m   Length: 22ft 10in/6.96m   Ceiling: 10,000ft/3,000m   Range: 450 miles/724km   Speed: 100mph/175kmph.
Total 2 impressed; no losses.

PITCAIRN (USA)

A little-known company which existed from 1925–40 and supplied seven examples of one type.

240. PA 39

A communications autogyro for the RAF, carrying the pilot and one passenger in tandem open cockpits.
In service during 1942 with 1447 Flt.
Powered by one 165hp Warner Super Scarab radial.
Serials: BW828–34 (7).
Rotor diameter: 41ft/12.5m   Length: 20ft 6in/6.25m   Ceiling: 12,000ft/3,600m   Range: n/k   Speed: 110mph/177kmph.
Total 7; 4 (57%) losses inc. 3 hostile.

PORTE (Felixstowe, Suffolk, UK)

An RN officer, John Porte, designed new hulls for the Curtiss flying boats (qv) and also had 21 examples built of his own design.

241. FB 2 Baby

A reconnaissance flying boat for the RNAS, with five crew and armed with one Lewis mg in the nose and dorsal positions, plus bombs underwing. It was a two-bay biplane with extended span upper wings braced by fabric-covered triangular kingposts and the tailplane mounted high on the fuselage; the wing floats were faired to the wing. Built by May, Harden & May.

In service 1916 at Felixstowe, used by five units (Catfirth, Felixstowe, Houton Bay, Killingholme, Stenness) until 1918, Catfirth.

Action: home waters.

Powered by two 225hp RR Eagle I tractors and one 275hp Green pusher, one 225hp RR Eagle I pusher and two 320hp Sunbeam Cossacks tractors, three 225hp Eagle I (one pusher), three 350hp Eagle VIII (one pusher), or three 275hp Eagle VII (one pusher) in-lines situated between the wings. The pusher was the centrally mounted engine.

Serials: 9801–9820 (21).

Span: 124ft/37.8m   Length: 63ft/19.2m   Ceiling: 8,000ft/2,400m   Endurance: n/k   Speed: 92mph/148kmph.

Total 21 but some not issued; 1 (8%) accidental loss.

POTEZ (France)

Formed in 1919 this famous company became part of SNCASE in 1940. Supplied six examples of two types.

242. 29

A single-bay biplane light transport taken over by the Free French and used for communications, with a cabin for two crew and five passengers; single fin/rudder and fixed undercarriage.

In service 1940 until 1941 with 2 F-F Flt.

Based overseas in West Africa, not operational in UK.

Powered by one 450hp Lorraine-Dietrich 2eb in-line.

Serials: AX678–79 (2).

Span: 47ft 6in/14.48m   Length: 34ft 9in/10.59m   Ceiling: 17,000ft/5,100m   Range: 310 miles/499km   Speed: 130mph/209kmph.

Total 2; 1 (50%) accidental loss.

243. 63-11

A low-wing twin-finned monoplane designed for reconnaissance but used for communications by the Free French, with three crew. It had a large glazed nose and a glazed canopy above the fuselage.

In service 1940–42 with 2 F-F Flt.

Based overseas in West Africa, not operational in UK.

Powered by two 670hp Gnome-Rhone 14m3-14 radials.

Serials: AX672–73 (2), AX680, AX691.

Span: 52ft 6in/16m   Length: 36ft 4in/11.08m   Ceiling: 29,500ft/8,850m   Range: 745 miles/1,199km   Speed: 277mph/446kmph.

Total 4; 2 (50%) accidental losses.

R.E.P. (France)

A short-lived company (1907–11) which supplied 12 examples of one type.

244. Parasol

A two-seat reconnaissance bomber for the RNAS, able to carry light bombs under fuselage. The parasol wing was strutted to the fuselage and braced by 'goalpost' kingposts and the deep fuselage had a steep angle down from the propeller hub.

In service 1915 with 1 Wing, used by three units (1W, 4W, Eastchurch) until 1916, Eastchurch.

Action: northern Europe.

Powered by one 110hp Le Rhone 9ja rotary.

Serials: 8454–8465 (12).
Span: 36ft/10.98m   Length: 26ft/7.92m   Ceiling and endurance: n/k   Speed: 70mph/113kmph.
Total 12; 3 (25%) losses inc. 1 hostile.

ROBEY (Lincoln, UK)

Assembled Short 184.

ROGOZARSKI (Yugoslavia)

Supplied one example of one type.

245. SIM-XIV-H

A three-seat low-wing general reconnaissance two-float seaplane, taken over from the Yugoslavian Navy.
Armament was 2xmg in a glazed nose position and one mg in the rear cockpit, plus 220lb/100kg of
bombs. The cockpit had a long 'greenhouse'-type canopy mounted midway along the fuselage top.
In service 1940 to 1942 with 2 (Y) Sqn.
Action: Mediterranean, not operational in the UK.
Powered by two 270hp Argus AS10 in-lines.
Serial: AX716.
Span: 49ft 10in/15.19m   Length: 36ft 9in/11.21m   Ceiling: 14,250ft/4,275m   Range: 522
miles/840km   Speed: 151mph/243kmph.
Total 1; 1 (100%) accidental loss.

ROOTES (Birmingham, Warwicks)

Assembled Bristol Blenheim and HP Halifax.

ROYAL AIRCRAFT FACTORY (Farnborough, Hants, UK)

A Government-owned enterprise which designed many types for the RFC, from its formation in 1910
until 1918 when it went out of design and construction and became an experimental and flight test
organisation. The vast majority of its designs were for reconnaissance or fighting with the RFC and will
be found in Vol. 1. In Factory parlance, FE stood for Farman Experimental (pusher types), H stood for
Hydroplane and RE for Reconnaissance Experimental. Supplied 16,179 examples of 19 types (all except
HRE 2 and FE 2B and 2C bombers, see Vol. 1); also assembled HP 0/400 and Vickers Vimy.

246. HRE 2

The only Factory seaplane to enter service with the RNAS, this was a two-seat, slightly staggered
two-bay biplane with two main floats and one under the tail, used for reconnaissance.
In service 1913–15 at Calshot.
Powered by one 70hp Renault WB/WC in-line.
Serial: 17.
Span: 39ft 6in/12.04m   Length: 32ft 3in/9.83m   Performance: n/k.
Total 1; 1 (100%) accidental loss.

247. FE 2B

Originally designed as a fighter and quite successful in this role (see Vol. 1), it began to be replaced by
more modern types and was switched to night bombing, initially with 100 Sqn the first night bombing
unit; it had increased fuel, two crew and was armed with two Lewis mg which could be fitted in various
positions around the front cockpit, and could carry 230lb/105kg of bombs under belly. (Some with 100
Sqn were fitted with one 1pdr quick-firing gun.) Had a simple V-strut undercarriage.
In service 1917 with 100 Sqn, used by nine sqns (38, 58, 83, 100. 101, 102, 148, 149, 166) until 1919 149
Sqn. Action: northern Europe.
Powered by one 160hp Beardmore pusher.
Serials: not known but likely to be late production in the B, C and D ranges.
Total not known.

247a. FE 2C

As the FE 2B but with the pilot in the front cockpit and the observer, with two Lewis mg, in the rear, plus 160lb/73kg of bombs.
In service from 1916 to 1918 with 100 Sqn and as a fighter by 25 Sqn. Action: northern Europe.
Serials: 6370–71 (2), A5744, B434, B445, B447, B449–50 (2), E7112–13 (2).
Span: 47ft 9in/14.55m   Length: 32ft 3in/9.83m   Ceiling: 11,000ft/3,353m   Endurance: 3hrs   Speed: 91mph/147kmph.
Total 10; losses not known.
Total FE 2 bombers not known; losses not known; nicknamed Fee.

FE 2b and C fighter see Vol. 1.

SAGE (Peterborough, Hunts, UK)

Assembled Short 184.

SAUNDERS (Cowes, IoW, UK)

Assembled Curtiss H4, Short 184, NT 2B, Felixstowe F2A and F5

SAUNDERS-ROE (SARO) (Cowes, IoW, UK)

A small company, formed in 1928 from Saunders (qv) in which Sir Alliot Verdon Roe had acquired a control-ling interest after he left Avro (qv). The company was nowhere near as successful as Avro, specialising in flying boats and, later, helicopters, none of which were ordered in large numbers; it was taken over by Westland (qv) in 1959. Supplied 133 aircraft of four types (Cloud and Skeeter, see Vol. 1); also assembled Supermarine Walrus.

248. London I

A general-reconnaissance flying boat for the RAF, with six crew and armed with one Lewis mg in nose, dorsal and tail positions, plus 1,600lb/725kg of bombs underwing.
In service 1936 with 209 Sqn, used by four sqns (201, 204, 209, 228) and the FBT Sqn until 1939, 204 Sqn.
Powered by two 620hp Bristol Pegasus IIIm3 radials.
Serials: K5257–63 (7).
Total 7; no losses.

RAF FE 2B, A5478, 100 Sqn. (Alastair Goodrum Collection)

Saro London I, K3560,
prototype. (Newark Air
Museum)

Saro Lerwick I, L7250.
(Air-Britain Archives)

248a. London II

As the Mk I but re-engined, with four- (later three-) bladed propellers and overwing exhausts.
In service 1936 with 204 Sqn, used by five sqns (201, 202, 204, 210, 240) until 1941, 202 Sqn; also served
with 1xAACU, 1xOTU and SPTSqn until 1942.
Based overseas in Gibraltar and Malta, action North and South Atlantic and Mediterranean.
Powered by two 980hp Pegasus X.
Serials: K5908–13 (6), K6927–32 (6), K9682–86 (5), L7038–43 (6).
Total 23 plus 7 conversions of the Mk I, making a total of 30; 9 accidental and three hostile losses.

	Span	Length	Ceiling	Range	Speed
Mk I	80ft/24.38m	57ft/17.37m	16,400ft/4,920m	1,740 miles/2,801km	145mph/233kmph
Mk II	"	"	18,700ft/5,610m	1,100 miles/1,771km	155mph/250kmph

Total Londons 30; in service 1936–42; 12 (40%) losses inc. 3 hostile.

249. Lerwick I

Saro's first, and last, monoplane GR flying boat, which was unsuccessful and soon withdrawn from operations; it had six crew and was armed with one Vickers mg in a FN-27 nose turret, two Brownings in a FN-8
dorsal turret and four Brownings in a FN-4a tail turret, plus 2,000lb/908kg of bombs in wing cells.
In service 1939 with 240 Sqn, used by three sqns (209, 240, 422) and 1xOTU until 1942, 422 Sqn.

Action: North Atlantic.

Powered by two 1,375hp Bristol Hercules I or II or 1,380hp Hercules IV radials.

Serials: L7250–7268 (19).

Span: 80ft 10in/24.63m   Length: 63ft 7in/19.4m   Ceiling : 25,600ft/7,680m   Range: 1,540 miles/2,479km   Speed: 213mph/344kmph.

Total 19; 14 (74%) losses inc. 1 hostile.

SAVAGE (King's Lynn, Norfolk, UK)

Assembled Airco DH 4 and Voisin LA.

SAVOIA-MARCHETTI (Italy)

A famous company, formed in 1915, which supplied four aircraft of one type.

250. SM 79K

This low-wing monoplane was a good bomber but was impressed for transport duties in North Africa with four crew plus passengers, and the armament removed.

In service 1941 with 117 Sqn, used by two sqns (117, 173) until 1944, 173 Sqn.

Based overseas in North Africa, not operational in the UK.

Powered by three 1,000hp Piaggio Stella PXIrc-40 radials.

Serials: AX702–05 (4).

Span: 69ft 7in/21.23m   Length: 53ft 2in/16.51m   Ceiling: 22,900ft/6,870m   Range: 1,243 miles/2,001km   Speed: 270mph/435kmph.

Total 4; 2 (50%) accidental losses.

SCOTTISH AVIATION (Prestwick, Scotland)

Formed in 1935 to undertake sub-contract and overhaul work but did not design its own aircraft until after the Second World War, these being quite successful. It then took over Jetstream production from the defunct Handley Page and Bulldog production from the defunct Beagle, after which it became part of British Aerospace in 1977. Supplied 239 examples of four types (Bulldog and Jetstream T 1, see Vol. 1); also assembled DH Queen Bee.

251. Pioneer CC 1

A STOL light transport designed for overseas work and also used for forward air-controlling; it carried a pilot and four passengers and was unarmed.

In service 1953 with 1311 Flt, used by six sqns (20, 78, 209, 215, 230, 267) and 1xmisc. unit until 1968, 209 Sqn and 1969 for forward air controlling, 20 Sqn.

Action: Aden, Malaya and Oman, also based overseas in the Gulf and Singapore.

Powered by one 540hp Alvis Leonides 502 or 504 radial.

Serials: XE512–15 (4), XG558–63 (6), XJ450–53 (4), XK367–70 (4), XL517–558 (10), XL664–706 (11).

Span: 49ft 9in/15.17m   Length: 34ft 4in/10.46m   Ceiling: 16,000ft/4,800m   Range: 300 miles/483km   Speed: 145mph/233kmph.

Total 39; 22 (56%) accidental losses.

252. Twin Pioneer CC 1

A twin-engined STOL light transport, again for overseas use; three crew, and 11 passengers or 3,400lb/1,545kg of freight. Could be armed with two Browning mg in the undercarriage sponsons and 2,000lb/910kg of bombs below the sponsons.

In service 1958 with 78 Sqn, used by five sqns (21, 78, 152, 209, 230) until 1968, 209 Sqn; also served with 1xFTU, SRCU, Twin Pioneer CU and 1xmisc. unit.

Action: Aden, Oman and Borneo; also based overseas in Kenya, Gulf, Malaya, Singapore and Guyana.

Powered by two 540hp Alvis Leonides 504 or 640hp Leonides 531 radials.

Serials: XL966–997 (12), XM284–91 (8), XM939–963 (12).

Total 32; 12 accidental losses.

Scottish Aviation
Pioneer CC 1, XL553,
78 Sqn. (Author's
Collection)

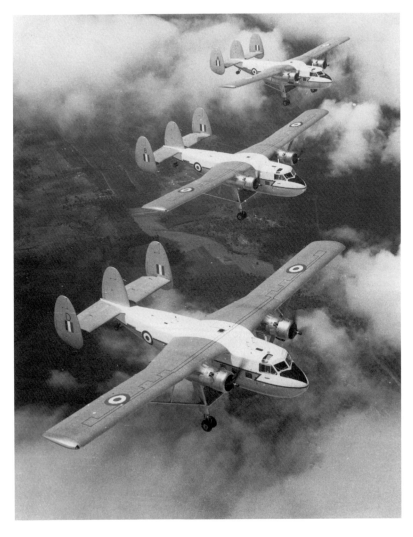

Scottish Aviation Twin
Pioneer CC 1, XM961
nearest, 21 Sqn.
(Newark Air Museum)

Scottish Aviation Jetstream
T 2, XX484, 750 Sqn.
(Author's Collection)

252a. Twin Pioneer CC 2

As the CC 1 but with structural changes.
In service 1959 with 230 Sqn, used by three sqns (152, 209, 230) until 1963, 230 Sqn; also served with
Twin Pioneer CU until 1967.
Action: Borneo, based overseas in the Gulf and Malaya.
Powered by two 640hp Leonides 531.
Serials: XN318–21 (4), XP293–95 (3).
Total 7 plus 2 conversions of the CC 1, making a total of 9; 4 accidental losses.
Both Marks: Span: 76ft 6in/23.31m   Length: 45ft 3in/13.8m   Ceiling: 20,000ft/6,000m   Range: 398
miles/641km   Speed: 165mph/266kmph.
Total Twin Pioneers 39; in service 1958–68; 16 (41%) losses; nicknamed Twin Pin.

253. Jetstream T 2

An FAA observer trainer and light transport, with MEL E190 radar in a nose radome and six crew.
In service 1978 with 750 Sqn, used by 1xObsTU until the present 2010 but due out of service in 2011.
Powered by two 913shp Turbomeca Astazou XVId turboprops.
Serials: ZA110–111 (2).
Total 2 plus 12 conversions of the T 1 (see Vol. 1) making a total of 14; 1 accidental loss to date.

253a. Jetstream T 3

A much-modified version based on the civil Jetstream 31 airliner; ordered as an observer trainer but mainly used
for communications. Radar was Racal ASR360 in an underbelly radome, replacing the nose radome of the T 2.
In service 1986 with 750 Sqn, used by 1xObsTU and 1xcomms. unit until 2008 HMS Heron Flight.
Powered by two 940shp Garrett-Airesearch TPE331-10 turboprops.
Serials: ZE438–441 (4).
Total 4; no losses.

	Span	Length	Ceiling	Range	Speed
T 2	52ft/15.85m	48ft 2in/14.4m	26,000ft/7,800m	1,382 miles/2,211km	285mph/456kmph
T 3	"	47ft 2in/14.1m	"	1,095 miles/1,752km	299mph/478kmph

**Total Jetstream T 2s and T 3s 6 plus 12 conversions making a total of 18; in service 1978–
present 2010; 1 (6%) loss to date.**

SHORT BROTHERS, later SHORTS (Eastchurch & Rochester, Kent, later Belfast, N.I.)

One of the oldest and longest-lived British companies, founded in 1908 and specialising in seaplanes and
naval types during the First World War. During the 1930s its flying boats, particularly the Empire types,
helped to popularise air travel and its Second World War boats played a large part in winning the Battle of
the Atlantic. Unfortunately post-Second World War success was not quite so forthcoming and the company was taken over by Bombardier of Canada in 1999 and now produces components only. Its seaplanes

and flying boats in the First World War were many and varied, so that the Short number (beginning with an S) is given for the early types for identification. Supplied 4,677 examples of 35 types (S 34, S 38, S 39, S 42, S 46, S 45, S 32, S 47, S 79, Sturgeon and Tucano, see Vol. 1); also assembled Airco DH 9 and 9A, Felixstowe F 3 and F 5, Bristol Bombay, HP Hampden and Hereford, and E.E Canberra.

254. Tractor Biplane Hydro S 41

A two-bay biplane seaplane for unarmed reconnaissance with the RNAS, with two crew; it had two main floats, two under the wings and one under the tail but could also be fitted with wheels. It had a long, narrow fuselage with the lower wing beneath and strutted to it; the upper wing had a longer span with angled bracing struts. There was no fin.
In service 1912 at Eastchurch, used by three units (Carlingnose, Eastchurch, 2W) until 1916, 2W.
Action: southern Europe.
Powered by one 80hp Gnome 7z Lambda rotary.
Serial: 10.
Total 1; 1 accidental loss.

254a. Improved S 41

As the above but with an improved wing-section, king-posts, ailerons, a fin and smaller floats; used for reconnaissance, as a seaplane.
In service 1913 at Grain, used by three units (Calshot, Eastchurch, Grain),until 1915, Calshot.
Powered by one 100hp Gnome 14 Omega-Omega rotary.
Serials: 20–21 (2).
Total 2. No losses.
Both Marks: Span: 50ft/15.24m   Length: 39ft/11.89m   Ceiling: n/k   Endurance: 5hrs   Speed: 60mph/97kmph.
Total S 41s 3; in service 1912–16; 1 (33%) loss.

255. Tractor Biplane Seaplane S 54

A two-bay biplane with two seats side-by-side for reconnaissance and training for the RNAS; no armament. The lower wing was mounted on the fuselage and the longer span upper wing had angled bracing struts; two main floats, two smaller underwing and one tail float.
In service 1913 to 1914 at Felixstowe.
Action: home waters.
Powered by one 160hp Gnome 14 Lambda-Lambda rotary.
Serial: 19.
Dimensions and performance n/k.
Total 1; 1 (100%) accidental loss.

256. Tractor Biplane Seaplane S 60

A two-bay biplane side-by-side two-seat unarmed reconnaissance seaplane for the RNAS, with two main floats and two smaller underwing but which could be fitted with a wheeled undercarriage. Longer span upper wing with angled support struts.
In service 1913 at Leven, used by seven units (Carlingnose, Dundee, Eastchurch Sqn, Leven, Morbeque, Ostend, 3N Sqn) until 1914, Ostend.
Action: home waters.
Powered by one 80hp Gnome 7z Lambda rotary.
Serial: 42.
Span: 48ft/14.63m   Length: 35ft/10.67m   Ceiling and endurance: n/k   Speed: 65mph/105kmph.
Total 1; 1 (100%) accidental loss.

257. Folder Seaplane S 64

A reconnaissance two-bay biplane seaplane for the RNAS with a longer span upper wing and angled support struts; a two-seater able to carry light bombs underwing. Two main floats, two underwing and one tail.

As the name suggests, the wings could be folded.

In service 1913, HMS Hermes, used by two units (Calshot, Westgate) until 1914, HMS Hermes; embarked on one cruiser and one AMC.

Action: home waters.

Powered by one 160hp Gnome 14 Lambda-Lambda rotary with a large exhaust above the cowling.

Serials: 81–82 (2).

Span: 56ft/17.07m   Length: 40ft/12.19m   Ceiling: n/k   Endurance: 5hrs   Speed: 78mph/126kmph.

Total 2; 2 (100%) losses inc. 1 hostile.

258. Tractor Biplane Seaplane S 73

A three-bay reconnaissance biplane for the RNAS, with two crew and able to carry light bombs or a torpedo underbelly. Two main floats, two underwing and one tail. The upper wing had a longer span with angled support struts.

In service 1914 at Grain, used by six units (Dundee, Felixstowe, Grain, Granton, Ostend, Westgate) until 1916, Dundee.

Action: home waters.

Powered by one 160hp Gnome 14 Lambda-Lambda rotary.

Serials: 78–80 (2).

Total 2; 1 accidental loss.

258a. Folder Tractor Biplane Seaplane Type 81

As the S 73 but with folding wings. Was the first British seaplane to launch a torpedo.

In service 1914 at Calshot, used by five units (Calshot, Felixstowe, Grain, Niorini, Westgate) until 1915, East Africa; embarked on one AMC and two cruisers.

Action: home waters, Indian Ocean.

Serials: 119–22 (4).

Total 4; 1 hostile loss.

	Span	Length	Ceiling	Endurance	Speed
S 73	57ft/17.37m	39ft/11.89m	n/k	5hrs	78mph/126kmph
Type 81	67ft/20.42m	42ft/12.8m	"	"	60mph/97kmph

Total S 73s 6; in service 1914–16; 2 (33%) losses inc. 1 hostile.

259. Gun-Carrying Pusher Seaplane

A reconnaissance three-bay biplane for the RNAS with two main floats and two underwing, this was a single-seater armed with one gun of varying types. It had a braced longer-span upper wing and twin rudders with small floats beneath.

In service 1914 at Calshot, used by three units (Calshot, Grain, Yarmouth) until 1915, Grain.

Powered by one 160hp Gnome 14 Lambda-Lambda rotary pusher.

Serial: 126.

Span: 67ft/20.42m   Length: 33ft 9in/10.29m   Ceiling: n/k   Endurance: 5hrs   Speed: 60mph/97kmph.

Total 1; no losses.

260. Type 74 Seaplane

A reconnaissance two-seater for the RNAS, which could carry light bombs underbelly. It had three-bay non-folding wings with the upper having a longer span braced by angled support struts, and two main, two underwing and one tail float. There was a large curved rudder and a small fin.

In service 1914 at Grain, used by seven units (Calshot, Dundee, Gibraltar, Granton, Leven, Scapa, Westgate) until 1915, Gibraltar; embarked on one cruiser.

Action: home waters and Mediterranean.

Powered by one 100hp Gnome 14 Omega-Omega rotary.

Serial: 74–77 (4), 183.

Total 5; 3 accidental and 1 hostile loss.

260a. Improved Type 74

As the above but had a deeper cowling and a smaller fin.

In service 1914 on HMS Riviera, used by five units (Bembridge, Blyth, Calshot, Dunkirk, Felixstowe) until 1916, Calshot; embarked on one cruiser and three seaplane carriers.

Action: home waters and Mediterranean.

Serials: 811–18 (8).

Total 8; 3 accidental and 1 hostile loss.

Both Marks: Span: 57ft/17.37m   Length: 39ft/11.89m   Ceiling: n/k   Endurance: 5hrs   Speed: 65mph/105kmph.

Total Type 74s 13; in service 1914–16; 8 (62%) losses inc. 2 hostile.

261. Type 135 Folder Tractor Seaplane

An RNAS reconnaissance two-bay biplane with a crew of two and able to carry light bombs or a torpedo under belly. The upper wing had a longer span, braced by angled support struts. Two main floats and one tail.

In service 1914 on HMS Riviera, used by two units (Calshot, Grain) until 1915, HMS Ark Royal; embarked on two seaplane carriers.

Action: home waters.

Powered by one 140hp Salmson B9 radial with a radiator above the cowling.

Serial: 135.

Span: 52ft/15.85m   Length: 37ft/11.28m   Ceiling: n/k   Endurance: 4.5hrs   Speed: 65mph/105kmph.

Total 1; 1 (100%) accidental loss.

262. Type 136 Folder Tractor Seaplane

Similar to the above but larger and re-engined this was an RNAS reconnaissance two-bay biplane with two crew and able to carry light bombs or a torpedo under belly. Two main floats and one tail.

In service 1914 on HMS Riviera, used by three units (Calshot, Felixstowe, 3W) until 1916, 3 Wing; embarked on two seaplane carriers.

Action: Mediterranean.

Powered by one 200hp Canton-Unne 2m7 in-line.

Serial: 136.

Span: 54ft 6in/16.61m   Length: 40ft/12.19m   Ceiling: n/k   Endurance: 4hrs   Speed: 72mph/116kmph.

Total 1; 1 losses.

263. Nile

An impressed three-bay biplane seaplane used for reconnaissance and training, with two crew and able to carry one torpedo or 100lb/45kg of bombs under belly. It had twin rudders with small floats beneath which were mounted under the tailplane and two main floats – there were no underwing floats.

In service 1914 at Grain, used by two units until 1914, HMS Hermes; embarked on one cruiser.

Action: home waters.

Powered by one 160hp Gnome 14 Lambda-Lambda rotary pusher.

Serial: 905.

Dimensions and performance n/k.

Total 1 impressed; no losses.

264. Type 166

An RNAS reconnaissance seaplane derived from the Short Type 136 (qv) with two crew and armed with a Lewis mg in the rear cockpit, plus 336lb/152kg of bombs or torpedo under belly. Could be fitted with a wheeled undercarriage. Built by Short and Westland.

In service 1915 on HMS Ark Royal, used by 10 units (Calshot, Felixstowe, Imbros, Killingholme, Mudros, Portland, Stavros, Suda Bay, Thassos, 2W) until 1918, Thassos; embarked on two monitors and three seaplane carriers.

Short 166, 163,
RNAS Thasos.
(G. Stuart Leslie)

Action: home waters, Mediterranean and southern Europe.
Powered by one 200hp Canton-Unne/Salmson 2m7 radial with only the upper half cowled.
Serials: 161–66 (6), 9751–9770 (20).
Span: 57ft 3in/17.47m   Length: 40ft 7in/12.39m   Ceiling: n/k   Endurance: 4hrs   Speed:
65mph/105kmph.
Total 26; 5 (19%) accidental losses.

265. Type 830

An RNAS reconnaissance seaplane derived from the Short Type 135 (qv), a two-seater armed with a
Lewis mg in the rear cockpit and light bombs under belly.
In service 1915 on HMS Engadine, used by five units (Dover, Dundee, Dunkirk, Felixstowe, Mudros) and
2xPTU until 1917, Dover; embarked on one cruiser and four seaplane carriers.
Action: home waters, Mediterranean and southern Europe.
Powered by one 140hp Salmson B 9 radial.
Serials: 819–821 (3), 828–830 (3), 1335–1346 (12), 9781–9790 (10).
Total 28; 6 accidental and 3 hostile losses.

265a. Type 827

As the 830 above but re-engined and with a longer wingspan. Built by Short, Brush, Fairey, Parnall and
Sunbeam.
In service 1915 with 8 Sqn on HMS Campania, used by 14 units (7N and 8NSqns, Calshot, Dover,
Dundee, Dunkirk, Felixstowe, Grain, Houton Bay, Killingholme, Portland, Scapa, Westgate, Yarmouth),
D Force RFC, one RAF sqn (269), 4xPTU and 1xTDS, until 1918, 269 Sqn; embarked on one monitor,
one AMC, one cruiser and two seaplane carriers.
Action: home waters, Mediterranean, Red Sea and East Africa.
Powered by one 150hp Sunbeam Nubian in-line.
Serials: 822–27 (6), 3063–3072 (10), 3093–3112 (20), 3321–3332 (12), 8218–8229 (20), 8250–57 (8), 8550–
8561 (12), 8630–8649 (20).
Total 108; 35 accidental and 2 hostile losses.

	Span	Length	Ceiling	Endurance	Speed
830	53ft 11in/16.43m	35ft 3in/10.75m	n/k	3.5 hrs	70mph/113kmph
827	61ft/18.59m	"	"	"	"

Total 830/827s 136; in service 1915–18; 46 (34%) losses inc. 5 hostile.

Short Type 827, 3331, RNAS Westgate. (Peter Green Collection)

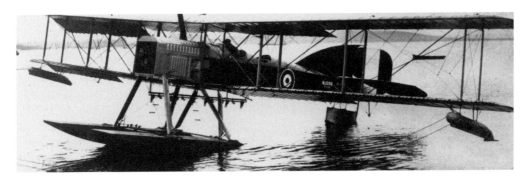

Short Type 184, N1098. (Peter Green Collection)

266. Type 184

The best-known of the many RNAS reconnaissance seaplanes designed by Short, this was also a bomber and torpedo bomber; it carried one or two crew and was armed with a Lewis mg in the rear cockpit (when a two-seater), plus 520lb/235kg of bombs or a 14in torpedo under fuselage. Built by Short, Brush, Mann-Egerton, Pheonix, Robey, Sage, Saunders and Westland.

In service 1915 on HMS Ben-my-Chree, used by 28 units (Bembridge, Calafrana, Calshot, Cattewater, Cherbourg, Dover, Dundee, Fishguard, Hornsea, Houton Bay, Killingholme, Mudros, Newhaven, Newlyn, Otranto, Portland, Port Said, Saint Maria de Leuca, Seaton Carew, Skyros, Strathbeg, Suda Bay, Syra, Torquay, Tresco, Westgate, Yarmouth, 6W), 27 RAF sqns (202, 219, 229, 230, 233, 234, 235, 237, 238, 239, 240, 241, 242, 243, 245, 246, 248, 249, 253, 263, 264, 266, 267, 268, 269, 270, 271), and two RAF flts, until 1920, 219 Sqn; also served with 4xRNAS PTU, SoAN, SoNCo-op, RAF&NCo-opSqn, SPTSqn and 2xTDS. Embarked on four monitors, four AMC, seven seaplane carriers and one cruiser.

Action: home waters, Mediterranean, Aden, Red Sea, East Africa and Estonia, also based overseas in Malta and Egypt.

Powered by one 200hp Sunbeam Mohawk, 260hp Sunbeam Maori III, or 220hp Renault 12fe in-line.

Serials: 184–85 (2), 841–850 (10), 8001–8105 (105), 8344–8391 (48), 9041–9060 (20), 9065–9094 (20), N1090–1099 (10), N1580–1589 (10), N1660–1689 (30), N1740–1839 (80), N2630–9303 (30), N2790–2894 (60), N2900–2999 (100), N9000–9229 (178), N9260 (14), N9290 (9).

Total 726; 168 accidental and 30 hostile losses.

266a. Intermediate Type 184

As the above but with detail improvements.
In service 1916–18.
Total and details included with the 184.

266b. Improved Type 184

As the 184 but with a larger tail float and other modifications. Built by Pheonix, Robey, Sage, Saunders and White.

In service 1917 at Calshot, used by 24 units (Bembridge, Calshot, Calafrana, Cattewater, Dover, Dundee, Dunkirk, Felixstowe, Fishguard, Hornsea, Houton Bay, Killingholme, Mudros, Newhaven, Newlyn, Portland, Port Said, Rosyth, Scapa, South Shields, Suda Bay, Suez, Westgate, Yarmouth) and 2xPTU until 1918. Embarked on one cruiser, eight seaplane carriers and one monitor.

Action: home waters, Mediterranean and Red Sea.

Powered by one 250hp Maori II, 260hp Maori III, 200hp Mohawk, or 220hp/240hp Renault 12fe, driving a four-bladed propeller.

Serials: N1080–1089 (10), N1130–1149 (20), N1220–1279 (60), N1590–1659 (95).
Total 185; 51 accidental and 8 hostile losses.

266c. Dover Type 184

As the 184 but with modifications to enable it to operate in rougher seas, these including larger main floats and more streamlined wing floats.

Action: home waters.

Unknown number of conversions of the 184.

All Marks: Span: 63ft 6in/19.35m   Length: 40ft 7in/12.37m   Ceiling: 9,000ft/2,700m   Endurance: 4.5 hrs   Speed: 88mph/142kmph.

Total 184s 911; in service 1915–20; 257 (28%) losses inc. 38 hostile; nicknamed Home-from-Home.

267. Bomber

A landplane RNAS bomber, based on the 184 above; it had two crew and was armed with one Lewis mg in the rear cockpit, plus 900lb/410kg of bombs under fuselage and wings. Built by Short, Mann-Egerton, Pheonix and Sunbeam.

In service 1916 with 7 (N) Wing, used by four units (7NSqn, 3W, 4W, H-P Sqn) and two TU until 1917, 5 Wing.

Action: northern Europe.

Powered by one 250hp RR Eagle II in-line.

Serials: 3706, 9306–9355 (50), 9476–9495 (20), 9771–9776 (6), 9831–9840 (6).

Span: 85ft/25.9m   Length: 45ft/13.72m   Ceiling: 9,500ft/2,850m   Endurance: 6hrs   Speed: 77mph/124kmph.

Total 83; 7 (8%) losses inc. 3 hostile.

268. Type 320

The last operational First World War design by Short, a reconnaissance and torpedo bomber seaplane for the RNAS/RAF; it was a two-seater armed with a Lewis mg in the rear cockpit and 660lb/300kg of bombs or an 18in torpedo under the fuselage. Built by Short and Sunbeam.

In service 1917 at Otranto, used by six units (6W, Calshot, Killingholme, Otranto, Taranto, Yarmouth) and six RAF sqns (229, 240, 248, 263, 266, 268), until 1919, 268 Sqn; also served with 1xTDS, 1xTorpAS and 1xTorpTS.

Action: home waters and Mediterranean, also based overseas in Malta.

Powered by one 320hp Sunbeam Cossack in-line.

Serials: N1150–1159 (10), N1300–1319 (20), N1360–1409 (50), N1480–1504 (25), N1690–1709 (20).

Span: 75ft/22.86m   Length: 45ft 9in/13.95m   Ceiling: 3,000ft/900m   Endurance: 3hrs   Speed: 72mph/116kmph.

Total 125; 32 (26%) losses inc. 3 hostile.

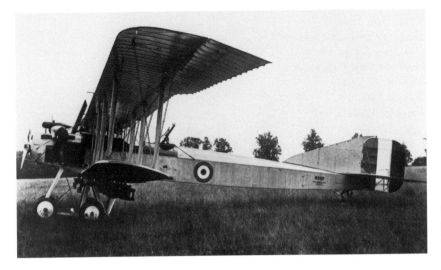

Short Bomber, 9357, 4 Wing RNAS. (Newark Air Museum)

191. Short 320, N1397, 268 Sqn. (G. Stuart Leslie)

Short Rangoon I, K2134, 203 Sqn. (Newark Air Museum)

269. Rangoon I

A general-reconnaissance flying boat for the RAF, with a crew of five and armed with one Lewis mg in the nose and each beam position, plus 1,000lb/454kg of bombs underwing.
In service 1931 with 203 Sqn, used by two sqns (203, 210) until 1936, 210 Sqn.
Based overseas in Gibraltar and Iraq.
Powered by three 550hp Bristol Jupiter XIf radials.
Serials: K2134, K2809, K3678, S1433–35 (3).
Span: 93ft/28.35m   Length: 66ft 9in/20.35m   Ceiling: 12,000ft/3,600m   Range: 650 miles/1,046km   Speed: 115mph/185kmph.
Total 6; no losses.

270. Singapore III

A general-reconnaissance flying boat for the RAF, with six crew and armed with one Lewis mg in nose, dorsal and tail positions, plus 2,000lb/908kg of bombs underwing.
In service 1935 with 205 Sqn, used by seven sqns (203, 205, 209, 210, 228, 230, 240) until 1941, 205 Sqn; also served with SPTSqn, FBTSqn and 1xOTU until 1942.
Based overseas in Malta, Iraq and Singapore, action Mediterranean.
Powered by two 700hp RR Kestrel IX tractors and two 700hp KestrelVIII pusher in-lines, in two nacelles.
Serials: K3592–95 (4), K4577–85 (9), K6907–6922 (16), K8565–68 (4), K8856–59 (4).
Span: 90ft/27.43m   Length: 64ft 2in/19.55m   Ceiling: 11,300ft/3,390m   Range: 1,000 miles/1,610km   Speed: 136mph/219kmph.
Total 37; 10 (27%) accidental losses.

271. Sunderland I

The most famous British military flying boat, very advanced for its time; it had 10 crew and was armed with one Vickers, later Browning, mg in a FN-11 nose turret, four Browning mg in a FN-13 tail turret and one manual Vickers or Browning in each beam position. 2,000lb/908kg of bombs or four, later eight, DC could be carried internally and winched out underwing for dropping and, later in service, it carried ASV-I or II radar with external aerials.
In service 1938 with 210 and 230 Sqns, used by seven sqns (95, 201, 202, 204, 210, 228, 230) until 1943, 204 Sqn; also served with 1xOTU until 1946.
Based overseas in Singapore, action North and South Atlantic, Mediterranean and Indian Ocean.
Powered by four 835hp Bristol Pegasus XXII radials.
Serials: L2158–2168 (11), L5798–5807 (10), N6133–35 (3), N9020–9050 (18), P9600–9624 (12), T9040–9078 (20).
Total 74; 36 accidental and 20 hostile losses.

Short Singapore III, K8858, 203
Sqn. (Newark Air Museum)

Short Sunderland I, L2163, 210 Sqn. (Newark Air Museum)

271a. Sunderland II

As the Mk I except that it had two Browning mg in an FN-7 dorsal turret to replace the beam guns, an FN4a tail turret, and ASV-II as standard. Built by Short and Blackburn.

In service 1941 with 201 Sqn, used by eight sqns (201, 202, 204, 228, 230, 330, 423, 461) and 1xFTU until 1944, 201 Sqn.

Action: North and South Atlantic, and Mediterranean.

Powered by four 815hp Pegasus XVIII.

Serials: T9083–9115 (15), W3976–3998 (23), W6000–04 (5), W6050–6064 (15).

Total 58; 37 accidental and 7 hostile losses.

271b. Sunderland III

The major production version, as the Mk II but with a redesigned hull bottom which had a smaller, sharper step; the nose turret was an FN-5, some had one 0.5in in the nose hatch, and this was sometimes augmented by four fixed Brownings in the forward fuselage sides and one manually operated Vickers mg in each beam position. Radar was ASV-II or -III with external aerials and eight reserve DCs could be carried in addition to those on the racks. Built by Short and Blackburn.

In service 1942 with 201 Sqn, used by 15 sqns (95, 119, 201, 202, 204, 228, 230, 246, 270, 330, 343, 422, 423, 461, 490) until 1945, 343 Sqn; also served with CC FIS, 2xFTU, OFIS and 2xOTU, until 1947.

Action: North and South Atlantic, Mediterranean and Indian Ocean.

Powered by four 815hp Pegasus XVIII or 835hp Pegasus XXII.

Serials: W3999–4027 (27), W6005–6033 (20), W6065–6080 (10), DD828–867 (40), DP176–200 (25), DV956–DW113 (45), EJ131–172 (35), EK572–596 (25), JM659–722 (42), ML725–795 (53).

Total 322; 120 accidental and 31 hostile losses.

271c. Sunderland IIIA

As the Mk III but had ASV-VIc radar in under-wingtip radomes.

In service 1944 to 1946 with 13 sqns (95, 201, 204, 205, 228, 230, 270, 330, 343, 422, 423, 461, 490), also used by 2xOTU and 2xFTU.

Action: North Atlantic.

Serials: ML796–884 (81), NJ170–194 (25), NJ253–58 (6), PP135–144 (10).

Total 122; 21 accidental and 2 hostile losses.

271d. Sunderland GR or MR 5

As the Mk IIIA but with new engines, a crew of 13, and armament of two Browning mg in the nose turret, four in the FN-13 tail turret and one manual 0.5in in each beam position to replace the dorsal turret when deleted (permanently after the Second World War finished); some also had the four fixed Brownings in the fuselage and the radar was ASV-VIc in the under-wingtip radomes. Built by Short and Blackburn.

In service 1945 with 230 Sqn, used by 11 sqns (88, 201, 204, 205, 209, 228, 230, 240, 259, 330, 461) and one flt until 1959, 205 Sqn, the RAF's last flying boat unit; also served with CCIS, 1xFTU, FBTSqn, 1xOTU and 1xOCU.

Action: North and South Atlantic, Indian Ocean, Berlin Airlift, Malaya, China and Korea, also based overseas in Norway, Ceylon, Singapore and Hong Kong.

Powered by four 1,200hp P&W Twin Wasp R1830-90 radials, with two exhausts above each engine.
Serials: NJ259–277 (19), PP103–164 (30), PP145–164 (20), RN264–306 (40), SZ559–599 (28), TX293, VB880–889 (10).

Total 148 plus 56 conversions of the Mk IIIA, making a total of 204; 49 accidental losses.

	Span	Length	Ceiling	Range	Speed
Mk I	112ft 8in/34.34m	85ft 4in/26m	20,500ft/6,150m	2,880 miles/4,637km	210mph/338kmph
Mk II	"	"	"	2,700 miles/4,347km	205mph/335kmph
Mk III	"	"	17,200ft/5,160m	"	210mph/338kmph
GR 5	"	"	17,900ft/5,370m	2,980 miles/4,798km	213mph/343kmph

Total Sunderlands 724; in service 1938–59; 323 (45%) losses inc. 60 hostile; nicknamed Flying Porcupine, Wonderland.

272. Scion I

A small unbraced-high-wing monoplane airliner impressed for communications work by the RAF, carrying the pilot and five passengers. It had a fixed undercarriage and a single fin/rudder, and the tailplanes were wire braced.

In service 1940 with 110 Wing, used by 2xcomms. units until 1941, 1 FPP.

Powered by two 84hp Pobjoy Niagara I or 85hp Niagara II radials with cylinder head cowlings.
Serials: W7419, X9375, AV981.

Total 3 impressed; 1 accidental loss.

272a. Scion II

As the Mk I but had an improved windscreen, with roof quarterlights, which sloped down more to the nose, improved cabin windows, carried six passengers and was impressed for communications duties by the RAF.
In service 1940 with 110 Wing, used by 1xAACU and 5xcomms. units until 1942, 4 ARU.
Based overseas in the Middle East and North Africa.
Powered by two 85hp Niagara II with a raised thrust-line so that the propeller shafts were level with the leading edges.

Short Sunderland
MR 5, SZ566.
(Air-Britain
Archives)

Serials: X9364, X9366, X9374, X9430, X9456, Z7189–90 (2), AV974, AV981, AV990.
Total 10 impressed; 3 accidental losses.

	Span	Length	Ceiling	Range	Speed
Mk I	42ft/12.5m	31ft 6in/9.6m	13,000ft/3,900m	380 miles/612km	125mph/201kmph
Mk II	"	31ft 4in/9.55m	"	390 miles/628km	128mph/206kmph

Total Scions 13; 4 (30%) accidental losses.

273. Scion Senior

Similar to the Mk II but larger with four engines and could thus carry 10 passengers; the wings were tapered with more pointed tips. Impressed for communications work and could be fitted with floats although it is doubtful if the RAF did this.
In service 1940 with Lydda SFlt, used by one sqn (173) and 1×comms. unit until 1943, 173 Sqn.
Based overseas in the Middle East, not operational in the UK.
Powered by four 85hp Niagara III with smooth cowlings.
Serials: Z7187, HK868.
Span: 55ft/16.46m   Length: 42ft/12.8m   Ceiling: 10,000ft/3,000m   Range: 400 miles/644km   Speed: 134mph/216kmph.
Total 2 impressed; 1 (50%) hostile loss.

273. S 30m Empire Flying Boat

A famous pre-war airliner, a high-wing monoplane with a single fin/rudder with underwing floats impressed for general-reconnaissance and transport work with the RAF; it had six or seven crew and was armed with seven manual Brownings on free mountings around the hull, and ASV-I radar with external aerials. Could carry 29 passengers.
In service during 1940 at Invergordon.
Action: North Atlantic.
Powered by four 835hp Bristol Pegasus XXII radials.
Serials: V3137–38 (2).
Total 2 impressed; 2 hostile losses.

274a. S 23m Empire Flying Boat

As the above but had four Brownings in BP-A dorsal and tail turrets, ASV-I, and could carry six DC underwing; 24 passengers could be carried.
In service 1940 with 119 Sqn, used by two sqns (119, 413) until 1941, 413 Sqn.
Action: North Atlantic.
Powered by four 835hp Pegasus Xc.
Serials: AX659–60 (2).
Total 2 impressed; 1 accidental loss.

	Span	Length	Ceiling	Range	Speed
S 30	114ft/34.75m	88ft/26.82m	20,000ft/6,000m	1,500 miles/2,415km	200mph/322kmph
S 23	"	"	"	760 miles/1,224km	"

Total Empire Boats 4; in service 1940–41; 3 (75%) losses inc. 2 hostile.

275. G-Class Flying Boat

A larger version of the Empire Flying Boat, a high-wing monoplane impressed by the RAF for general-reconnaissance with a crew of seven or eight and armed with four Browning mg in two BP-A dorsal turrets (fore and aft) and a BP-A tail turret; 2,000lb/908kg of bombs or six DC underwing and ASV-II radar with external aerials. Named Golden Hind.
In service 1940 with 119 Sqn, used by one sqn and one flt, until 1941, 119 Sqn.
Action: North Atlantic.
Powered by four 1,500hp Bristol Hercules XIV radials.

Serials: X8273–75 (3).
Span: 134ft 4in/40.95m   Length: 103ft 2in/31.44m   Ceiling: n/k   Range: 3,200
miles/5,152km   Speed: 209mph/336kmph.
Total 3 impressed; 1 (33%) accidental loss.

276. Stirling I Series I

An RAF heavy bomber, its first with four engines; it was very manoeuvrable but had a poor ceiling and
a weak undercarriage. Seven or eight crew and armed with two Browning mg in a FN-5 or 5A nose
turret and FN-25 ventral turret and four Brownings in a FN-20 or -4A tail turret, plus one in each beam
position; 14,000lb/6,350kg of bombs internally and in wing cells.
In service 1940 with 7 Sqn, used by two sqns (7, 15) and 1xmisc. unit, until 1941, 15 Sqn.
Action: northern Europe.
Powered by four 1,375hp Bristol Hercules II or 1,400hp Hercules III radials.
Serials: N3636–3661 (19), N6000–6049 (46).
Total 65.

276a. Stirling I Series II

As the Series I but had two Brownings in each beam position and the ventral turret was deleted.
In service during 1941, used by four sqns (7, 15, 149, 214), training to 1944.
Powered by four 1,590hp Hercules XI in shorter Short-designed nacelles.
Total included in the Series I.

276b. Stirling I Series III

The main Mk I production, as the Series II but with two Brownings in a FN-7 dorsal turret (some later
had a Mk III style FN-50) replacing the beam positions and four Brownings in a FN-20 tail turret. The
engine nacelles were a different Bristol design.
In service 1941 with 7 Sqn, used by seven sqns (7, 15, 75, 90, 149, 214, 218) and one transport sqn (620)
until 1944, 214 Sqn; Mk Is of all series also served with 14xCU, ECFS, 1xBATFlt, PNTU, 1xFTU,
1xTTFlt and 1xmisc. unit.
Action: northern Europe.
Serials: N3663–3769 (72), N6066–6129 (36), R9141–9358 (150), W7426–7639 (150), BF309–454 (115),
BK592–647 (42), DJ972–77 (6), EE871–EF316 range (61).
Total 632; Mk I all series had 249 accidental and 308 hostile losses.

276c. Stirling III

As the Mk I Series III but had two Brownings in a FN-5 nose turret, two in a FN-50 (more rounded and
streamlined) dorsal turret as standard, and four in a FN-20 tail turret, with 14,000lb/6,350kg of bombs;
some had H2S in a radome under the rear fuselage.
In service 1943 with 149 Sqn, used by 11 sqns (7, 15, 75, 90, 149, 214, 218, 196, 513, 622, 623), two RCM
sqns (171, 199) and two transport sqns (570, 620), until 1944, 149 Sqn; also served with CNS, 8xCU,
EANS, ECFS, PNTU, 1xTTFlt and 2xmisc. units until 1945.
Action: northern Europe.
Powered by four 1,615hp Hercules XVI, with long intakes above the cowlings and longer exhausts.
Serials: BF455–580 (85), BK649–818 (108), EE871–EF316 range (362), EH875–EJ127 (120), LJ440–670
range (136), LK375–624 (166), MZ260–264 (5).
Total 982; 225 accidental and 257 hostile losses.

276d. Stirling A IV

Although superseded as a bomber the Stirling became a useful airborne forces transport and glider-
tug; the nose turret was replaced by a clear Perspex nose and the dorsal turret was deleted, leaving
just four Brownings in the FN-20 tail turret. There was a paratroop exit in the lower rear fuselage,
glider-towing gear around the tail, and it carried six crew and either 24 passengers or 9,450lb/4,290kg
of freight.

Short Stirling III, BF509. (Newark Air Museum)

Short Stirling C V, PK117, 51 Sqn. (Newark Air Museum)

In service 1944 with 299 and 190 Sqns, used by 11 sqns (46, 51, 158, 190, 196, 242, 295, 299, 570, 620, 624), and three SD sqns (138, 148, 161), until 1946, 196 Sqn; also served with CNS, 4xCU and the ORTU.
Action: northern and southern Europe, also based overseas in North Africa.
Serials: EF317–23 range (7), LJ557–670 range (39), LJ810–LK370 (384), PK225–237 (13), PW255–266 (12), PW384–599 (70), TS261–266 (6).
Total 531 plus 44 conversions of the Mk III, making a total of 575; 109 accidental and 73 hostile losses.

276e. Stirling C V

A dedicated transport version with all armament and turrets deleted and faired-over, the nose being more pointed with a Perspex tip; it had cabin windows and a large freight door on the starboard side. Five crew and 40 passengers or 10,000lb/4,540kg of freight which could be loaded through the hinged nose.
In service 1945 with 46 Sqn, used by six sqns (46, 51, 158, 196, 242, 299), four flts and 1xmisc. unit until 1946, 46 Sqn.
Based overseas in Egypt and India.
Serials: PJ878–PK186 (161).
Total 161; 29 accidental and 1 hostile loss.

	Span	Length	Ceiling	Range	Speed
Mk I	99ft 1in/30.21m	87ft 3in/26.6m	15,000ft/4,500m	2,330 miles/3,751km	260mph/419kmph
Mk III	"	"	17,000ft/5,100m	2,010 miles/3,236km	270mph/435kmph
C V	"	"	18,000ft/5,400m	3,000 miles/4830km	280mph/4,508kmph

Total Stirlings 2,371; in service 1940–46; 1,251 (53%) losses inc. 639 hostile.

Shorts Belfast C 1, XR368,
53 Sqn. (Charles Parker)

277. Seaford GR 1

Intended to replace the Sunderland, to which it bore a strong resemblance (being originally the Mk IV), it saw little use because the Second World War had ended and it offered little or no improvement over the Sunderland GR 5; 10 crew but was not fitted with turrets during its RAF service though it could carry these in nose and tail, plus 4,960lb/2,250kg of stores internally and ASV-VIc in underwing radomes.
In service during 1946 with 201 Sqn.
Powered by four 1,800hp Bristol Hercules XIX radials.
Serials: NJ200–207 (8).
Span: 112ft 9in/34.37m   Length: 88ft 7in/27m   Ceiling: 13,000ft/3,900m   Range: 2,800 miles/4,508km   Speed: 242mph/3,896kmph.
Total 8; no losses.

278. Belfast C 1

The RAF's largest British-designed aircraft, the Belfast was primarily a freighter for the 'Empire routes', carrying six crew and 77,500lb/34,960kg of freight, though 150 passengers could be carried if required. In service 1966 to 1976 with 53 Sqn, it was retired prematurely due to defence cuts. Nicknamed Belslow and Dragmaster.
Powered by four 5,730shp RR Tyne R-TY-12-10 turboprops.
Serials: XR362–371 (10).
Span: 158ft 9in/48.39m   Length: 136ft 5in/41.59m   Ceiling: 30,000ft/9,000m   Range: 3,600 miles/5,796km   Speed: 346mph/557kmph.
Total 10; no losses.

SIDDELEY-DEASY (Coventry, Warwicks, UK)

Assembled Airco DH 10.

SIKORSKY (USA)

A pioneer helicopter company formed in 1923 and still extant. Supplied 103 examples of three types (Hoverfly, see Vol. 1).

279. Whirlwind HAR 21 (HRS-2)

When the first Westland-built Whirlwinds were found lacking in hot-weather performance, the American version was ordered for transport duties with the FAA, carrying two crew and 10 passengers; it was unarmed.
In service 1952–56 with 848 Sqn.
Action: Malaya.
Powered by one 600hp P&W Wasp R1340-40 radial.
Serials: WV189–198 (10).
Total 10; 5 accidental losses.

279a. Whirlwind HAS 22 (HO4S-3)

Similar to the HAR 21 but re-engined and performing FAA anti-submarine duties, with three crew and sonar gear; it was also used for communications duties, with two crew and 10 passengers.

In service 1953 with 706 Sqn, used by two sqns (845, 848), one flt, 2xCU, 1xATU and 1xcomms. unit, until 1970, 781 Sqn; embarked on six carriers.

Action: Suez, also based overseas in Malta.

Powered by one 700hp Wright Cyclone R1300-3 radial.

Serials: WV199–225 (15).

Total 15; 7 accidental losses.

	Rotor diameter	Length	Ceiling	Range	Speed
HAR 21	53ft/16.15m	42ft 2in/12.88m	9,800ft/2,940m	405 miles/652km	105mph/169kmph
HAS 22	"	"	10,600ft/3,180m	360 miles/580km	112mph/180kmph.

Total US Whirlwinds 25; in service 1952–70; 12 (48%) losses.

For British Whirlwinds see Westland.

SLINGSBY (Kirbymoorside, Yorks, UK)

Britain's major builder of gliders and sailplanes from 1934 until the 1970s when it switched to light aircraft and component production; in earlier times its successful Firefly trainer would have been with the RAF but it now trains military pilots with a civilian contractor. Supplied 955 examples of 13 types (Falcon, Kirby Kite, Primary, Gull, Cadet, King Kite, Sedbergh, Prefect, Grasshopper, Swallow, Regal and Venture, see Vol. 1).

280. Hengist I

An assault glider carrying a pilot and 15 passengers, but only used for trials. It had a high unbraced wing and the cockpit was faired into the nose ; single fin/rudder.

In service 1943 with the GPEU, used by GPEU and 2xmisc. units, until 1946, AFEE.

Serials: DG572–73 (2), DG673–76 (4).

Span: 80ft/24.38m   Length: 56ft 5in/17.2m.

Total 6; no losses.

SOPWITH (Kingston, Surrey, UK)

Formed in 1912 by T. O. M Sopwith, a pioneer airman, and became one of the best-known early British companies, particularly for the Camel. However it did not long outlast the First World War due to financial problems and went out of business in 1920. Like those of Short Bros, its early designs were many and varied. Supplied 13,735 examples of 26 types (School Biplane, Tractor Seaplane, Tabloid, Gunbus, Gordon Bennet, Two-Seater Scout, Schneider, Baby, Strutter fighters, Pup, Triplane, Camel, Dolphin, Snipe and Salamander, see Vol. 1).

281. Bat Boat No.1

A small two-bay biplane reconnaissance flying boat for the RNAS with two underwing floats and a bow-mounted elevator, carrying two crew and able to carry light bombs underwing. It had a very long marine-wood nose with the lower wing mounted on top of the fuselage.

In service during 1913 at Calshot.

Powered by one 90hp Austro-Daimler in-line pusher mounted midway between the wings.

Serial: allocated 38 but never carried it.

Unnumbered; total 1; 1 accidental loss.

281a. Bat Boat No. 1

As the above, probably using the same hull, but was an amphibian, with wheels on the fuselage side, and a revised tail unit with a single triangular fin and oval rudder. An increased dihedral on the lower wing gave better sea clearance.

In service 1914 at Calshot, used by three units (Calshot, Scapa, Yarmouth) until 1915, Calshot.

Action: home waters.

Serial: 38.

Total 1; 1 accidental loss.

281b. Bat Boat Type 1A

A revised amphibious version with twin rudders and no fins.

In service 1913–14 at Calshot.

Action: home waters.

Powered by one 120hp Green E6 in-line pusher much larger in appearance then the earlier versions, with a fuel tank above.

Serial: 118.

Total 1; 1 accidental loss.

281c. Bat Boat Type 2

A civil version impressed by the RNAS for reconnaissance, similar to the Mk IA but re-engined. It had three-bay staggered wings with the lower wing above and strutted to the fuselage.

In service 1914 at Calshot, used by two units (Calshot, Yarmouth) until 1915, Calshot.

Action: home waters.

Powered by one 200hp Sunbeam Mohawk radial pusher.

Serial: 879.

Total 1 impressed; no losses.

	Span	Length	Ceiling	Endurance	Speed
No.1	41ft/12.5m	32ft/9.75m	n/k	5hrs	65mph/105kmph
No.2	55ft/16.46m	35ft/10.67m	"	"	78mph/126kmph
Type 1A	"	30ft 4in/9.24m	"	"	"
Type 2	"	"	"	"	"

Total Bat Boats 3 plus 1 impressed making a total of 4; in service 1913–15; 3 (75%) losses.

282. Tractor Biplane (RG)

A reconnaissance type for the RNAS and RFC, with two or three crew and unarmed. A two-bay biplane of equal span and without a fin; there were fuselage windows.

In service 1913 at Eastchurch, used by three RNAS units (Eastchurch Sqn, Killingholme, 3NSqn), one RFC sqn (5) and CFS until 1915, Eastchurch.

Powered by one 80hp Gnome 7z Lambda rotary.

Serials: 33, 103–04 (2), 246–48 (3), 300, 315, 319, 324–25 (2).

Span: 40ft/12.19m   Length: 29ft/8.84m   Ceiling: 12,900ft/3,870m   Endurance: 2.5hrs   Speed: 70mph/113kmph.

Total 11 plus 1 rebuild of the School Biplane (Vol. 1) and 1 impressed, 906, making a total of 13 (4 RNAS); 1 accidental RNAS loss.

283. Pusher Seaplane

A two-seat, unarmed reconnaissance four-bay biplane for the RNAS with two main floats and one under the tail.

In service 1914 at Grain, used by three units (1 and 2NSqns, 3W) until 1915, Grain.

Powered by one 100hp Anzani radial pusher.

Serials: 123–24 (2).

Dimensions and performance: n/k.

Total 2; no losses.

284. Two-Seater

An RNAS bomber and trainer two-bay biplane with enlarged ailerons, two crew side-by-side and able to carry light bombs. The tailplanes were curved as was the rudder (no fin) and it had a two-skid undercarriage.

In service 1914 at Hendon, used by two units until 1914, Antwerp. Nicknamed Sociable, Tweenie and Churchill.

Action: northern Europe.

Powered by one 100hp Gnome-Monosoupape 9b-2 rotary, fully cowled.

Span: 36ft/10.98m   Length: 24ft 3in/7.42m   Ceiling: n/k   Endurance: 3hrs   Speed: 90mph/145kmph.

Serial: 149.

Total 1; 1 (100%) hostile loss.

285. Tractor Seaplane Type 137 (or Type C)

A reconnaissance two-bay biplane seaplane for the RNAS, an unarmed two-seater with two main floats and one tail. There was a fuel tank mounted in front of the cockpits between the wing and fuselage.

In service 1914–15 at Calshot; embarked on one cruiser.

Action: home waters.

Powered by one 120hp Austro-Daimler or 200hp Canton-Unne 2M7 in-line.

Serials: 137–38 (2), 157–59 (3).

Dimensions and performance: n/k.

Total 5; 1 (20%) accidental loss.

286. Tractor Biplane Seaplane

A two-seat unarmed reconnaissance three-bay biplane for the RNAS, with two main floats and one tail, and a fuel tank as on the Type 137 above. Nicknamed Circuit.

In service 1914 at Calshot, used by two units (Calshot, Grain) until 1914, Grain.

Powered by one 120hp Green E6 in-line.

Serial: 151.

Span: 36ft/10.98m   Length: 29ft/8.84m   Ceiling and endurance: n/k   Speed: 80mph/129kmph.

Total 1; 1 (100%) accidental loss.

287. Hydro-Biplane Type S

A reconnaissance seaplane for the RNAS, with two crew and armed with one 1.5 pdr Vickers in the nose position. It had four-bay wings of equal span and the nacelle was mounted on the lower wing, while the tailplane was high set on the booms. Two main floats and a tail.

In service during 1914 at Calshot. Nicknamed Gunbus.

Powered by one 200hp Salmson 2m7 radial pusher.

Serial: 93.

Span: 80ft/24.3m   Other dimensions and performance: n/k.

Total 1; no loss.

Sopwith Type 137, 138, RNAS Calshot. (Peter Green Collection)

Sopwith Type
807. (G. Stuart
Leslie)

288. Type 880 Pusher Seaplane

Originally ordered by the Greek Government, and impressed by the RNAS, this was a reconnaissance and home defence two-seater which could be fitted with wheels and was armed with a Lewis mg in the front cockpit and light bombs underwing. It had four-bay staggered wings, a single fin beneath the tailplane with the curved rudder top protruding above and a two-skid land undercarriage when fitted.

In service 1914 at Calshot, used by six units (Calshot, Eastchurch, Killingholme, Westgate, Yarmouth, 3NSqn) until 1915, Eastchurch.

Action: home waters and northern Europe.

Powered by one 100hp Gnome-Monosoupape 9b-2 rotary pusher with a large radiator behind the aft cockpit.

Serials: 897–901 (5).

Span: 50ft/15.24m   Length: 31ft/9.45m   Ceiling and endurance: n/k   Speed: 80mph/129kmph.

Total 5; 3 (66%) accidental losses.

289. Type 807 Folder Seaplane

A reconnaissance seaplane for the RNAS, a two-seater able to carry light bombs on the float bracing struts. It was a two-bay biplane with jury struts close to the fuselage.

In service 1914 at Calshot, used by two units (Bembridge, Calshot), and Force D RFC until 1917, Basrah; embarked on one cruiser, one AMC and four seaplane carriers.

Action: home waters, Middle East, Mediterranean and East Africa.

Powered by one 100hp Gnome-Monosoupape 9b-2 rotary driving a propeller mounted on struts forward of the cowling.

Serials: 807–810 (4), 919–926 (8).

Span: 36ft/10.98m   Length: n/k   Ceiling: n/k   Endurance: 3.5hrs   Speed: 80mph/129kmph.

Total 12; 7 (58%) accidental losses.

290. Type 860

A torpedo-bomber seaplane for the RNAS with two crew, armed with a Lewis mg in the rear cockpit and able to carry a 14in torpedo under the fuselage. It was a two-bay biplane with the usual three floats and a fuel tank between the fuselage and upper wing.

In service 1915 at Calshot, used by five units (Calshot, Dover, Dundee, Felixstowe, Grain) until 1917, Grain.

Action: home waters and Mediterranean. Embarked on three seaplane carriers.

Powered by one 200hp Sunbeam Mohawk in-line with radiators each side.

Serials: 851–860 (10), 927–938 (6).

Dimensions and performance n/k.

Total 16; 4 (25%) accidental losses.

Sopwith Type 860, 931.
(Alastair Goodrum Collection)

Sopwith 9700 One and Half
Strutter, N5201, 2 Wing.
(G. Stuart Leslie)

291. Type 9700 1½ Strutter

A bomber variant of the Type 9400 fighter (Vol. 1) for the RNAS, a single-seater with the pilot in the front cockpit and the rear cockpit faired over to provide an internal bomb bay carrying 260lb/120kg of bombs; one Vickers mg above the cowling.

In service 1916 with 3 Wing, used by 11 units (Dunkirk, Eastchurch, Mullion, Pembroke, Prawle Point, 2W, 3W, 5W, 2, 5 and 7NSqns), one RAF sqn (233), 6xPTU, 1xATU, 1xMObsS and Fleet SoAF&G, until 1919. Action: northern and southern Europe.

Powered by on 110hp Clerget 9z or 130hp Clerget 9b rotary.

Serials: 9650–9750 range (30), A6901–7000 (100), N5080–5119 range (21), N5120–5169 (50), N5200–5219 (20), N5500–5549 (38), N5600–04 (5), N5630–34 (5), other N numbers (33).

Total 302; 26 accidental and 4 hostile losses.

291a. Ship's Strutter

An RNAS/RAF reconnaissance variant, with flotation bags in the fuselage and other naval equipment for catapulting from ships; a two-seater armed with a Lewis mg in the modified rear cockpit.

In service 1918 at Rosyth, used by four units (Donisbristle, Rosyth, Smoogroo, Turnhouse) until 1920, HMS *Argus*; embarked on one carrier and 18 battleships.

Action: Estonia.

Powered by one 140hp Clerget 9bf.

Serials: F2210–2229 (20), F7547-7596 (50).

Total 70 plus 88 conversions of the Type 9400 (Vol. 1) and 9700, making a total of 158; losses not known.

	Span	Length	Ceiling	Endurance	Speed
9700	33ft 6in/10.21m	25ft 3in/7.7m	13,000ft/3,900m	4.5hrs	102mph/164kmph
Ship's	"	"	15,000ft/4,500m	3.75hrs	"

Total 1½ Strutters 372 plus 88 conversions making a total of 460; in service 1916–20; losses not known.

For Type 9400 Fighter Strutters see Vol. 1.

292. B 1

A two-bay biplane bomber for the RNAS, a single-seater with one Vickers on the cowling and 560lb/255kg of bombs carried internally behind the cockpit; it was developed into the Grain Griffin (qv).
In service 1917 with 5 Sqn, used by four units (5NSqn, Dover, Turnhouse, Grain) until 1919, Grain.
Action: northern Europe.
Powered by one 200hp Hispano-Suiza 8ba or 200hp Wolseley Adder in-line.
Serial: N50.
Span: 38ft 6in/11.73m   Length: 27ft 6in/8.38m   Ceiling: 21,000ft/6,300m   Endurance: 3.5 hrs   Speed: 118mph/190kmph.
Total 1; no losses.

293. Cuckoo I

The RAF's first new torpedo-bomber, a single-seater able to carry an 18in torpedo under the fuselage but with no other armament.
In service 1918 with TorpAS and 185 Sqn, used by three sqns (185, 186, 210) until 1923, 210 Sqn; also served with TorpAS, 1xFS, 1xTorpTS, 2xTTSqns, 1xTSqn and 1xTDS.
Powered by one 200hp Sunbeam Arab I in-line.
Serials: N6900–7099 (120), N7150–7199 (24), N7982–8079 (18).
Total 162 (but some not issued); 4 accidental losses.

293a. Cuckoo II

A re-engined version.
In service in 1919 with 185 Sqn and used by two sqns (185, 210) until 1923, 210 Sqn.
Powered by one 200hp Wolseley Viper in-line.
Seventeen conversions of the Mk I; 1 accidental loss.

	Span	Length	Ceiling	Endurance	Speed
Mk I	46ft 9in/14.25m	28ft 6in/8.68m	12,100ft/3,630m	4hrs	103mph/166kmph
Mk II	"	"	13,700ft/4,110m	"	92mph/148kmph

Total Cuckoos 162; in service 1918–23; 5 (3%) losses.

Sopwith Cuckoo I, N6966, 201
TDS. (G. Stuart Leslie)

SPARTAN (Cowes, IoW, UK)

A small company formed in 1928 and going out of business in 1935. Supplied three examples of one type.

294. Cruiser II

A small low-wing monoplane airliner impressed by the RAF as a light transport, carrying two crew and six passengers; unarmed. It had a wire-braced single fin/rudder and a heavy-looking strutted undercarriage.
In service 1940 with 6 AACU, used by 2xAACU until 1941, 7 AACU.
Powered by three 120hp DH Gipsy III in-lines, one in the nose.
Serials: X9431, X9433.
Total 2 impressed; no losses.

294a. Cruiser III

A developed version with a longer fuselage, revised strut-braced fin/rudder, revised cockpit and cabin windows and a spatted undercarriage. In service 1940 with 6 AACU, used by 2xAACU until 1940, 7AACU.
Serial: X9432.
Total 1 impressed; no losses.

	Span	Length	Ceiling	Range	Speed
Mk II	54ft/16.46m	39ft 2in/11.94m	15,000ft/4,500m	360 miles/499km	135mph/217kmph
Mk III	"	41ft/12.5m	"	550 miles/885km	"

Total Cruisers 3 impressed; no losses.

SPARTAN (USA)

A small American company, formed in 1928, which supplied one example of one type.

295. 7W Executive

A low-wing cabin monoplane impressed for communications with the RAF, carrying the pilot and five passengers. Three cabin windows each side with a sturdy-legged fixed undercarriage and single fin/rudder.
In service 1940–41 with 1 PRU.
Powered by one 450hp P&W Wasp Junior R985-SB3 radial.
Serial: AX666.
Span: 38ft 11in/11.86m   Length: 26ft 10in/8.17m   Ceiling: 24,200ft/7,260m   Range: 1,000 miles/1,610km   Speed – 212mph/341kmph.
Total 1 impressed; 1 accidental loss (100%).

STAMPE et RENARD (Belgium)

Formed in the 1930s and out of business in 1957; one example of this company's well-known trainer escaped the Germans and was taken on charge.

296. SV 4B

A two-seat basic trainer, a single-bay biplane similar to the Tiger Moth but with swept rounded wings, used by the RAF for communications work.
In service 1942 with 24 Sqn, used by 2xcomms. units until 1945, MCommsSqn.
Powered by one 140hp Renault 4PEI in-line.
Serial: MX457.
Span: 27ft 6in/8.07m   Length: 22ft 10in/6.96m   Ceiling: 19,000ft/5,700m   Range: 250 miles/402km   Speed: 110mph/177kmph.
Total 1; no losses.

STANDARD MOTORS (Coventry, Warwicks, UK)

Assembled DH Mosquito.

STINSON (USA)

A company formed in 1926 and well-known for its light aircraft, becoming part of Vultee in 1940. Supplied 519 examples of three types.

297. 105 Voyager

A high-wing cabin monoplane impressed by the RAF as an artillery spotter but not successful in this role and used mainly for communications, with the pilot and one passenger.

In service 1940 with 651 Sqn, used by two AOP flts, 1xOTU and 1xcomms. unit, until 1945, 595 Sqn.

Powered by one 75hp Continental A80-9 in-line.

Serials: X1050, X5324.

Span: 34ft/10.36m   Length: 22ft 3in/6.81m   Ceiling: 12,000ft/3,600m   Range: 380 miles/612km   Speed: 105mph/169kmph.

Total 2 impressed; no losses.

298. Junior

A cabin monoplane impressed for communications work by the RAF; it had a high wing braced by four struts and a strutted undercarriage.

In service 1940–41 with the ATA, carrying the pilot and three passengers.

Powered by one 165hp Wright Whirlwind radial.

Serial: X8522.

Span: 41ft 8in/12.7m   Length: 29ft/8.84m   Ceiling: 13,500ft/4,050m   Range: 400 miles/644km   Speed: 125mph/201kmph.

Total 1 impressed; no losses.

299. Reliant I

A civil design ordered as a navigation trainer and communications type for the FAA, unarmed, and carrying four crew as a trainer and the pilot and four passengers as a transport.

In service 1942 with 752 Sqn, used by 5xCU, 1xPTU, 8xATU, 3xObsTU, ECFS, 1xRAF OTU, 1xRAF SoTT, 6xFAA and 4xRAF comms. units, and 7xRAF and 2xFAA misc. units, until 1946, 747 Sqn.

Based overseas in North America, Far East, BWI and Ceylon.

Powered by one 290hp Lycoming R680-13 radial.

Serials: FB523–772 (250), FK814–FL163 (250) plus 16 RAF impressed – W5791, W7978–84 (7), X8518–21 (4), X9596, BS803, HM593, MA960.

Span: 41ft 11in/12.78m   Length: 29ft 6in/8.99m   Ceiling: 14,000ft/4,200m   Range: 700 miles/1,127km   Speed: 135mph/217kmph.

Total 500 plus 16 impressed making a total of 516; 33 (6%) accidental losses.

Stinson Reliant I,
FK832, 752 Sqn.
(Newark Air Museum)

Supermarine Seagull III, N9647, 440 Flt. (Newark Air Museum)

SUNBEAM (Wolverhampton, Staffs, UK)

Assembled Short 827, Bomber and 320.

SUPERMARINE (Southampton, Hants, UK)

Formed from Pemberton-Billing in 1916, and became Vickers-Supermarine in 1928, though popularly still called Supermarine; known originally for its flying boats, the company became almost immortal as that responsible for the Spitfire, which was by far the best of its designs. The company became part of the British Aircraft Corporation in 1960. Supplied 22,399 examples of 11 types (Spitfire, Seafire, Attacker, Swift and Scimitar, see Vol. 1); also assembled the AD Flying Boat and Short 184.

300. Seagull III

A spotter and reconnaissance biplane amphibian for the FAA, with three crew and armed with a Lewis mg in the dorsal position.
In service 1923 with 440 Flt, used by one flt, SoNCo-op and 2xRAF misc. units until 1928, Malta; embarked on one carrier.
Based overseas in Malta.
Powered by one 470hp Napier Lion V in-line.
Serials: N9562–66 (5), N9603–07 (5), N9642–9654 (11).
Span: 46ft/14.02m   Length: 37ft 9in/11.51m   Ceiling: 9,100ft/2,730m   Endurance: 4.5hrs   Speed: 98mph/158kmph.
Total 21; no losses.

301. Southampton I

A general-reconnaissance flying boat, carrying five crew and armed with one Lewis mg in the nose and each beam position; had a wooden hull and the outer wing sections were slightly swept. It was able to carry 1,000lb/454kg of bombs underwing.
In service 1927 with the 480 Flt, used by six sqns (201, 203, 204, 205, 209, 210) and two flights until 1929, 201 Sqn; also served with Air Pilotage S, NavS and SoNCo-op, until 1932.
Powered by two 470hp Napier Lion V in-lines.
Serials: N9896–9901 (6), S1036–1045 (10), S1058–59 (2), S1121–28 (6).
Total 24; 1 accidental loss.

301a. Southampton II

As the Mk I but with a metal rather than wooden hull and straight wings; two had enclosed cockpits and some had sweep on the outer wings, these probably being the converted Mk Is.

In service 1927 with the Flying Boat Flt, used by six sqns (201, 203, 204, 205, 209, 210) until 1936, 201 Sqn; also served with the SPTFlt, NavS, 1xAOS and SoNCo-op.

Based overseas in Egypt, Iraq and Singapore.

Powered by two 500hp Lion Va.

Serials: S1127–28 (2), S1149–53 (5), S1159–62 (4), S1228–35 (8), S1248–49 (2), S1298–1302 (5), S1420–23 (4), S1464, S1643–47 (5), K2889, K2964–65 (2).

Total 39 plus 17 conversions of the Mk I, making a total of 55; 6 accidental losses.

	Span	Length	Ceiling	Range	Speed
Mk I	75ft/22.86m	51ft 1in/15.57m	n/k	500 miles/805km	90mph/145kmph
Mk II	"	48ft 8in/14.83m	5,900ft/1,770m	550 miles/885km	95mph/153kmph

Total Southamptons 63; in service 1925–36; 7 (11%) losses.

302. Scapa I

A general-reconnaissance flying boat for the RAF, with five crew and armed with one Lewis mg in the nose and each beam position and able to carry 1,000lb/454kg of bombs underwing.

In service 1935 with 202 Sqn, used by four sqns (202, 204, 228, 240) until 1939, 240 Sqn; also served with the SPTSqn and FBTSqn.

Supermarine Southampton I, S1125. (Newark Air Museum)

Supermarine Scapa I, K7306, 228 Sqn. (Air-Britain Archives)

Based overseas in Malta and Egypt.
Powered by two 535hp RR Kestrel IIIms in-lines.
Serials: K4191–4200 (10), K4565, K7304–05 (2).
Span: 75ft/22.86m   Length: 53ft/16.15m   Ceiling: 15.500ft/4,650m   Range: 1,000
miles/1,610km   Speed: 141mph/227kmph.
Total 13; 3 (23%) accidental losses.

303. Walrus I

A spotter and reconnaissance amphibian for the FAA, designed to operate from the RN's capital ships
and cruisers and later used for ASR by the FAA and RAF; it had three or four crew, was armed with a
Lewis (later Vickers) mg in nose and dorsal positions and could carry 760lb/345kg of bombs or two DCs
underwing.
In service 1936 with 702 Flt, used by three flts, 11 sqns (700, 701, 702, 710, 711, 712, 714, 715, 716, 836,
1700), 1xFAA PTU, 9xFAA ATU, 5xFAA ObsTU, 1xFAA TAGTU, some RAF sqns as the Mk II below,
2xRAF PAFU, RAF SoASR, 1xRAF AACU, 1xRAF FTS, 1xRAF METS, SoNCo-op, 1xRAF OTU,
SPTSqn and 3xFAA comms. units, until 1945, 1700 Sqn, training to 1946. Embarked on four carriers, 12
battleships, one battle-cruiser, 39 cruisers, four escort carriers and one seaplane carrier.
Action: North and South Atlantic, Mediterranean, Indian Ocean and Pacific, based overseas in Malta, China,
Singapore, Middle East, North, East, West, and South Africa, BWI, New Zealand, Ceylon and Hong Kong.
Powered by one 620hp Bristol Pegasus IIm2 or 690hp Pegasus VI radial pusher.
Serials: K4797, K5773–5783 (11), K8338–45 (8), K8537–8564 (28), L2169–2336 (168), P5646–5720 (50),
R6543–6591 (25), W2670–3101 (195), X9460–9558 (65).
Total 551 (131 RAF); 116 accidental and 15 hostile losses.

303a. Walrus II

An ASR version for the FAA and RAF, as the Mk I but with a wooden rather than metal hull, an
uncowled tail wheel and no provision for bombs; crew often reduced to two thus increasing the number
of survivors able to be rescued. Built by Saro.
In service 1940 with 700 Sqn, used by 14 RAF (Mk I and II) Sqns (89, 269, 275, 276, 277, 278, 281, 282,
283, 284, 292, 293, 294, 624) and three FAA sqns (700, 701, 1700), three ASR flts, SARTU, 4xFAA CU,
3xFAA ObsTU, 1xFAA TAGTU and 4xFAA misc. units until 1946, 293 Sqn. Embarked on five battle-
ships, eight cruisers and one seaplane carrier.
Action: northern and southern Europe and Mediterranean, also based overseas in North America, BWI,
North, East, West and South Africa, Far East, Denmark and Singapore.
Powered by one 690hp Pegasus VI.
Serials: W 2670–3101 range (5), X9559–9593 (35), Z1755–1823 (50), HD804–936 (100).
Total 190 (99 RAF); 63 accidental and 1 hostile loss.
Both Marks: Span: 45ft 10in/13.97m   Length: 37ft 7in/11.46m   Ceiling: 18,500ft/5,550m   Range:
600 miles/966km   Speed: 135mph/217kmph.
**Total Walruses 741; in service 1936–46; 195 (26%) losses inc. 16 hostile; nicknamed Shagbat
and Pusser's Duck.**

304. Stranraer II

The RAF's last GR biplane flying boat, with five crew, armed with a Lewis mg in nose, dorsal and tail
positions and able to carry 1,000lb/454kg of bombs underwing. Nicknamed Strainer and Strany.
In service 1935 with 209 Sqn, used by four sqns (209, 210, 228, 240) until 1941, 240 Sqn; also served with
FBTSqn, SPTSqn and 1xOTU until 1942.
Based overseas in Gibraltar, action North and South Atlantic and Mediterranean.
Powered by two 980hp Bristol Pegasus X radials.
Serials: K7287–7303 (17).
Span: 85ft/25.9m   Length: 54ft 10in/16.71m   Ceiling: 18,500ft/5,550m   Range: 1,000
miles/1,610km   Speed: 165mph/266kmph.
Total 17; 11 (65%) losses inc. 1 hostile.

Above: Supermarine Walrus I. (Peter Green Collection)

Right: Supermarine Stranraer II, K7287. (Charles Parker)

305. Sea Otter I

An FAA spotter and reconnaissance, communications and ASR amphibian to replace the Walrus, with three or four crew and armed with one Vickers mg in the nose position and two in the dorsal position, plus 1,000lb/454kg of bombs or two DC underwing. The FAA's last fixed-wing ASR type.

In service 1944 with 1700 Sqn, used by five sqns (810, 1700, 1701, 1702, 1703), RAF sqns as the Mk II, 2xCU, 1xPTU, 5xATU, SoASR, ASRTU, SARTU, 5xcomms. units and 1xmisc. unit, until 1952, 781 Sqn. Embarked on one carrier.

Action: North Atlantic and Pacific, also based overseas in Ceylon and Hong Kong.

Powered by one 810hp Bristol Mercury XXX radial.

Serials: JM740–JN257 (248).

Total 246 (139 RAF); 36 accidental losses.

Supermarine Sea Otter ASR 1, JN180, 781 Sqn. (Newark Air Museum)

305a. Sea Otter ASR II

A dedicated ASR version for the RAF, as the Mk I except that the armament was deleted and handrails were installed on the fuselage sides, plus other detail changes; it was the RAF's last fixed-wing ASR type. In service 1943 with 277 Sqn, used by seven sqns (276, 277, 278, 279, 281, 282, 292), two flts, 1xFAA ATU, 3xcomms. units and 6xmisc. units, until 1955, 278 Sqn.

Action: North Atlantic and Indian Ocean, also based overseas in Malta and Singapore.

Serials: RD869–922 (40).

Total 40 plus 82 conversions of the Mk I, making a total of 122 (20 FAA); 7 accidental and 1 hostile loss.

Both Marks: Span: 46ft/14.02m   Length: 39ft 11in/12.17m   Ceiling: 17,000ft/5,100m   Range: 690 miles/1,111km   Speed: 163mph/262kmph.

Total Sea Otters 286; in service 1943–55; 44 (15%) losses inc. 1 hostile.

TAYLORCRAFT (USA)

A manufacturer of light aircraft from 1936–46, on which designs British Taylorcraft types (see Vol. 1) were based. Supplied 25 examples of three types (Plus D and Plus C, see Vol. 1)

306. BL 2

A development of the Plus C (Vol. 1) which was impressed by the RAF for communications work, carrying the pilot and one passenger side-by-side. The high wing was braced by V-style struts and it had a curved fin and pointed tailplanes.

In service 1942 with 172 Wing, used by 3xcomms. units until 1945, India.

Based overseas in India, not operational in the UK.

Powered by one 65hp Lycoming 0-145-B2 inline.

Serials: MA920, MA924.

Span: 36ft/10.97m   Length: 22ft/6.71m   Ceiling: 17,000ft/5,100m   Range: 500 miles/800km   Speed: 100mph/160kmph.

Total 2 impressed; no losses.

TIPSY (Belgium)

Existed from 1934–39 and known for its pre-Second World War light aircraft; supplied two examples of one type.

307. B 2

Impressed by the RAF for communications work, this was a low-wing monoplane with two-seats side-
by-side in an open cockpit.
In service 1941 with the ATA, used by 1xPAFU and ATA until 1945, 15 PAFU.
Powered by one 62hp Walter Mikron 2 in-line.
Serial: HM494.
Total 1 impressed; no losses.

307a. Trainer

As the B 2 but with increased auw.
In service 1942 with 221 Gp CommsFlt, used by 2xcomms. units until 1943, Bengal SFlt.
Based overseas in India, not operational in the UK.
Serial: MA930.
Total 1 impressed; 1 accidental loss.

	Span	Length	Ceiling	Range	Speed
B 2	31ft 2in/9.5m	21ft 8in/6.6m	19,700ft/5,910m	450 miles/724km	124mph/200kmph
Trainer	"	"	19,000ft/5,700m	400 miles/644km	110mph/177kmph

Total B 2s 2 impressed; in service 1941–45; 1 (50%) loss.

VEGA (USA)

Assembled Lockheed Ventura.

VICKERS-ARMSTRONG (Weybridge, Surrey, UK)

A well-known arms manufacturer which started aircraft production in 1913, though its First World War
fighter designs were not terribly successful apart from the FB 5. However, its multi-engined types found
favour during the 1920s and '30s and the company produced the famous Wellington, built in larger numbers than any other British bomber. Post-Second World War it was airliners, or military versions of these,
which mainly occupied the company, apart from the Valiant, and it became part of the British Aircraft
Corporation in 1960. Supplied 14,402 examples of 21 types (Boxkite, EFB, FB 5, FB 9, ES 1, FB 12, FB
19, FB 14 and Vampire, see Vol. 1); also assembled Hawker Hart and Avro Lancaster.

308. Vimy IV

Too late to see the First World War service, this was the RAF's main bomber type through the early
1920s, and a modified civil version was the first aircraft to cross the Atlantic non-stop; in its military
form it carried three crew and was armed with one or two Lewis mg in nose and dorsal positions, plus
2,476lb/1,125kg of bombs underwing.
In service 1919 with 58 Sqn, used by nine sqns (7, 9, 45, 58, 70, 99, 100, 216, 502) until 1928, 502 Sqn; also
served with 1xTDS, 4xFTS, 1xParaTS, RAFC, 1xA&GS and 1xmisc. unit.
Based overseas in Egypt and Iraq.
Powered by two 350hp RR Eagle VIII in-lines.
Serials: F701–711 (12), F2915–2944 (27), F2996–98 (3), F3146–3195 (41), F8596–8645 (50), F9146–9200
(50), H5065–5100 (25), H9963, J7238–7247 (10), J7440–7454 (15).
Total 234; 19 accidental losses from 1920.

308a. Vimy DC

A variant for advanced and parachute training, as the Mk IV but with dual-controls, armament deleted
and re-engined.
In service 1928, used by 1xFTS and 1xParaTS until 1931, Henlow.
Based overseas in Egypt.
Powered by two 430hp Bristol Jupiter IV or 385hp A-S Jaguar IV radials.
Serials: J7701–05 (5).
Total 5 plus an unknown number of conversions of the Mk IV; losses in the above.

Vickers Vimy
IV. (Peter Green
Collection)

	Span	Length	Ceiling	Range	Speed
Mk IV	68ft 1in/20.76m	43ft 6in/13.26m	14,000ft/4,200m	900 miles/1,449km	112mph/180kmph
DC	"	"	5hrs	"	"

Total Vimys 239; in service 1919–31; losses not known.

Vimy Ambulance – see Vernon.

309. Vimy Ambulance

Developed from the Vimy Commercial, itself a development of the bomber but with a large oval fuse-lage, which held four stretchers or eight sitting cases plus two attendants and two pilots. They were altered to Vernon III (qv) standard during service.
In service 1922 with 45 Sqn and 70 Sqn then became Vernons.
Action: Iraq, not operational in the UK.
Powered by two 350hp RR Eagle VIII in-lines mounted between the wings.
Serials: J6904–5 (2), J7143–44 (2).
Total 4; 1 accidental loss.

309a. Vernon I

Derived from Vimy Ambulance, this bomber-transport used the wings and tail surfaces of the Vimy; it carried two crew and 12 passengers, or 2,476lb/1,125kg of bombs underwing, and was responsible for pioneering air routes in the Middle East.
In service 1922 with 45 Sqn, used by two sqns (45, 70) until 1926, 45 Sqn.
Action: Iraq, also based overseas in Egypt; not operational in the UK.
Serials: J6864–6883 (20).
Total 20; 1 accidental loss.

309b. Vernon II

A re-engined version.
In service 1924 with 45 Sqn, used by two sqns (45, 70) and 1xFTS until 1927, 45 Sqn.
Action: Iraq, not operational in the UK.
Powered by two 500hp Napier Lion II in-lines, mounted on the lower-wing.
Serials: J6884–93 (9), J6976–80 (5), J7133–7142 (10).
Total 24 plus 3 conversions of the Mk I, making a total of 27; 5 accidental losses.

309c. Vernon III

As the Mk II but with the nose wheel deleted and with two fuel tanks beneath the upper-wing. In service 1925 with 70 Sqn, used by two sqns (45, 70) until 1927, 45 Sqn.
Action: Iraq, not operational in the UK.
Powered by two 500hp Lion II.
Serials: J7539–7548 (10).
Total 10 plus 5 conversions of the Vimy Ambulance and Mk II, making a total of 15; 3 accidental losses.

	Span	Length	Ceiling	Range	Speed
Mk I	68ft 1in/20.76m	43ft 8in/13.31m	10,500ft/3,150m	450 miles/724km	98mph/158kmph
Mk II	"	"	11,700ft/3,510m	320 miles/515km	118mph/190kmph
Mk III	"	"	"	n/k	"

Total Vernons 58; in service 1922–27; 10 (17%) losses.

310. Virginia II

The first of a line of biplane night-bombers for the RAF, with four crew and armed with one Lewis mg in nose and dorsal positions, plus 890lb/405kg of bombs.
In service 1924 to 1927 with 7 Sqn.
Powered by two 500hp Napier Lion II in-lines.
Serial: J6857.
Total 1; no losses.

310a. Virginia III

As the Mk II but had dihedral on the lower-wing, dual-controls and carried 1,196lb/545kg of bombs.
In service 1924 with 7 Sqn, used by two sqns (7, 58) and 1xmisc. unit, until 1926, 58 Sqn.
Serials: J6992–93 (2), J7219–20 (3).
Total 5 plus 1 conversion of the Mk I; no losses.

Vickers Vernon III. (Alastair Goodrum Collection)

310b. Virginia IV

As the Mk III but carrying 1,300lb/590kg of bombs and with additional electrical equipment.
In service 1924 with 7 and 9 Sqns, used by two sqns (7, 9) until 1927, 9 Sqn.
Powered by two 500hp Lion II or 470hp Lion V.
Serials: J7274–75 (2).
Total 2; no losses.

310c. Virginia V

As the Mk IV but had a third, central, fin.
In service 1925 with 9 Sqn, used by three sqns (7, 9, 58) and 1xmisc. unit, until 1926, 58 Sqn.
Powered by two 470hp Lion V.
Serials: J7418–7439 (22).
Total 22; no losses.

310d. Virginia VI

As the Mk V but with dihedral on both upper and lower-wings.
In service 1925 with 9 Sqn, used by three sqns (7, 9, 58) until 1927, 58 Sqn.
Engines as Mk IV.
Serials: J7558–7567 (10), J7706–7720 (15).
Total 25 plus 6 conversions of the Mk V, making a total of 31; 2 accidental losses.

310e. Virginia VII

As the Mk VI but with the bomb load increased to 2,320lb/1,055kg, a new nose design, and sweep on the outer wings; one aircraft carried a Lewis mg in each of two 'pulpits' sited on the upper-wing for a time and this had straight wings.
In service 1926 with 9 Sqn, used by three sqns (7, 9, 58) until 1933, 7 Sqn.
Serials: J8236–41 (6), J8326–30 (5).
Total 11 plus 38 conversions of earlier Mks, making a total of 49; 2 accidental losses.

310f. Virginia IX

As the Mk VII but with a tail gunner's position housing a Lewis mg in addition to the nose and dorsal positions, a longer nose, and the central fin deleted.
In service 1927 with 58 Sqn, used by three sqns (7, 9, 58) until 1934, 58 Sqn.
Serials: J8907–14 (8).
Total 8 plus 27 conversions of the Mk VII, making a total of 35; 3 accidental losses.

Vickers Virginia V,
J7427. (Mike Blakey
via Charles Parker)

Vickers Virginia
X, K2665, 9 Sqn.
(Newark Air
Museum)

310g. Virginia X

The ultimate Virginia, armed with one Lewis mg in the nose and two in the tail position, the dorsal position being deleted; the bomb load was now 3,000lb/1,360kg. It had a metal frame, HP slots on the upper-wing, and late production had a tail wheel.
In service 1928 with 7 Sqn, used by 9 sqns (7, 9, 10, 51, 58, 75, 214, 500, 502) until 1938, 51 Sqn; also served with 1xParaTS, 1xSoTT and 2xmisc. units, until 1941.
Powered by two 540hp Lion XI.
Serials: K2321–2339 (19), K2650–2680 (31).
Total 50 plus 53 conversions of earlier Mks making a total of 103; 19 accidental losses.

	Span	Length	Ceiling	Range	Speed
Mk II	86ft 6in/26.36m	50ft 7in/15.42m	8,700ft/2,610m	1,000 miles/1,610km	95mph/153kmph
Mk VII	87ft 8in/26.72m	"	7,500ft/2,250m	980 miles/1,579km	104mph/167kmph
Mk IX	"	62ft 3in/18.98m	"	"	"
Mk X	"	"	15,300ft/4,590m	985 miles/1,586km	108mph/174kmph

Total Virginias 124; in service 1924–41; 26 (21%) losses; nicknamed Ginnie.

311. Victoria I

A transport development of the Virginia, with a new oval fuselage married to the Virginia's wings and tail unit; two crew and 22 passengers, bomb racks underwing if required. Dihedral on lower wing only.
In service 1924 with 70 Sqn, used by two sqns (70, 216) until 1926, 216 Sqn.
Based overseas in Iraq, not operational in the UK.
Powered by two 500hp Napier Lion II in-lines, mounted on the lower-wing.
Serial: J6860.
Total 1; no losses.

311a. Victoria II

As the Mk I but with rounded engine cowlings.
In service 1925 with 216 Sqn, used by one sqn and 1xFTS until 1928, 4 FTS.
Based overseas in Egypt, not operational in the UK.
Serial: J6861.
Total 1; no losses.

311b. Victoria III

As the Mk II but with dihedral on all wings, which had swept outer-sections.
In service 1926 with 70 Sqn, used by two sqns (70, 216) until 1935, 216 Sqn.
Action: Iraq, also based overseas in Egypt, not operational in the UK.
Powered by two 500hp Lion II mounted mid-way between the wings.
Serials: J7921–7935 (15), J8226–8235 (10).
Total 25; 10 accidental losses.

311c. Victoria IIIA

As the Mk III but with metal-framed wings.
In service 1926 with 216 Sqn, used by two sqns (70, 216) until 1934, 70 Sqn.
Based overseas in Egypt, not operational in the UK.
Serials: J8061–66 (6), J8915–8929 (15).
Total 21; 1 accidental loss.

Vickers Victoria VI,
K3159 (nearest) and
Victoria V, K2808.
(Alastair Goodrum
Collection)

311d. Victoria IV

As the Mk IIIA but with HP slots, no fins and two fuel tanks beneath the upper-wing.
In service 1928 with 70 Sqn, used by two sqns (70, 216) until 1934, 70 Sqn.
Based overseas in Iraq, not operational in the UK.
Powered by two 480hp Lion IIb.
Serial: J9250.
Total 1 plus 17 conversions of earlier Mks, making a total of 18; 3 accidental losses.

311e. Victoria V

As the Mk IV but with an all-metal frame and able to carry 23 passengers.
In service 1929 with 216 Sqn, used by two sqns (70, 216), Air Pilotage S, EWS, 1xcomms. unit and
2xmisc. units, until 1935, 70 Sqn.
Based overseas in Egypt, Iraq, and India.
Powered by two 530hp Lion XIa.
Serials: J9760–66 (7), K1310–15 (6), K2340–45 (6), K2791–2808 (18).
Total 37 plus 8 conversions of earlier Mks, making a total of 45; 3 accidental losses.

311f. Victoria VI

A re-engined Victoria V, very similar to the Valentia (qv).
In service 1931 with 70 Sqn, used by two sqns (70, 216) until 1935, 216 Sqn.
Based overseas in Egypt and Iraq, not operational in the UK.
Powered by two 590hp Bristol Pegasus Im3 radials.
Serials: K3159–3169 (11).
Total 11 plus 24 conversions of earlier Mks, making a total of 35; 4 accidental losses.

	Span	Length	Ceiling	Range	Speed
Mk I	87ft 4in/26.62m	59ft 6in/18.13m	n/k	400 miles/644km	106mph/171kmph
MkV	"	"	16,200ft/4,860m	770 mile/1,240km	130mph/209kmph
MkVI	"	"	18,300ft/5,490m	800 miles/1,288km	"

Total Victorias 97; in service 1924–35; 21 (22%) losses.

312. Vildebeest I

A two-seat land-based torpedo-bomber for the RAF, armed with one Vickers mg in the top port cowl-
ing and one Lewis mg in the rear cockpit plus 1,100lb/500kg of bombs underwing, or one torpedo
under the fuselage.
In service 1932 with 100 Sqn, used by three sqns (22, 42, 100) until 1939, 22 Sqn; also served with
1xAACU, CDTFlt, 1xTorpTFlt and 1xmisc. unit, until 1941.
Based overseas in Malta and Singapore.
Powered by one 590hp Bristol Pegasus Im3 radial.
Serials: K2810–2822 (13), S1707–15 (9).
Total 22; 4 accidental losses.

312a. Vildebeest II

As the Mk I but with a spatted main undercarriage and the ventral fin deleted.
In service 1933 to 1941 with 100 Sqn, also served with 1xAACU and the CDTFlt.
Based overseas in Singapore.
Powered by one 620hp Pegasus IIm3.
Serials: K2917–2945 (29).
Total 29; 18 accidental losses.

312b. Vildebeest III

As the Mk II but with three crew, a third cockpit being installed just behind the pilot's; these obsolete
torpedo-bombers were sent on a suicide operation against the Japanese fleet invading Malaya in 1942.

In service 1934 with 22 Sqn, used by five sqns (22, 36, 42, 100, 273) until 1942, 273 Sqn; also served with 1xAACU, SoNCo-op, 1xTorpTS and 1xmisc. unit.

Based overseas in Malta and Singapore, action Far East.

Serials: K4156–4188 (33), K4588–4614 (27), K6369–6407 (39).

Total 99; 39 accidental and 12 hostile losses.

312c. Vildebeest IV

A re-engined Mk III, but with the third crew member and seat deleted.

In service 1937 with 42 Sqn, used by two sqns (22, 42), 1xAACU and 1xmisc. unit, until 1940, 42 Sqn.

Powered by one cowled 745hp Bristol Perseus VIII radial, driving a three-bladed propeller.

Serials: K6408–14 (7), K8078–8087 (10).

Total 17; 3 accidental losses.

	Span	Length	Ceiling	Range	Speed
Mk I	49ft/14.94m	36ft 8in/11.18m	19,000ft/5,700m	1,250 miles/2,012km	140mph/225kmph
Mk III	"	"	"	"	143mph/230kmph
Mk IV	"	37ft 8in/11.48m	"	1,625 miles/2.616km	156mph/251kmph

Total Vildebeests 167; in service 1932–42; 76 (46%) losses inc. 12 hostile; nicknamed Beast.

313. Vincent I

A general-purpose biplane for colonial work, based on the Vildebeest and very similar to it. It had two crew and was armed with one Vickers mg in the port top cowling and a Lewis mg in the rear cockpit, plus 1,000lb/454kg of bombs (or for GR work two DC) underwing, and could carry a long-range tank under the fuselage; a message hook was fitted to the axle.

In service 1934 with 84 Sqn, used by eight sqns (8, 45, 47, 55, 84, 207, 223, 244), 8xcomms. units and 6xmisc. units until 1944, Aden CommsFlt.

Based overseas in Aden, Egypt, Jordan, Sudan, Kenya and North Africa.

Action: Iraq, Middle East and western Indian Ocean; not operational in the UK.

Powered by one 620hp Bristol Pegasus IIm3 radial.

Serials: K4106–4155 (50), K4615–19 (5), K4656–4750 (95), K4883–85 (3), K6326–6368 (43).

Span: 49ft/14.94m   Length: 36ft 8in/11.18m   Ceiling: 17,000ft/5,100m   Range: 625 miles/1,006km   Speed: 142mph/229kmph.

Total 196; 59 (30%) losses inc. 5 hostile.

314. Valentia I

A development of the Victoria VI (qv) and very similar to it except that it was re-engined and had a tail wheel; it carried two crew, and 22 passengers or 2,200lb/1,000kg of freight, but could instead carry 2,200lb/1,000kg of bombs under the centre section when required. In the mid-1930s six aircraft were fitted with a Lewis mg in improvised nose and dorsal positions for the Abyssinian crisis.

In service 1935 with 216 Sqn, used by three sqns (31, 70, 216), ALS (India), 1xANS, 1xEWS, 1xFTS, 1xOTU, 1xSS, 3xcomms. units and 2xmisc. units, until 1944, Iraq & Persia CommsFlt.

Based overseas in Iraq, Egypt, India and East Africa.

Action: North Africa, Middle East and Far East.

Powered by two 625hp Bristol Pegasus IIL2 radials.

Serials: K3599–3614 (16), K4630–35 (6), K5605, K8848–52 (5).

Span: 87ft 4in/26.62m   Length: 59ft 6in/18.13m   Ceiling: 16,200ft/4,860m   Range; 800 miles/1,288km   Speed: 120mph/193kmph.

Total 28 plus 40 conversions of the Victoria, making a total of 68; 16 (24%) accidental losses.

315. Wellesley I

A light bomber also used for general-reconnaissance and the first RAF type to use Barnes-Wallis' geodetic construction; a modified version gained the world long-distance record for Britain. In RAF service it had two crew and was armed with one fixed Browning mg in the starboard wing, one Vickers mg

Vickers Vildebeest III,
K4163, Gosport Base.
(Scott Collection)

Vickers Vincent
I, K4123, 84 Sqn.
(Air-Britain Archives)

Vickers Valentia I,
K3601, EWS.
(Newark Air Museum)

in the rear cockpit and carried 2,000lb/908kg of bombs in underwing panniers. Some aircraft were modified to have a long greenhouse canopy instead of two separate positions.

In service 1937 with 76 Sqn, used by 10 sqns (7, 14, 35, 45, 47, 76, 77, 148, 207, 223), one GR sqn (47) and two transport sqns (117, 267) until 1943, 47 Sqn; also served with 1xATC, 2xOTU, TU&RPl, 3xcomms. units and 1xmisc. unit.

Based overseas in Egypt, Jordan, Sudan and Kenya, action East and North Africa and Mediterranean.

Powered by one 835hp Bristol Pegasus XX radial.

Serials: K7713–7791 (79), K8520–8536 (17), L2637–2716 (80).

Span: 74ft 7in/22.74m   Length; 39ft 3in/11.97m   Ceiling: 33,000ft/9,900m   Range: 2,480 miles/3,993km   Speed: 228mph/367kmph.

Total 176; 107 (61%) losses inc. 39 hostile.

316. Wellington I

The Wellington was the most successful of the early Second World War trio of night bombers (the others being the Handley Page Hampden and Armstrong-Whitworth Whitley [qv]); the Mk I had five crew and was armed with one Browning mg in a Vickers A nose turret, two in a Vickers A tail turret and 4,500lb/2,045kg of bombs carried internally.

In service 1938 with 99 Sqn, used by 11 sqns (9, 37, 38, 75, 99, 109, 115, 148, 149, 214, 215) until 1941, 109 Sqn; also served with ATA AFS, CGS, 6xBATFlts, 2xOTU, 1xFAA RTU and 3xmisc. units, until 1945.

Action: northern Europe, based overseas in East and West Africa.

Powered by two 815hp Bristol Pegasus XVIII radials.

Serials: L4212–4391 (172), R2699–2703 (5).

Total 177 (2 FAA); 62 accidental and 7 hostile losses.

316a. Wellington IA

As the Mk I but had two Brownings in an FN-5 nose turret, two in an FN-25 retractable ventral turret and two in an FN-10 tail turret, with increased auw and larger main wheels.

In service 1939 with 9 Sqn, used by 11 sqns (9, 37, 38, 57, 75, 99, 115, 149, 150, 214, 215) and one flt until 1940, 150 Sqn; also served with 1xAAS, CGS, 3xFTU, 3xTTFlts, 1xGpTFlt, 3xBATFlts, 4xOTU and 3xmisc. units, until 1945.

Action: northern Europe, based overseas in Far East.

Serials: L7770–7786 (17), N2865–3019 (120), P2515–2532 (18), P9205–9236 (32).

Total 187; 80 accidental and 28 hostile losses.

Vickers Wellesley I, 14 Sqn. (Scott Collection)

Vickers Wellington
IC, 108 Sqn.
(G. Stuart Leslie)

316b. Wellington DW I Series I

A variant of the Mk IA for sweeping acoustic mines, with a circular degaussing ring connecting nose, wingtips and tail; the armament was deleted and the turrets faired over.
In service 1940 with 1 GRU, used by three GR flts until 1943, 1 GRU.
Action: North Africa.
Four conversions of the Mk IA; losses included with the Mk IA.

316c. Wellington DW I Series II

As the above but with improved degaussing gear.
In service 1941 with 1 GRU, used by one sqn, three GR flts and 1xAFTU until 1944, 162 Sqn.
Action: North Africa.
Eleven conversions of the Mk I and IA, and four conversions of the DWI Series I; losses included with the Mk I and IA.

316d. Wellington IC

The most widely-used of the Mk I variants, for bombing, GR, torpedo-bombing, PR and RCM work. As the Mk IA but with the ventral turret replaced by a manually operated Vickers mg in each beam position and an FN-5 tail turret replacing the FN-10; five or six crew. The 4,500lb/2,045kg bomb load could be replaced by two torpedos, four DC, or six cameras, and the GR version had ASV-II radar with external aerials. Other changes were 24v electrics, and the main wheels protruded below the nacelles.
In service 1940 with 9 Sqn, used by 25 sqns (9, 15, 37, 38, 40, 57, 75, 99, 101, 103, 108, 115, 148, 149, 150, 156, 214, 215, 218, 300, 301, 304, 305, 311, 419) and one flt, three GR sqns (36, 221, 458) and two GR flts, one NF sqn (93), three RCM sqns (109, 162, 192), one PR flt, one ASR sqn (294) and one ASR flt, until 1943, 215 Sqn; also served with 1xAAS, AGS (India), ASRTU, 1xAPC, CGS, 5xFTU, 6xBDTFlts, 2xTT-Flts, 2xGpTFlts, 4xMETS, 22xOTU, 1xTorpBS, 1xGCFlt, 1xOTFlt, SoGR, 1xPTS, 1xRef.FU, Warwick TU, 6xcomms. units and 16xmisc. units, until 1945.
Action: northern and southern Europe, North Africa, Far East, North Atlantic and Mediterranean.
Powered by two 815hp Pegasus XVIII without intakes above.
Serials: L7790–899 (80), N2735–2859 (100), P9237–9300 (50), R1000–1806 range (525), R3150–3299 (100), T2458–3000 (300), W5612–5735 (77), X3160–3221 (50), X9600–Z1181 range (368), Z8702–9116 range (231), AD589–653 (50), BB455–516 range (43), DV411–953 (425), ES980–995 (15), HD942–HF146 (85), HF829–922 (63), HX364–786 range (123), LA965–LB257 range (16).
Total 2,701; 1,129 accidental and 750 hostile losses.

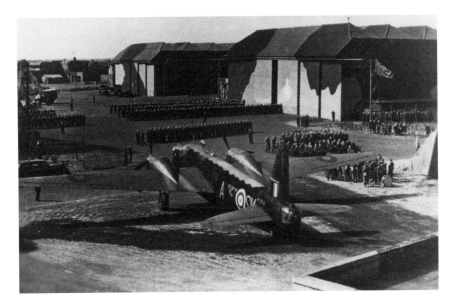

Vickers
Wellington II,
W5590, 305
Sqn. (P. Brych
via Peter
Green)

316e. Wellington II

As the Mk IC but, in case of a shortage of Pegasus engines, it had Merlins. Five crew and armed with two Brownings in an FN-5 nose turret, a manually operated Vickers mg in each beam position and two Brownings in a FN-10 tail turret, plus 4,000lb of bombs; unlike the Mk Is this could be a single bomb as the bomb bay was modified to take it.

In service 1940 with 12 Sqn, used by 14 sqns (9, 12, 38, 57, 99, 104, 142, 148, 158, 214, 218, 305, 406, 466) until 1943, 104 Sqn; also served with 1xOTU, 3xFTU, 1xMETS, 1xRef.FU, 1xFAA CU and 3xmisc. units. Action: northern Europe and North Africa.

Powered by two 1,145hp RR Merlin X in-lines.

Serials: W5352–5611 (200), Z8328–8646 (200).

Total 400 plus 2 conversions of the Mk IA, making a total of 402; 148 accidental and 186 hostile losses.

316f. Wellington III

As the Mk IC except that it had two Brownings in an FN-5 nose turret, a manually operated Vickers in each beam position and two Brownings in an FN-5 rear turret, (later four in an FN-4 turret), plus 4,500lb/2,045kg of bombs internally. The long fuselage transparency was replaced by smaller, triangular, windows, there were cable-cutters in the leading-edges and windscreen wipers were fitted.

In service 1941 with 9 Sqn, used by 26 sqns (9, 12, 37, 40, 57, 70, 75, 99, 101, 115, 142, 150, 156, 162, 166, 196, 199, 300, 419, 420, 424, 425, 426, 427, 428, 429), one RCM sqn (192) and one GR flt, until 1944, 99 Sqn; also served with 5xAGS, AN&BS, BCIS, CGS, ECFS, 2xFTU, 2xTTFlts, 1xMETS, 29xOTU, 6xcomms. units and 3xmisc. units, until 1946.

Action: northern and southern Europe, North Africa and Far East; also based overseas in the Middle East.

Powered by two 1,590hp Bristol Hercules XI radials with small intakes above the cowlings.

Serials: W range (1), X3222–4003 (449), Z1562–1751 (137), BJ581–BK564 (600), DF542–DG197 (150), HF112, HF609–816 range (125), HZ102–JA654 range (61).

Total 1,524; 495 accidental and 419 hostile losses.

316g. Wellington IV

A Mk IC fitted with American engines in case of a shortage of Pegasus.

In service 1941 with 300 Sqn, used by five sqns (142, 300, 301, 305, 460), one GR sqn (458) and one PR sqn (544), until 1943, 305 Sqn; also served with 2xPAFU, 2xOTU, 1xOTFlt and 1xTTFlt.

Action: northern Europe.

Powered by two 1,050hp P&W Twin Wasp R1830-S3c4-g radials, with smaller intakes above the cowlings.
Serials: N2735–3019 range (19), R1220–1806 range (25), Z1182–1751 range (195).
Total 239; 54 accidental and 124 hostile losses.

316h. Wellington VIA

A high-altitude bomber with four crew in a pressurised cabin, the pilot under an off-set bubble canopy,
and the nose turret replaced by a metal, rounded nose; armament was four Browning mg in a FN-20 tail
turret and it carried 4,500lb/2,045kg of bombs.
In service during 1942 with 109 Sqn, but saw no operational use.
Powered by two 1,280hp Merlin 60 in-lines.
Serials: W5795–96 (2), DR485–600 range (29).
Total 31 (but some not issued); 1 accidental loss.

316j. Wellington VIG

As the MkVIA but with the rear turret deleted and faired over; 4,500lb/2,045kg of bombs and Oboe equipped.
Used by 109 Sqn during 1942.
Serials: DR480–600 range (6).
Total 6; no losses.

316k. Wellington VIII

Although Mk ICs were used by Coastal Command the Mk VIII was the first dedicated general-reconnaissance version of the Wellington, adapted from the Mk IC and also used as a torpedo-bomber, with six
crew. The nose turret was deleted and replaced with a Perspex nose and there were two Browning mg in
an FN-5 tail turret, plus two torpedoes or four DC internally; it was fitted with ASV-Ib or -II radar with
external aerials and some carried a Leigh-Light under the rear fuselage. It had the long fuselage windows.
In service 1942 with 221 Sqn, used by nine sqns (36, 38, 69, 172, 179, 221, 458, 547, 612) and two flts
until 1943; also served with CNS, 2xFTU, 2xMETS, 6xOTU, 1xRef.FU, 3xTorpTFlts, 1xOTFlt and
3xcomms. units, until 1946.
Action: North and South Atlantic, Mediterranean and Indian Ocean, also based overseas in North and
East Africa, and southern Europe.
Powered by two 815hp Pegasus XVIII.
Serials: W5612–725 range (23), Z8328–99114 range (21), BB455–656 range (7), ES986, HF828–922 range
(21), HX364–786 range (177), LA964–LB251 range (144).
Total 394; 133 accidental and 47 hostile losses.

316l. Wellington X

A medium bomber with more powerful engines and triangular or long fuselage windows, also much
used for operational training; it had five or six crew and was armed with two Brownings in an FN-5 nose
turret, one manually operated Vickers in each beam position, four Brownings in an FN-20 or 120 tail
turret and 4,000lb/1,815kg of bombs.
In service 1942 with 196 Sqn, used by 23 sqns (37, 40, 70, 99, 104, 142, 150, 166, 196, 199, 215, 300, 305, 420,
424, 425, 426, 427, 428, 429, 431, 432, 466), two GR sqns (36, 305), one GR flt, two RCM sqns (62, 192), one
cal. sqn (527) and one PR flt until 1945, 40 Sqn; also served with 1xAAS, AI CFlt, AB&GS, 6xAGS, AN&BS,
ASRTU, 2xTTFlts, BCIS, CGS, CNS, CC FIS, 2xCU, ECFS, 4xFTU, Staff PTU, 2xBDTFlts, 2xFIS,
GpScreened PTU, OATS, 33xOTU, 1xPTS, 2xRef.FU, 11xcomms. units and 20xmisc. units until 1946.
Action: northern and southern Europe, North Africa and Far East, also based overseas in East Africa,
Palestine and Malta.
Powered by two 1,615hp Hercules XVI or 1,725hp Hercules XVII, with long intakes above the cowlings.
Serials: HE147–HF606 range (816), HZ102–JA645 range (303), LN157–LR210 (1,382), ME870–MF742
range (299), MS470–496 (27), NA710–NB766 (263), NC414–ND133 range (329), PF820–PG422 range
(164), RP312–RR178 range (179).
**Total 3,762 (3 FAA), plus 4 conversions of earlier Mks, making a total of 3,766; 811 accidental
and 457 hostile losses.**

Vickers Wellington X, MF560, 11 OTU. (Author's Collection)

316m. Wellington T 10 (originally T 19)

A post-Second World War crew trainer with six crew, the nose turret deleted and faired over, the guns removed from the tail turret and carrying practice bombs only.

In service 1945, used by 2xAFS, 1xAGS, 6xANS, CNS, CNCS, EAAS, EANS, EFS, 3xFRefS, RAFFC, 1xRef.FU, and 1xRAF and 1xFAA misc. unit, until 1953, 2 ANS, the last RAF Wellingtons.

Serials: NA710–NB766 range (54), NC414–ND133 range (33), PF820–PG422 range (44), RP312–RR178 range (27).

Total 158; 84 accidental losses.

316n. Wellington GR XI

A general-reconnaissance and torpedo-bomber type developed from the Mk X; it had six crew, with a Perspex nose replacing the front turret and sometimes carrying a 0.5in mg, four Brownings in an FN-20A tail turret and it carried two 18in torpedoes or three DC, with ASV-II radar with external aerials or ASV-III in a chin radome. Triangular and rectangular fuselage windows.

In service 1943 with 407 Sqn, used by six sqns (36, 38, 221, 344, 407, 547), one flt and one ASR sqn (294) until 1945, 344 Sqn; also served with 1xBATFlt, 4xOTU, 1xRef.FU, 1xTorpTU, 1xParaTS, 1xFAA CU, 1xFAA PTU, 1xFAA ATU, 1xcomms. unit and 1xRAF and 1xFAA misc. unit.

Action: North and South Atlantic and Mediterranean, also based overseas in North and West Africa and Malta.

Powered by two 1,615hp Hercules XVI.

Serials: HF100–606 range (24), HZ102–JA645 range (69), MP502–825 range (105).

Total 198 (9 FAA); 42 accidental and 21 hostile losses.

316p. Wellington GR XII

As the GR XI but with a Leigh-Light in the rear fuselage, two torpedoes or six DC, and four Brownings in an FN-4 tail turret; ASV-II with external aerials or ASV-III in a chin radome.

In service 1942 with 172 Sqn, used by five sqns (36, 38, 172, 221, 407) until 1944, 407 Sqn; also served with ASVTU, CNS, 2xOTU and 1xmisc. unit until 1945.

Action: North and South Atlantic and Mediterranean, also based overseas in North Africa.

Serials: HF113–120 (8), MP502–825 range (48).

Total 56; 25 accidental and 10 hostile losses.

316q. Wellington GR XIII

A general and night-reconnaissance and torpedo-bomber based on the GR XII but with two Brownings in an FN-5 nose turret (though some had a Perspex nose for night-recc.), four in an FN-4 tail turret and able to carry two 18in torpedoes or six DC, plus ASV-II with external aerials or ASV-III in a chin radome. The fuselage windows were split and diamond shaped and it did not carry a Leigh-Light. Nicknamed Fishington.

In service 1943 with 612 Sqn, used by 16 sqns (8, 36, 38, 69, 203, 221, 244, 304, 344, 415, 458, 524, 547, 612, 621, 13[Greek]), one night-recc.sqn (69) and two ASR sqns (281, 294), until 1945, 344 Sqn; also served with 1xAAS, ASV TU, CGS, CNS, EAAS, EANS, 2xFTU, LoranTU, 7xOTU, 1xRef.FU, Staff Nav.S, 1xTorpTU, 6xcomms. units and 7xmisc. units, until 1946.

Action: North and South Atlantic, Mediterranean, western Indian Ocean and northern Europe; also based overseas in the Middle and Far East, BWI and East Africa.

Powered by two 1,725hp Hercules XVII.

Serials: HZ102–JA645 range (417), ME870–MF742 range (297), MP502–825 range (42), NB772–NC234 (292), NC414–ND133 range (83).

Total 1,131 but some not issued; 202 accidental and 77 hostile losses.

316r. Wellington GR XIV

A general-reconnaissance development of the Mk X, with a Perspex nose (but some had an FN-5 nose turret and two Brownings), four Brownings in an FN-4 tail turret, four DC internally and eight RP underwing, with a retractable Leigh-Light aft of the bomb bay and ASV-III or -VIA radar in a chin radome. The engines were low-rated.

In service 1943 with 407 Sqn, used by nine sqns (14, 36, 38, 172, 179, 304, 407, 458, 524) and one flt until 1946, 38 Sqn; also served with 1xAGS, ASV TU, CNS, EAAS, 1xFTU, 6xOTU, 1xRef.FU, 1xTorpTU, 1xFAA ATU, 2xcomms. units and 1xmisc. unit.

Action: North and South Atlantic and Mediterranean, also based overseas in the Middle East, North Africa, BWI, Malta, Egypt and Palestine.

Engines as Mk X.

Serials: HF121–451 (242), ME870–MF742 range (4), MP502–825 range (54), NB767–70 (5), NC414–ND133 range (86), PF820–PG422 range (163).

Total 554; 102 accidental and 38 hostile losses.

Vickers Wellington
GR XIV, MP714.
(Peter Green
Collection)

316s. Wellington XV

A transport conversion of the Mk IA with turrets deleted and faired over, and sometimes with the fairings painted to look like turrets. Four crew and carried freight on a strengthened floor.
In service 1943, used by one comms. unit and 1xmisc. unit until 1945.
Based overseas in the Far East.
Powered by two 815hp Pegasus XVIII.
Fourteen conversions of the Mk IA; losses included with the Mk IA.

316t. Wellington XVI

A passenger version of the Mk XV able to carry 18 passengers.
In service 1943 with 232 Sqn, used by three sqns (24, 232, 242), 1xCU, 1xcomms. unit and 1xmisc. unit, until 1946, 242 Sqn.
Fifteen to one hundred conversions of the Mk IC; losses included in the Mk IC.

316u. Wellington T XVII

A radar trainer for night-fighter crews, fitted with AI-10 radar in a Mosquito-type nose radome, and all armament deleted; it had four to six crew and was based on the GR XI.
In service 1944 with 51 OTU, used by 4xOTU, 1xFAA CU and 1xFAA RTU until the late 1940s.
Powered by two 1,615hp Hercules XVI.
Ten conversions of the GR XI (5 FAA).

316v. Wellington T XVIII

An AI-10 or SCR720 radar trainer, as the above but with nine crew.
In service 1944, used by 3xOCU, 3xOTU, AI CFlt and 2xmisc. units, until 1952, 228 OCU.
Powered by two 1,725hp Hercules XVII.
Serials: PF820–PG422 range (29), RP312–RR178 range (20).
Total 49 plus 28 conversions, making a total of 77; 8 accidental losses.

Wellington T 19 – see T 10.

	Span	Length	Ceiling	Range	Speed
Mk I	85ft 10in/ 26.15m	60ft 6in /18.44m	21,800ft /6,540m	2,200 miles /3,542km	245mph /394kmph
Mk IA	"	64ft 7in/ 19.68m	26,300ft/ 7,890m	"	265mph/ 427kmph
Mk IC	"	"	18,000ft /5,400m	1,800 miles/ 2,898km	235mph/ 378kmph
Mk II	"	60ft 10in /18.54m	23,500ft/ 7,050m	1,570 miles/ 2,528km	254mph/ 409kmph
Mk III	"	64ft 7in /19.68m	22,000ft/ 6,600m	1,540 miles/ 2,479km	255mph/ 411kmph
Mk IV	"		21,200ft/ 6,360m	1,510 miles/ 2,431km	299mph/ 481kmph
MkVIA	86ft 2in/ 26.26m	61ft 9in/ 18.82m	38,500ft/ 11,550m	1,590 miles/ 2,560km	300mph/ 483kmph
MkVIII	85ft 10in/ 26.15m	64ft 7in/ 19.68m	19,000ft/ 5,700m	2,550 miles/ 4,105km	235mph/ 378kmph
Mk X	"	"	22,000ft/ 6,600m	1,885 miles/ 3,035km	255mph/ 411kmph
GR XI	"	"	19,000ft/ 5,700m	1,400 miles/ 2,254km	256mph/ 412kmph

GR XIII	"	"	16,000ft/ 4,800m	1,390 miles/ 2,238km	250mph/ 402kmph
Mk XV	"	"	21,800ft/ 6,540m	2,000 miles/ 3,220km	245mph/ 394kmph
Mk XVI	"	"	18,000ft/ 5,400m	1,800 miles/ 2,898km	235mph/ 378kmph
T XVII	"	"	22,000ft/ 6,600m	1,470 miles/ 2,367km	255mph/ 411kmph
T XVIII	"	"	16,000ft/ 4,800m	1,390 miles/ 2,238km	250mph/ 402kmph

Total Wellingtons 11,567; in service 1938–53; 5,540 (48%) losses inc. 2,164 hostile; nicknamed Wimpey.

317. Warwick B I

Resembling a larger Wellington, the Warwick was designed as a bomber but was overtaken by the various four-engined types coming into service, so the B I was relegated to crew training; it carried six crew and was armed with two Brownings in an FN-5 nose turret and FN-50 dorsal turret, and four in an FN-20 tail turret.
In service 1943 with 5 OTU, used by 2xOTU until 1945, 5 OTU.
Powered by two 1,850hp P&W Double-Wasp R2800 S14g radials.
Serials: BV214–531 range (16).
Total 16.

317a. Warwick ASR I (Bomber/ASR)

As the type was in production other roles were needed and long-range air-sea rescue seemed to be a possibility, so this variant was as the B I but able to carry Lindholme ASR gear internally. Nicknamed Bastard Bomber.
In service 1943–44 with 279 Sqn.
Action: North Atlantic.
Serials: BV214–242 range (40).
Total 40.

317b. Warwick ASR I (Stage A)

As the above but carried two Lindholme sets and could also carry an Airborne Lifeboat Mk I under the bomb bay.
In service 1943–44 with 280 Sqn.
Action: North Atlantic.
Serials: BV214–531 range (10).
Total 10.

317c. Warwick ASR I (Stage B)

As the above but the tail turret was changed to an FN-120 and ASV-II radar with external aerials was fitted.
In service 1943 to 1944 with 281 Sqn.
Action: North Atlantic.
Serials: BV214–531 range (20).
Total 20.

317d. Warwick ASR I (Stage C), later ASR I

The standard ASR Mk I, as the Stage B but with one Lindholme gear, one Lifeboat Mk II and extra fuel.
In service 1943 with 280 Sqn, used by 14 sqns (38, 269, 276, 277, 278, 279, 280, 281, 282, 283, 284, 292, 293, 294), four flts, two met. sqns (251, 520) and four transport sqns (167, 301, 304, 525) until 1946, 38 Sqn; also served with Warwick TU, ASRTU, 1xFTU, 2xOTU, SARTU, 1xcomms. unit and 7xmisc. units.
Action: North and South Atlantic, Mediterranean and Indian Ocean, also based overseas in North Africa, Far East and Malta.

Vickers Warwick
ASR I, 280 Sqn.
(Peter Green
Collection)

Powered by two 1,850hp Double-Wasp R2800-47.
Serials: BV226–531 range (141), HF938–HG134 (126).
Total 267 plus conversions of earlier ASR versions; all Mk I losses – 108 accidental and 4 hostile.

317e. Warwick C I
A transport version with turrets faired over, cabin windows and a strengthened floor; it had four crew
and carried 9,600lb/4,360kg of freight.
In service 1944 with 525 Sqn, used by three sqns (301, 304, 525) and 1xmisc. unit, until 1945, 301 Sqn.
Based overseas in India.
Serials: BV243–256 (14).
Total 14; 6 accidental losses.

317f. Warwick GR II
A conversion trainer for the general-reconnaissance sqns but saw little use; it had six crew and was
armed with one 0.5in Browning in a Perspex nose, two Brownings in an FN-50 dorsal turret, four in an
FN-120a tail turret, and 12,000lb/5,448kg of stores, including three torpedoes or DCs, in the bomb bay.
Radar was ASV-III or -IVb in a chin radome and the fuselage windows were split straight and triangular.
In service 1944 with 6 OTU, used by CCIS, 2xOTU and EANS, until 1945, 6 OTU.
Powered by two 2,300hp Bristol Centaurus IV radials, driving four-bladed propellers.
Serials: HG341–539 (126).
Total 126 but some not issued; 2 accidental losses.

317g. Warwick C III
A transport version of the B I with streamlined nose and tail fairings (the turrets being deleted), a freight
pannier beneath the bomb bay and late aircraft with a dorsal fin; it had four crew and carried 26 passengers or 6,700lb/3,040kg of freight.
In service 1944 with 525 Sqn, used by five sqns (167, 301, 304, 353, 525) until 1946, 301 Sqn; also served
with 2xOTU, 3xcomms. units and 1xmisc. unit.

Action: northern Europe and Far East.

Powered by two 1,850hp Double-Wasp R2800-47, driving three-bladed propellers.

Serials: HG215–340 (100).

Total 100; 24 accidental losses.

317h. Warwick GR V

A much-modified general-reconnaissance version which would have replaced Coastal Command's Wellingtons had the war lasted longer; it carried seven crew and was armed with one 0.5in Browning in a Perspex nose, four Brownings in an FN-120a tail turret, and one manually operated 0.5in in each beam position. 8,000lb/3,672kg of stores were carried internally and radar was ASV-III, -VIb or -XVII in a radome under the nose, plus a Leigh-Light in a ventral, retractable housing. It had split fuselage windows and a dorsal fin.

In service 1944 with 179 Sqn, used by two sqns (179, 621) until 1946, 621 Sqn; also served with ECFS, JASS, 2xOTU, 1xcomms. unit and 1xmisc. unit.

Action: North Atlantic and Palestine, also based overseas in Egypt.

Powered by two 2,400hp Centaurus VII driving four-bladed propellers.

Serials: LM777–909 (106), PN702–825 (91).

Total 197; 25 accidental losses.

317j. Warwick GR VI

The ultimate Warwick which, with the war's end, saw little use.

In service 1945 with 281 Sqn, used by one met. sqn (520), three ASR sqns (269, 280, 281) and 1xCU until 1946, 281 Sqn.

Powered by two 1,850hp Double-Wasp R2800-47.

Serials: PN826–862 (22).

Total 22 but some not issued; no losses.

	Span	Length	Ceiling	Range	Speed
B I	96ft 8in/29.46m	72ft 3in/22.03m	21,500ft/6,450m	2,300 miles/3,703km	224mph/361kmph
ASR I	"	"	28,200ft/8,460m	"	"
C I	"	"	"	"	"
GR II	"	68ft 6in/20.88m	19,000ft/5,700m	3,050 miles/4,910km	262mph/422kmph
C III	"	70ft 6in/21.49m	28,200ft/8,460m	2,300 miles/3,703km	224mph/361kmph
GR V	"	73ft/22.25m	19,000ft/5,700m	3,050 miles/4,910km	298mph/480kmph

Total Warwicks 812; in service 1943–46; 169 (21%) losses inc. 4 hostile.

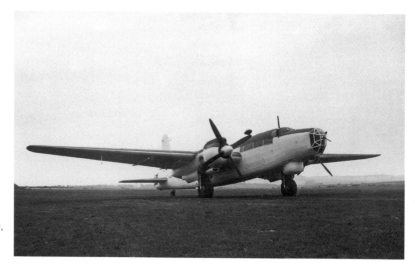

Warwick GR V, PN697, AAEE. (Peter Green Collection)

318. Viking C 1A

The Viking was a quite successful post-Second World War airliner, from the Wellington lineage, and was ordered for the King's Flight as a VIP transport; the C 1A was unarmed and had six crew, carrying up to 27 passengers.

In service 1946–48 with the King's Flt for suitability trials.

Powered by two 1,690hp Bristol Hercules 634 radials.

Serials: VL226–27 (2).

Total 2; 1 accidental loss.

318a. Viking C 2

As the C 1A but VL231-3 had a strengthened floor and freight door for the Royal baggage, with five crew and up to 21 passengers; VL246-7 were the Royal aircraft carrying eight passengers, VL245 carried 21 passengers and VL248 was a mobile workshop.

In service 1947 with the King's Flight until 1957, the Queen's Flight.

Serials: VL231–33 (3), VL245–48 (4).

Total 7; 1 accidental loss.

Both Marks: Span: 89ft 3in/27.21m   Length: 65ft 2in/19.86m   Ceiling: 23,700ft/7,110m   Range: 1,700 miles/2,737km   Speed: 210mph/338kmph.

Total Vikings 9; in service 1946–57; 2 (22%) losses.

319. Valetta C 1

Not surprisingly, the Viking was wholly militarised to become the RAF's first post-Second World War transport, the Valetta, replacing the Douglas Dakota (qv). A pointed tailcone was optional and it carried four crew and 34 passengers or 8,000lb/3,672kg of freight; it could tow a glider.

In service 1948 with 240 OCU, 1949 with 204 Sqn, used by 13 sqns (24, 30, 48, 52, 70, 84, 110, 114, 115, 204, 216, 233, 622) and one PR sqn (683) until 1966, 52 Sqn; also served with AES, 1xANS, EAAS, 1xFTU, 4xOCU, Para&GTU, 1xParaTS, CAW, RAFFC, 15xcomms. units and 12xmisc. units.

Action: Malaya, Suez and Aden, also based overseas in Germany, Malta, Cyprus, Egypt, Iraq, Kenya and Singapore.

Powered by two 1,925hp Bristol Hercules 230 radials.

Serials: VL249–282 (15), VW140–206 (53), VW803–864 (59), VX483–563 (51), WD157–171 (13), WJ492–499 (8).

Total 199; 63 accidental losses.

Vickers Valetta C 1, Aden Comms. Sqn. (Author's Collection)

319a. Valetta C 2

A VIP version, with four crew and nine to 15 passengers, the pointed tailcone being standard; it also carried extra fuel.

In service 1949 with Southern CommsSqn, used by 15xcomms. units and RAFFC until 1969, RAF Germany Comms Flt.

Action: Suez, also based overseas in Germany, Malta, Cyprus, Egypt, Aden and Singapore.

Serials: VX571–590 (10), WJ504.

Total 11; 2 accidental losses.

318b. Valetta T 3

A navigation trainer variant of the C 1, with five astrodomes on the cabin roof and 14 crew.

In service 1951 with 1 ANS, used by 1xAFS, AES, 4xANS, 2xOCU, RAFC, RAFFC, 3xcomms. units and 3xmisc. units, until 1968, 2 ANS.

Based overseas in Malta, Cyprus and Egypt.

Serials: VX564, WG256–267 (12), WJ461–487 (27).

Total 40; 5 accidental losses.

319c. Valetta T 4

A radar trainer conversion of the T 3 used for training Javelin navigators on AI-17 radar, which was housed in a long nose-radome; the astrodomes were reduced to one.

In service 1956–58 with 228 OCU; also served with 1xANS.

Eighteen conversions of the T 3; one accidental loss.

	Span	Length	Ceiling	Range	Speed
C 1	89ft 3in/27.21m	62ft 11in/19.18m	22,200ft/6,660m	1,460 miles/2,351km	258mph/415kmph
C 2	"	"	"	2,000 miles/ 3,220km approx.	"
T 3	"	"	"	1,460 miles/2,351km	"
T 4	"	67ft 3in/20.5m	"	"	"

Total Valettas 250; in service 1948–69; 71 (28%) losses; nicknamed Pig.

320. Varsity T 1

A crew trainer developed from the Valetta, with up to nine crew and able to carry 600lb/270kg of light bombs in an under-fuselage pannier which also housed a bomb-aimer's position; it had H2S in a nose radome. The Varsity's ECM duties included electronic 'eavesdropping' whilst transiting the Berlin air corridors.

In service 1951 with 201 AFS, used by six ECM sqns (97, 115, 116, 151, 192, 527), two ferry sqns (173, 187), 1xAFS, AES, AE&AEngS, AAITS, 5xANS, BCBS, CNCS, 5xFTS, 1xRef.FS, RAFC, CAW, 1xRS, RAF Tech.Coll, SCBS, 2xSoTT, 4xcomms. units and 9xmisc. units, until 1976, 6 FTS.

Based overseas in Cyprus, Egypt and Australia.

Powered by two 1,950hp Bristol Hercules 264 radials.

Serials: WF324–429 (59), WJ886–950 (48), WL621–709 (46), XD366.

Span: 95ft 8in/29.16m   Length: 67ft 6in/20.57m   Ceiling: 28,700ft/8,610m   Range: 2,665 miles/4,291km   Speed; 288mph/464kmph.

Total 154; 29 (19%) accidental losses.

321. Valiant B 1

The RAF's first nuclear-armed strategic jet bomber and the first of the famous V-bombers; it carried five crew, the pilots on MB-3a ejector seats, and had no defensive armament but could carry 21,000lb/9,535kg of bombs internally, including Blue Danube, Red Beard and US Mk5, 15/39, 28 and 43 nuclear weapons. Radar was H2S in a radome in the lower front fuselage.

In service 1955 with 138 Sqn, used by seven sqns (7, 18, 49, 138, 148, 207, 214) and one ECM sqn (199), until 1965, 3 Gp, when metal fatigue in the wing spar saw its premature withdrawal; also served with 1xOCU and 1xmisc. unit.

Vickers Varsity T 1, 5 FTS.
(Author's Collection)

Action: Suez.
Powered by four 9,500lb st RR Avon 204, or 10,000lb st Avon 205 jets.
Serials: WP206–222 (13), WZ361–375 (12).
Total 25; 5 accidental losses.

321a. Valiant B (PR) 1
A bomber which could also be used for strategic reconnaissance, with the bomb load being replaced by eleven cameras in the bomb bay with ports in the doors, plus six more, with ports, in the rear fuselage.
In service 1955 with 543 Sqn, used by one PR sqn (543) and seven bomber sqns (7, 49, 90, 138, 148, 207, 214), until 1965, 543 Sqn.
Serials: WP217, WP219, WP221, WP223, WZ377–384 (7).
Total 11; 1 accidental loss.

321b. Valiant B (PR) K 1
As the above but could also carry refuelling gear and act as a tanker.
In service 1956 with 543 Sqn, used by one PR sqn (543) and five bomber sqns (7, 90, 138, 148, 214) until 1965, 543 Sqn.
Serials: WZ389–405 (17).
Total 17; 3 accidental losses.

321c. Valiant BK 1
A bomber or tanker without the reconnaissance capability and with a flight-refuelling probe on the nose.
In service 1956 with 138 and 207 Sqns, used by seven sqns (7, 49, 90, 138, 148, 207, 214) until 1965, 49 Sqn.
Dropped the UK's first H-bomb.
Based overseas in Australia and Christmas Island.
Serials: WZ400, XD812–893 (38).
Total 39; 2 accidental losses.
All Marks: Span: 114ft 4in/34.85m   Length: 108ft 3in/33m   Ceiling: 49,000ft/14,700m   Range: 4,500 miles/7,245km   Speed: 567mph/913kmph.
Total Valiants 92; in service 1955–65; 11 (12%) losses.

VICTORY AIRCRAFT (Canada)
Assembled Avro Lancaster.

VOISIN (France)
A pioneer company which went out of aircraft production in 1920. Supplied 110 examples of one type.

322. Type LA
A bomber for the RNAS and RFC, with two crew and armed with one Lewis mg in the front cockpit and able to carry 110lb/50kg of bombs under the fuselage. Built by Voisin and Savage.
In service 1915 with 1 (N) Sqn, used by six RNAS units (1, 7 and 8NSqns, 1W, 3W, 4W), five RFC sqns (4, 5, 7, 12, 16), and 2xTSqns, until 1917.
Action: northern and southern Europe, and Middle East.
Powered by one 120hp Canton-Unne in-line pusher.
Serials: 1856, 1858, 1860, 1864–65 (2), 1867–68 (2), 1877, 1879, 1883, 1889–90 (2), 3821–3832 (12), 4787–4836 (50), 5001, 5010–11 (2), 5013–14 (2), 5017, 5026, 5066, 5097, 7458, A5169.
Total 85; 1 RNAS accidental and 9 RNAS hostile losses.

322a. Type LAS
A development used mainly by the RNAS, with vertical struts and equipped with W/T.
In service 1915 with 3 Wing, used by seven units (1N, 7N, 8N, 1W, 3W, 4W), one RFC sqn (30) and 2x PTU, until 1917, 8 Sqn.
Action: southern Europe, Middle East and East Africa.
Powered by one 140hp Canton-Unne pusher, mounted higher and inclined for some downward thrust.
Serials: 5025, 5028, 8501–09 (9), 8518–23 (6), 8700–07 (8).
Total 25 (2 RFC); 13 accidental and 1 hostile loss.

Vickers Valiant
BK 1, XD815.
(Author's
Collection)

Voisin LA,
8144. (Alastair
Goodrum
Collection)

	Span	Length	Ceiling	Endurance	Speed
LA	52ft 4in/15.95m	31ft 7in/9.63m	n/k	124 miles/200km	65mph/105kmph
LAS	"	"	"	4hrs	68mph/109kmph

Total Type LA 110; in service 1915–17; total losses not known.

VOUGHT-SIKORSKY (USA)

Formed in 1939 and renamed just Sikorsky in 1943. Supplied 150 examples of two types.

323. Chesapeake I

A two-seat dive-bomber for the FAA, taken over from a French contract and intended to operate from escort carriers but found unsuitable for this and instead relegated to training; it was armed with four Browning mg in the wings and one in the rear of the canopy, and had a 1,500lb/681kg bomb load under the fuselage.

In service during 1941 with 811 Sqn, also served with 1xCU, 3xATU, 1xcomms. unit and 4xmisc. units, until 1944.

Powered by one 750hp P&W Twin Wasp Junior R1535 SB4g radial.

Serials: AL908-956 (50).

Span: 42ft/12.8m   Length: 34ft/10.36m   Ceiling: 22,700ft/6,810m   Range: 1,340 miles/2,157km   Speed: 257mph/414kmph.

Total 50; 17 (34%) accidental losses.

324. Kingfisher I (OS2U-3)

A sea or land plane reconnaissance type, mainly used by the FAA for catapult operations from armed merchant cruisers of the RN; it had a crew of two and was armed with one Browning mg in the nose and one in the rear cockpit, with 240lb/110kg of bombs underwing.

In service 1942 with 703 Sqn, used by two sqns (700, 703), 1xPTU, 3xATU, 1xObsTU and 3xmisc. units, until 1944, 777 Sqn, when all catapult seaplanes were retired. Embarked on two cruisers, one seaplane carrier and three AMC.

Action: Indian Ocean also based overseas in West and South Africa and BWI.

Powered by one 450hp P&W Wasp Junior R985-SB3 radial.

Serials: FN650–709 (100).

Span: 35ft 11in/10.95m   Length: 33ft 8in/10.26m   Ceiling: 18,200ft/2,930m   Range: 908 miles/1,462km   Speed: 121mph/195kmph.

Total 100; 9 (9%) accidental losses.

Vought-Sikorsky Chesapeake I.
(Air-Britain Archives)

Vought-Sikorsky Kingfisher
I, FN656 in landplane form.
(Air-Britain Archives)

Vultee Vigilant I, HL432.
(Alastair Goodrum Collection)

VULCAN MOTOR & ENGINEERING (Southport, Lancs, UK)

Assembled Airco DH 4 and DH 9A.

VULTEE-STINSON (USA)

Formed 1940 from Vultee and Stinson, became part of Consolidated in 1943. Supplied 118 examples of two types.

325. Vigilant I (O-49 or L-1)

Ordered by the RAF for artillery observation but was found to be too big and was used instead for communications. It had two crew and was unarmed.

In service 1942 with 651 Sqn, used by one sqn, one flt, 1xOTU, 1xFIS and 8xcomms. units, until 1945, BAFO TCW.

Based overseas in southern Europe, North Africa and Germany.

Powered by one 295hp Lycoming R680-9 radial.

Serials: HK925–30 (6), HL429–432 (4).

Total 10; 2 accidental losses.

325a. Vigilant IA (L-1A)

As the above but with detail changes.

In service 1941 with 651 Sqn, used by one sqn, 1xOTU, 1xFIS, 6xcomms. units and 1xmisc. unit until 1947, SHAEF CommsFlt.

Based overseas in Germany.

Serials: BZ100–108 (8).

Total 8; 4 accidental losses.

Vultee-Stinson Sentinel I, preserved example in US markings. (Author's Collection)

	Span	Length	Ceiling	Range	Speed
Mk I	51ft/15.54m	34ft/10.36m	20,000ft/6,000m	350 miles/563km	123mph/198kmph
Mk IA	"	34ft 3in/10.44m	12,800ft/3,840m	280 miles/450km	122mph/196kmph

Total Vigilants 18; in service 1942–47; 6 (33%) losses; nicknamed Viggy.

326. Sentinel I (L-5)

A type widely used by the Americans and ordered by the RAF for AOP work but used instead for communications in the Far East. A two-seater without armament.

In service 1944 with 221Gp CommsFlt, used by 8xcomms. units and 1xmisc. unit, until 1947, 221Gp CommsFlt.

Based overseas in the Far East, India and Singapore, not operational in the UK.

Powered by one 185hp Lycoming O-435-1 in-line.

Serials: KJ368–407 (39).

Total 39; 15 accidental losses.

326a. Sentinel II (L-5B)

As the above but could carry a stretcher in the rear fuselage, loaded through a hatch in the starboard fuselage side, giving a slightly different rear fuselage and canopy shape, and was used for casualty evacuation as well as communications.

In service 1944 with 221Gp CommsFlt, used by four sqns (27, 117, 194, 357), 4xcomms. units and 4xmisc. units, until 1947, Malaya CommsSqn.

Action: Far East and DEI, also based overseas in Malaya and Singapore, not operational in the UK.

Serials: KJ408–467 (61).

Total 61; 13 accidental losses.

Both Marks: Span: 34ft/10.36m   Length: 24ft 1in/7.35m   Ceiling: 15,800ft/4,740m   Range: 280 miles/451km   Speed: 120mph/193kmph.

Total Sentinels 100; in service 1944–47; 28 (28%) losses; nicknamed Flying Jeep.

WACO (USA)

A pre-Second World War manufacturer of sporty biplanes followed by wartime gliders; formed in 1929 and out of business 1947. Supplied 1,042 examples of three types (ZGC-7 and YKC, see Vol. 1)

Waco Hadrian II. (Air-Britain Archives)

327. Hadrian I (CG-4)

The USAAF's standard assault glider, smaller than its British counterpart the Horsa and used in the Far East by the RAF and GPR; it carried two crew, and 14 passengers or 4,000lb/1,816kg of freight which was loaded through a lifting nose.
In service 1943 with 21 HGCU, used by 3xCU and 2xmisc. units, until 1946, 21 HGCU.
Based overseas in the Far East.
Serials: FR562–580 (18).
Total 18; 5 accidental and 2 hostile losses.

327a. Hadrian II (CG-4A)

The operational version, which had a cantilever undercarriage, a rounder nose, and internal changes; intended for large-scale airborne operations in the Far East but little used before the war's end.
In service 1944 with 669 Sqn, used by six sqns (668, 669, 670, 671, 672, 673), 2xHGCU, 1xOTU, TSTU (India), Glider Pick-up TFlt, 1xcomms. unit and 1xmisc. unit, until 1946, India.
Action: Far East.
Serials: FR581–778 (197), KH871–992 (122), KK569–968 (353), VJ120–413 (200), VJ426–VK874 (144).
Total 1,016; 140 accidental losses.
Both Marks: Span: 83ft 4in/25.4m   Length: 48ft 4in/14.73m.
Total Hadrians 1,034; in service 1943–46; 147 (14%) losses inc. 2 hostile.

328. CG-13A

A larger high-wing assault glider which was supplied to the RAF but only used for trials work; it carried two crew and 30-42 passengers or 10,200lb/4,627kg freight. It had a rounded nose which lifted for loading, a large fin/rudder and the high wing was braced by triangular struts as were the tailplanes.
In service 1944–46 with the AFEE.
Based overseas in the Far East.
Serials: KL162–67 (6).
Span: 85ft 7in/26.08m   Length: 54ft 3in/16.54m.
Total 6; no losses.

WARING & GILLOW (London, UK)

Assembled Airco DH 9.

WEIR (Glasgow, Scotland, UK)

Assembled Airco DH 9.

WESTLAND (Yeovil, Somerset, UK)

One of the longest-lasting British aircraft manufacturers, formed in 1915 when it assembled other companies' designs, but just after the First World War it started to build its own aircraft. During the Second World War the company again concentrated on other companies' designs but post-war became the UK's largest helicopter company, taking over Bristol's and Saro's designs and building Sikorsky designs under license, often improving on the originals. An Anglo-French agreement saw Westlands building two French designs whilst the French built the Lynx and the company became GKN-Westland in the 1990s, merging with the Italian company Agusta to become Agusta-Westland in 2000, until taken over again by the Italian Finmeccanica in 2004, though retaining the Agusta-Westland name. Supplied 4,457 examples of 19 types (Lysander, Whirlwind fighter, Welkin, Wyvern, Scout, Gazelle, Lynx AH and Apache, see Vol. 1); also assembled Airco DH 4, 9 and DH 9A, Short 166 and 184, Vickers Vimy and Fairey Barracuda.

329. Walrus I

Based on the DH 9A, which the company had built during the First World War, this was a spotter-reconnaissance type for the FAA, with three crew and armed with a Vickers mg on the port fuselage side and a Lewis mg in the rear cockpit.
In service 1922 with 3 Sqn, used by one sqn and three FAA flts (420, 421, 423) until 1925, 421 Flt; embarked on one carrier.
Powered by one 480hp Napier Lion IIb in-line.
Serials: N9500–9535 (36).
Span: 46ft 2in/14.07m   Length: 29ft 9in/9.07m   Ceiling: 19,000ft/5,700m   Endurance: n/k   Speed: 124mph/200kmph.
Total 36; 11 accidental losses (31%).

330. Wapiti I

Based on the DH 9A but heavily modified, this was a general-purpose biplane for the RAF with two crew and armed with a Vickers mg on the port fuselage side and a Lewis mg in the rear cockpit, plus 580lb/265kg of bombs underwing. It had wooden-framed wings and rear fuselage.
In service 1928 with 84 Sqn, used by 11 sqns (5, 11, 30, 39, 60, 84, 100, 600, 601, 602, 605), and one comms sqn (24) until 1933, 601 Sqn.

Westland Walrus I,
N9513. (Ron Brittain
via Peter Green)

Westland Wapiti IIA, K1125, 55 Sqn. (Air-Britain Archives)

Action: Iraq.
Powered by one 420hp Bristol Jupiter VI radial.
Serials: J9078–9102 (23).
Total 23; 7 accidental and 1 hostile loss.

330a. Wapiti IA

As the Mk I but was for VIP communications, with a headrest for a modified rear cockpit and armament deleted; it had a metal-skinned fuselage.
In service 1928 with 24 Sqn, used by three sqns (24, 604, 605) until 1934, 605 Sqn.
Powered by one 440hp Jupiter VIII.
Serials: J9095–96 (2).
Total 2; no losses.

330b. Wapiti II

A general-purpose type like the Mk I but with a composite frame and HP slots on the upper-wing leading-edges.
In service 1929 with 84 Sqn, used by three sqns (55, 84, 601) and 1xcomms. unit until 1933, 84 Sqn.
Action: Iraq.
Powered by one 460hp Jupiter VIIIf without reduction gear on the engine front.
Serials: J9239–9247 (8).
Total 8; 2 accidental losses.

330c. Wapiti IIA

The major production version, with an all-metal frame and a revised undercarriage, and was a general-purpose type, otherwise as the Mk I.
In service 1928 with 11 Sqn, used by 20 sqns (5, 11, 20, 27, 28, 30, 31, 39, 55, 60, 84, 501, 600, 601, 602, 603, 604, 605, 607, 608) until 1940, 27 Sqn; also served with 1xAAS, 1xAACU, 1xA&GS, 1xATC, 1xATU, EWS, 2xFTS, SoNCo-op, SoP, TB Leuchars, 3xcomms. units and 2xmisc. units, until 1943.
Action: Iraq and India, also based overseas in Egypt and the Far East.
Powered by one 440hp Jupiter VIII, 460hp Jupiter VIIIf, or 480hp Jupiter Xfa.
Serials: J9380–9414 (35), J9481–9514 (34), J9592–9636 (45), J9708–9724 (17), J9835–9871 (37), K1122–1157 (36), K1254–1309 (56), K1316–1415 (100), K2252–2320 (69).
Total 429; 91 accidental and 1 hostile loss.

330d. Wapiti V

An army co-operation version, with a message-hook, wider chord rudder, wheel brakes and a tail wheel.
In service 1930 with 27 Sqn, used by seven sqns (5, 11, 20, 27, 28, 31, 60) and 1xcomms. unit, until 1940,
5 Sqn; second-line to 1943.
Action: India, not operational in UK.
Powered by one 480hp Jupiter Xfa.
Serials: J9725–9759 (35).
Total 35; 19 accidental losses.

330e. Wapiti VI

An advanced trainer variant of the Mk IIA, with armament deleted and dual-controls in a revised rear cockpit.
In service 1932 with 605 Sqn, used by 10 sqns (501, 502, 504, 600, 601, 602, 603, 604, 605, 607) until 1937,
502 and 504 Sqns.
Powered by one 550hp Jupiter IXf.
Serials: K2236–2247 (12).
Total 12; no losses.

	Span	Length	Ceiling	Range	Speed
Mk I	46ft 5in/14.15m	29ft 9in/9.07m	n/k	n/k	n/k
Mk II	"	"	22,700ft/6,810m	"	133mph/214kmph
Mk IIA	"	31ft 8in/9.65m	20,600ft/6,180m	500 miles/805km	140mph/225kmph
Mk V	"	34ft 2in/10.41m	"	"	"
Mk VI	"	31ft 8in/9.65m	"	"	"

Total Wapitis 509; in service 1928–43; 121 (24%) losses inc. 2 hostile; nicknamed Wap, What a Pity.

331. Wallace I

Derived from the Wapiti this was a general-purpose biplane later much used for target-towing; it had two
crew and the armament, in its GP role, was one Vickers mg in the port fuselage side and a Lewis mg in the
rear cockpit, with 580lb/265kg of bombs underwing. As a target tug it had a winch on the port side.
In service 1933 with 501 Sqn, used by four sqns (501, 502, 503, 504) until 1937, 504 Sqn; also served with
3xAAS, 7xAOS, 6xAACU, 6xATC, 5xATS, 6xB&GS, EWS, 2xFTS, GDGS, 1xSS and the RAF Reg.S,
until 1943.
Powered by one 620hp Bristol Pegasus IIm3 radial.
Serials: K3562–3573 (12), K3664–3677 (14), K3906–13 (8), K4012–20 (9), K4337–45 (9), K5071–5082 (12).
Total 64, of which many were rebuilt Wapitis with new serials; 21 accidental losses.

331a. Wallace II

As the Mk I but had a glazed canopy; it was also widely used as a target-tug with the winch on the port side.
In service 1936 with 502 Sqn, used by three sqns (501, 502, 504) until 1939, 501 and 504 Sqns; also served
with 2xAAS, 9xAOS, 7xAACU, 4xATC, 4xATS, 6xB&GS, EWS, 4xFTS, GDGS, 1xSS, RAF Reg.S,
1xSoTT and TngC PracticeFlt, until 1943.
Powered by one 700hp Pegasus IV driving a larger diameter propeller.
Serials: K4346–48 (3), K5116, K6012–6086 (75), K8674–8702 (29).
Total 108; 30 accidental losses.

	Span	Length	Ceiling	Range	Speed
Mk I	46ft 5in/14.15m	34ft 2in/10.41m	n/k	n/k	n/k
Mk II	"	"	24,100ft/7,230m	470 miles/757km	158mph/254kmph

Total Wallaces 172; in service 1933–43; 51 (30%) losses; nicknamed Nellie.

332. Dragonfly HR 1

The first really operational Service helicopter, based on the American Sikorsky S-51; it carried one or
two crew and three or four passengers and was used for ASR and communications by the FAA.

Westland Wallace II, K6020, 1 Air Observer's School. (Newark Air Museum)

In service 1950 with 705 Sqn, used by carrier rescue flts, 1xPTU and 1xmisc. unit until 1953, 705 Sqn. Embarked on all operational carriers.
Action: Korea.
Powered by one 500hp Alvis Leonides 521/50 radial.
Serials: VX595–600 (6), VZ961–66 (6).
Total 12; 4 accidental losses.

332a. Dragonfly HC 2
The RAF version, for communications and casualty evacuation in Malaya, and for the latter duty it could carry a stretcher externally; it had composite rotor blades.
In service 1950 with the Casualty Evacuation Flt, used by one sqn (194), one flt and 1xmisc. unit, until 1956, 194 Sqn.
Action: Malaya, also based overseas in Singapore, not operational in the UK.
Serials: VZ960, WF308–10 (3).
Total 4; 4 accidental losses.

332b. Dragonfly HR 3
A development of the HR 1 for the FAA, with metal rotor blades and hydraulic servo-control.
In service 1952 with 705 Sqn, used by 1xPTU, 1xATU and 1xmisc. unit until 1960, Britannia RN College Flt. Embarked on one carrier, plus a rescue flt on all operational carriers.
Action: Korea and Suez, also based overseas in Malta.
Serials: WG661–754 (34), WH989–92 (4), WN492–500 (9), WP493–510 (12).
Total 59; 9 accidental losses.

332c. Dragonfly HC 4
The RAF version of the HR 3, carrying a stretcher externally and also used for training.
In service 1953 with 194 Sqn, used by one sqn (194), CFS and 3xmisc. units, until 1961, CFS Helicopter Sqn.
Action: Malaya.
Serials: WT845–46 (2), WX953, WZ749, XB251–56 (6), XF259–61 (3).
Total 13; 10 accidental losses.

Westland Dragonfly HR 3, WN496, Eglinton SF. (Charles Parker)

332d. Dragonfly HR 5

An FAA conversion of earlier Mks, with a more powerful engine and modified instruments and radio.
In service 1957 with 705 Sqn, used by one flt, 2xPTU and 1xmisc. unit, until 1967, Britannia RN
College Flt; embarked on three carriers, plus rescue flts, and one survey ship.
Powered by one 540hp Leonides 523.
Twenty-five conversions of the HR 1 and HR 3; eight accidental losses.

	Rotor diameter	Length	Ceiling	Range	Speed
HR 1	48ft/14.63m	41ft 1in/12.53m	12,400ft/3,720m	300 miles/483km	95mph/153kmph
HR 3	49ft/14.94m	"	13,200ft/3,960m	"	"
HC 4	"	"	12,400ft/3,720m	"	"

Total Dragonflies 88; in service 1950–67; 35 (40%) losses.

333. Whirlwind HAR 1

Based on the Sikorsky S-55, this was a transport and ASR helicopter for the FAA but was considerably
heavier than its US parent and consequently suffered a performance penalty. It was unarmed and had a
crew of two plus eight passengers, but in hot climates carried several less!
In service 1954 with 705 and 848 Sqns, used by two sqns (829, 848), one flt, 1xPTU, 1xcomms. unit and
2xmisc. units, until 1966, 829 Sqn; embarked on one carrier and one ice-patrol ship.
Action: Malaya.
Powered by one 600hp P&W Wasp R1340-40 radial.
Serials: XA862–70 (10).
Total 10; 2 accidental losses.

333a. Whirlwind HAR 2

As the HAR 1 but used by the RAF for search and rescue, with appropriate modifications and carrying
three crew and up to eight passengers.
In service 1955 with 22 Sqn, used by three sqns (22, 228, 275) and one flt until 1963, 228 Sqn.
Based overseas in Cyprus, Aden and Australia.
Serials: XJ429–30 renumbered from XD serials (2), XJ432–36 renumbered from XD serials (5), XJ725–
30 (6), XJ756–61 (6), XJ762–66 (5), XK968–91 (9).
Total 33; 11 accidental losses.

333b. Whirlwind HC 2

As the HAR 2 but used as a transport, with the SAR winch and specialised equipment removed, so carrying two crew and eight passengers.
In service 1954 with JEHU, used by one sqn (225) and 3xmisc. units until 1962, 225 Sqn.
Four conversions of the HAR 2; losses with the HAR 2.

333c. Whirlwind HAR 3

A more powerful development of the HAR 1 for the FAA; some were fitted with sonar and some, later, had a drooped tail boom.
In service 1955 with 701 Sqn, used by two sqns (815, 845), one flt, 1xCU, 1xPTU, 1xATU, 1xcomms. unit and 2xmisc. units, until 1966, 705 Sqn; embarked on one carrier.
Action: Suez, also based overseas in Malta.
Powered by one 700hp Wright Cyclone R1300-3 radial.
Serials: XG572–86 (14), XJ393–401 (10).
Total 24; 10 accidental losses.

333d. Whirlwind HC 4

As the HC 2 but a tropicalized transport for the RAF.
In service 1954 with 155 Sqn, used by two sqns (110, 155) and 1xmisc. unit until 1960, 110 Sqn.
Action: Malaya, also based overseas in Aden and Guyana.
Powered by one 600hp Wasp R1340-57 with an increased supercharger ratio.
Serials: XJ407–414 renumbered from XD serials (8), XJ426–28 (3) renumbered from XD serials, XJ431 renumbered, XJ437 renumbered, XJ723–24 (2), XJ761, XL109–13 (5).
Total 21 plus 1 conversion of the HC 2, making a total of 22; 4 accidental losses.

333e. Whirlwind HAR 4

An SAR version of the HC 4, with three crew, eight to ten passengers and a rescue winch; it was not tropicalized.
In service 1958 with 217 Sqn, used by three sqns (217, 228, 275) and one flt until 1962, 228 Sqn.
Fourteen conversions of the HC 4; three accidental losses.

Westland Whirlwind HAR 2, XJ430, 22 Sqn. (Scott Collection)

333f. Whirlwind HAS 7

An anti-submarine version for the FAA, its first front-line helicopter and the first Whirlwind with a British engine which, in its early service, often failed! The HAS 7 had three or four crew and was armed with sono buoys and a torpedo in a bay under the fuselage; it had a drooped tail boom as standard, and horizontal stabilizers. In service 1957 with 700 and 845 sqns, used by seven sqns (814, 815, 819, 820, 824, 825, 829) and one flt until 1967, 829 Sqn; also served with 2xCU, 1xATU, 1xcomms. unit and 2xmisc. units, until 1976. Embarked on seven carriers.

Powered by one 780hp Alvis Leonides Major 755 radial.

Serials: XG589–598 (12), XK906–945 (20), XL833–900 (45), XM660–687 (15), XN258–314 (25), XN357–387 (15).

Total 132; 62 accidental losses.

333g. Whirlwind HC 7

An assault transport based on the above, with the anti-submarine gear, weapons bay and torpedo removed; carried two crew and eight passengers.

In service 1959 with 848 Sqn, used by four sqns (845, 846, 847, 848) and 1xCU until 1966, 848 Sqn. Embarked on two carriers.

Action: Borneo.

Unknown number of conversions of the HAS 7; losses included with the HAS 7.

333h. Whirlwind HCC 8

A VIP version of the HC 7 for the RAF, with two crew, and four passengers in a VIP cabin with extra windows.

In service 1959 to 1964 with the Queen's Flt.

Powered by one 780hp Leonides Major 755.

Serials: XN126–27 (2).

Total 2; no losses.

333j. Whirlwind HAR 9

A major development of the Whirlwind, with the piston engine replaced by a turboprop in a redesigned longer nose without the intake grills around the top and one large exhaust on the port side. It had a rescue winch, a tail-rotor pylon of increased sweep and chord, and a drooped boom. The HAR 9 was used by the FAA for search and rescue and communications, with three crew and five passengers or two crew and eight passengers.

In service 1964 with HMS Hermes, used by one sqn (829) and carrier rescue flights until 1977, 781 Sqn; embarked on two ice-patrol ships and one RFA.

Powered by one 1,050shp B-S Gnome H1000 turboprop.

Sixteen conversions of the HAS 7; 3 accidental losses.

333k. Whirlwind HAR 10

As the HAR 9, a similar version for the RAF as its standard SAR type.

In service 1962 with 22 Sqn, used by three sqns (22, 202, 228), three flts and SARTU, until 1981, 22 Sqn. Based overseas in Libya and Singapore.

Serials: XP299–405 (52), XR453–485 (15), XS412.

Total 68, plus 43 conversions of the HC 2, HC 4 and HCC 8, making a total of 111; 35 accidental and 1 hostile loss.

333l. Whirlwind HC 10

An RAF transport version of the above, without the SAR gear and able to carry a 7.62mm gpmg in the cabin door and four Nord AS 11 AGMs on fuselage pylons. Two crew and eight passengers.

In service 1961 with 225 Sqn, used by six sqns (28, 84, 103, 110, 225, 230) until 1982, 84 Sqn; also served with 1xFTS, 1xcomms. unit and 3xmisc. units.

Action: Borneo, also based overseas in Germany, Cyprus, Malaya, Singapore, Hong Kong and Guyana.

Total and losses included with the HAR 10.

Westland Whirlwind HAR 10,
XJ729 converted from HAR 2,
22 Sqn. (Author's Collection)

333m. Whirlwind HCC 12

An RAF VIP transport version with two crew, and four passengers in a VIP cabin which had extra windows and steps to its door.

In service 1964 with the Queen's Flt, used by one sqn (32) and one flt until 1981, 32 Sqn.

Serials: XR486–87 (2).

Total 2; 1 accidental loss.

For HAS 21 and HAR 22, see Sikorsky.

	Rotor diameter	Length	Ceiling	Range	Speed
HAR 1	53ft/16.15m	41ft 8in/12.7m	8,600ft/2,580m	320 miles/515km	99mph/159kmph
HAR 3	"	"	"	"	106mph/171kmph
HC 4	"	"	"	"	99mph/159kmph
HAS 7	"	"	13,000ft/3,900m	334 miles/538km	109mph/175kmph
HAR 9	"	44ft 2in/13.46m	16,600ft/4,980m	300 miles/483km	110mph/177kmph

Total British Whirlwinds 292; in service 1954–82; 132 (45%) losses inc. 1 hostile; nicknamed Whirlybird.

334. Wessex HAS 1

An adaption of the Sikorsky S-58 for use by the FAA as an anti-submarine and SAR helicopter; it had three or four crew and was armed with sonar and two A-S torpedoes or DC on fuselage-side sponsons.

In service 1960 with 700H Sqn, 1961 with 815 Sqn, used by six sqns (814, 815, 819, 820, 826, 829) until 1970, 829 Sqn; also served with two SAR sqns, 2xCU and 1xATU, until 1979. Embarked on six carriers, six destroyers and one RFA.

Powered by one 1,450shp Napier Gazelle 161 turboprop, with twin, downward-angled exhausts each side of the nose.

Serials: XL727–29 (3), XM299–331 (9), XM832–876 (40), XP103–160 (40), XS115–154 (20), XS862–889 (28).

Total 140; 48 accidental losses.

334a. Wessex HC 1

An assault helicopter version of the above, with anti-sub. gear deleted and carrying two crew and 16 passengers; armament was one manually-operated 0.5in Browning in the cabin door, one 7.62mm gpmg on each undercarriage strut and two Nord AS 11 AGMs on the sponsons.

In service 1962–65 with 845 Sqn, also served with 3xCU until 1979. Embarked on two carriers.

Action: Borneo.

Serials not known.

Total 12 plus unknown number of conversions of the HAS 1; losses included with the HAS 1.

Westland Wessex HC 2, XT678, 28 Sqn.
(28 Sqn)

Westland Wessex HAS 3, 737 Sqn. (Scott
Collection)

334b. Wessex HC 2

A RAF transport development, with twin engines and a large, single, upwards-angled exhaust on each side of the nose; it had two or three crew, and 16 passengers or 4,000lb/1,816kg of freight, and could be armed with one 0.5in Browning or 7.62mm gpmg in the door and two Nord AS 11 or SS 12 AGMs on the sponsons.

In service 1963 with the Wessex TU, 1964 with 18 Sqn, used by six sqns (18, 28, 72, 78, 84, 103) until 2003, 84 Sqn; also served with the Wessex TU, Air Transport Sqn, 1xFTS, Helicopter OCU, SRCU, 1xcomms. unit and 1xmisc. unit.

Action: Aden, Oman and North Ireland, also based overseas in Germany, Cyprus, the Gulf, Singapore and Hong Kong.

Powered by two 1,350shp B-S Gnome H1200-110 or 111 turboprops.

Serials: XR497–529 (29), XR588, XS674–79 (6), XT601–07 (7), XT667–681 (15), XV719–731 (12).

Total 70; 8 accidental losses.

334c. Wessex HAR 2

As the HC 2 but with the armament replaced by a winch and other SAR gear, plus extra navigational equipment; it carried four crew and 20 passengers.

In service 1970 with Bahrein SFlt, used by two sqns, (22, 202), three flts and SARTU, until 1997, 22 Sqn. Based overseas in the Gulf.

Twenty conversions of the HC 2; two accidental losses.

334d. Wessex HAS 3

As the HAS 1, an anti-submarine version for the FAA but with Ekco-Mel ARI-5955 radar in a dorsal radome, a 'hump' behind the main rotor, and no window in the door, plus internal changes. Armed with two A/S torpedoes or DC.

In service 1967 with 700H and 814 Sqn, used by five sqns (814, 819, 820, 826, 829) until 1971, 819 Sqn;

also served with 2xCU and 1xmisc. unit, until 1984, 772 Sqn . Embarked on two carriers, one cruiser, eight destroyers and six RFA.

Action: Falklands.

Powered by one 1,600shp Gazelle 165 with exhausts as the HAS 1.

Serials: XT255–257 (3).

Total 3 plus 41 conversions of the HAS 1 making a total of 44; 17 accidental and 1 hostile loss.

334e. Wessex HCC 4

A VIP transport adaptation of the HC 2 for the RAF, with three crew and six passengers in a VIP cabin with extra windows; no armament.

In service 1969 with the Queen's Flt, used by one flt and one sqn (32) until 1998, 32(The Royal) Sqn.

Powered by two 1,350 shp Gnome H1200-110.

Serials: XV732–33 (2).

Total 2; no losses.

334f. Wessex HU 5

An assault helicopter for the FAA, similar to the HC 2 but with two 7.62mm gpmg in the door, two RP pods, four SS 11 or SS 12 AGMs on the sponsons, naval equipment and detail changes.

In service 1963 with 700V Sqn, 1964 with 848 Sqn, used by five sqns (829, 845, 846, 847, 848) until 1986, 845 Sqn; also served with 1xCU, 1xRAF FTS, 1xcomms. unit and 3xmisc. units. Embarked on four carriers, two assault ships, one helicopter training ship, one destroyer and 10 RFA.

Action: Borneo, Aden and Falklands.

Serials: XS479–523 (40), XT448–487 (40), XT755–774 (20).

Total 100; 20 accidental and 6 hostile losses.

334g. Wessex HAR 5

An FAA search and rescue variant of the HU 5, with armament deleted and a winch fitted over the door.

In service 1979 with 771 Sqn, used by two sqns and 1xmisc. unit, until 1988, 772 Sqn.

A few conversions of the HU 5.

334h. Wessex HU 5C

A version of the HU 5 used by the RAF for SAR and transport duties, so had RAF equipment and SAR gear; could be armed with a 7.62mm gpmg in the door.

In service 1985–95 with 84 Sqn.

Based overseas in Cyprus, not operational in the UK.

Five conversions of the HU 5; one accidental loss.

	Rotor diameter	Length	Ceiling	Range	Speed
HAS 1	56ft/17.07m	48ft 4in/14.73m	14,100ft/4,230m	645 miles/1,038km	132mph/213kmph
HC 2	"	50ft/15.24m	12,000ft/3,600m	478 miles/770km	120mph/193kmph
HAS 3	"	48ft 4in/14.73m	"	302 miles/486km	127mph/204kmph
HCC 4	"	50ft/15.24m	17,400ft/5,220m	478 miles/770km	132mph/213kmph

Total Wessex 327; in service 1960–2003; 103 (31%) losses inc. 7 hostile.

335. Belvedere HC 1

The RAF's first twin-rotor helicopter, originally designed by Bristol (qv), and used for transport duties, in which its reputation varied from bad to good depending on the operational theatre; reliability was poor but it served in harsh conditions. It carried two or three crew and 25 passengers or 6,000lb/2,725kg of freight, and was unarmed. Nicknamed the Flying Longhouse.

In service 1960 with the Belvedere Trials Unit, 1961 with 66 Sqn, used by three sqns (26, 66, 72) and the SR OCU until 1969, 66 Sqn.

Action: Borneo and Aden, also based overseas in Singapore.

Powered by two 1,650shp Napier Gazelle NGA2 turboprops.

Westland Belvedere HC 1,
XG466, 26 Sqn. (Newark Air
Museum)

Westland Wasp HAS 1, 829 Sqn.
(Author's Collection)

Serials: XG449–476 (23).
Rotor diameter: 49ft 11in/15.22m   Length: 54ft 4in/16.56m   Ceiling: 13,400ft/4,020m   Range: 445
miles/716km   Speed: 138mph/222kmph.
Total 23; 7 (30%) accidental losses.

336. Wasp HAS 1

Designed by Saro, this was the naval version of the P531, similar to the Scout (see Vol. 1) but with a four-
wheeled undercarriage; it was the FAA's first small-ship anti-submarine and general duties helicopter
and carried two crew and three passengers. Armament was two A/S torpedoes, 2xDC or four Nord AS
11 or 12 ASMs under the fuselage.
In service 1963 with 700W Sqn, 1964 with 829 Sqn, used by three sqns (829, 845, 848) until 1988, 829
Sqn; also served with 2xCU, 2xPTU and 2xmisc. units. Embarked on 49 frigates, one destroyer, five
survey ships, one ice-patrol ship, one assault ship and four RFA.
Action: Borneo and Falklands.
Powered by one 968shp RR Nimbus 103 turboprop.
Serials: XS463, XS476, XS527-545 (30), XT414-443 (30), XT778-795 (18), XV622-639 (18).
Rotor diameter: 32ft 3in/9.83m   Length: 32ft 4in/9.85m   Ceiling: 12,200ft/3,660m   Range: 303
miles/488km   Speed: 120mph/193kmph.
Total 98; 19 (19%) accidental losses.

337. Sea King HAS 1

A British-built and modified Sikorsky S-61 used by the FAA for anti-submarine duties, with a crew of four and armed with four A/S torpedoes or DC on fuselage sponsons and Ekco AW391 radar in a dorsal radome. In service 1969 with 700S Sqn, 1970 with 824 Sqn, used by five sqns (814, 819, 820, 824, 826) until 1978, 819 Sqn; also served with 3xCU. Embarked on three carriers, two cruisers and six RFA.
Powered by two 1,500shp RR Gnome H1400 turboprops.
Serials: XV642–714 (56).
Total 56; 9 accidental losses.

337a. Sea King HAS 2

As the HAS 1 but with a faster fuel jettison, a stronger transmission system, a six-bladed tail-rotor and FOD guards to the engine intakes; it could be used as a transport carrying 24 passengers.
In service 1976 with 820 Sqn, used by six sqns (814, 819, 820, 824, 825, 826) until 1985, 819 Sqn; also served with 2xCU. Embarked on four carriers, two cruisers and seven RFA.
Powered by two 1,660shp Gnome H1400-1T.
Serials: XZ570–582 (13), XZ915–922 (8).
Total 21; 1 accidental loss.

337b. Sea King HAS 2A

The HAS 1 modified to HAS 2 standard. A strake was added to the port rear fuselage for service in the Falklands. Action: Falklands.
In service 1977, used by six sqns (814, 819, 820, 824, 825, 826) until 1985, 819 Sqn; also served with 2xCU. Embarked on three carriers, two cruisers and seven RFA.
Forty-five conversions of the HAS 1; one accidental loss.

337c. Sea King HAS 2 (AEW), later AEW 2

Developed hastily to remedy the FAA's lack of early warning radar, which cost the RN dear in the Falklands; it was an HAS 2 or 2A with the anti-submarine equipment removed and replaced by a console for a Searchwater radar, the radome being an inflatable, rotatable bag on the starboard fuselage side, plus improved avionics. The increased weight reduced the crew to three, a pilot and two observers. Nicknamed Whisky or Bag.
In service 1982 with 824 Sqn, used by two sqns (824, 829) until 2003, 849 Sqn. Embarked on three carriers and one RFA.
Powered by two 1,500shp Gnome H1400-1T.
Twelve conversions of the HAS 2 and 2A; no losses.

337d. Sea King HAR 3

An RAF version for search and rescue with the appropriate gear, avionics changes, and the A/S equipment and weapons deleted; it has extra cabin windows. Four crew and 18 passengers. Will be replaced shortly by civilian registered Sikorsky S-92s
In service 1978 with the Sea King IFTU and 202 Sqn, used by two sqns (78, 202) and one flt until the present, 2010; also served with Sea King TU, 1xOCU and 1xRSqn.
Based overseas in the Falklands.
Powered by two 1,660shp Gnome H1400-1.
Serials: XZ585–599 (15), ZA105, ZE368–70 (3).
Total 19; 1 accidental loss.

337e. Sea King HAR 3A

As the HAR 3 but with composite rotors, a 'glass' cockpit, improved avionics and night capable; it also has a limited defensive capability. Also to be replaced as above.
In service 1996 with the Sea King TU, 1997 with 22 Sqn until the present, 2010, also served with 1xOCU and 1xRSqn.
Serials: ZH540–45 (6).
Total 6; no losses to date.

Westland Sea King
HAR 3, XZ594,
202 Sqn. (Author's
Collection)

Westland Sea King
HC 4, 846 Sqn. (Mike
French)

337f. Sea King HC 4

A much-modified Sea King, sometimes called a Commando, which is an assault helicopter for the FAA, carrying three crew, and 27 passengers or 6,000lb/2,725kg of freight; it can be armed with one 7.62mm gpmg in the door. The floats are deleted and it has a fixed undercarriage on the sponsons, there is no dorsal radome or radar and there are extra cabin windows; it has NVG and GPS. Nicknamed Junglie.

In service 1979 with 846 Sqn, used by three sqns (845, 846, 848) until the present, 2010; also served with 2xCU and 1xSAR unit. Embarked on three carriers, two assault ships, one helicopter carrier and seven RFA.

Action: Falklands, Bosnia, Iraq and Afghanistan.

Serials: ZA290–314 (15), ZD476–80 (5), ZD625–27 (3), ZE425–28 (4), ZF115–124 (10), ZG820–22 (3).

Total 40; 4 accidental and 3 hostile losses to date.

337g. Sea King HC 4 plus

A development of the HC 4 for service in Afghanistan, with new main rotor blades, giving an increased ceiling, new tail rotor, new defensive aids, new NVG and FLIR in a nose turret. (One wonders why it is not known as the HC 4A).

In service 2007 with 846 Sqn, used by two sqns (845, 846) to the present, 2010.

Action: Afghanistan.

Fourteen conversions of the HC 4; no losses to date.

337h. Sea King HAS 5

An FAA anti-submarine development of the HAS 2 with Seasearcher radar in a larger, flat-topped dorsal radome, MAD gear in the starboard sponson, improved avionics, and a larger radar cabin in a strengthened airframe. Weapons and crew as the HAS 2.

In service 1980 with 820 Sqn, used by six sqns (810, 814, 819, 820, 824, 826) until 1993, 819 Sqn; also served with 2xCU and RAF Sea King TU until 2004. Embarked on four carriers, four frigates and 10 RFA.

Action: Falklands.

Powered by two 1,500shp Gnome H1400-1.

Serials: ZA126–137 (12), ZA166–70 (5), ZD630–37 (8), ZE418–22 (5).

Total 30 plus 52 conversions of the HAS 2 and 2A, making a total of 82; 11 accidental and 2 hostile losses.

337j. Sea King HU 5

An SAR and utility transport for the FAA with three crew and 19 passengers, and weapons and A/S gear deleted and replaced by SAR gear; there is a step on the starboard side and a convex window. To shortly be replaced by civilian registered Sikorsky S-92s.

In service 1987 with 771 Sqn, used by one sqn, and 1xCU until the present, 2010.

Nineteen conversions of the HAS 5; no losses to date.

337k. Sea King HAS 6

A development of the HAS 5 with improved avionics and sonar, composite blades, and an improved airframe, with weapons and radar as the HAS 5. Nicknamed Jez.

In service 1988 with 824 (Trials) Sqn, 1989 with 819 Sqn, used by six sqns (810, 814, 819, 820, 824, 826) until 2004, 771 Sqn; also served with 2xCU. Embarked on three carriers, one assault ship, four frigates, one aviation trng ship and seven RFA.

Powered by two 1,500 shp Gnome H1400-1T.

Serials: ZG816–19 (4), ZG875.

Total 5 plus 52 conversions of the HAS 5 making a total of 57; 3 accidental losses.

Westland Sea
King HU
5, 771 Sqn.
(Author's
Collection)

Westland Sea King
ASaC 7, 849 Sqn.
(Author's Collection)

337l. Sea King HAS 6 (CR)

A transport version of the above with A/S gear, radar and radome removed and the undercarriage fixed down but still having the HAS 6 float u/c sponsons. It has a defensive arms suite and carries a 0.5in mg in the door. Capacity as the HC 4 with a strengthened cabin floor for freight.

In service 2004 with 820 Sqn, used by four sqns (820, 825, 846, 848) until the present, 2010, embarked on one RFA.

Action: Iraq.

Five conversions of the HAS 6; no losses to date.

337m. Sea King ASaC 7

An updated AEW 2, with Searchwater 2000 radar in the 'bag', GPS, JTIDS and improved avionics; the dorsal radome is deleted. Nicknamed Bag. Some have been given similar improvements to the HC 4 plus (qv).

In service 2002 with 849 Sqn, used by three sqns (849, 854, 857) to the present, 2010. Embarked on two carriers.

Action: Iraq and Afghanistan.

Twelve conversions of the AEW 2, HAS 5 and HAS 6; 2 accidental losses to date.

	Rotor diameter	Length	Ceiling	Range	Speed
HAS 1	62ft/18.9m	55ft 10in/16.71m	10,000ft/3,000m	690 miles/1,111km	137mph/221kmph
HAS 2	"	"	"	764 miles/1,230km	"
AEW 2	"	"	"	"	140mph/225kmph
HAR 3	"	"	14,000ft/4,200m	"	170mph/274kmph
HC 4	"	"			
HAS 5	"	"			

Total Sea Kings 177; in service 1969–present, 2010; 37 (21%) losses inc. 5 hostile to date.

338. Puma HC 1

A British-built Aerospatiale design ordered as a transport for the RAF, with two or three crew and 16 passengers or 5,500lb/2,500kg of freight; it can be armed with two 7.62mm gpmg in the cabin doors. The Puma has had several updates without changing its Mk number.

In service 1971 with 240 OCU and 33 Sqn, used by three sqns (33, 72, 230) and two flts until the present, 2010; also served with Helicopter OCU, 1xOCU, and 1xRSqn.

Action: Northern Ireland, the Gulf, Bosnia and Iraq, also based overseas in Germany and Belize.

Powered by two 1,320shp Turbomeca Turmo III, or 1,435shp Turmo IIIC-C4 turboprops.
Serials: XW198–237 (40), ZA934–41 (7), ZE449, ZJ954–57 (4).
Total 52; 12 accidental and 1 hostile loss to date.

338a. Puma HC 2
An improved and re-engined Puma with a glass cockpit and new communications and ECM.
In service 2010.
Powered by two 2,104shp Turbomeca Makila 1A2 turboprops.
30 conversions of the HC 1.
HC 1: Rotor diameter: 49ft 2in/14.99m   Length: 46ft 1in/14.05m   Ceiling: 15,700ft/4,710m   Range:
390 miles/628km   Speed: 174mph/280kmph.
HC 2: Dimensions as HC 1, performance not yet known.
Total Pumas 52; in service 1971–present 2010; 13 (20%) losses to date inc. 1 hostile.

339. Lynx HAS 2
The FAA version of the Lynx for anti-submarine and anti-surface shipping roles and communications
duties, operating from small ships. The skids on the AH 1 (Vol. 1) were replaced by a tricycle wheeled
undercarriage mounted on fuselage-side sponsons and it had a folding tailcone. Two crew and nine pas-
sengers, and it was armed with Seaspray radar in a nose radome, and two A/S torpedoes, two Stingray
ASMs, two DC or four Sea Skua ASMs on fuselage sponsons.
In service 1976 with 700L Sqn, 1978 with 702 Sqn, used by three sqns (702, 815, 829) until 1988, 815 Sqn;
also served with 1xCU and 1xmisc. unit. Embarked on one carrier, 14 destroyers, 23 frigates and four RFA.
Powered by two 900shp RR Gem 2 turboprops.
Action: Falklands.
Serials: XZ227–257 (30), XZ689–736 (30).
Total 60; 2 accidental and 3 hostile losses.

339a. Lynx HAS 3
A development of the HAS 2 with more powerful engines.
In service 1982 with 815 Sqn, used by two sqns (815, 829) and one CU until the 1990s; also served with
1xCU and 1xmisc. unit. Embarked on 14 destroyers, 32 frigates and three RFA.
Action: the Gulf.
Powered by two 1,135shp Gem 41-2.

Westland Puma HC 1, XW228 early production without FOD guards, 230 Sqn. (Author's Collection)

Westland Lynx HAS 3, ZD252, 815 Sqn. (Author's Collection)

Serials: ZD249–268 (20), ZD565–67 (3), ZF557–59 (3).
Total 26, plus 53 conversions of the HAS 2 making a total of 79; 1 accidental loss to date.

339b. Lynx HAS 3S (= speech secure)

As the HAS 3 but with flotation bags in the nose and improved avionics including secure radio.
In service 1987 with 815 Sqn, used by two sqns (815, 829) and 1xCU until the present, 2010. Ships as the HAS 3.
Action: the Gulf.
Serials: ZF560–63 (4).
Total 4 plus 40 conversions of the HAS 3 making a total of 44; 2 accidental losses to date.

339c. Lynx HAS 3 (ICE)

A standard HAS 3 modified for duties with the Antarctic patrol ship, having less-sophisticated avionics, and special equipment including a survey camera.
In service 1988 to the present, 2010. Embarked on two ice-patrol ships.
Four conversions of the HAS 3; one accidental loss to date.

339d. Lynx HAS 3 GMS (= Gulf modification)

As the HAS 3s but with better cooling for operations in the Gulf, armed with four Stingray or Sea Skua ASMs plus a 7.62mm gpmg in the cabin door; has FLIR, improved ECM and flare and chaff dispensers.
In service 1992 with 815 Sqn, used by one sqn to the present, 2010. Embarked on one destroyer and frigates.
Action: the Gulf.
Thirty-six conversions of the HAS 3; four accidental losses to date.

339e. Lynx HAS 8, later HMA 8

An anti-shipping and liason type for the FAA with a new nose holding Seaspray 2000 radar in a chin radome and a Sea Owl thermal imager in a ball above the nose; it has improved avionics, BERP composite rotor blades, a Central Tactical System, extra flotation bags and the tail-rotor rotates in the opposite direction to the HAS 3. Armament as the HAS 3.

In service 1994 with 815 (OEU) Sqn, 1996 with 815 Sqn, used by one sqn and 1xCU to the present, 2010. Powered by two 1,135shp Gem 42-200. Embarked on 11 frigates.

Forty-four conversions of the HAS 3 variants; two accidental losses to date.

339f. Lynx HMA 8 (SRU)

This variant carries the Saturn radio upgrade, improved avionics, a GPS navigational suite and a defensive aids suite.

All surviving HMA 8 (DAS) were converted.

	Rotor diameter	length	ceiling	range	speed
HAS 2	"	39ft 2in	8,500ft	388 miles	144mph
HAS 3	"	"	"	390 miles	"

Total FAA Lynxes 235; in service 1977–present 2010; 31 (13%) losses inc. 5 hostile to date.

Future Lynx see Wildcat under Agusta-Westland.

340. Merlin HM 1

An FAA anti-submarine and shipping strike helicopter, developed jointly with Agusta under the European Helicopters brand name. It has four crew and can carry up to 12 passengers, is armed with four Stingray or Harpoon ASMs or four DC or A-S torpedoes on fuselage sponsons, and has Blue Kestrel radar in a under forward fuselage radome.

In service 1998 with the IFTU, 2000 with 824 (Trials) Sqn, and 2002 with 814 Sqn, used by four sqns (814, 820, 824, 829) to the present, 2010. Embarked on two carriers, one RFA and five frigates.

Action: Iraq.

Powered by three 2,312shp RR-Turbomeca RTM322-01 turboprops.

Serials: ZH821–864 (44).

Total 44; 1 accidental loss to date.

Westland Lynx HMA 8, XZ236 converted from HAS 3, 815 Sqn. (Author's Collection)

Westland
Merlin
HM 1.
(Author's
Collection)

340a. Merlin HM 2

An improved HM 1 which will give the Merlin a surface attack capability as well as anti-submarine ;
it will have a defensive aids suite and improved avionics and its main weapon will be the future air-to-
surface guided weapon plus a 0.5in mg in the cabin door.
In service from 2012.
Total 30 conversions of the HM 1.

340b. Merlin HC 3

An RAF transport version, with the radar and armament deleted, non-folding rotors and tail boom, a
FLIR turret beneath the nose, strengthened floor, extra cabin windows, refuelling probe, improved navi-
gational equipment, rear-loading ramp and a double-wheel main undercarriage. It carries three crew and
24 passengers or 10,000lb/4,540kg of freight.
In service 2001 with 28 Sqn, used by one sqn and two flights to the present, 2010.
Action: Iraq and Afghanistan, based overseas in Bosnia.
Powered by three 1,863shp RTM322-12/8.
Serials: ZJ117–138 (22).
Total 22; no losses to date.

340c. Merlin HC 3A

The conflicts in Iraq and Afghanistan have left the RAF short of heavy-lift helicopters so six Merlins
originally ordered by the Royal Danish Air Force were purchased for the RAF. They differ from the
HC 3 in having an improved cockpit, NVG, laser obstruction avoidance, weather radar in a small nose
radome and have advanced BERP IV rotor blades.
In service 2007 with 78 Sqn, used by one sqn to the present, 2010.
Serials: ZJ990, ZJ992, ZJ994–995 (2), ZJ998, ZK001.
Total 6; no losses to date.

	Rotor diameter	Length	Ceiling	Range	Speed
HM 1	61ft/18.59m	74ft 9in/22.79m	15,000ft/4,500m	1,150 miles/1,851km	200mph/322kmph
HC 3	"	"	12,800ft/3,840m	"	173mph/279kmph

Total Merlins 72; in service 2000–present, 2010; 1 (2%) loss to date.

WHITE & THOMPSON (Middleton-on-Sea, Sussex, UK)

A small firm, founded in 1912, which became Norman-Thompson (qv) in 1915. Supplied 101 examples
of two types, also assembled Short 184s.

341. No. 2 Flying Boat

An impressed reconnaissance and training type for the RNAS, unarmed and with two crew. It was an unstaggered two-bay biplane with an almost circular fabric fin on the centre of the upper wing and a long dorsal fin on the fuselage with the tailplane mounted on its top; two underwing floats.
In service 1914 at Calshot, used by two units until 1915, Felixstowe.
Powered by one 120hp Beardmore in-line pusher mounted just below the upper wing.
Serial: 882.
Total 1 impressed; 1 accidental loss.

341a. No. 3 Flying Boat or NT 2

A reconnaissance boat for the RNAS, as the above but with a Lewis mg in the port side of the cockpit and 150lb/70kg of bombs underwing. The central upper wing fin was replaced by two smaller above the inner struts and the longer upper wings were braced by 'goalpost' kingposts – wing tips were slightly rounded. There was an additional small fin mounted over the tailplane.
In service 1914 at Dover, used by six units (Bembridge, Dover, Dundee, Dunkirk, Fort George, 1NSqn) and 1xPTU until 1918, Calshot. Embarked on one seaplane carrier.
Action: home waters.
Serials: 1195–1200 (6).
Total 6; 1 accidental and 1 hostile loss.

341b. NT 2A

As the NT 2 but with a new hull and with the armament deleted, used for reconnaissance and training.
In service 1915–18 at Calshot.
Action: home waters.
Powered by one 120hp Beardmore or 150hp Hispano-Suiza 8aa in-line pusher.
Serials: 3807–08 (2).
Total 2 plus 4 conversions of the NT 2, making a total of 6; 1 hostile loss.

Westland Merlin HC 3, 28 Sqn. (Andrew Nowland)

341c. NT 2B

A development of the NT 2A used for training by the RNAS/RAF, but engine problems delayed its entry into service. It had two crew in an enclosed cockpit, dual control, and could carry 200lb/91kg of bombs underwing. Built by Saunders and Supermarine.

In service 1917 at Calshot, used by 2xPTU, 2xRAF TDS and the RAF&NCo-opS, until 1919, 209 TDS. Powered by one 120hp Beardmore, 150hp Hispano-Suiza 8aa, or 200hp Sunbeam Arab I in-line pusher.

Serials: N1180–189 (10), N2260–2359 (20), N2400–2429 (30), N2555–2579 (24), N2760.

Total 85 but many not issued; 2 accidental losses.

	Span	Length	Ceiling	Endurance	Speed
No. 2	45ft/13.72m	27ft 6in/8.38m	n/k	6hrs	70mph/113kmph
No. 3	"	"	"	"	85mph/137kmph
NT 2A	"	"	"	"	"
NT 2B	48ft 4in/14.73m	"	11,400ft/3,420m	n/k	"

Total NT 2s 93 plus 1 impressed making a total of 94; in service 1914–18; 6 (6%) losses inc. 2 hostile.

WHITEHEAD (Richmond, Surrey, UK)

Assembled Airco DH 9 and 9A.

WIGHT (Actually J.S.White) (Cowes, IoW, UK)

A small-scale manufacturer of seaplanes, formed in 1913, which supplied 119 examples of four types. Also assembled Short 184

342. 1914 Navyplane

A four-bay biplane reconnaissance seaplane for the RNAS with two crew and no armament. It had two long main floats only, heavily strutted, and the rudder was beneath the tailplane.

In service 1913 at Calshot, used by three units (Calshot, Dover, Fort George) until 1915, Fort George. Action: home waters.

Powered by one 160hp Gnome 14 Lambda-Lambda rotary pusher.

Serials: 128–29 (2), 155, 884.

Total 4; 4 accidental losses.

342a. Improved Navyplane

As the above but re-engined.

In service 1914 on HMS *Ark Royal*, used by three units (Calshot, Dover, Dunkirk) until 1916, Dover; embarked on one seaplane carrier.

Action: home waters and Mediterranean.

Powered by one 200hp Salmson 2m7 radial pusher.

Serials: 171–77 (7).

Total 7 plus 2 impressed, 893–95 (3), making a total of 9; 4 accidental losses.

	Span	Length	Ceiling	Endurance	Speed
1914	63ft/19.2m	n/k	n/k	n/k	79mph/127kmph
Improved	"	"	"	"	72mph/116kmph

Total Navyplanes 13; in service 1913–16; 8 (61%) losses.

343. Type 840

A three-bay biplane two-seater torpedo bomber for the RNAS, armed with one torpedo or light bombs under the fuselage.

In service 1915 on HMS *Campania*, used by six units (Calshot, Dundee, Dunkirk, Gibraltar, Scapa, Yarmouth) until 1917, Gibraltar. Embarked on one seaplane carrier.

Action: home waters and Mediterranean.

Powered by one 200hp Sunbeam Mohawk in-line.

White & Thompson NT 2B, N2575, 210 TDS. (S. Taylor via G. Stuart Leslie)

Wight 840, 9022, RNAS Gibraltar. (Peter Green Collection)

Serials: 831–840 (10), 1300–1319 (20), 1351–54 (4), 1400–1411 (12), 8281–8285 (5), 9021–28 (8).
Span: 61ft/18.59m   Length: 41ft/12.5m   Ceiling: n/k   Endurance: 7hrs   Speed: 81mph/130kmph.
Total 59 (but some not issued); 14 (21%) losses inc. 2 hostile.

344. Converted Seaplane
A reconnaissance sea or land plane for the RNAS/RAF, a two-seater with a Lewis mg in the rear cockpit and able to carry 448lb/205kg of bombs underwing.
In service 1917 at Eastchurch, used by four RNAS units (Calshot, Cattewater, Houton Bay, Scapa) and two RAF sqns (241, 243), until 1919, 241 Sqn; also served with 1xRNAS PTU, 1xRNAS ObsTU and 1xRAF TDS.
Action: home waters.

Wight Converted Seaplane. (Air-Britain Archives)

Powered by one 275hp RR Eagle VI or VII, or 250hp Sunbeam Maori II in-line.
Serials: 9841–9860 (20), N1280–1289 (10), N2180–2229 (15).
Span: 65ft 6in/19.96m   Length: 44ft 8in/13.61m   Ceiling: 9,600ft/2,880m   Endurance:
3.5hrs   Speed: 85mph/137kmph.
Total 45; 8 (18%) accidental losses.

ZLIN (Czechoslovakia)
A company which has produced light aircraft since 1935. Supplied one example of one type.

345. Z XII/12
An impressed tandem two-seat low-wing monoplane for communications work by the RAF with a
greenhouse-style canopy, a triangular fin & rudder and a strutted undercarriage.
In service 1942 with 221Gp CommsFlt, used by 2xcomms. units until 1943, Bengal CommsFlt.
Based overseas in India, not operational in the UK.
Powered by one 50hp Persy II in-line.
Serial: MA926.
Span: 32ft 9in/9.98m   Length: 25ft 7in/7.8m   Ceiling: 13,100ft/3,930m   Range: 280
miles/451km   Speed: 155mph/250kmph.
Total 1 impressed; no losses.

Appendix 1: Aircrew

Throughout this book the number of crew for each type is given and this section gives a brief outline of how the aircrew categories have developed over the years.

Every aircraft must, of course, have a pilot (although this may not be the case in future!) so that a pilot can always be assumed to be part of the crew. The crew of early two-seaters were usually both pilots until it was realised that this was wasteful and from 1913 the RFC began to think about using full-time observers and began to recruit these from 1914 on; they were trained, on the job, in aerial reconnaissance, photography, artillery spotting and the use of the Lewis gun. In 1915 an observer badge was instituted and in 1916 formal training courses began. As night bombing developed from 1916 observers became responsible for bomb-aiming by 1917 and then navigation, for which specialist training started in 1918.

Two-seat fighters did not require the skills of the observer but did need a gunner and, from 1916, NCOs and other ranks were recruited for this task, with formal training being started from the end of 1916 and a badge was awarded from 1917. However, in 1918 all gunners were retitled observers (although not so highly trained as the observers proper).

The RNAS initially used pilots and groundcrew in their two-seaters but its first observers were recruited in 1915 and studied naval gunnery, signals, navigation and fleet tactics; a badge was awarded from 1917. Specialist training was undertaken at various establishments until observer schools were started in late 1917. The RNAS observers flew in two-seaters but the flying boats continued to fly with two pilots. Gunners in the RNAS were initially called aerial gunlayers, in best naval tradition.

With the establishment of the RAF some standardisation took place and in the RAF the pilots took over navigation, the observer role disappearing by the mid-1920s (although reinstated in 1934); gunners were groundcrew tradesmen who received flying pay when actually flying but still had to do their normal job and also sometimes acted as bomb-aimers. The Fleet Air Arm of the RAF, however, bowed to Admiralty pressure and observers flew in FAA two-seaters from 1921 onwards and, as most FAA spotter-reconnaissance types were three-seaters, they were joined by telegraphist/air gunners (T/AG) from 1923 for W/T and gunnery; all of these 'back-seaters' being RN personnel. As more sophisticated aircraft entered service with the RAF during the 1930s it became apparent that pilots could not do all the jobs of navigation, bomb-aiming, etc. as well as pilot, so in 1934 the air observer was re-introduced with responsibility for gunnery and bomb-aiming (pilots were still navigators); a flying badge was awarded in 1937 and observers took over navigation in 1939. Full-time air gunners were also appointed from 1939. Wireless-operators had been used by the RNAS and part of the job of the T/AG in the FAA was to operate the wireless. The role reappeared in the RAF during the late 1930s as wireless-operator/air gunner (WOP/AG).

At the beginning of the Second World War, therefore, light bombers were crewed by a pilot, an observer and WOP/AG, and medium-bombers by two pilots (usually), an observer, and three WOP/AGs. Coastal Command long-range types, because of their long endurance patrols, carried two pilots and two navigators, while the gunners were also trained fitters. As four-engined heavy bombers entered service it was decided, in 1941, that two pilots, who had taken many months to train and who would both be lost should the aircraft be shot down, were a luxury and thus one pilot became the norm. A new category of flight engineer was introduced to maintain the engines and fuel tanks; they were also classified as pilot assistants – able to fly the aircraft straight and level (if still controllable) should the pilot be killed or wounded, thus giving the crew a chance to bale out.

During 1942 observers changed their titles to navigators, more accurately reflecting their role, and the bomb-aiming part of their former job, in heavy bombers, became the responsibility of an air-bomber. Therefore the 'heavies' coming into service consisted of a crew of seven as standard (at least in those of British design) – pilot, air-bomber, flight engineer, navigator, WOP/AG and two 'straight' air-gunners. In American-designed bombers, two pilots and an extra gunner were required, making a total of ten. In light- and medium-sized bombers bomb-aiming was still carried out by the navigator. Air-bombers were not used after 1944, as navigators regained this responsibility; two were carried in heavy bomber crews. Two-seat light bombers, such as the Mosquito, carried the pilot and a navigator. In Coastal Command, flight engineers were added to the crew and the gunners also acted as radar operators.

Mid-war transport types normally had a crew of four, with two pilots, a navigator and engineer and, for supply dropping, carried a party from the RASC (not counted as crew in this book but an important part of the team) and, for para-dropping, an RAF dispatcher, often the WOP/AG. The FAA continued to use an observer in its two-seaters, plus a T/AG in three seaters.

In 1946 WOPs became air signallers but the general crew categories remained the same. The new jet bombers, not having defensive armament, led to the demise of the air gunner role. The V-bombers that entered service in the 1950s required specialist training because of their complex electronics (and, it was said, only officers and gentlemen could drop nuclear weapons!), so NCO air signallers were either promoted or solely employed in Coastal Command and transports. Air electronics officers became part of the V-bomber crews from 1956; co-pilots reappeared and a V-bomber crew consisted of a pilot, co-pilot, navigator (plotter), navigator (radar) and AEO. NCO signallers became air electronics operators in 1962 but the air-signaller role was reintroduced from 1979 for service in ECM and AEW types. The Canberras had a pilot and two navigators.

In Transport Command the new, more sophisticated types coming into service created a need for air stewards – this role had been previously fulfilled by the signaller – and was standardised by the creation of air quartermasters in 1962; this position was retitled as 'air loadmasters' from 1970, which more accurately reflected the new roles appearing in Hercules and transport helicopters.

With the advent of the Sentry AEW, which has a very large crew, two new flying badges appeared (perhaps unofficially), fighter controller and air technician and, ironically, together with the Sentinel's image analyser (see Vol. 1) may soon be the only specialist non-pilot brevets to be displayed – during 2006 flight engineers ceased to be trained and navigators, AEOs, loadmasters and signallers all became weapons systems officers or operators, though those aircrew holding the previous brevets will still wear them.

In effect navigators became weapons systems officers, who operate navigation, weapon and radar systems while weapons systems operators are NCOs who specialise as WSOp (Acoustics) on anti-submarine types, WSOp (crewman) – formerly air loadmasters – on transports, and as SAR winchmen (and gunners on helicopters), WSOp (electronic warfare) on AEW types, and WSOp (linguistic) on electronic surveillance.

The Fleet Air Arm continued with pilots and observers but TAGs were replaced with aircrewmen, who are recruited from within existing personnel and specialise as anti-submarine warfare or commando aircrewmen; they are also the SAR winchmen.

Finally, the army still supplies despatchers from the Royal Logistics Corps for supply dropping, while paratroop despatchers are RAF parachute jump instructors.

Appendix 2: Engines

ADC (UK)
Cirrus IIIa
4-cylinder, 90hp, Miles Hawk.
See also Cirrus.

Allison (USA)
250-C-20
420shp, Eurocopter Twin Squirrel.
T-56A turboprop
4,050shp, Lockheed Hercules C 1, C 3; 4,910shp, Lockheed Hercules C 1, C 3.
See also Rolls-Royce Allison.

Alvis (Coventry, Warwicks, UK)
Leonides
9-cylinder radial, 501–520hp, Percival Sea Prince C 1; 502–540hp, SA Pioneer CC I; 503/125–540hp,

Percival Sea Prince T 1, C 2; 503/127–560hp, Hunting Pembroke C 1; 504–540hp, SA Pioneer CC 1, Twin Pioneer CC 1; 521/50–500hp, Westland Dragonfly HR 1-HR 4; 523–540hp, Westland Dragonfly HR 5; 524–520hp, Bristol Sycamore HR 10 – HR 14; 531–640hp, SA Twin Pioneer CC 1, CC 2.

Leonides Major
14-cylinder radial, 755–780hp, Westland Whirlwind HAS 7, HCC 8.

Anzani (France)
80hp 6-cylinder radial, Depperdussin Monoplane.
100hp 10-cylinder radial, Caudron G IV, Curtiss H 4, Sopwith Pusher SP.

Argus (Germany)
AS 10e
8-cylinder in-line, 270hp, Messerschmidt Aldon, Rogosarski SIM-XIV.

Armstrong Siddeley (Coventry, Warwicks, UK)
Jaguar
14-cylinder radial, IV–385hp, Vickers Vimy DC.
Lynx
7-cylinder radial, IVc–225hp, Airspeed Courier, Avro Commodore, Avro 642/4m.
Mongoose
5-cylinder radial, III–155hp, Parnall Peto.
Cheetah
7-cylinder radial, IX–310hp, Airspeed Envoy, Avro Anson I, X; XV–420hp, Avro Anson XII, C19, T 20, T 21, T 22;   XIX–395hp, Avro Anson I, X, XI.
Panther
14-cylinder radial, IIa–605hp, Fairey Gordon, Seal.
Tiger
14-cylinder radial, IV–720hp, Blackburn Shark I; VI–760hp, Blackburn Shark II, III; VIII–860hp, A-W Whitley II; VIII (S)–920hp, A-W Whitley III; IX–810hp, A-W Whitley I.
Double-Mamba turboprop
100–2,950shp, Fairey Gannet AS 1, T 2; 101–3,035shp, Fairey Gannet AS 4, T 5; 112–3,875shp, Fairey Gannet AEW 3.
Sapphire turbojet
202–10,500lb st, HP Victor B 1; 207–11,050lb st, HP Victor B 1.

Austro-Daimler (Austria)
90hp 6-cylinder in-line, Sopwith Bat Boat I.
120hp 6-cylinder in-line, Sopwith 137.

AVCO-Lycoming (USA)
T-55 turboprop
L-II–3, 750shp, Boeing-Vertol Chinook HC 1.
ALF-502R turbofan
6,970 lb st, BAe 146 CC 1, CC 2.
See also Textron-Lycoming.

Beardmore (UK)
120hp 6-cylinder in-line, Wight & Thompson No.2, No.3, NT 2A.
160hp 6-cylinder in-line, Royal Aircraft Factory FE 2, Wight & Thompson NT 2B.

Bentley (UK)
BR 2
9-cylinder rotary, 200hp, Grain Griffin, Parnall Panther.

Berliet (France)
100hp in-line, Coastal Class airship, Coastal Star.

BHP (UK)
Galloway Adriatic
6-cylinder in-line, 230hp, Airco DH 9.
Galloway Atlantic
12-cylinder in-line, 500hp, HPV/1500.

Blackburne (UK)
Tomtit
3-cylinder radial, 26hp, DH Humming Bird.

BMW (Germany)
132n
12-cylinder in-line.
900hp, Heinkel He 115.

BMW Rolls-Royce (International)
BR710 turbofan
101–11,995lb st, BAe Nimrod MA 4.

Bristol (UK)
Lucifer
3-cylinder radial, IV–140hp, Parnall Peto.
Jupiter
9-cylinder radial, IV–430hp, Vickers Vimy DC; VI–520hp, Westland Wapiti I; VIII–440hp, B-P Sidestrand II, Westland Wapiti IA, IIA; VIIIf–460hp, B-P Sidestrand III, HP Hinaidi, Westland Wapiti II, IIA; IX–525hp, HP Clive II; XIf–550hp, Short Rangoon, Westland Wapiti VI; Xfa–480hp, Westland Wapiti IIa,V; XIf– 550hp, HP 42.
Pegasus
9-cylinder radial, Im-3–590hp, Blackburn Baffin, Vickers Victoria VI, Vildebeest I; IIL-2–625hp, Vickers Valentia; IIm-2–620hp, Supermarine Walrus I; IIm–3 620hp, Blackburn Baffin, B-P Overstrand, Vickers Vincent, Vickers Vildebeest II, III, Westland Wallace I; IIIm–3 620hp, Fairey Swordfish I, II, Saro London I; IV–700hp, Westland Wallace II; VI–690hp, Supermarine Walrus I, II; X–980hp, HP Harrow I, Saro London II, Supermarine Stranraer II; Xc–835hp, Short S23m; XVIII–815hp, Short Sunderland II, III, Vickers Wellington I, VIII, XV, XVI; XX–835hp, HP Harrow II, Vickers Wellesley; XXII–835hp, Bristol Bombay, HP Hampden I, Short S30m, Short Sunderland I, III; XXX–775hp, Swordfish II, III, IV.
Mercury
9-cylinder radial, VIII–825hp, Blenheim I; XV–825hp, Blenheim IV; XXV–825hp, Blenheim V. XXX–810hp, Bristol Blenheim V, Supermarine Sea Otter.
Perseus
9-cylinder radial, VIII–745hp, Vildebeest IV; X–750hp, Botha I; XA–860hp, Botha I; XIIc–815hp, Flamingo; XVI–745hp, Hertfordshire.
Taurus
14-cylinder radial, II–1,060hp, Beaufort I, Albacore; VI–1,060hp, Beaufort I; XII–985hp, Beaufort I, Albacore; XVI–985hp–Beaufort I.
Hercules
14-cylinder radial, I–1,375hp, Lerwick I; II–1,375hp, Lerwick I, Stirling I; III–1,400hp, Stirling I; IV–1,380hp, Lerwick I; XI–1,590hp, Albemarle, Stirling I, Wellington III; XIV–1,500hp, Short G-Class; XVI–1,615hp, Lancaster II, Halifax III, VII, A9, Wellington X, XI, XII, XIII, TXVII, Stirling III, IV; XVII–1,725hp, Wellington X, XIV, TXVIII; XIX–1,800hp, Seaford GR 1; 100–1,675hp, Halifax VI, C8; 101–1,615hp, Hastings C 1; 106–1,675hp, Hastings C 1A, C 2, T 5; 216–1,675hp, Hastings C1a, C2; 634–

1,690hp, Viking C 1A, C 2; 230–1,925hp, Valetta; 264–1,950hp, Varsity T 1; 736–1,675hp, Hastings C 4.
Centaurus
18-cylinder radial, IV–2,300hp, Warwick II; VII–2,400hp, Buckingham, Warwick V; 57–2,470hp,
Brigand; 173–2,625hp, Beverley; 175–2,625hp, Beverley.
Proteus turboprop
255–4,445shp, Britannia.

Bristol-Siddeley (UK)
Olympus turbojet
100–9,750lb st, Vulcan B1; 101–11,000lb st, Vulcan B 1; 104–12,000lb st, Vulcan B 1; 200–16,000 st,
Vulcan B2; 201–17,000lb st, Vulcan B 2; 301–20,000lb st, Vulcan B 2.
Viper turbojet
203–2,500lb st, Shackleton MR 3; 300–3,120lb st, Dominie T 1; 301–3,000lb st, HS 125 CC 1; 520–
3,310lb st, Dominie T 1; 601–3,750lb st, HS 125 CC 2.
Gnome turboprop
H 1000–1,050shp, Whirlwind HAR 9, 10, HCC 12; H 1200–1,350shp, Wessex HC 2, HCC 4, HU 5.
See also Rolls-Royce.

Canton-Unne (France)
80 hp radial–Eta, 110 hp radial, Breguet Biplane, MF SP, 120 hp radial, Voisin LA.
B 9
9-cylinder radial, 140 hp, HF 27, Voisin LAS.
R 9
9-cylinder radial, 160 hp, HF 27.
2m7
14-cylinder radial, 200 hp, De Chasse, Short Type 136, Short 166, Sopwith 137.

Chenu (France)
In-line 80 hp, Breguet biplane.
In-line 210 hp, Astra-Torres.

Cirrus (UK)
Cirrus
4-cylinder radial, IIIA–90hp, Miles Hawk; Cirrus Minor I–82hp, Swallow II.
Hermes
4-cylinder in-line, II–110hp, Desoutter I; III–115hp, Koolhoven FK 43.

CFM (International)
56 turbofan
2a-3–24,000lb st, Sentry AEW 1.

Clerget (France)
9
9-cylinder rotary, 9Z–110hp, Hamble Baby, 1½ Strutter; 9B–130hp, Hamble Baby, Convert, 1 ½ Strutter;
9BF–140hp, Ship's Strutter,

Continental (USA)
A-50
4-cylinder in-line, 50hp, Chief.
A-65/0-173
4-cylinder in-line, 65hp, Cub, Cub Coupe, Plus C, Plus D.
A-75-8
4-cylinder in-line, 75hp, Cruiser.

A-80-9
4-cylinder in-line, 75hp, Stinson 105.
0-470
6-cylinder in-line, 213hp, Bird Dog.

Curtiss (USA)
OX-5 8-cylinder in-line, 90hp, Curtiss H-1.
OXX 12-cylinder in-line, 100hp, Curtiss H-1, H-4.
VX 12-cylinder in-line, 160hp, R-2.
D-12 12-cylinder in-line, 480hp, Fox I.

De Havilland (UK)
Gipsy
4-cylinder in-line, II–108hp, Ferry; III–110hp, Ferry, Desoutter II; 12–425hp, Albatross.
Gipsy Minor
4-cylinder in-line, I 90hp, Moth Minor.
Gipsy Six
6-cylinder in-line, I–200hp, DH 89, Nighthawk, Mentor, Falcon Six, Hendy Heck, Gull Six; II–205hp, Rapide, Dominie, DH 86, Pheonix, Vega Gull, Petrel.
Gipsy Major
4-cylinder in-line, I–130hp, Eagle II, Puss Moth, Dragonfly, Fox Moth, Hornet Moth, Leopard Moth, Dragon, Moth Major, Warferry, Monospar ST 12, Falcon Major, Hawk Major, Monarch, Whitney Straight, Messenger, Spartan Cruiser.
Gipsy Queen
6-cylinder in-line, II–210hp, Proctor; 30–240hp–Heron, Sea Heron; 70–340hp, Devon C 1, Sea Devon; 71–330hp, Marathon. 175–400hp, Devon C 2.
Gipsy King
6-cylinder in-line, I–425hp, Don.

Europrop (International)
TP400-D6 turboprop
11,000shp, A400M.
Fiat (Italy)
6-cylinder in-line, 240hp, Coastal Star Class, North Sea Class.
A 12
6-cylinder in-line, 60hp, DH 4, DH 9.

Garrett-Airesearch (USA)
TFE 731 turbofan
3,700shp, HS 125 CC1, 2; 5r–4,300shp, H-S 125 CC3.
TPE 331 turboprop
940shp, Jetstream T3.

Gnome (France)
7 Gamma
7-cylinder rotary, 70hp, Deperdussin.
7Z Lambda
7-cylinder rotary, 80hp, Avro 504, Borel, TB 8, Donnet-Leveque, Farman F22, Short S41, Short S60, Sopwith Tractor Biplane.
Monosoupape 9B-2
9-cylinder rotary, 100hp, Deperdussin, Sopwith 2-Seater, Sop 880, Sop 807.
14 Omega-Omega
14-cylinder rotary, 100hp, Short Improved S 41, Short Type 74.

14
14-cylinder rotary, 120hp, Farman F22.
14 Lambda–Lambda
14-cylinder rotary, 160hp, Short S 54, Short S 64, Short S 73, Nile, Short Gun-Carrying Pusher Seaplane, Wight 1914 Navyplane.

Gnome-Rhone (France)
14m3
14-cylinder radial, 670hp, Potez 63-11.

Green (UK)
E6
6-cylinder in-line, 120hp, SS & SSPClass, Coastal Class, Batboat IA, Sopwith Tractor Biplane Seaplane.
12-cylinder in-line, 275hp, Porte Baby.

Hispano-Suiza (Spain)
8
8-cylinder in-line, 8Aa–150hp, AAD FB, NT 2A, 2B, 4; 8Ba–200hp, Sopwith B 1; 8Bb–200hp, AAD-FB, NT 4A.
12
12-cylinder in-line, 720hp, Loire 130; 12Y-31–860hp, M-S 406; 12YBRS–860hp, Dornier 22.

Isotta-Fraschini (Italy)
6-cylinder in-line, 160hp, FBA H.

Itala (Italy)
180hp in-line, SR-1.

Le Rhone (France)
9
9-cylinder rotary, 9C–80hp, Bristol TB 8, Caudron G-IV; JA–110hp, REP.

LHTEC (International)
CTS800-4N turboprop
1,316shp, Agusta-Westland Lynx Wildcat.

LIBERTY (USA)
12A
12-cylinder in-line, 400hp, DH 9A, Amiens, Caproni 42.

Lorraine-Dietrich (France)
2eb
6-cylinder in-line, 450hp, Potez 29.

Lycoming (USA)
O-145
4-cylinder in-line B2, 65hp, Taylorcraft BL2.
O-435
6-cylinder in-line, 185hp, Sentinel.
R680
9-cylinder radial, 290hp, Reliant; 295hp, Vigilant.

Maybach (Germany)

180hp in-line, Parseval, 240hp in-line, HMA 9r, R 23.
See also Wolseley.

Menasco (USA)

Buccaneer
6-cylinder in-line, 200hp, Mohawk.

Mercedes (Germany)

D-1
12-cylinder in-line, 100hp, Albatros B II, Mars Arrow, DFW B II.

Napier (UK)

Lion
12-cylinder in-line; II–500hp, Bison I, Fawn II, V-1500, Vernon II, III, Virginia II-IV, Victoria I, II, III;
IIB–480hp, Dart, Blackburn I, Fairey IIID, Hyderabad, Victoria IV, Walrus; V–470hp, Bison II, Dart,
Blackburn II, Hyderabad, Seagull III, Southampton I, Virginia IV-IX; VA–500hp, Fairey IIID, IIIF, Fawn I,
II, Southampton II; VI–525hp, Fawn III; X–460hp, Ripon IIA; XI–540hp, Ripon II, Fairey IIIF, Virginia
X; XIA–530hp, Ripon IIA, IIC, Fairey IIIF, Victoria V.

Rapier
16-cylinder in-line, VI–365hp, Seafox.

Dagger
24-cylinder in-line, VIII–955hp, Hereford.

Gazelle turboprop
NGA 2–1,650shp, Belvedere; 161–1,450shp, Wessex HAS 1; 165–1,600shp, Wessex HAS 3.

Persy (Czechoslovakia)

II
4-cylinder in-line, 50hp, Zlin Z 12.

Piaggio (Italy)

Stella PXI-rc-40
14-cylinder radial, 1,000hp, SM-79K.

Pobjoy (UK)

R
7-cylinder radial, 85hp, Monospar ST 4, ST 6.

Niagara
7-cylinder radial, I–84hp, Monospar ST 10, Scion I; II–85hp, Scion I, II; III–85hp, Monospar ST 25,
Scion Senior; IV–98hp, ST 25.

Pratt & Whitney (Canada)

PT6T Twin-PAC turboprop
3B–1,800shp, Griffin HAR 2.

PTC6C turboprop
1,530shp, Agusta-W 139.

Pratt & Whitney (USA)

Hornet
9-cylinder radial, 800hp, Fairchild 91, R1690, 750hp, Lodestar IA.

Wasp
9-cylinder radial, 420hp, Ford Trimotor; T 181–525hp, Fokker XXII; R1340-40–600hp, Whirlwind
HAR 21, HAR 1, 2, HC 4.

Wasp Junior R985
9-cylinder radial, 450hp, Traveller, Navigator, Expeditor, Goose, Model 12A, Electra, Spartan Executive, Kingfisher.

Twin Wasp Junior R1535
14-cylinder radial, 750hp, Chesapeake.

Twin Wasp R1830
14-cylinder radial, 1,050hp, Catalina I-III, Boston I, Hudson IV, Wellington IV; 1,200hp, Beaufort II, Catalina IB, IV, VI, Liberator I, II, III, V, VI, VII, VIII, Coronado, DC 3, Dakota I-IV, Hudson V, VI, Model 18, Maryland, Sunderland V; 1,300hp, Liberator V, C IX, R2000–1,380hp, Skymaster.

Double Wasp R2800
18-cylinder radial, 1,850hp, Ventura I, Marauder I, Warwick I, III, VI; 2000hp, Ventura II, V, Marauder IA-III.

F 117 turbofan
41,700lb st, Globemaster III C 1.

Ranger (USA)

L440
6-cylinder in-line, 5–200hp, Widgeon; 7–200hp, Argus III.

V 770
12-cylinder in-line, 8–520hp, Seamew.

Renault (France)

WB/WC
8-cylinder in-line, 70hp, SS class, HRE 2.
12-cylinder, 110hp, F37; 160hp in-line, F40.

12Fe
12-cylinder in-line, 220hp, Coastal Class, Coastal ★ Class, De Chasse, Concours, Short 184, Improved 184; 240hp, Improved 184.

4PEI
4-cylinder in-line, 140hp, Stampe SV-4.

Bengali
6-cylinder in-line, 6q–220hp, Goeland, Simoun.

Rolls-Royce (UK)

Hawk
6-cylinder in-line, I–75hp, SS Class, SSP Class, SSZ Class, SST Class.

Eagle
12-cylinder in-line, I–225hp, North Sea Class, H 12, 0/100, Porte Baby; II–250hp, R 23, R 24, R 27, Concours, Short Bomber; III–250hp, DH 4, R 31; IV–284hp, DH 4, Campania, Fairey IIID, Felixstowe F2A, 0/400, R 27; VI–275hp, DH 4, Campania, Wight CV SP; VII–275hp, DH 4, Porte Baby, Wight Cv SP; VIII–350hp, North Sea Class, DH 4A, H-12b, H-16, R 27, 0/400, Porte Baby, Campania, Fairey IIIC, F 2A, F 3, F 5, V/1500, Porte Baby, Fairey IIID, FE 2D, Vimy, Vimy Ambulance, Vernon I; IX–360hp, Fairey IIID.

Falcon
12-cylinder in-line, II–250hp, Kangaroo.

Condor
12-cylinder in-line; III–670hp, Andover, Aldershot, Horsley I; IIIB–650hp, Iris III, Horsley II, III.

Buzzard
12-cylinder in-line; IIMS–825hp, Iris V, Perth.

Kestrel
12-cylinder in-line; IB–480hp, Hart, Hardy; IIA–490hp, Fox IA; IIIMS–535hp, Scapa; IIIS–480hp, Heyford I; V–695hp, Hart (I), Hind; VI–695hp, Hendon, Heyford II, III; VIII–700hp, Singapore III; IX–700hp, Singapore III; X–545hp, Hart, Hardy; X (D)–520hp, Hart (S).

Merlin
12-cylinder in-line; I–1,030hp, Battle; II–1,030hp, Battle; III–1,030hp, Battle; IV–1,030hp, Whitley IV; X–1,145hp, Whitley IVA,V,VII, Halifax I,Wellington II; 20–1,390hp, Lancaster, Halifax I, II; 21–1,390hp, Mosquito IV; 22–1,390hp, Lancaster I, Halifax II,V; 23–1,390hp, Mosquito IV; 24–1,610hp, Lancaster I, 7,York, Lancastrian II; 26–1,610hp, Hurricane IV; 30–1,300hp, Barracuda I; 32–1,620hp, Barracuda II, III; 60–1,280hp, Wellington VI; 68–1,315hp, Lincoln B 2; 72–1,280hp,-Mosquito IX; 76–1,280hp, Mosquito IX, XVI; 77–1,280hp, Mosquito IX, XVI; 85–1,635hp, Lancaster VI, Lincoln B 1, B 2; 113–1,535hp, Mosquito 35; 114–1,535hp, Mosquito 35.

Vulture
24-cylinder in-line; II–1,760hp, Manchester I.

Griffon
12-cylinder in-line; 37–2,020hp, Barracuda BR 5; 57–2,500hp, Shackleton MR 1; 57A–2,500hp, Shackleton MR 1, 1A, MR 2,T 4; 58–2,500hp, Shackleton MR 2C, MR 3; 59–2,500hp, Firefly T 7; 74–2,245hp, Firefly AS5,AS 6.

Dart turboprop
101–2,680shp, Argosy; 201–3,245shp, Andover C I, E 3; 531–2,105shp, Andover CC 2.

Tyne turboprop
RTY-12-10–5,730shp, Belfast C 1.

Nimbus turboprop (originally Bristol–Siddeley)
103–968shp, Wasp.

Gnome turboprop (originally Bristol–Siddeley)
H 1400–1,500shp, Sea King HAS 1 – ASaC 7.

Gem turboprop
2–900shp, Lynx HAS 2; 41-2–1,135shp, Lynx HAS 3; 42–1,135shp, Lynx HAS 8.

AVON turbojet
101–6,500lb st, Canberra 2, 11, 17, 19; 109–7,500lb st, Canberra B 6, 8, 15,16,T 17; 117 -7,530lb st, Comet C 2; 118–7,530lb st, Comet C 2; 204 – 9,500lb st, Valiant B 1; 205–10,000lb st, Valiant B 1; RA 29–10,500lb st, Comet C 4.

Conway turbojet
201–20,000lb st,Victor B 2, K 2; 210–20,000lb st, Victor B 2R; 301–22,500lb st. VC 10.

Spey turbojet
250–12,160lb st, Nimrod MR 1, 2.

RB-211 turbofan
524–50,000lb st, Tristar.

Trent turbofan
71,000lb st,A330-200.

Rolls-Royce Allison (UK)
AE 2100 turboprop
D3–4,591shp, Hercules C 4, 5.

Rolls-Royce Continental (USA)
G 10 in-line; 470–310hp, Basset.

Rolls-Royce Packard (USA)
Merlin
12-cylinder in-line; 28–1,390hp, Lancaster III, X; 31–1,390hp, Mosquito 20; 33–1,390hp, Mosquito 20; 38–1,480hp, Lancaster III, X; 224–1,610hp, Lancaster III; 225–1,610hp, Mosquito 25.

Rolls-Royce Turbomeca (International)
RTM 322 turboprop
01–2,312shp, Merlin HM 1; D4/8–1,863shp, Merlin HC 3.

Royal Aircraft Factory (UK)

3A
12-cylinder in-line; 200hp, DH 4.

Salmson (France)

B 9
9-cylinder radial; 140hp, Short Type 135, Short Type 830; 9nD–175hp, Bloch 81.
2M7
9-cylinder radial; 200hp, Breguet de Chasse, Short Type 166, Sopwith Hydro BSP, Improved Navyplane.
See also Canton-Unne.

Siddeley-Deasy (UK)

Puma
6-cylinder in-line; 230hp, DH 4, 9.

Sunbeam (UK)

In-line–100hp, SST Class.
Amazon
6-cylinder in-line; 160hp, Coastal Class.
Nubian
8-cylinder in-line; 150hp, Avro 510, Curtiss R 2, Short Type 827, Sopwith 806.
Mohawk
12-cylinder in-line; 200hp, De Chasse, Concours, De Bombe, Mann-Egerton B 2, Short Type 184, Improved 184, Batboat II, Sopwith 860, Wight 840.
Arab
8-cylinder in-line; I–200hp, Curtiss R 2, Cuckoo I, NT-2B; II–200hp, Grain Griffin.
Cossack
12-cylinder; 320hp, HP 0/100, Porte Baby, Short Type 320.
Maori
12-cylinder in-line; II–250hp, Improved 184, Wight Converted SP; III–260hp, HP 0/400, Campania, Fairey IIIA-B, 184, Improved 184; IV–260hp, R 33.

Textron-Lycoming (USA)

T 55 turboprop
L 712–4,500shp, Chinook HC 2, HC3.
See also Avco-Lycoming.

Turbomeca (France)

Turmo turboprop
III–1,320shp, Puma HC 1; IIIC–1,435shp, Puma HC 1.
Arriel turboprop
1C1–724shp, Dauphin.
Arrius turboprop
2K1–900shp, Agusta 109E.
Astazou turboprop
XVId–913shp, Jetstream T2.
Makila turboprop
1A2–2,104shp, Puma HC 2.

Walter (Czechoslovakia)

Mikron
4-cylinder in-line; II–62hp, Tipsy B 2, Trainer.

Warner (USA)
Scarab
7-cylinder radial; 145hp, Airmaster, Fairchild 24.
Super Scarab R 500
7-cylinder radial; 165hp, Argus I, II, Harlow PC5A, Pitcairn PA39.

White & Popple (UK)
In-line 105hp, Delta.

Wolesley (UK)
Viper
8-cylinder in-line; 200hp, Cuckoo II.
Adder
8-cylinder in-line; 200hp, Sopwith B1-Maybach diesel; 180hp, Parseval, HMA 9r, 230hp, R 80.

Wright (USA)
Whirlwind R 975
9-cylinder radial; 165hp, Stinson Junior; 300hp, Pacemaker; 450hp, Fokker T 8W.
Cyclone R1820
9-cylinder radial; 820hp, Super Electra; 875hp, DC-2, Cleveland; 1,000hp, Fortress I; 1,100hp, Hudson I, II, N3P-B; 1,200 hp, Fortress IIA, Dauntless, Hudson III, Lodestar II; 1,380hp, Fortress II, III; R 1300.
700hp, Whirlwind HAR 22, HAR 3, HC 4.
Double-Row Cyclone R 2600
14-cylinder radial; 1,600hp, Boston III, IIIA, IV, Baltimore I, II; 1,650hp, Helldiver, Baltimore III, IV; 1,700hp, Boston V, Baltimore V, Mariner, Mitchell; 1,750hp, Avenger I, II; 1,850hp, Avenger III-AS 6.
Turbo-Cyclone R 3350
18-cylinder radial; 2,200hp, Washington; 2,700hp, Skyraider; 3,250hp, Neptune.

Appendix 3: Weapons

Guns: First World War–1930s
The first aircraft of the First World War carried no fixed armament (pilots equipping themselves with rifles) but in 1915, Lewis drum-fed machine guns, using 0.303in ammunition, were mounted on two-seaters in whichever cockpit was not occupied by the pilot. As a propeller-interrupter gear had not been developed at this stage, forward-firing Lewis guns were mounted on the upper-wing centre section, meaning that the pilot had to be very acrobatic when changing a drum; this was simplified later in the war when a Foster Mounting allowed the gun to be pulled down towards the cockpit, as on the SE 5A. Some Lewises were mounted on the fuselage side, angled to fire outside the arc. The lack of a propeller-interrupter gear in the RFC gave rise to the several 'pusher' designs these giving the gunner in the front cockpit an excellent field of fire, still using the Lewis.

When a satisfactory interrupter gear was developed the standard fixed forward-firing machine gun became the Vickers belt-fed, still of 0.303in calibre, mounted on or in the fuselage, and firing through the propeller on tractor designs. Meanwhile, the Lewis was used in the main for rear defence from 1917 onwards, usually mounted on a Scarff ring in the rear cockpit of two-seaters and in other defensive positions on multi-crewed bombers and flying-boats.

This armament remained standard in the RAF and FAA into the late 1930s although the Fairey High-Speed mounting supplemented the Scarff ring.

Guns: Second World War

From the late 1930s onwards the Browning 0.303in-calibre belt-fed machine gun replaced the Vickers as the fixed forward-firing gun, normally wing-mounted, while the Vickers K gas-operated drum-fed mg replaced the venerable Lewis on the new designs. However, with the advent of faster aircraft it had been found that the gunner could not fight the slipstream so powered turrets, mainly supplied by Armstrong-Whitworth, Boulton-Paul, Bristol and Fraser-Nash, were fitted to the new bombers and, after a spell with the Vickers K, Browning belt-fed guns became the standard turret armament, although the Vickers K survived for defensive use in non-turret aircraft.

Guns: 1940s–Present

Gun turrets now had 0.5in Brownings rather than the puny 0.303in, and some carried the 20mm cannon, but turrets and air-gunners had been phased out from the RAF by 1960, as had all rearwards defensive armament. However, defensive guns have made something of a comeback in RAF and FAA helicopters today, most of which can carry, when required, the army's standard belt-fed 7.62mm General Purpose MG in the cabin door. The Chinook can also mount an automatic M134 7.62mm minigun in this position.

Bombs: First World War, 1920s and 1930s

Weights were 20lb/9kg, 50lb/23kg, 65lb/31kg, 112lb/50kg, 230lb/105kg, 250lb/113kg, 336lb/152kg, 520lb/236kg, 550lb/250kg and 1,650lb/743kg.

Bombs: 1930s, Second World War and after

General purpose (GP): 40lb/18kg, 250lb/113kg, 500lb/227kg, 1,000lb/454kg, 1,900lb/855kg, 4,000lb/1,816kg.
Armour piercing (AP): 1,600lb/720kg, 2,000lb/908kg.
Semi-armour piercing (SAP): 250lb/113kg, 500lb/227kg.
Anti-submarine (AS): 100lb/45kg, 250lb/113kg, 500lb/227kg, 600lb/270kg.
Incendiary: 4lb/2kg, 30lb/14kg, 30lb/14kg J, 250lb/113kg, 500lb/227kg.
Medium capacity (MC): 250lb/113kg, 500lb/227kg, 1,000lb/454kg, 4,000lb/1,816kg, 12,000lb/5,448kg Tallboy, 22,000lb/9,988kg Grand Slam.
High capacity (HC): 2,000lb/908kg Cookie, 4,000lb/1,816kg, 8,000lb/3,600kg Super Cookie, 12,000lb/5,448kg.
Specialised: 500lb/227kg JW Johnny Walker, 1,000lb/454kg spherical, 1,280lb/577kg Highball, 9,150lb/4,154kg Upkeep (Dams raid).

Bombs: Post-Second World War–Present

GP, 500lb (length: 6ft 6in/1.48m, diameter: 13in/0.32m).
GP, 1,000lb (length: 7ft 4in/1.21m, span: 1ft 5in/1.33m).

Bombs, Nuclear: 1950s–1990s

Violet Club 9,000lb/4,086kg 0.5mt, carried by Vulcan B 1.
Blue Danube 10,250lb/4,613kg, 20kt carried by Valiant B1, Vulcan B 1 & Victor B 1.
Yellow Sun Mk 1 7,250lb/3,291kg, 400kt, carried by Vulcan B 1 & Victor B 1.
Yellow Sun Mk 2 7,250lb/3,291kg 1mt, carried by Vulcan B 1 & B2, Victor B 1 & B 2.
WE 177A 600lb/270kg 200kt, carried by Buccaneer S2A & S2B, Jaguar GR 1.
WE 177B 950lb/428kg 500kt, carried by Vulcan B 2, Tornado GR 1.
Red Beard 1,750lb/794kg 15-25kt, carried by Canberra B 6, B 15 & 16, Vulcan B 2, Victor B 1.
US Mk 5 6,000lb/2,724kg carried by Vulcan B 1.
US Mk 7 carried by Canberra B (I) 6 and B (I) 8.
US Mk 15/39 6,600–7,500lb/2,997–3,405kg, carried by Valiant B 1
US Mk 43 2,100lb/953kg, carried by Canberra B (I) 6, B (I) 8 and Valiant.

Torpedos: First World War–1950s

Fist World War: 80lb/36kg (14in/0.36m diameter).

First and Second World Wars: 1,440–1,800lb/648–810kg (18in/0.45m diameter).

Second World War and after: Mk 24 680lb/306kg. Mk 24 Homing (Nicknamed Fido, Wandering Willie).

Mines: Second World War

1,000lb/454kg.

1,500lb/681kg.

Depth Charges: Second World War

Mk VIII 250lb/113kg.

Mk VII 450lb/203kg.

Rocket Projectiles: Second World War and after

25lb/11kg (3in/7.62mm diameter).

60lb/28kg.

Air to Air Missiles: 1950s–Present

Raytheon/Loral Sidewinder AIM-9 (length – 9ft 5in/2.87m, span – 2ft 1in/0.91m, speed Mach 2+, range – 10+ miles/16km), carried by Nimrod MR2.

Air to Ground Missiles: 1950s–Present

Nord AS 11 (length: 3ft 9in/1.14m, span: 1ft 6in/0.45m, speed: 360mph/579kmph, range 2 miles/3km), carried by Whirlwind HC 10, Wessex HC2 and HU5.

Nord AS 12 (length: 6ft 4in/1.93m, span: 2ft 1in/0.64m, speed: 230mph/370kmph, range: 3 miles/5km), carried by Wessex HC 2 and HU 5, Nimrod MR 1, Lynx HAS 2.

Nord AS 30 (length: 12ft 7in/3.84m, range: 7.5 miles/11km), carried by Canberra B (I) & B 16.

Boeing/M-D Harpoon AGM-84 (length: 12ft 7in/3.84m, span: 3ft/0.91m, speed: Mach 0.85, range: 75 miles/120km), carried by Nimrod MR2 and 4, Merlin HMA 1.

MBDA Martel (length: 13ft 5in/3.96m; 12ft 7in/3.66m TV variant, span: 3ft 9in/1.14m, speed: Mach 1, range: 37 miles/60km), carried by Nimrod MR 1.

Air to Surface Missiles: 1950s–Present

AS 11 and AS 12 (see above).

Martel (see above).

BAe Sea Eagle (length: 13ft 6in/3.96m, span: 3ft 9in/1.14m, speed: Mach 0.85, range: 68 miles/109km), carried by Nimrod MR 2.

Harpoon (see above).

BAe Sea Skua (length: 8ft 2in/2.52m, span: 2ft 3in/0.69m, speed: M0.8, range: 9+ miles/14km), carried by Lynx HAS 2, 3.

Anti-Radar Missiles: 1950s–Present

Raytheon Shrike AGM-45 (length: 10ft/3.04m, span: 3ft/0.91m speed: Mach 2+, range: 25 miles/40km), carried by Vulcan B2.

Torpedos: 1950s–Present

Raytheon Mk 46 (length: 8ft 6in/2.59m, diameter: 12ft 6in/3.81m, speed: 55mph/89kmph, range: 7 miles/11km), carried by Whirlwind HAS 7, Wessex HAS 1, HAS 3, Wasp HAS 1, Sea King HAS 1, 2, 5, 6, Lynx HAS 2.

BAe Stingray (length: 8ft 5in/2.6m, diameter: 1ft 3in/0.34m, speed: 47mph/45kmph, range: 40+ miles/11km), carried by Sea King HAS, Lynx HAS 2, 3, Nimrod MR 1, 2 & MRA 4, Merlin HMA1.

Mines: 1950s–Present
BAe Stonefish 2,183lb/990kg (length: 8ft 2in, diameter: 1ft 7in) carried by Nimrod MR, Hercules C.

Depth charges: 950s–Present
BAe Mk II (length: 4ft 7in, diameter: 11in) carried by Sea King HAS, Nimrod MR.

Rocket Projectiles (Unguided) 1950s–Present
TDA SNEB pod 68mmx 18 (length: 2ft 7in, diameter 2ft 8in) carried by Canberra B (I) 6 & B 15.

Appendix 4: Roles and Types of Aircraft

Bombers, general purpose, torpedo-bombers
Bombs were first dropped from aircraft in anger by the Italians against the Turks in North Africa in 1911 but the RFC, when formed a year later, did not see bombing as one of its roles. The RNAS, however, following the RN's doctrine of taking the war to the enemy, did pursue it and carried out the first strategic bombing raid in history when three Avro 504s severely damaged the Zeppelin sheds at Friedrichshafen in November 1914. This policy of strategic bombing was continued until the formation of the RAF on 1 April 1918 by which time the RFC too was using bombers, mainly on tactical targets close behind the German lines. The RNAS had issued a specification for a large twin-engined 'bloody paralyser of a bomber' and this, the Handley-Page 0/100, entered service in 1917 and was taken over by the RAF at the merger of the two Services; Trenchard capitalised on this by forming the Independent Force, RAF, whose role was solely bombing using single-engined day-bombers and twin-engined night bombers.

Thus developed the concept of a strategic heavy bomber force which was kept alive between the wars but not used operationally, whereas the general-purpose types, developed during the 1920s to exercise 'air control' in the Middle East and north-west India, saw constant action against dissident tribesmen.

At the outbreak of the Second World War only one of the RAF's three heavy bombers was a night-bomber, the Whitley, whilst the Hampden and Wellington flew by day. Early Second World War daylight raids soon dispelled the myth that 'the bomber would always get through' and thereafter the RAF switched to night bombing for the remainder of the war, with grave affects on bombing accuracy until 1943; from 1940 its first four-engined bomber, the Stirling, joined the offensive. Light and medium bombers continued to fly in daylight, attacking tactical targets, particularly in France, the Low Countries, North Africa and Italy. In the Far East Wellingtons and Blenheims were the main types until the Liberator came into service, but this theatre also saw the RAF's only use of a dive-bomber, the Vengeance. From 1943 onwards the RAF's new heavies, the Lancaster and Halifax, together with new navigational aids and a single-minded AOC, began to cause severe damage to German cities and industry, albeit suffering heavy casualties in return.

The RAF still saw strategic bombing as a vital role of the post-war RAF but it was not until 1951 that Bomber Command received its first jet, the excellent Canberra and, four years later, the first of the V-bombers, our nuclear deterrent. The Canberra replaced the Mosquito as the service's light bomber, the medium bomber having disappeared at the end of the Second World War, and the V-bombers replaced Lincolns and Washingtons as heavy bombers, providing a very powerful force until the nuclear deterrent role was passed to the Royal Navy's Polaris submarines in 1971. Canberras served in the UK, Germany and the Middle and Far East, where they did see action, but during the 1970s strike and ground-attack types (see Vol. 1) took over the light bomber role and it disappeared. Heavy bombers, in the shape of the Vulcan, carried on in a tactical nuclear and conventional bombing role until 1982 when it was used operationally, for the first and only time, during the Falklands war. Following this the Vulcan was retired and the bomber as such disappeared from the RAF's inventory.

Just as the RNAS pioneered conventional bombing in the First World War so it developed air-dropped torpedoes and the aeroplanes to do this and torpedo attacks were made during the war. Torpedoes could cause much more damage to a ship than bombs and were easier to aim and the role was adopted by the

RAF when the RNAS and RFC merged but, with the creation of the Fleet Air Arm, carrier-borne aircraft took on the torpedo bomber role in addition to the RAF's landplane equivalents. As other anti-shipping weapons, such as rocket projectiles, were introduced during the Second World War the torpedo bomber gradually disappeared although after the war homing torpedoes became an important weapon against submarines, now carried by FAA helicopters and the RAF's Nimrods.

1910–14

Breguet Biplane 1912–14, Avro 504 1914–14, Bristol TB 8 1914–, Sopwith Two-Seater 1914–14.

1914–19

Avro 504 to 1915, Bristol TB 8 to 1916, Breguet II/V 1915–16, Henri Farman 27 1915–18, Voisin LA 1915–17, Caudron G-IV 1916–17, Henri Farman 40/56 1916–17, REP Parasol 1915–16, Sopwith 860 (TB) 1915–17, Short Bomber 1916–17, Sopwith 9700 Strutter 1916–17, Airco DH 4 1917–20, HP 0/100 1917–18, RAF FE 2B 1917–19, Sopwith B 1 1917–19, Airco DH 9 1918–20, Airco DH 9A 1918–, Airco Amiens 1918–, Caproni CA 42 1918–18, Fairey IIIA 1918–19, Grain Griffin 1918–20, HP 0/400 1918–, HP V1500 1918–20, Sopwith Cuckoo (TB) 1918–, Vickers Vimy 1919–.

1920–29

DH 4 to 1920, Airco DH 9 to 1920, Airco DH 9A, Airco Amiens to 1923, Griffin to 1920, HP 0/400 to 1921, HP V1500 to 1920, Cuckoo (TB) to 1923, Vimy to 1928, Blackburn Dart (TB) 1922–, Avro Aldershot III 1924–25, Fairey Fawn 1924–29, Vickers Virginia II 1924–27, Virginia III 1924–26, Virginia III 1924–27, HP Hyderabad 1925–, Vickers Virginia IV 1925–26, Virginia VI 1925–27, Fairey Fox 1926–, Hawker Horsley I 1926–30, Vickers Virginia VII 1926–, Fairey IIIF Mk IV 1927–, Virginia IX 1927–, Boulton-Paul Sidestrand 1928–, Fairey IIIF Mk I 1928–, Vickers Virginia X 1928–, Westland Wapiti (GP) 1928–, Ripon (TB) 1929–, HP Hinaidi 1929–, Hawker Horsley II (TB) 1929–.

1930–39

Airco DH 9A to 1930, Dart (TB) to 1934, Hyderabad to 1934, Fox to 1931, Sidestrand to 1936, Wapiti (GP), Ripon (TB) to 1935, Hinaidi to 1934, Horsley I to 1930, Horsley II (TB) to 1934, Virginia VII to 1933, Fairey IIIF Mk IV to 1937, Virginia IX to 1934, Fairey IIIF Mk I to 1937, Virginia X to 1938, Hawker Horsley III (TB) 1930–35, Fairey Gordon (GP) 1931–39, Vickers Vildebeest (TB) 1932–, HP Heyford I 1933–39, Hawker Hart 1933–38, Westland Wallace (GP) 1933–39, Blackburn Baffin (TB) 1934–38, Vickers Vincent (GP) 1934–, Blackburn Shark (TB) 1935–37, Boulton-Paul Overstrand 1935–39, HP Heyford II 1935–39, Heyford III 1935–39, Hawker Hart Special (GP) 1935–, Hawker Hardy (GP) 1935–, Hawker Hind 1935–40, Fairey Hendon II 1936–39, Fairey Swordfish I (TB) 1936–, AW Whitley I 1937–39, Whitley II 1937–39, Bristol Benheim I 1937–, Fairey Battle 1937–, HP Harrow 1937–39, Vickers Wellesley 1937–, Whitley III 1938–40, HP Hampden 1938–, Vickers Wellington I 1938–, Whitley IV 1939–40, Whitley V 1939–, Bristol Blenheim IV 1939–, Bristol Beaufort (TB) 1939.

1940–45

Wapiti (GP) to 1940, Vildebeest (TB) to 1942, Vincent (GP) to 1944, Hart Special (GP) to 1940, Hardy (GP) to 1941, Hart to 1940, Swordfish I (TB) to 1943, Blenheim I to 1942, Battle to 1941, Wellesley to 1942, Whitley III to 1940, Hampden to 1942, Wellington I to 1943, Whitley IV to 1940, Whitley V to 1942, Blenheim IV to 1943, Beaufort (TB) to 1944, Avro Manchester 1940–42, Avro Lancaster 1942–, Lincoln 1945–, Blackburn Botha (TB) 1940–40, Fairey Albacore (TB) 1940–43, HP Halifax I 1940–42, Martin Maryland 1940–42, Short Stirling I 1940–44, Vickers Wellington II 1940–43, Boeing Fortress I 1941–42, Consolidated Liberator II 1941–43, DH Mosquito IV 1941–45, Douglas Boston III 1941–45, HP Halifax II 1941–45, Vickers Wellington III 1941–44, Wellington IV 1941–43, Consolidated Liberator III 1942–45, Bristol Blenheim V 1942–44, Fairey Barracuda 1942–45, HP Hampden TB 1942–43, HP Halifax V 1942–45, Lockheed Ventura I/II 1942–43, Martin Baltimore I-III 1942–44, Martin Marauder I (TB) 1942–44, NA Mitchell II 1942–45, Vickers Wellington X 1942–45, DH Mosquito IX 1943–45, Grumman Avenger I-III 1943–, HP Halifax III 1943–45, Martin Baltimore IV/V 1943–, Short Stirling III 1943–44, Consolidated Liberator VI 1944–, Liberator VIII 1944–45, Curtiss Helldiver 1944–44, DH

Mosquito XIV 1944–, Mosquito XX 1943–, Mosquito XXV 1944–, Douglas Boston IV/V 1944–, HP Halifax VII 1944–45, Martin Marauder III 1944–, NA Mitchell III 1944–45, HP Halifax VI 1945–45.

1946–49
Lancaster, Lincoln, Baltimore IV/V to 1946, Liberator VI to 1946, Avenger I-III to 1946, Mosquito B 16 to 1948, Mosquito B 20 to 1946, Mosquito B 25 to 1948, Boston IV/V to 1946, Marauder III to 1946, DH Mosquito B 35 1947–.

1950–59
Lancaster to 1950, Lincoln to 1956, Mosquito B 35 to 1953, Boeing Washington B 1 1950–54, EE Canberra B 2 1951–, Canberra B 6 1954–, Vickers Valiant B 1 1955–, Avro Vulcan B 1 1956–, EE Canberra B (I) 6 1956–, Canberra B (I) 8 1956–, HP Victor B 1 1957–.

1960–69
Canberra B 2 to 1962, Canberra B 6 to 1963, Canberra B (I) 6 to 1969, Canberra B (I) 8, Valiant B 1 to 1965, Vulcan B 1 to 1968, Victor B 1 to 1966, Avro Vulcan B 2 1960–, HP Victor B 2 1961–64, Canberra B 15 1962–, Canberra B 16 1962–69.

1970–79
Vulcan B 2, Canberra B (I) 8 to 1972, Canberra B 15 to 1970.

1980–89
Vulcan B 2 to 1984.

Electronic warfare, long-range reconnaissance and surveillance
The night bombing offensive in the latter stages of the Second World War saw the beginning of electronic countermeasures as the Germans began to be able to home in on the RAF's bombers, necessitating the development of counter measures carried by specially equipped Lancasters, Halifaxes, Fortresses and Liberators. These, together with electronic spying to discover radar and radio frequencies, were carried on after the Second World War against the USSR by the RAF and FAA until the end of the Cold War and several variants of existing types have been in service to train our own defences against similar probing from prospective enemies. The end of the Cold War changed the major threat to terrorism and electronic aural surveillance assumed greater importance, done by Nimrods and by smaller types such as the AAC's Defender and the new Shadows of the RAF (see Vol. 1). It is likely that this aspect of air warfare will become even more important in the future.

Long-range reconnaissance (i.e. against the forces of the USSR and its allies) became vitally important after the Second World War and the wartime Mosquitos and Spitfires were replaced by Canberras for shorter range work (see Vol. 1) but for strategic reconnaissance versions of the three V-bombers came into service, using traditional photographic methods and also electronic imagery. However, the end of the Cold War removed the need for long-range aircraft and, in any case, the role is being taken over by UAVs.

The threat of low-level air attack by Soviet forces, below the cover of ground-based radar, provided the impetus for an airborne radar and consequently the Shackleton was converted for this and served for many years until replaced by the Sentry. The Royal Navy's ships faced a similar threat and the FAA had AEW, in the shape of the Skyraider and subsequently the Gannet AEW 3, long before the RAF; however, the RAF's assertion that it could provide the RN with radar cover after the Gannet was withdrawn was proved false by the Falklands war and the FAA quickly received an AEW conversion of the Sea King helicopter to remedy the problem and, if the two new carriers are procured, will have to look at new types to replace this.

1939–45
Short Stirling III 1943–44, Vickers Wellington X 1943–45, Boeing Fortress III 1944–, Consolidated Liberator VI 1944–.

1946–59

Fortress III to 46, Liberator VI to 46, Avro Lincoln PR 2 1950-56, Douglas Skyraider AEW 1 1951–, Lockheed Neptune MR 1MOD 1952–56, Vickers Varsity T 1 1953–, EE Canberra B 6BS 1954–, Boeing Washington B 1 1955–58, Vickers Valiant B (PR) 1 1955–, Grumman Avenger ECM 1956–59, DH Comet 2RC 1957–, EE Canberra B 6RC 1958–, Fairey Gannet AEW 3 1959–.

1960–69

Skyraider AEW 1 to 1960, Varsity T 1 to 1965, Comet 2RC, Canberra B 6BS, Canberra B 6RC, Gannet AEW 3, Valiant B 1 to 65, EE Canberra T 17 1967-94, Fairey Gannet AS 6 ECM 1960–71, HP Victor SR 2 1965–74, H-S Argosy E 1 1968–78.

1970–79

Comet 2RC to 75, Canberra B 6BS to 74, Canberra B 6RC to 75, Gannet AEW 3 to 78, Canberra T 17, Gannet AS 6 ECM to 71, Victor SR 2 to 74, Argosy E 1 to 78, EE Canberra E 15 1970-94, H-S Nimrod R 1 1971–present, Avro Shackleton AEW 2 1972–, Avro Vulcan B2 MRR 1973–, H-S Andover E 3 1976–.

1980–89

Canberra T 17, Canberra E 15, Nimrod R 1, Shackleton AEW 2 , Vulcan B 2 MRR to 1982, Andover E 3, Westland Sea King AEW 2 1982–.

1990–99

Canberra T 17 to 94, Canberra E 15 to 94, Nimrod R 1, Shackleton AEW 2 to 91, Andover E 3 to 93, Sea King AEW 2, Boeing Sentry AEW 1 1991–present.

2000–10

Sentry AEW 1, Nimrod R 1, Sea King AEW 2 to 03, Westland Sea King ASaC 7 2002–present.

Transport and Communications

Aircraft were first used as transports by the British to drop supplies to the besieged garrison at Kut-al-Amara in Mesopotamia in 1916; the swiftly advancing British army in France, August 1918, was also supplied with air-dropped ammunition and food but it was in 1919 that passenger carrying started, with a shuttle service from London to the Armistice negotiations in Paris.

During the 1920s aircraft designed as transports entered service in the Middle East and in India, where the RAF evacuated many British residents from Kabul in Afghanistan in the world's first major airlift. However, transports were only used in the Empire although in the UK a few modified bombers were used by 24 Sqn to carry VIPs and senior officers around the country.

With war looking inevitable the RAF began to order transports and communications (air-taxi) types and on the outbreak of war impressed (requisitioned) numerous airliners and light aircraft which saw extensive use in these roles during the first years of the Second World War. However, these were not really military aircraft and soon, reacting to the demands of airborne warfare and the distances involved in the war in the Middle and Far East, aircraft designed for the job entered service, notably the Dakota, although converted bombers also saw extensive service as did the troop/cargo carrying gliders of the Glider Pilot Regiment. The end of the Second World War saw Transport Command a very large force, flying all over the world.

The Dak remained in service after the war and began to be replaced by British-designed types but there were never enough of these and they were only adequate for the job, their shortcomings being exposed by the Suez war. This resulted in the ordering of modern types as replacements and air-trooping replaced the dreaded troopships to the outposts of Empire; in these outposts helicopters replaced the light transports. Transport Command (later Air Support Command) was then at its zenith but defence cuts and the closure of overseas bases saw a large reduction in the number of its aircraft by 1980.

The Suez war was the first in which helicopters were used as assault transports, resulting in the Royal Marine Commandos becoming an air and sea-borne force, with its own FAA helicopters.

Another war, this time in the Falklands, emphasised the need for transports, both fixed-wing and rotary, and some very long distances were flown, with new aircraft (although not new designs) being ordered. Since then Support Command, later Strike Command and now Air Command, has been involved in wars in the Gulf, Sierra Leone, Iraq and Afghanistan, in all of which transports have played an indispensable role, and in which there have never been enough, particularly helicopters. The present fleet is soon to be modernised, not before time as some of the older aircraft are getting very tired.

1919–29

Airco DH 4A 1919–19, Vickers Vimy Ambulance/Vernon 1922–27, Avro Andover I 1924–25, DH Humming Bird 1924–27, Vickers Victoria I 1924–26, Victoria II 1925–28, Victoria III 1926–, Victoria IV 1928–, Victoria V 1929–.

1930–39

Victoria III to 34, Victoria IV to 34, Victoria V to 35, DH Puss Moth 1930–, Fairey IIIF (C) 1930–35, Victoria VI 1931–35, HP Clive 1930–34, Hawker Hart (C) 1934–, Vickers Valentia I 1935–, DH Don 1937–, Fairchild Argus 1937–, Miles Nighthawk 1937–39, Parnall Hendy Heck 1937–, Airspeed Envoy III 1938–, Avro 642/4m 1938–, DH Dragon Rapide 1938–, Percival Vega Gull 1938–, Airspeed Courier 1939–, Bristol Bombay 1939–, DH Dragonfly 1939–, DH Fox Moth 1939–, DH Hornet Moth 1939–, DH Leopard Moth 1939–, DH Moth Minor 1939–, GAL Monospar 1939–, HP Harrow 1939–, Lockheed Electra Junior 1939–, Miles Mentor I 1939–, Miles Hawk Major 1939–, Miles Whitney Straight 1939–, Miles Monarch 1939–, Percival Petrel I 1939–.

1940–45

Puss Moth, Valentia I to 44, Don I to 40, Argus, Hendy Heck to 44, Envoy III to 45, Avro 642/4m to 40, Dragon Rapide, Vega Gull to 45, Courier to 44, Bombay to 44, Dragonfly to 44, Fox Moth to 44, Hornet Moth, Leopard Moth, Moth Minor, Monospar to 44, Harrow to 45, Electra Junior to 45, Mentor I to 44, Hawk Major, Whitney Straight, Monarch, Petrel I, DH 86 1940–45, DH Flamingo 1940–45, Airspeed Ferry 1940–41, Bloch 81 1940–40, BA Swallow II 1940–43, BA Eagle II 1940–43, Caudron Goeland 1940–42, Caudron Simoun 1940–42, Curtiss Cleveland 1940–44, DH Dragon 1940–, DH Hertfordshire 1940–40, DH Albatross 1940–42, DH Moth Major 1940–44, Ford 5AT 1940–40, HP 42 1940–41, Heston Pheonix 1940–45, Lockheed Super Electra 1940–45, Lockheed 18/Lodestar 1940–, Loire 130 1940–41, Messerschmidt Aldon 1940–45, Miles Falcon Six 1940–45, Miles Falcon Major 1940–45, Percival Gull Six 1940–45, Percival Proctor I 1940–, Potez 29 1940–41, Potez 63-11 1940–42, Short Scion 1940–42, Scion Senior 1940–43, Spartan Cruiser 1940–41, Spartan Executive 1940–41, Stinson Voyager 1940–45, Stinson Junior 1940–41, Aeronca Chief 1941–43, Avro Commodore 1941–42, Bellanca Pacemaker 1941–45, Desoutter 1941–45, Lockheed Hudson I 1941–42, Hudson III 1941–45, A-W Whitley V 1941–42, Cessna Airmaster 1941–42, Consolidated Liberator LB 30 1941–44, Douglas DC 2 1941–43, Fokker XXII 1941–43, Foster-Wicko Warferry 1941–45, Harlow PC 5 1941–45, Lockheed Electra 1941–44, Miles Hawk 1941–45, Miles Mohawk 1941–, Piper Cub Coupe 1941–45, Savoi-Marchetti SM 79 1941–44, Tipsy B2 1941–45, Airspeed Horsa 1942–, A-W Albemarle 1942–, Beech Traveller 1942–, Douglas DC 3 1942–45, Koolhoven FK 43 1942-45, Lockheed Hudson V 1942-44, Hudson VI 1942-45, Piper Cruiser 1942-44, Pitcairn PA 39 1942–42, Stampe SV4C 1942–45, Stinson Reliant I 1942–, Taylorcraft BC12 1942–45, Vultee Vigilant 1942–, Zlin Z12 1942–43, Avro Anson X 1943–, Avro York C 1 1943–, Beech Expeditor 1943–, Douglas Dakota 1943–, GAL Hamilcar 1943–, Grumman Widgeon I 1943–45, HP Halifax A V 1943–45, Miles Messenger 1943–, Piper Cub 1943–, Slingsby Hengist 1943–, Vickers Wellington XV 1943–45, Wellington XVI 1943-, Waco Hadrian 1943–, Avro Anson C XI 1944–, Anson C XII 1944–, Consolidated Coronado I 1944–, Douglas Dauntless 1944–, Douglas Skymaster I 1944–, Grumman Goose I 1944–45, HP Halifax A III 1944–, Percival Proctor II 1944–, Proctor III 1944–, Proctor IV 1944–, Short Stirling III 1944–45, Stirling A IV 1944–, Vickers Warwick C I 1944–45, Warwick C III 1944–, Vultee-Stinson Sentinel 1944–, Waco CG-13 1944–, Avro Lancastrian C 2 1945–, Bristol Buckingham I 1945, Consolidated Liberator VI 1945–, Liberator VII 1945–, Liberator VIII 1945–, Liberator IX 1945–, DH Dominie 1945–, HP Halifax C VI 1945–45, HP Halifax A VII 1945–, Short Stirling C V 1945–.

1946–49

Puss Moth to 46, Argus to 47, Dragon Rapide to 47, Hornet Moth to 46, Leopard Moth to 46, Moth Minor to 46, Hawk Major to 46, Whitney Straight to 47, Monarch to 48, Petrel I to 46, Horsa, Albemarle to 46, Anson C 10, Anson C 11, Anson C 12, York C 1, Liberator C 6 to 46, Liberator C 7 to 46, Liberator C 8 to 46, Liberator C 9 to 46, Coronado C 1 to 46, Dakota, Skymaster C 1 to 46, Hamilcar I to 49, Halifax A 3 to 46, Halifax A 7 to 47, Lodestar to 47, Stirling A 4 to 46, Stirling C 5 to 46, Hengist to 46, Wellington C XVI to 46, Warwick C 3 to 46, Hadrian to 46, Waco CG-13 to 46, Traveller to 46, Expeditor, Dominie, Dragon to 46, Dauntless to 46, Mohawk to 46, Messenger to 48, Proctor CC 2, Proctor CC 3, Proctor CC4, Cub to 46, Reliant I to 46, Vigilant to 47, Lancastrian C 2, Buckingham I to 46, Avro Anson C 19 1946–, HP Halifax C 8 1946–46, Halifax A 9 1946–48, Vickers Viking 1946–, DH Devon C1/2 1948–, HP Hastings C 1 1948–, Vickers Valetta C 1 1948–, Valetta C 2 1949–.

1950–59

Horsa to 50, Anson C 10 to 51, Anson C 11 to 51, Anson C 12 to 57, York C 1 to 57, Dakota, Expeditor to 55, Dominie to 55, Proctor C 2 to 54, Proctor CC 3 to 51, Proctor CC4 to 55, Anson C 19, Hastings C 1, Valetta C 1, Valetta C 2, Devon C 1/2, Lancastrian C 2 to 50, Viking to 57, Avro Anson C 21 1950–, Percival Sea Prince C 1 1950–, Westland Dragonfly HC 2/4 1950–, Bristol Sycamore 1951–, HP Hastings C 2 1951–, Hastings C 4 1951–, Cessna Bird Dog 1952–54, Sikorsky Whirlwind 21 1952–56, Percival Sea Prince C 2 1953–, SA Pioneer CC 1 1953–, DH Heron 1954–, Hunting Pembroke C 1 1954–, Westland Whirlwind HAR 1 1954–, Whirlwind HC 2 1954–, Whirlwind HC 4 1954–, DH Sea Devon C 1 1955–, Sikorsky Whirlwind 22 1955–, Blackburn Beverley C 1 1956–, DH Comet 1956–, SA Twin Pioneer CC 1 1958–, Bristol Britannia 1959–, Westland Whirlwind HC 8 1959–, Whirlwind HAR 9 1959–.

1960–69

Dakota, Anson C 19 to 68, Anson C 21 to 68, Beverley C 1 to 67, Sea Prince C 1 to 65, Dragonfly HC to 67, Sycamore, Britannia, Comet, Hastings C 1 to 68, Valetta C 1 to 66, Valetta C 2 to 69, Devon C 1 /2, Hastings C 2 to 68, Hastings C 4 to 68, Sea Prince C 2, Pioneer CC 1 to 68, Pembroke C 1, Whirlwind HAR 1 to 66, Whirlwind HC 2 to 62, Whirlwind HC 4 to 60, Heron, Sea Devon C 1, Twin Pioneer CC 1 to 68, Whirlwind 22, Whirlwind HCC 8 to 64, Whirlwind HAR 9 to 66, Westland Belvedere HC 1 1960–69, DH Sea Heron C 1 1961–, Fairey Gannet COD 4 1961–, H-S Argosy C 1 1961–, Westland Wessex HC 1 1962–65, Wessex HC 2 1963–, Wessex HU 5 1963–, H-S Andover CC 2 1964–, Westland Whirlwind HAR 9 1964–, BAC VC 10 C1 1966–, H-S Andover C 1 1966–, Short Belfast C 1 1966–, Lockheed Hercules C 1 1967–, Westland Wessex HCC 4 1969–.

1970–79

Dakota to 70, Devon C 1/2, Heron, Sea Prince C 2 to 73, Pembroke C 1, Sea Devon C 1, Sycamore to 72, Britannia to 76, Comet to 75, Whirlwind 22 to 70, Sea Heron C 1, Gannet COD 4 to 74, Argosy C 1 to 75, Wessex HC 2, Wessex HU 5, Andover CC 2, Whirlwind HAR 9 to 77, VC 10 C1, Andover C 1, Belfast C 1 to 76, Hercules C 1, Wessex HCC 4, H-S 125 CC 1 1971–, Westland Puma HC 1 1971–, H-S 125 CC 2 1973–, Westland Sea King HC 4 1979–.

1980–89

Devon C 1 /2 to 84, Heron to 89, Pembroke C 1, Sea Devon C 1 to 89, Sea Heron C 1 to 89, Wessex HC 2, Wessex HU 5 to 86, Andover CC 2, VC 10 C 1, Andover C 1, Hercules C 1, Wessex HCC 4, 125 CC 1, Puma HC 1, 125 CC 2, Sea King HC 4, Boeing Chinook HC 1 1980–, Lockheed Hercules C 3 1980–, BAe 146 CC 1 1983–84, H-S 125 CC 3 1983–, Lockheed Tri Star 1985–85, Tri Star KC 1 1985–, Tri Star C 2 1985–, Westland Wessex HU 5C 1985–, BAe 146 CC 2 1986–, SA Jetstream T 3 1986–08.

1990–99

Pembroke C 1 to 90, Wessex HC 2, Andover CC 2 to 95, VC 10 C 1 to 96, Andover C 1 to 94, Hercules C 1, Wessex HCC 4 to 98, 125 CC 1 to 94, Puma HC 1, 125 CC 2 to 98, Sea King HC 4, Chinook HC 1 to 94, Hercules C 3, 125 CC 3, Tri Star KC 1, Tri Star C 2, Wessex HU 5C to 95, BAe 146 CC 2, SA

Jetstream T 3, Boeing Chinook HC 2 1994–, BAC VC 10 C1K 1994–, Eurocopter Twin Squirrel HCC 1 1996–, Eurocopter Dauphin 1996–.

2000–10
Wessex HC 2 to 03, Hercules C 1, Puma HC 1, Sea King HC 4, Hercules C 3, 125 CC 3, Tri Star KC 1, Tri Star C 2, BAe 146 CC 2, VC 10 C1K , Chinook HC 2, Jetstream T 3 to 08, Twin Squirrel HCC 1 to 06, Dauphin, Lockheed Hercules C 4 2000–, Hercules C 5 2001–, Boeing Globemaster C 1 2001–, Westland Merlin HC 3 2001–, Bell Griffin HAR 2 2003–, Westland Sea King HU 6 2003–.

Tankers

The first experiments in air-to-air refuelling were carried out during the late 1930s by Sir Alan Cobham but it was not used during the Second World War and only the advent of the V-bombers and the nuclear deterrent saw it become part of the RAF's operations, with tanker versions of the V-bombers refuelling their bomber compatriots; in addition the short range of the Lightning fighter made AAR vital in air defence too and tankers became an indispensable part of the RAF. The FAA also used it but by carrying AAR pods on Sea Vixens, Scimitars and Buccaneers. The British forces adopted the 'probe and drogue' method in which the receiving aircraft controls the hook-up to the tanker.

The Falklands war, fought at great range from any air bases, put severe pressure on the tankers because transports too needed fuel, and were fitted with AAR probes to get them to the Islands so VC 10s and Tri Stars were hastily converted into tankers to supplement (and eventually replace) the venerable Victors. These continue to serve today, once more overstressed by the conflicts in Iraq and Afghanistan, and the new Airbus 330 tanker/transports due shortly will be most welcome.

1955–69
Vickers Valiant BK 1 1956–65, HP Victor K 1 1965–.

1970–79
HP Victor K 2 1974–.

1980–89
Victor K 2, Avro Vulcan K 2 1982–84, Lockheed Hercules C 1 (K) 1982–, BAC VC 10 K 2 1983–. BAC VC 10 K 3 1985–, Lockheed Tri Star K 1 1986–.

1990–99
Victor K 2 to 93, Hercules C 1 (K) to 96, VC 10 K 2, VC 10 K 3, TriStar K 1, BAC VC 10 K 4 1994–.

2000–10
VC 10 K 2 to 01, VC 10 K 3, Tri Star K 1, VC 10 K 4.

Crew Trainers

During the First World War and between the world wars the only non-pilot aircrew were observers and gunners and both were trained on existing operational types. However, the multi-crewed bombers and flying boats coming into service in the late 1930s meant more specialist training was required and new types began to come into service, notably the ubiquitous Anson, devoted to training navigators, air bombers, wireless operators and gunners. Theses categories were then drawn together at Operational Training Units, equipped with versions of the aircraft they would fly in combat.

This pattern continued after the Second World War for a while but the number of aircrew 'trades' decreased and so, therefore, did the number of types required and by the 1980s the Dominie was the only non-pilot trainer in use by the RAF with the Jetstream T2 training Observers for the FAA; the Jetstream is soon to be replaced by King Air 350s and it is likely that this type will also replace the RAF's venerable Dominies in the very near future.

1930–39

Blackburn Shark III 1938–, DH Dominie I 1939–, DH 86B 1938–, Miles Mentor I 1938–.

1940–45

Shark III to 43, Dominie I, DH 86B to 41, Mentor I to 41, Blackburn Botha I 1940–43, HP Hereford I 1940–41, Percival Proctor I 1940–45, Proctor II 1940–45, Avro Anson I 1941–, Fokker XXII 1941–41, Percival Proctor III 1941–45, Grumman Goose IA 1942–45, Stinson Reliant I 1942–, Curtiss Seamew I 1943–45, Percival Proctor IV 1943–, Vickers Wellington X 1943–, Fairey Swordfish IV 1944–, Vickers Wellington XVII 1944–, Wellington XVIII 1944–, Vickers Warwick GR II 1944–45, Vickers Wellington T 10 1945–.

1946–49

Dominie I to 48, Anson T I, Reliant I to 46, Proctor IV to 46, Wellington X to 46, Swordfish IV to 46, Wellington T 17, Wellington T 18, Wellington T 10, Avro Anson T 20 1948–, Anson T 21 1948–, Anson T 22 1949–.

1950–59

Anson T 1 to 55, Wellington T 17 to 50, Wellington T 18 to 52, Wellington T 10 to 53, Anson T 20 to 57, Anson T 21, Anson T 22, Bristol Brigand T 4/5 1951–58, Vickers Valetta T 3 1951–, Vickers Varsity T 1 1951–, HP Hastings T 5 1953–, HP Marathon T 1 1953-58, Percival Sea Prince T 1 1953–, Vickers Valetta T 4 1956–58, Avro Shackleton T 4 1957–, EE Canberra T 11 1959–.

1959–69

Anson T 21 to 65, Anson T 22 to 60, Valetta T 3 to 68, Varsity T 1, Hastings T 5, Sea Prince T 1, Shackleton T 4 to 68, Canberra T 11 to 69, H-S Dominie T 1 1965–, Avro Shackleton T 2 1968–70.

1970–79

Varsity T 1 to 76, Hastings T 5 to 77, Sea Prince T 1 to 79, Dominie T 1, Shackleton T 2 to 70, EE Canberra T 22 1973–, SA Jetstream T 2 1978–.

1980–89

Dominie T 1, Canberra T 22 to 85, Jetstream T 2.

1990–91

Dominie T 1, Jetstream T 2.

2000–10

Dominie T 1, Jetstream T 2.

Over-sea reconnaissance and anti-submarine types, ASR

The first requirement of the RNAS was for reconnaissance, looking for surface ships and U-boats, and float-planes were quickly developed which could be carried in seaplane carriers and, later, cruisers, battlecruisers and battleships. A logical development of this was a ship which could carry, launch and retrieve wheeled aircraft and the aircraft carrier was in service with the RN shortly after the First World War. Longer over-sea patrols became the province of the flying boat which was bigger and thus carried more fuel giving a longer range, these being supplemented in areas not likely to see enemy fighters by airships, which could patrol for up to 24 hours and performed vital convoy escort work; inshore patrols were flown by land-based types.

The formation of the RAF saw the RNAS disappear but the Fleet Air Arm of the RAF was formed to fly the catapult aircraft and carrier-borne types for the Royal Navy and between the wars the aircraft carrier became an indispensable part of the Fleet. However, land-based aircraft remained with the RAF and in 1937, when the Royal Navy regained control of the Fleet Air Arm, the RAF retained Coastal Command, still controlling land-based torpedo-bombers, general-reconnaissance types and the flying boats, a somewhat unsatisfactory compromise which persists to this day.

In the Second World War both the FAA and Coastal Command expanded although Coastal was somewhat of the Cinderella Command when compared to Bomber and Fighter, even though the UK's survival depended on it stopping the U-boats cutting our shipping supply lines. The FAA played an equal part as escort carriers were introduced, enabling patrols to be flown around convoys, while the RAF's long-range Liberators, and extra Atlantic bases such as the Azores, meant that Coastal Command could close the dreaded Atlantic gap in which many ships had been torpedoed. After a very close shave the FAA and Coastal Command, working together, defeated the U-boats and the advent of the escort carrier had seen the end of the catapult seaplane during 1944.

The withdrawal of all American-built aircraft after the Second World War saw Coastal Command lose its most effective types and it wasn't until the Shackleton entered service that it had a modern aircraft, a long-serving type constantly updated to counter the menace of Soviet submarines until it was replaced by the jet-powered Nimrod. The end of the Cold War meant that there was no credible submarine threat and Coastal Command became part of Strike Command, now Air Command, and by 2010 had no squadrons, due to defence costs. The FAA still relied on carrier types for anti-submarine work after the Second World War but quickly saw the benefits of helicopters, these taking over from the late 1950s and being of two types, the larger and more sophisticated flying from carriers whilst the catapult aircraft concept was re-introduced by small helicopters which operate from the RN's small ships.

As the non-maritime RAF aircraft began to operate over the Channel and the North Sea from early in the Second World War it became obvious that an air-sea-rescue organisation was vital to retrieve downed aircrew; initially it consisted of operational types but the Walrus amphibian began to play a large part and later in the war long-range ASR aircraft such as the Warwick, able to carry an airborne lifeboat in or beneath their bomb bay, flew over all the oceans where the RAF operated – although outside the scope of this book, the RAF's ASR launches and the RN's rescue motor launches also played a vital role.

The Walrus's successor, the Sea Otter, continued to provide ASR post-Second World War but the Korean war hastened the introduction of helicopters and these swiftly replaced fixed-wing types in RAF and FAA service and have continued in service ever since, providing cover both for civilians and the military; they are to be replaced by civilian-registered types very shortly, some with RAF/FAA crews.

1907-13
Delta airship 1912–, Deperdussin Monoplane 1912–, Donnet-Leveque FB 1912–13, Short S 41 1912–, Eta airship 1913–, Astra-Torres airship 1913–, Parseval airship 1913–, Borel Seaplane 1913–, Bristol TB 8 1913–, DFW Mars Arrow 1913–, RAF HRE 2 1913–, Short S 54 1913–, Short S 60 1913–, Short S 64 1913–, Sopwith Bat Boat 1913–, Sopwith Tractor BP 1913–, Wight Navyplane 1913–.

1914-19
Delta airship to 15, Eta airship to 14, Astra-Torres airship to 16, Parseval airship to 16, Borel to 14, Bristol TB 8 to 16, Deperdussin to 16, Mars Arrow to 14, RAF HRE 2 to 15, Short S 41 to 16, Short S 54 to 14, Short S 60 to 14, Short S 64 to 14, Bat Boat to 15, Sopwith Tractor BP to 15, Navyplane to 16, Albatross BII 1914–17, Avro 510 1914–17, Curtiss H 1 1914–16, DFW B II 1914–15, Henri Farman HF 22 1914–15, Short S 73/81 1914–16, Short Gun-carrying PSP 1914–15, Short 74 1914–16, Short 135 1914–15, Short 136 1914–16, Short Nile 1914–14, Sopwith Pusher SP 1914–15, Sopwith 137 1914–15, Sopwith Tractor BP SP 1914–14, Sopwith Type S 1914–14, Sopwith 880 1914–15, Sopwith 807 1914–17, White & Thompson NT 2 1914–18, SS airship 1915–19, Curtiss H 4 1915–18, Short 166 1915–18, Short 830/827 1915–18, Short 184 1915–20, Wight 840 1915–17, Coastal airship 1916–19, Curtiss R 2 1916–17, Mann-Egerton B 1916–17, Porte Baby 1916–18, Norman Thompson NT 4 1917–18, Curtiss H 12 1916–19, Maurice Farman MF 37 1916–16, HMA 9r airship 1917–18, R 23 airship 1917–19, SSP airship 1917–19, SSZ airship 1917–18, North Sea airship 1917–, AD Flying Boat 1917–18, Fairey Campania 1917–19, Fairey Hamble Baby 1917–18, Felixstowe F 2A 1917–, FBA H 1917–18, Short 320 1917–19, Sopwith Strutter 1917–19, Wight Converted SP 1917–19, SST airship 1918–19, SR 1 airship 1918–19, R 27 airship 1918–19, R 31 airship 1918–, Blackburn Kangaroo 1918–18, Curtiss H 16 1918–19, Fairey IIIB 1918–, Fairey IIIC 1918–, Felixstowe F 3 1918–, Felixstowe F 5 1918–, Sopwith Ship's Strutter 1918–19, R 33 airship 1919–, Parnall Panther 1919–.

1920-29
North Sea airship to 21, R 31 airship to 20, Fairey IIIB to 20, Fairey IIIC to 21, Felixstowe F 2A to 23,

Felixstowe F 3 to 21, Felixstowe F 5 to 25, Ship's Strutter to 20, R 33 airship to 20, Panther to 24, Short 184 to 20, R 80 airship 1921–22, Fairey IIID 1922–33, Westland Walrus 1922–25, Avro Bison 1923–29, Supermarine Seagull III 1923–28, Blackburn Blackburn 1926–, Parnall Peto 1926–, Suipermarine Southampton I 1927–29, Southampton II 1927–, Fairey IIF Mk III 1928–.

1930–39
Blackburn to 31, Fairey IIID to 33, Fairey IIF Mk III to 37, Southampton II to 36, Blackburn Iris 1930–34, Short Rangoon 1931–36, Blackburn Perth 1935–37, Supermarine Scapa 1935–39, Supermarine Stranraer 1935–, Avro Anson I 1936–, Fairey Swordfish 1936–, Saro London 1936–, Supermarine Walrus I 1936–, Fairey Seafox 1937–, Short Sunderland I 1938–, Lockheed Hudson I 1939–, Saro Lerwick 1939–.

1940–45
Anson I to 41, Swordfish to 45, Seafox to 43, London to 41, Hudson I to 42, Lerwick to 42, Sunderland I to 43, Walrus I to 45, Stranraer to 41, DH Hornet Moth 1940–40, Fairey Battle 1940–41, Fokker T8W 1940–40, Lockheed Hudson III 1940–45, Rogozarski SIM XIV 1940–42, Short Empire Flying Boat 1940–41, Short G-Class 1940–41, Supermarine Walrus II 1940–, AW Whitley VII 1941–43, Consolidated Catalina 1941–, Consolidated Liberator I 1941–43, Dornier Do 22 1941–42, Fairchild 91 1941–43, Heinkel He 115 1941–42, Lockheed Hudson II 1941–42, Hudson IV 1941–42, Hudson V 1941–44, Northrop N3P-B 1941–43, Short Sunderland II 1941–44, Vickers Wellington Ic 1941–43, Boeing Fortress I 1942–42, Boeing Fortress II 1942–, Consolidated Liberator III 1942–45, HP Halifax GR II 1942–45, Lockheed Hudson VI 1942–45, Short Sunderland III 1942–, Vickers Wellesley 1942–43, Vickers Wellington GR VIII 1942–43, Wellington GR XII 1942–44, Vought-Sikorsky Kingfisher 1942–44, Bristol Blenheim V 1943–44, Consolidated Liberator V 1943–45, HP Halifax Met V 1943–45, Lockheed Ventura V 1943–, Martin Baltimore GR IV 1943–45, Baltimore GR V 1943–, Martin Mariner I 1943–43, Supermarine Sea Otter 1943–, Vickers Wellington GR XIII 1943–45, Wellington GR XIV 1943–, Vickers Warwick ASR 1 1943–, Consolidated Liberator GR VI 1944–, Consolidated Liberator GR VIII 1944–, Vickers Warwick GR V 1944–, Avro Lancaster ASR/MR 3 1945–, Fairey Barracuda III 1945–, HP Halifax Met III 1945–, Halifax Met 6 1945–, Short Sunderland GR 5 1945–, Vickers Warwick GR 6 1945–.

1946–49
Lancaster MR 3, Fortress II to 47, Catalina to 47, Liberator GR VI to 46, Liberator GR 8 to 47, Barracuda AS 3, HP Halifax Met III to 46, Halifax Met 6 , Ventura V to 46, Baltimore GR V to 46, Sunderland III to 46, Sunderland GR 5, Walrus ASR 2 to 46, Sea Otter, Wellington GR 14 to 46, Warwick ASR 1 to 46, Warwick GR 5 to 46, Warwick GR 6 to 46, Fairey Firefly AS 5/6 1948–, Bristol Brigand MET 3 1949–, HP Halifax GR 6 1946–.

1950–59
Lancaster MR 3 to 54, Brigand MET III to 54, Barracuda AS 3 to 53, Firefly AS 5/6 to 56, Halifax GR 6 to 52, Sunderland GR 5 to 59, Sea Otter to 55, Avro Shackleton MR I 1951, Lockheed Neptune MR 1 1952–57, Avro Shackleton MR 2 1953–, Grumman Avenger AS 4/5 1953–57, Sikorsky Whirlwind HAS 22 1953–55, Fairey Gannet AS 1/4 1954–58, Westland Whirlwind HAR 1 1954–, Whirlwind HAR 2 1955–, Whirlwind HAR 3 1955– Avro Shackleton MR 3 1957–, Westland Whirlwind HAS 7 1957–, Westland Whirlwind HAR 4 1958–.

1960–69
Shackleton MR 1 to 62, Shackleton MR 2, Whirlwind HAR 1 to 66, Whirlwind HAR 2 to 63, Whirlwind HAR 3 to 66, Shackleton MR 3, Whirlwind HAS 7 to 67, Whirlwind HAR 4 to 62, Westland Wessex HAS 1 1960–, Westland Whirlwind HAR 10 1962–, Westland Wasp HAS 1 1963–, Wessex HAS 3 1967–, Westland Sea King HAS 1 1969–.

1970–79
Shackleton MR 2 to 72, Shackleton MR 3 to 72, Whirlwind HAR 10, Wessex HAS 1 to 70, Wessex HAS 3, Sea King HAS 1 to 78, H-S Nimrod MR 1 1970–, Westland Sea King HAS 2 1976–, Sea King HAR 3 1978–, Westland Lynx HAS 2 1976–, H-S Nimrod MR 2 1979–.

1980–89

Whirlwind HAR 10 to 81, Wessex HAS 3 to 84, Nimrod MR 1 to 84, Sea King HAS 2 to 85, Sea King HAR 3, Nimrod MR 2, Westland Sea King HAS 5 1980–, Sea King HAR 5 1987–, Sea King HAS 6 1988–, Lynx HAS2 to 88, Westland Lynx HAS 3 1982–.

1990–99

Sea King HAR 3, Nimrod MR 2, Sea King HAS 5 to 93, Sea King HAR 5, Sea King HAS 6, Lynx HAS 3, Westland Lynx HMA 8 1994 to present.

2000–10

Sea King HAR 3-, Nimrod MR 2-2010, Sea King HAR 5, Sea King HAS 6 to 04, Lynx HAS 3-, Lynx HMA 8-, Agusta–Westland Merlin HM 1 2002–.

Appendix 5: Abbreviations

A	Airborne forces transport (role prefix)
AAC	Army Air Corps
AACU/Flt	Anti-Aircraft Co-Operation Unit/Flight
AAEE	Aircraft & Armament Experimental Establishment
AAITS	Airman Aircrew Initial Training School
AAM	Air-to-Air Missile
AAR	Air-to-Air Refuelling
AAS	Air Armament School
AB&GS	Air Bombing and Gunnery School
ACFE	Air Command Far East
ADGB	Air Defence of Gt Britain
AEFlt	Air Electronics Flt
AE&AEngS	Airman Aircrew and Air Engineer's School
AES	Air Electronics School
AEW	Airborne Early Warning (role prefix)
AFEE	Airborne Forces Experimental Establishment
AFS	Advanced Flying School
AFTS	Advanced Flying Training School
AFTU	Advanced Flying Training Unit
AFU	Advanced Flying Unit
A&GS	Armament & Gunnery School
AG&BS	Air Gunnery & Bombing School
AGM	Air-to-Ground Missile
AGS	Air Gunnery School
AHQ	Air Headquarters
AI	Airborne Interception Radar
AIS	Air Interception School
ALS	Air Landing School
AMC	Armed Merchant Cruiser
AMRAAM	Advanced Medium Range AAM
AN&BS	Air Navigation & Bombing School
ANS	Air Navigation School
AndTFlt	Andover Training Flt
AONS	Air Observer's Navigation School
AOS	Air Observer's School

APC/S	Armament Practice Camp/Station
Art&InfCo-opS	Artillery & Infantry Co-operation School
ArtObsS	Artillery Observation School
ARU	Aircraft Repair Unit
AS	Anti-Submarine (role and role prefix)
ASaC	Airborne Surveillance and Control (role prefix)
ASH	Air-Surface Homing (radar)
ASM	Air-to-Surface Missile
ASR	Air-Sea-Rescue
ASRAAM	Advanced Short Range Anti-Aircraft Missile
ASRTU	Air-Sea-Rescue Training Unit
ASS	Air Signals School
ASV	Air-Surface Vessel Radar
ASWDU	Anti-Submarine Warfare Development Unit
ATA	Air Transport Auxiliary
ATC/S	Armament Training Camp/Station
ATU	Armament Training Unit (Army or Naval)
A-W	Armstrong-Whitworth (gun turret)
AWAC	Airborne Warning & Control
B	Bomber (role prefix)
B	Bristol (gun turret)
BAe	British Aerospace
BAFO	British Air Force of Occupation
BANS	Basic Air Navigation School
BAS	Beam Approach School
BATFlt	Beam Approach Training Flight
BATTS	Beam Approach Technical Training School
BBMF	Battle of Britain Memorial Flight
BC	Bomber Command
BCATP	British Commonwealth Air Training Plan
BCBS	Bomber Command Bombing School
BCInstR&EFlt	Bomber Command Instrument Rating & Examination Flight
BCIS	Bomber Command Instructor's School
BCJetCFlt/U	Bomber Command Jet Conversion Flight/Unit
BDTFlt	Bomber Defence Training Flight
BERP	British Experimental Rotor Project
B&GS/Flt	Bombing and Gunnery School/Flight
B (I)	Bomber Intruder (role prefix)
B (K)	Bomber (Tanker) (role prefix)
BP	Boulton-Paul (gun turret)
B (PR) K	Bomber, (Photo-Reconnaissance), Tanker (role prefix)
BR	Bomber Reconnaissance (role prefix)
BS	Bomber Support (role prefix)
B-S	Bristol-Siddeley
BWI	British West Indies
C	Transport (role prefix)
C & CU	Check and Conversion Unit
CAACU	Civilian Anti-Aircraft Co-Operation Unit
Cal	Calibration
CANS	Civilian Air Navigation School
CArtCo-opU/S/Flt.	Coastal Artillery Co-Operation Unit/School/Flight
CATCS	Central Air Traffic Control School

CAW	College of Air Warfare
CC	Communications (role prefix)
CC	Coastal Command
CC FIS	Coastal Command Flying Instructor's School
C&CFlt/U	Check & Conversion Flt/Unit
CCGS	Coastal Command Gunnery School
CCIS	Coastal Command Instructor's School
CCTU	Coastal Command Trials Unit
CDCo-opFlt	Coastal Defence Co-Operation Flt
CDTFlt	Coastal Defence Training Flight
CFCS	Central Flying Control School
C Flt/U	Conversion Flight/Unit
CFS	Central Flying School
CGS	Central Gunnery School or Central Gliding School
CLE	Central Landing Establishment
CNCS	Central Navigation & Control School
CNS	Central Navigation School
COD	Carrier On Board Delivery (role prefix)
Coll	College
Comms	Communications (as in transport)
CR	Commando Role (role suffix)
DAF	Desert Air Force
DC	Depth Charge
DEI	Dutch East Indies
DERA	Defence Engineering Research Establishment
DF	Direction Finding
DH	De Havilland
E	Electronic Intelligence Trainer (role prefix)
EAAS	Empire Air Armament School
EANS	Empire Air Navigation School
ECFS	Empire Central Flying School
ECM	Electronic Countermeasures
EFS	Empire Flying School
Elint	Electronic Intelligence
ERFTS	Elementary & Reserve FTS
ERS	Empire Radio School
ETPS	Empire Test Pilot's School
EWS	Electrical & Wireless School
FAA	Fleet Air Arm
FBTS/Flt	Flying Boat Training Squadron/Flight
FC	Fighter Command
FE	Far East
FEAF	Far East Air Force
F-F	Free-French
F-FAF	Free-French Air Force
FinS	Finishing School
FIS	Flying Instructor's School
Fleet SoAF&G	Fleet School of Aerial Fighting and Gunnery
FLIR	Forward Looking Infra-Red
Flt	Flight

FN	Fraser-Nash (gun turret)
FPP	Ferry Pilot's Pool
FPTFlt/U	Ferry Pilot's Training Flt/Unit
FR	Flight Refuelling
FRADU	Fleet Requirements & Direction Unit
FRefS	Flying Refresher School
FRU	Fleet Requirements Unit
FS	Fighting School
Ft	Feet
FTS	Flying Training School
FTU/Flt	Ferry Training Unit/Flight
FU	Ferry Unit
FWS	Fighter Weapons School
GCo-opFlt	Gunnery Co-Operation Flt
GCAOpsS	Ground Controlled Approach Operator's School
GDGS	Ground Defence Gunner's School
GE	General Electric Company
GGFlt	Ground Gunnery Flight
GIS/Flt	Glider Instructor's School/Flight
Gp	Group
GPEU	Glider Pilot Exercise Unit
GPFlt	Glider Pilot Flt
GPMG	General purpose machine gun
GpPl	Group Pool
GPR	Glider Pilot Regiment
GPS	Ground Positioning System
GpTFlt	Group Training Flight
GR	General Reconnaissance (also role prefix 1940s)
GRS	General Reconnaissance School
GRU	Gunnery Research Unit
GTS	Glider Training School
HAR	Helicopter Air Rescue (role prefix)
HAS	Helicopter Anti-Submarine (role prefix)
HC	Helicopter Transport (role prefix) or Home Command
HDU	Hose-Drum Unit
HF	High Frequency radio
HGCU	Heavy Glider Conversion Unit
HM	Helicopter Marine (role prefix)
HMA	Helicopter Marine Attack (role prefix) or His Majesty's Airship
HMS	Her/His Majesty's Ship
HP	Handley-Page
Hp	Horse-power
HT	Helicopter Training (role prefix)
HTF	Heavy Transport Flight
HU	Helicopter Utility (role prefix)
IFTS	Initial Flying Training School
Inst	Instrument
InstFTS/U/Sqn	Instrument Flying Training School/Unit/Squadron
ITS	Initial Training School
JASS	Joint Anti-Submarine School

JEHU	Joint Experimemtal Helicopter Unit
JHTU	Joint Helicopter Trials Unit
JTIDS	Joint Tactical Information Display System
K	Tanker (role prefix)
Kg	Kilogram
Km	Kilometre
LancasterFinS	Lancaster Finishing School
Lb	Pounds (thrust or weight)
M	Metre
MAD	Magnetic Anomaly Detector
MB	Martin-Baker
MC	Maintenance Command
MCommsSqn	Metropolitan Communications Squadron
MCU	Mosquito Conversion Unit or Meteor Conversion Unit
ME	Middle East
MEAF	Middle East Air Force
ME C&CS/U	Middle East Check & Conversion School/Unit
Met	Meteorological
METS	Middle East Training School
Mg	Machine Gun
Misc	Miscellaneous
Mk	Mark (number)
Mm	Millimetre
MObsS	Marine Observer's School
MOTU	Maritime Operational Conversion Unit
MR	Maritime Reconnaisance (role prefix)
MRR	Maritime Radar Reconnaissance (role suffix)
MU	Maintenance Unit
N	Naval
Nav	Navigation
NavS	Navigation School
NSqn	Naval Squadron
NTSqn	Night Training Squadron
NVG	Night Vision Goggles
NW	Naval Wing
OAFU	Overseas Aircraft Ferry Unit
OAFU	Observer's Advanced Flying Unit
OAPU	Overseas Aircraft Preparation Unit
OATS	Officer's Advanced Training School
ObsS	Observer's School
ObsSoR&AP	Observer's School of Reconnaissance & Aerial Photography
ObsSoAG	Observer's School of Aerial Gunnery
ObsTU	Observer's Training Unit (Naval)
OCTU	Officer Cadet Training Unit
OCU	Operational Conversion Unit
ORTU	Operational & Refresher Training Unit
OTU/Flt	Operational Training Unit/Flight
PAFU	Pilot's Advanced Flying Unit

Para&GS	Parachute & Gliding School
Para&GTS/U	Parachute & Glider Training School/Unit
ParaTS/U	Parachute Training School/Unit
Pl	Pool
PNTU	Pathfinder Navigation Training Unit
PR	Photo-Reconnaissance (and role prefix)
PRU	Photo-reconnaissance Unit
PT&RPl	Pilot Training and Re-inforcement Pool
PTU	Pilot Training Unit (Naval & AAC)
P&W	Pratt & Whitney
Qv	Which see
R	Electronic Reconnaissance (role prefix)
RAE	Royal Aircraft Establishment
RAF	Royal Air Force or Royal Aircraft Factory
RAFC	RAF College
RAFFC	RAF Flying College
RAFRegS	RAF Regiment School
RAFTC	RAF Technical College
RAFVR	RAF Volunteer Reserve
RATFlt	Radio Aids Training Flight
RATGp	Rhodesian Air Training Group
RAuxF	Royal Auxiliary Air Force
RCM	Radio Countermeasures
RDFS	Radio Direction-Finding School
RE	Royal Engineers
RFA	Royal Fleet Auxiliary
RefFU/S	Refresher Flying Unit/School
RFC	Royal Flying Corps
RFS	Reserve Flying School
RN	Royal Navy
RNAS	Royal Naval Air Service
RP	Rocket Projectile
RR	Rolls-Royce
RRFlt	Radar Reconnaissance Flight
RS	Radio School
RSqn	Reserve Squadron
RTFlt	Radio Training Flight
R/TSqn	Reserve later Training Squadron
RTU	Radio & radar Training Unit (FAA)
RWE	Radio Warfare Establishment
RWR	Rearward Warning Radar
S	School
SAAF	South African Air Force
SAR	Search & Rescue
SARTU	SAR Training Unit
SASIObs	School for Anti-Submarine Inshore Patrol Observers
SC	Strike Command
SCBS	SC Bombing School
SCR584TU	SCR584 (radar) Training Unit
SD	Special Duties

SFlt	Station Flight
SFTS	Service Flying Training School
SHAEF	Supreme Headquarters Allied Expeditionary Force
Shp	Shaft Horse-power
SLAIS	Special Low-Attack Instructor's School
SMObs	School for Maritime Observers
SMOP	School for Maritime Operational Pilots
SMR	School of Maritime Reconnaissance
SoACo-op	School of Army Co-Operation
SoAF	School of Aerial Fighting
SoAF&G	School of Aerial Fighting & Gunnery
SoAG	School of Aerial Gunnery
SoAN	School of Aerial Navigation
SoAS	School of Air Support
SoASR	School of Air-Sea-Rescue
SoAT	School of Air Transport
SoFC	School of Flying Control
SoGR	School of General Reconnaissance
SoLAW	School of Land-Air Warfare
SoMR	School of Maritime Reconnaissance
SoN&BD	School of Navigation & Bomb Dropping
SoNCo-op	School of Naval Co-Operation
SoNCo-op&AN	School of Naval Co-operation and Aerial Navigation
SoP	School of Photography
SoTT	School of Technical Training
SPTS/Flt	Seaplane Training Squadron/Flight
Sqn	Squadron
SR	Strategic Reconnaissance (role prefix)
SRFlt	Sea Rescue Flight
SRCU	Short-Range Conversion Unit
SS	Signals School
STOL	Short Take-Off and Landing
SU	Support Unit or Servicing Unit
T	Trainer (role prefix)
TAF	Tactical Air Force
TAGTU	Telegraphist-Air Gunner's Training Unit (FAA)
TB	Training Base or Torpedo Bomber (role prefix)
TC	Transport Command
TCDU	TC Development Unit
TCPU	TC Practice Unit
TDS	Training Depot Station
TEU	Tactical Exercise Unit
TFP	Training Ferry Pool
TFR	Terrain Following Radar
TFSqn/Flt	Target Facilities Squadron/Flight
TorpAS	Torpedo Aircraft School
TorpBS	Torpedo Bomber School
TorpTU/Flt/S	Torpedo Training Unit/Flt/School
TorpU	Torpedo Unit
TSCU	Transport Support Conversion Unit
TSPC	Transport Support Practice Camp
TSqn/Flt	Training Squadron/Flight

TSTU	Transport Support Training Unit
TTC	Technical Training Command
TTFlt/Sqn/U	Target Towing Flight/Squadron/Unit
TU	Training Unit
TU&RPl	Training Unit & Reserve Pool
UASqn	University Air Squadron
UAV	Unmanned Aerial Vehicle
UHF	Ultra-High Frequency radio
USAAF	US Army Air Force
USAF	US Air Force
USAAS	United States Army Air Service
USN	US Navy
VHF	Very High Frequency radio
VIP	Very Important Person
VS	Vickers-Supermarine
W	Wing
W&ObsS	Wireless & Observer's School
WS	Wireless School

Corrections and Additions to Volume 1

Into all books creep some typing errors and, occasionally, wrong information, leading to some anguish on the part of the author. Fortunately, in a two-volume work, there is a chance to correct these and also to include some additional information which has become available since the publication of Vol. 1 in November 2008.

The title should have included 'pilot trainers and target tugs'

Page 37 Entry 27 Husky T 1. – should read '5AExFlt' not 5 xAExFlt.

Page 23 Photos – caption to A-W FK 8 to read 'B4200 rebuild'.

Page 40 Entry 31 Griffin T 1. Correct engines to read – 'Two P&W Canada PT6T-3d turboprops in Twin-Pac configuration giving 1,800shp'.

Page 47 Entry 41 Sentinel R 1 – add 'Action Afghanistan'.

Page 70 Entry 67 Defender 4S AL 1 – add the following – '67a. Defender AL 2.

An improved version of the AL 1; no further details available.

In service 2009 with 651 Sqn until the present 2010.

Serials ZH001–003. Total 3. No losses to date.

67b. Defender T 3. A trainer version of the above for the AAC.

In service 2009.

Serial ZH004. Total 1. No losses to date.

Total Defenders = 8. No losses to date'. Britten-Norman thus supplied 'eight aircraft of one type'

Page 71 Delete 'Brush Coachworks' and substitute 'Brush Electrical Engineering'.

Page 78 Caption to photo of JN 4A to read B1922 not D1922.

Page 113 Entry 98 – add one accidental loss in 2009 so to read '5 accidental losses to date'; total Squirrel losses to read '6 (15%) losses to date'. Add to serials 'ZK199–200 (2)' making the total 28 and total Squirrels 40.

Page 115 Entry 100 Typhoon. The total Typhoon order now seems likely to be reduced to 174 but the mix of Marks has not yet been revealed. Add 'Based overseas in the Falklands' and 'Two sqns (6,11) and one Flight' to the FGA4.

Page 122 Entry 105 Seaplane. Add 'Action home waters'.

Page 139 Entry 125 Vigilant T 1. Delete serials ZJ960–68 and substitute ZJ960–63 (4), ZJ967–68 (2). ZZ192–94 (3). Total Vigilants to read 66.

Page 173 Entry 150c Hawk T 2 – add 'In service 2009 with 4 FTS'. 'Serials ZK010–037'.

Page 178 Entry 155 Lightning II – 'Serials ZM135–200' (all that is allocated at present).

Page 202 Entry 190a Tornado GR 1 (T) – after 'Total 50' add 'serials in the GR 1'.

Page 207 Entry 196a Defender AL 2 – delete (transferred to Entry 67). Islander CC 2 becomes entry 196a, Islander CC 2A becomes entry 196b, Islander CC 2B becomes entry 196c. Entry 196 Islander CC 1 serials to read 'ZG844-48 (5), ZG993-94 (2)'; the total thus becomes 7. New entry 196c delete 'Serial ZH 537' and substitute 'One conversion of the CC 2'. 'Total 1' to read 'Total one conversion'. Thus 'Total Islanders' to read 10 not 19 so loss rate is 10% not 5%. Total aircraft supplied by Pilatus-Britten-Norman to read 10 not 19.

Page 208 Entry 196a King Air 350, should read 197a and the name should be changed to 'Shadow R 1'; add – 'It has cabin roof aerials, an under-belly 'boat' fairing, two ventral fins under the rear fuselage and wingtip winglets'.

Page 274 Photo caption to read 'FB 19 Mk II' not 'Mk I'.

Page 285 Entry 295 Lynx – add new entry 195d 'Lynx AH 9A'.

As the AH 9 but with more powerful engines to enable it to operate in hot and high areas such as Afghanistan. The new engines have large upward-curved exhausts.

In service 2009.

Powered by two 1,361shp LHTEC CTS800-4n turboprops.

Total 12 conversions of the AH 9: no losses to date.

Page 287 Entry 295d – the Future Lynx is to be known as 'Lynx Wildcat AH 2 (or AH 1 depending on which Mark number the FAA Wildcat is given). It will enter service in 2014. The total to be supplied is 34 and the entry number changed to 295e.

Page 293 Add new entry under LHTEC CTS800-4n – 'Lynx AH 9A.

In Limbach entry include 'Slingsby Venture T 2'.

Page 294 Pratt & Whitney – amend PT6T to give 1,800shp.

Page 298 Bombs: Post-second World War–present. Paveway IV, should read Tornado GR 4 not 6R 41.

Add complete new entries

Diamond Aircraft (Austria)

Twin Star (R 1?)

A twin-engined four-seater which will be used for IR imaging and ground mapping. It has a large pannier under the centre section. No further details.

In service with 5 Sqn 2009.

Powered by two 135hp Thierlet Centurion turbo-diesels, although these may be changed due to Thierlet going bankrupt.

Serials: ZA179–80 (2).

Span: 44ft/13.42m Length: 27.8ft/8.5m Ceiling: 18,000ft/5,480m Range: 1,055 miles/1,693km Speed: 222mph/356kmph.

Under engines add new entry – 'Thierlet (Germany)'.

Centurion four-cylinder in-line turbo-diesel, 135hp, Twin Star (R 1?).'

Mil (Russia)

Mi-17.

Two examples of this large helicopter were used by Joint Helicopter Command to train Afghan pilots on the type. Three crew and thirty passengers or 8,800lb/4000kg of freight plus more underslung.

In service with Special Duty Sqn during 2009.

Powered by two 2,225shp Klimov TV3 turboshafts.

Serials: ZB697–698 (2).

Rotor diameter: 69ft 10in/21.35m Length: 60ft 5in/18.42m Ceiling: 19,690ft/6,000m Range 594 miles/950km Speed: 156mph/250kmph.

Index of Aircraft Names and Nicknames

This gives the entry number (not page) for each type.

Arabic numbers

0/100 (Handley-Page)	174
0/400	175
No.2 Flying Boat (White & Thompson)	381
No.3 Flying Boat	341A
5 AT (Ford)	165
9r 16	
12A (Lockheed)	205
18 (Lockheed)	206
24 (Fairchild)	137
29 (Potez)	242
63-11	243
74 (Short)	260
81 (Bloch)	63
81 (Short)	258A
91 (Fairchild)	138
105 (Stinson)	297
108 (Messerschmidt)	218
115 (Heinkel)	200
125 (Hawker-Siddeley)	198A
130 (Loire)	212
135 (Short)	261
136	262
137 (Sopwith)	285
139 (Agusta-Westland)	4
146 (BAe)	82
166 (Short)	264
184	266
320 (Short)	268
504 (Avro)	33
510	34
642/4m (Avro)	39
807 (Sopwith)	289
827 (Short)	265A
830	265
840 (Wight)	343
860 (Sopwith)	290
880	288
1914 Navyplane	342
9700	291

Also published by The History Press

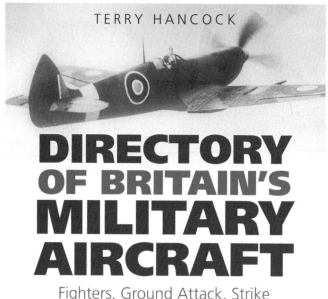

TERRY HANCOCK

DIRECTORY OF BRITAIN'S MILITARY AIRCRAFT

Fighters, Ground Attack, Strike and Overland Reconnaissance

This dictionary details all the aircraft, airships and gliders which have served the UK's forces throughout the 100 years of flight since the first powered flight, the airship *Nulli Secundus*, in 1907. Broken up alphabetically, this volume focuses on Fighters, Bombers, Ground Attack, Strike and Over-land Reconnaissance. Intending to create a quick and useful reference book, author Terry Hancock details every type of manned aircraft that has carried military serials and seen service with the operational squadrons or training and support units of the British armed forces, the RFC, RNAS, RAF, Fleet Air Arm and Army Air Corps (excluding types designed for record breaking, carrying civil registrations, types used solely by the Commonwealth, temporary serials, types retained for ground training, tethered balloons and man-carrying kites).

Visit our website and discover thousands of other History Press books.

www.thehistorypress.co.uk

The History Press